Naming Your Baby

Making an appropriate choice

The choice of a name for a child is made long before the child is old enough to have an opinion about names or anything else—but the decision you make could affect your child's whole outlook and personality. Certainly, most people want to choose a name that is associated with good qualities and a happy and successful life. It should not be bizarre or old-fashioned, but on the other hand perhaps not too boring or obvious either.

If, like the late Frank Zappa, you invent a way-out name like *Dweezil* or *Moon Unit*, you have to be confident that your child will be resilient enough to cope with the inevitable stream of reactions (amazement, horror, delight, fascination, bullying, or teasing, as the case may be) that such a name will provoke. Jokey names are equally suspect. When Mr and Mrs Wall choose the names *Brick* and *Stone* for their sons, or when the Streets name their child *High*, the choice may provoke a moment's mirth, but the joke can very soon wear thin for the bearer. For most of us, these are inappropriate choices.

Equally inappropriate are names which, due to some historical accident, have acquired irrelevant or distracting connotations. An example is *Gay*. Until two or three decades ago this was a well-established girl's name, growing in popularity, meaning 'happy' or 'cheerful'. But during the 1960s the vocabulary word dramatically changed its meaning, effectively killing its use as a given name. For this reason, it does not appear in this book. Whether you support or oppose homosexual liberation, you probably do not want to choose a name that would seem to imply a choice of sexual orientation on your child's behalf.

So the first priority must be to choose a name that is appropriate and has good connotations. So much is easy to say. Making the right choice is more difficult. Some parents pass on to their child their own name or that of some close relative, admired friend, or prospective godparent. To them this little book can offer, not a range of choices, but supplementary information about the background to the name chosen, and confirmation that it is an appropriate choice, with the right sort of associations.

To others, who want a wide range of names to choose from, it offers information about the history, original meaning, and associations of names. It not only describes the linguistic origins of all the usual English names; it also mentions the famous people with whom particular names are associated, and it offers a number of new or unusual choices for those who wish to be more adventurous.

Traditional choices

A few hundred English names are chosen every year by vast numbers of parents. These are the safe, well-

BABIES' NAMES

BABIES' NAMES

Patrick Hanks

OXFORD
UNIVERSITY PRESS

OXFORD
UNIVERSITY PRESS

Great Clarendon Street, Oxford OX2 6DP

Oxford University Press is a department of the University of Oxford.
It furthers the University's objective of excellence in research, scholarship,
and education by publishing worldwide in

Oxford New York

Auckland Cape Town Dar es Salaam Hong Kong Karachi
Kuala Lumpur Madrid Melbourne Mexico City Nairobi
New Delhi Shanghai Taipei Toronto

With offices in

Argentina Austria Brazil Chile Czech Republic France Greece
Guatemala Hungary Italy Japan Poland Portugal Singapore
South Korea Switzerland Thailand Turkey Ukraine Vietnam

Oxford is a registered trade mark of Oxford University Press
in the UK and in certain other countries

Published in the United States
by Oxford University Press Inc., New York

© Pamela Gulleford 2005
Appendix material Oxford University Press 2005

The moral rights of the author have been asserted
Database right Oxford University Press (makers)

First published 1995
Revised edition with new appendix material 2005

British Library Cataloguing in Publication Data
Data available

Library of Congress Cataloging in Publication Data
Data available

ISBN 0-19-861098-X
ISBN 978-0-19-861098-4

10 9 8 7 6 5 4 3 2

Typeset by Selwood Systems
Printed in Italy by Legoprint S.p.A.

established names with which it is almost impossible to go wrong. Among the most popular boys' names are *David*, *John*, *William*, *James*, *Michael*, *Andrew*, and *Peter*, while for girls they include *Susan*, *Sarah*, *Ann*, *Elizabeth*, and *Mary*. There are fewer than a thousand of these perennial favourites, and most of them go back to the Bible. *David*, for example, has been in use since at least a thousand years before Christ, in honour of the biblical king who bore the name. The ever-popular *Susan* goes back to the biblical story of Susannah, whose virtue triumphs over the lust of the elders.

The most important names in the New Testament are those of the four evangelists—*Matthew*, *Mark*, *Luke*, and *John*—and the apostles, principally *Peter*, *James*, *Andrew*, *Thomas*, *Philip*, *Bartholomew*, *John*, *Matthew*, and *Simon*, closely followed by *Paul*. *John* is trebly important: the name was borne by an apostle (the son of Zebedee), by the author of the fourth gospel, and by the forerunner of Christ, John the Baptist. The frequency of forms of *Johannes* or *John* among early Christians ensured that the name was borne by some early saints, which further reinforced its popularity. *Michael* owes its popularity to the archangel, captain of the angelic host, mentioned in the Book of Revelation.

With the exception of Mary, the mother of Jesus, very few women play a major role in the gospels. This helps to explain why the set of conventional girls' Christian names is even smaller than that for boys, and why *Mary* has been so popular. It is borne by others in the New Testament—principally Mary

Magdalene, a woman who 'had been healed of evil spirits and infirmities' (Luke 8), and who was identified in Christian tradition with the repentant sinner of Luke 7. *Anne* and *Elizabeth* were traditionally accepted as the names of the mother and sister respectively of the Virgin Mary, although the biblical evidence is thin. *Anne* is itself derived from an Old Testament name, *Hannah*.

Of other biblical names, the popularity of *Hannah*, *Sarah*, *Adam*, and *Nathan* continues unabated, although others, such as *Dinah*, *Zillah*, *Edna*, *Job*, *Amos*, *Abner*, and *Enoch*, are now out of fashion. These Old Testament names have always had high status among Jews. On the other hand, they have never been officially used by Roman Catholics. Among Low-Church Protestants, they were popular in the seventeenth and nineteenth centuries and some are now undergoing a revival.

Saints' names

A large number of very widely used names owe their importance to the fact that they were borne by early, famous, or canonized Christians, ranging from learned Church fathers (*Basil*, *Ambrose*, *Jerome*, *Augustine*, and *Gregory*) through innumerable martyrs (*Agatha*, *Agnes*, *Laurence*, *Sebastian*), mystics, ascetics, and visionaries (*Anthony*, *Simeon*, *Francis*, *Teresa*), founders of religious orders (*Benedict*, *Bernard*, *Dominic*), to the simple nineteenth-century French peasant girl (*Bernadette*) whose visions of the Virgin Mary led to the foundation of a healing shrine at Lourdes. What they all have in common is that at some time during the past two millennia a cult grew up around them. They are particularly popular among Roman Catholics. In some cases (*Christopher*, *George*, *Katherine*) it is now recognized that the legends of the cult have obscured any basis of historical fact that may once have existed, but this latter-day scepticism has done nothing to impair the popularity of the names.

There are a few names which are borne almost exclusively by Roman Catholics. Examples include *Aloysius*, *Ferdinand*, *Xavier*, and *Carmel*.

Jewish names

The traditional Jewish names in the English-speaking world are, as we have seen, derived from the Bible. *Abraham*, *Jacob*, *Benjamin*, *Esther*, and *Hannah* are traditional Jewish names, although they are by no means confined to Jews. By contrast, *Moses*, *Israel*, *Isaac*, *Hyam*, and *Solomon* are much more common among Jews than Gentiles, while a few names (*Ephraim*, *Zipporah*) are almost exclusively Jewish. The popularity of *Moss*, *Montague*, and *Morton* as Jewish names is a reminder of the long-established Jewish practice of choosing like-sounding Gentile names as equivalents or reminders of true Jewish names—in this case, *Moses*.

Royal and aristocratic names

The most important group of English names after biblical names consists of those introduced by the Normans following the invasion of 1066. Many of them were borne by royalty—*William*, *Henry*, and *Richard* in particular—while others (*Robert*, *Ralph*, *Humphrey*, *Hugh*, *Raymond*, *Reginald*, *Matilda*, *Millicent*, *Rosalind*, *Rosamund*) were associated with the Norman nobility.

This group of names has a fascinating history. They are pagan names, originating thousands of years ago among the Germanic tribes of central Europe. They have strange meanings like 'will-protection' (*William*), 'homeland-power' (*Henry*), 'fame-bright' (*Robert*), and 'might-battle' (*Matilda*).

Normally, pagan names fell out of use in the Christian era unless they happened to be borne by an early Christian saint. So, for example, the Roman names *Antonius* and *Marcus* survived because there were saints bearing these names; *Tiberius* and *Gaius* didn't because there weren't. Similarly, most Old English names (*Athelstan*, *Wulfstan*, etc.) died out after the Norman Conquest, although a few, such as *Edward* and *Audrey*, survived—again because of famous local saints bearing these names.

So how did *William*, *Henry*, *Richard*, and other pagan names become so common in the English-speaking world? The answer, surprisingly enough, lies at the court of the Frankish king Charlemagne at Aachen in the ninth century. The native language of the Franks was a form of Old High German, and they bore Germanic names—*Willihelm*, *Haimric*, *Richard*, etc. These names continued in use at the Frankish court even though its official language was a form of Latin (and subsequently French) rather than German. Thus they became fashionable names in medieval France. Now the scene shifts to northern France a hundred years later. The Norse raiders who settled in Normandy (the 'land of the Norsemen') in northern France went native. They abandoned their Norse language and instead picked up French customs, the French language—and even French names. So in 1066, when William the Conqueror, bastard son of Robert, Duke of Normandy, landed at Hastings in 1066 and set himself up as king of England, he and his followers were French-speaking and brought their traditional Germano-French royal and aristocratic names with them. In the course of the next hundred years, the Normans spread these names throughout England, Wales, Ireland, and Scotland, and they have enjoyed great popularity ever since, spreading far beyond the British Isles.

Vogues and trends in traditional names

There are definite vogues for given names; they come into fashion and go out again for reasons that can sometimes be recorded: for example, a name may experience a sudden increase in use after it has been used for a character in a popular book, film, or television series. More seriously, a particular set of names may be associated with a religious sect or cult.

The popularity of the more common names ebbs and flows regularly with the generations, often in cycles or waves over a period of about fifty to eighty years. Boys' names such as *William*, *George*, and *Henry* were particularly popular choices in the 1920s and 30s, rather less so after the Second World War. For this reason, they are now back in vogue, having just the right combination of familiarity and apparent distinctiveness to ensure that they will be widely chosen. The irony is that for this very reason—since everyone else is busy choosing them—they will rapidly lose their distinctiveness.

Names that are currently very popular but may soon become rather less so include *Andrew*, *Jack*, *Thomas*, *Henry*, and *Jake* for boys and *Sophie*, *Charlotte*, *Olivia*, *Amy*, and *Jessica* for girls. Conversely, *Anthony*, *Brian*, *Howard*, and *Terence* for boys and *Margaret*, *Kathleen*, *Dorothy*, *Patricia*, and *Jean* for girls are examples of well-established names that enjoyed rather more popularity in the 1940s; they are currently somewhat out of fashion and may therefore be due for revival.

Celtic affinities

At present, ancient Celtic names are enjoying a tremendous vogue. Anyone with even a drop of Celtic blood in their veins and even none at all, it seems, stands a good chance of receiving a traditional Irish, Scottish, or Welsh name. This book contains a selection of over 300 Irish or Scottish Gaelic names and a further 150 Welsh names. Some of the former, for example *Mairenn* and *Mór*, are almost entirely confined to Ireland or Scotland. Others are now used throughout the world by people who may be only vaguely aware, if at all, of their derivation: for example *Bridget*, *Donald*, *Duncan*, *Ian*, *Kenneth*, *Kevin*, *Neil*, and *Sheila* from Gaelic; *Gareth*, *Gladys*, *Gwendolen*, and *Trevor* from Welsh. Other Celtic names exist in an Anglicized form, but are still used mainly by people conscious of their Celtic ancestry, for example *Brendan*, *Fintan*, *Cormac*, and *Declan* from Gaelic and *Branwen*, *Dilys*, *Evan*, *Olwen*, and *Wyn* from Welsh.

In Ireland, Gaelic names such as *Aedh*, *Cathal*, *Caitlín*, and *Gráinne* have been widely revived since independence in their original form, unscrambling the garblings due to Anglicization. (*Aedh*, for example, had been Anglicized as *Hugh*, and *Gráinne* as *Grace*, English names with which they have no connection.) Because of the differences in phonology and spelling, Gaelic names can look very different from English names even when they are in fact quite closely equivalent. For example, the Irish Gaelic form of *George* is *Seoirse*; the Gaelic form of *John* is *Seán*. Irish *Séamas* and Scottish *Seumas* are the Gaelic equivalents of English *James*.

A striking feature of the Gaelic naming tradition is the antiquity of its independence and folklore. *Meadhbh* (*Maeve*) recalls a first-century queen of Connacht, leader of the famous cattle raid of Cooley. The name *Deirdre* recalls the tragic story of a beautiful girl betrothed against her will to Conchobhar (*Connor*), her elopement with her beloved Naoise, and Conchobhar's pursuit of the lovers throughout Ireland and Scotland.

In Scotland, where the Gaels settled from the fifth

century onwards, particular names are often associated with particular clans. Thus, the name *Somerled* (*Somhairle* in Scottish Gaelic, sometimes Anglicized phonetically as *Sorley*) is traditionally associated with clan MacDonald, the kindred of the Lords of the Isles. *Gillespie* and *Archibald* are particularly associated with clan Campbell. There was considerable interplay in the Middle Ages between Gaelic names and Norse (Scandinavian) names. Gaelic *Somhairle*, *Úisdean*, and *Raghnall* (*Ronald*) are from Norse, while Norse names such as *Njall* and *Birgit* are from Gaelic. One of the more surprising developments in recent years is the standardization of the clan name *Mackenzie* as a girl's given name in North America.

Welsh names are likewise of great antiquity, though fewer traditional names survive in Welsh than in Gaelic. Many of the ancient names that are now in use or being revived are found in the *Mabinogi*, a medieval collection of traditional legends. These include *Branwen*, *Lleu*, *Geraint*, *Heilyn*, *Iorwerth*, *Rhiannon*, *Urien*, *Ynyr*, and *Pryderi*. Another group of traditional Welsh names commemorates heroes and princes who led resistance variously to the Romans (*Caradoc*), the Saxons (*Cadwaladr*), and the English (*Llewelyn*, *Glyndŵr*). The most important Welsh source of names is the cycle of legends associated with the court of King Arthur, legendary defender of the Britons against the Saxon invaders. Names derived from this tradition include *Elaine*, *Enid*, *Gavin* (*Gawain*), *Guinevere*, *Lancelot*, *Merlin* (*Myrddin*), *Percival*, and *Tristan* (*Tristram*). The last century witnessed not only a revival of traditional Welsh names but also an influx of new coinages. These are mainly from vocabulary elements (e.g. *Eirwen* 'snow-pure', *Glenda* 'clean-good'), but also from placenames such as *Trefor*.

Using a family name as a given name

Increasingly, people seeking a non-traditional given name for a child will use a family name, often the name of a family with which the child has some connection. In earlier times, a first-born child would be christened with the mother's maiden name, especially if she came from a rich and powerful family; the conjunction of the two names would be taken as symbolic of the union between the two families. Several names that were originally family names are now well established as first names in their own right (e.g. *Clifford*, *Dudley*, *Stanley*, *Fraser*, and *Lennox*). Examples of female names that originated as family names include *Beverley*, *Lesley*, *Kelly*, and *Kimberley*, while other names such as *Courtney* and *Kendall* are borne by both sexes.

In North America, family names are often given as first names, not because of any family connection, but out of admiration for some great historical or contemporary figure (*Washington*, *Lincoln*, *Bradford*, *Wesley*, *Winthrop*). Examples of American girls' names derived from family names include *Brooke* and *Paige*. Many more are used for either sex, so that it is not possible to determine the gender of a bearer from the name alone.

Pet forms and nicknames as names in their own right

Pet forms are more often used as first names in their own right in America than Britain; one should not assume that a *Pam* is necessarily to be addressed more formally as *Pamela*, nor *Bobby* or *Rob* as *Robert*. Some short forms or pet forms are now more commonly used than the more formal version, as in the case of *Reg*. In the same way some informal nicknames have come to be bestowed as official first names (*Bud*, *Ginger*, *Rusty*), especially in America. Words denoting ranks of the nobility such as *Duke*, *Earl*, and *Prince* are also regularly used as first names in North America.

Names from overseas

Names from other countries have been enthusiastically adopted in the English speaking world, beginning in the nineteenth century with French and German names, followed in the early twentieth century by Russian names, often introduced via France (*Vera*, *Tanya*, *Natasha*). A couple of decades later, there was a vogue for names of Scandinavian origin (*Ingrid*, *Astrid*). Over 7,000 names are recorded in the *Dictionary of First Names* (Oxford, 1990), some 4,000 of them being of foreign origin.

TV, film, literature, and music as sources for names

Works of literature have long had an influence on name choices, but nowadays their influence is probably surpassed by the names of characters in television soap operas and famous films.

From Shakespeare's heroines we get *Rosalind*, *Olivia*, *Portia*, *Perdita*, *Imogen*, *Juliet*, *Ophelia*, and *Cordelia*. On the whole, however, Shakespeare has been less influential than might have been expected. Other writers have influenced particular names. Thus, *Pamela* and *Clarissa* owe much of their popularity to Richardson; *Amelia* to Fielding; *Nicol* to Scott; *Justine* to Durrell; *Leila* to Byron and Lord Lytton; *Christabel* to Coleridge; *Maud* and *Vivien* to Tennyson; and *Pippa* to Browning. In the nineteenth century, the male given name *Shirley* changed sex from male to female after publication of Charlotte Brontë's novel *Shirley* in 1849.

In the past hundred years, works of popular literature have been equally if not more influential: *Janice*, for example, derives from a novel by Paul Leicester Ford, published in 1899, which is hardly ever read nowadays. *Gone with the Wind* (1936) gave us *Scarlett* and *Rhett* among other names.

Films and film stars have had a great influence on the choice of names. *Trac(e)y*, for example, underwent a surge of popularity as a female name after the 1956 film *High Society*, in which Grace Kelly played a character called Tracy Lord. It was reinforced by the birth of Jean Simmons's daughter Tracey, named for her friend Spencer Tracey. *Greer*, *Cary*, and *Spencer* have been chosen as names in honour of Greer Garson, Cary Grant, and Spencer Tracy, while the popular status of *Clark* was noticeably influenced by Gable, *Trevor* by Howard, *Jean* by Harlow, *Jane* by Russell, and *Marilyn* by Monroe.

The influence of opera and classical music on naming has been negligible, but several modern names owe their popularity to the worlds of rock, pop, and folk music. This, too, is a present-day tendency: the rise of *Dylan*, *Kylie*, and *Madonna* is clearly traceable, but we can only guess how many Johns and Pauls owe their name to Lennon and McCartney.

Other sources of names

There are many other sources from which a personal name may be derived. Sometimes a vocabulary word denoting a desirable quality for the life ahead is bestowed on a baby, as in the case of the names *Hope*, *Patience*, *Prudence*, and more recently *Joy* and *Happy*.

Since the nineteenth century, words denoting precious and semi-precious stones (*Beryl*, *Ruby*, and more recently *Amber*, *Jade*, and *Crystal*) have come to be used as given names. The little group of nineteenth-century flower names (*Daisy*, *Primrose*, *Marigold*, etc.) has been expanded in recent years to include other plants (*Bryony*, *Fern*, *Poppy*), birds (*Lark*, *Kestrel*, *Teal*), and natural features (*Storm*, *Rainbow*, *River*).

Where a placename is also found as a given name, it is usually by way of being a family name, but a few have been taken directly from the names of the Western Isles and other places, e.g. *Ailsa*, *Isla(y)*, and *Iona*.

Creating a new name

It remains to be said that in the English-speaking world (though not in some other countries) it is permissible to make up names on the basis of other words and names. Formerly regarded as typical of the US, this practice is now becoming more and more widespread, especially for girls' names. Strategies include fanciful respellings (*Kathryn* (a popular form in America), *Madalynne*, *Ilayne*); recombining syllables from other names (*Jolene*, *Lolicia*); and elaborations with productive feminine suffixes: *-elle*, *-ette*, *-ice*, *-inda*, *-lyn(ne)*. Where such coinages have become established, they are recorded and (as far as possible) explained in this book. It is often tempting to invent a name that nobody else has ever borne, but it needs to be said that inventions of this sort are not always felicitous, and may become tiresome or even an embarrassment in later life. People want to belong; they rarely want a name that sets them aside from the rest of society. Safer choices for a child's name lie in the traditional categories outlined above and explained in the pages that follow.

Acknowledgements

This book is largely derived from *A Concise Dictionary of First Names*, by Patrick Hanks and Flavia Hodges

(Oxford, 1992). It is appropriate here to pay tribute to the contribution of my former colleague Flavia Hodges and to repeat our thanks to the various scholars (Tomás de Bhaldraithe, Ronald Black, Gwynedd Pierce, Joe Reif, and others), who read, corrected, and improved earlier drafts of that work. I would also like to thank Kate Hardcastle for additional research and editing to help create the present book.

P. W. H.
Easter 1995

A

Aaron M Biblical name borne by the brother of Moses, who was appointed by God to be Moses' spokesman and became the first High Priest of the Israelites (Exodus 4:14–16, 7:1–2). The origin and meaning are uncertain: most probably, like **»Moses**, it is of Egyptian rather than Hebrew origin. The traditional derivation from Hebrew *har-on* 'mountain of strength' is no more than a folk etymology. The name has been in regular use from time immemorial as a Jewish name, and was taken up by the Nonconformists as a Christian name in the 17th century.

Abbie F Pet form of **»Abigail**. Also spelled **Abby**, **Abbey**.

Abel M Biblical name borne by the younger son of Adam and Eve, who was murdered out of jealousy by his brother Cain (Genesis 4:1–8). The Hebrew form is *Hevel*, of which the origin is uncertain. It is generally associated with the vocabulary word *hevel* 'breath' or 'vapour' and taken to imply vanity or worthlessness. Abel is considered by the Christian Church to have been a pre-Christian martyr (cf. Matthew 23:35). The name enjoyed a vogue among Puritans and Nonconformists from the 17th century onwards.

Abigail F Biblical name (meaning 'father of exaltation' in Hebrew), borne by one of King David's wives, who had earlier been married to Nabal (1 Samuel 25:3), and by the mother of Absalom's captain Amasa (2 Samuel 1:25). Popular in the 17th century, it has regained favour since the 1990s.

a **Abner** M Mainly North American: Biblical name (meaning 'father of light' in Hebrew) of a relative of King Saul, commander of Saul's army (1 Samuel 14:50; 26:5). It is not common in England, but did enjoy some popularity in North America until the end of the 19th century, having been brought in at the time of the earliest Puritan settlements.

Abraham M Biblical name borne by the first of the Jewish patriarchs, with whom God made a covenant that his descendants should possess the land of Canaan. The Hebrew form is *Avraham*, of uncertain derivation. In Genesis 17:5 it is explained as 'father of a multitude (of nations)' (Hebrew *av hamon (goyim)*). It has always been a popular Jewish given name and was also chosen by Christians, especially among 17th-century Puritans and other fundamentalists. Various early saints of the Eastern Roman Empire bore this name.

Ada F Of uncertain origin; it became popular in the late 18th century. It may be a Latinate variant of the biblical name »**Adah**. However, it has also been explained as a pet form of »**Adele** and »**Adelaide**.

Adah F Biblical name (meaning 'adornment' in Hebrew), borne by the wives of Lamech (Genesis 4:19) and of Esau (Genesis 36:2). See also »**Ada**.

Adam M Biblical name, borne by the first man, according to Genesis 2–3. This probably derives from the Hebrew word *adama* 'earth': it is a common feature of creation legends that a god fashioned the first human beings from earth or clay and breathed life into them.

Addison M Transferred use of the surname, which is derived from *Addie* or *Adie*, a medieval (and occasional modern) pet form of »**Adam**. It is now quite popular, especially in the United States.

Adela F Latinate form of »**Adele**.

Adelaide F Of Germanic origin (via French **Adélaïde**), from *adal* 'noble' + *heid* 'kind', 'sort'. St Adelaide

(c.931–999) was the wife of the Holy Roman Emperor **a**
Otto the Great and became regent after his death. She
was noted for her beauty, goodness, and nobility of
character.

Adele F From French **Adèle**, an ancient name of
Germanic origin, from *adal* 'noble'. This was borne by
a 7th-century saint, a daughter of the Frankish king
Dagobert II. It was also the name of William the
Conqueror's youngest daughter (c.1062–1137), who
became the wife of Stephen of Blois. The name went
out of use in England in the later Middle Ages, and was
revived in the 19th century.

Adeline F French pet form of *Adèle* (see **»Adele**). The
Latinate form **Adelina** is also found occasionally as an
English name.

Adlai M Biblical name borne by a minor character, the
father of one of King David's herdsmen (1 Chronicles
27:29). It is an Aramaic contracted form of the Hebrew
name *Adaliah* 'God is just', and is one of the biblical
names taken up by the Puritans in the 17th century.
Many of them, including *Adlai*, were brought to New
England by the early settlers and have survived in North
America. *Adlai* is particularly associated with the
American statesman and Democratic presidential
candidate Adlai Stevenson (1900–65), in whose family
the name was traditional: it was also borne by his
grandfather (1835–1914), who was vice-president in
1893–7.

Adrian M Usual English form of the Latin name
Hadriānus 'man from Hadria'. Hadria was a town in
northern Italy, which gave its name to the Adriatic Sea.
The name was borne by the Roman emperor Publius
Aelius Hadrianus, during whose reign (AD 117–38)
Hadrian's Wall was built across northern England. In
the Christian era it was the name of at least one
Christian martyr and was adopted by several early

popes, including the only English pope, Nicholas Breakspeare (Adrian IV).

Adrianne F Modern feminine form of **»Adrian**, less common than **»Adrienne**.

Adrienne F French feminine form of **»Adrian**, now also found in the English-speaking world.

Aed M Traditional spelling of the Irish name **»Aodh**.

Aengus M Usual Irish form of **»Angus**.

Africa F Name adopted in the 20th century among African-Americans, in acknowledgement of their ancestral heritage in the continent of Africa.

Agatha F Latinized version of the Greek name *Agathē*, from the feminine form of the adjective *agathos* 'good'. This was the name of a Sicilian martyr of the 3rd century.

Agnes F Latinized version of the Greek name *Hagnē*, from the feminine form of the adjective *hagnos* 'pure', 'holy'. This was the name of a young Roman virgin martyred in the persecutions instigated by the Roman emperor Diocletian in AD 303. She became a very popular saint in the Middle Ages. Her name was associated early on with Latin *agnus* 'lamb', leading to the consistent dropping of the initial *H-* and to her representation in art accompanied by a lamb.

Aidan M Anglicized form of the ancient Gaelic name **Áedán**, a pet form of *Áed* (see **»Aodh**). The name was borne by various early Irish saints, notably a bishop of Ferns (d. 626), who was noted for his kindness and generosity, and the St Aidan (d. 651) who brought Christianity to the English settlers of 7th-century Northumbria, founding the monastery on the island of Lindisfarne.

Aileen F Scottish variant spelling of **»Eileen**.

Ailie F Scottish pet form of **»Aileen** or an Anglicized spelling of **»Eilidh**.

Ailsa F Modern Scottish name derived from *Ailsa Craig*, a
a high rocky islet in the Clyde estuary off the Ayrshire
coast, by the ancient estates of the Kennedys. The name
of this islet is actually Norse, not Gaelic (from Old
Norse *Alfsigesey* 'Alfsigr's island'), but use as a given
name has been influenced by *Ealasaid*, the Gaelic form
of **»Elizabeth**.

Aimée F French: originally a vernacular nickname
meaning 'beloved', from French *aimer* 'to love' (Latin
amāre; cf. **»Amy**).

Aine F Irish: traditional name, pronounced 'ah-na',
from an old vocabulary word meaning 'delight' or
'radiance'. This was the name of the queen of the
Munster fairies.

Ainsley M, occasionally F Transferred use of the Scottish
surname, also spelled *Ainslie*, borne by an important
family in the Scottish borders. It was originally a local
name, taken north by Norman barons in the 12th
century from either *Annesley* in Nottinghamshire or
Ansley in Warwickshire.

Aisling F Irish Gaelic, pronounced 'ash-ling': from the
vocabulary word *aisling* 'dream', 'vision'. This was not
in use as a given name during the Middle Ages, but was
adopted as part of the Irish revival in the 20th century.

Alan M Of ancient Celtic origin and uncertain
derivation. In Scotland and Ireland it is taken to be
from the Gaelic name *Aillén*, a diminutive of *ailill* 'spirit',
'elf'. This has become inextricably mixed with a Breton
name, *Alain* (said to be a diminutive of a word meaning
'rock'), introduced into England by followers of William
the Conqueror. The most notable of these was Alan,
Earl of Brittany, who was rewarded for his services with
vast estates in different parts of England. The spellings
»Allan and **»Allen** are used mainly for the surname, but
in North America they are also common
spellings of the given name. See also **»Alun**.

a **Alana** F Latinate feminine form of »**Alan**; a comparatively recent coinage. The spelling **Alanna** is also found.

Alanda F Recent coinage, a feminine form of »**Alan** influenced by »**Amanda**.

Alannah F Variant of »**Alana**, possibly influenced by names of Hebrew origin such as »**Hannah** and »**Susannah** or by the Anglo-Irish term of endearment *alannah* (Gaelic *a leanbh* 'O child').

Alasdair M Scottish Gaelic form of »**Alexander**, of which the usual Anglicized form is »**Alistair**.

Alban M From the Latin name *Albānus*, which is of uncertain origin. It may be an ethnic name from one of the numerous places in the Roman Empire called *Alba* 'white', or it may represent a Latinized form of a British name derived from the Celtic word *alp* 'rock', 'crag'. Christian tradition has it that St Alban was the first martyr in Roman Britain, who was executed, probably in 209, at Verulamium (now known as St Albans). A Benedictine abbey was founded there and dedicated to the saint by King Offa. Derivation from *Albion*, a poetic name for Britain, is also a possibility.

Albert M From an Old French name of Germanic (Frankish) origin, *Adalbert*, from *adal* 'noble' + *berht* 'bright', 'famous'. This was a princely name throughout Europe, and was adopted by the Normans and introduced by them to England. Its popularity in England in the 19th century was largely in honour of Queen Victoria's consort, Prince Albert of Saxe-Coburg-Gotha.

Aldous M Of uncertain origin; probably from a medieval short form of any of various Norman names, such as *Aldebrand*, *Aldemund*, and *Alderan*, containing the Germanic word *ald* 'old'. It is now rare, known mainly as the given name of the novelist Aldous Huxley (1894–1963).

Alec M Scottish short form of »**Alexander**.

Alethea F A learned coinage which came into use in the 17th century, from the Greek word *alētheia* 'truth'. See also »**Althea**.

Alex M, F Short form of »**Alexander**, »**Alexandra**, and »**Alexis**; also used as a given name in its own right.

Alexa F Short form of »**Alexandra** or variant of »**Alexis** as a girl's name.

Alexander M From the Latin form of the Greek name *Alexandros* 'defender of men'. Its use as a Christian name was sanctioned by the fact that it was borne by several characters in the New Testament and some early Christian saints. However, its tremendous popularity throughout Europe is due mainly to the exploits of the conqueror Alexander the Great (356–23 BC), around whom a large body of popular legend grew up in late antiquity, much of which came to be embodied in the medieval 'Alexander romances'.

Alexandra F Latinate feminine form of »**Alexander**. This name owes its sudden rise in popularity in Britain at the end of the 19th century to Queen Alexandra, Danish wife of Edward VII.

Alexia F Variant of »**Alexis**.

Alexis F, M Variant of *Alexius*, the Latin spelling of Greek *Alexios*, which is a short form of various compound personal names derived from *alexein* 'to defend'. St Alexius was a 5th-century saint of Edessa, venerated in the Orthodox Church as a 'man of God'. *Alexis* was originally a boy's name, but is now more commonly given to girls.

Alfred M From an Old English name meaning 'elf counsel'. This was quite common in England before the Norman Conquest, being borne most notably by Alfred the Great (849–99), King of Wessex. Along with *Edward*, it is one of the few distinctively Old English names to spread widely on the Continent. It was a revived in the 19th century, along with other names of pre-Conquest historical figures.

Alger M Transferred use of the surname, which is ultimately derived from an Old English personal name derived from *ælf* 'elf' + *gār* 'spear'. This form absorbed other Old English names with different first elements: *æthel* 'noble', *ēald* 'old', and *ēalh* 'temple'. Never popular, it is now rarely used.

Algernon M Of Norman French origin, originally a byname meaning 'with a moustache' (from Old French *grenon*, *gernon* 'moustache'). The Normans were as a rule clean-shaven, and this formed a suitable distinguishing nickname when it was applied to William de Percy, a companion of William the Conqueror. In the 15th century it was revived, with a sense of family tradition, as a byname or second given name for his descendant Henry Percy (1478–1527), and thereafter regularly used in that family. It was subsequently adopted into other families connected by marriage with the Percys, and eventually became common property.

Alice F Originally a variant of ≫**Adelaide**, being the Old French form of the Germanic name *Adalheidis*. However, it was regarded as a distinct name when it was revived in the 19th century. It was the name of the child heroine of Lewis Carroll's *Alice's Adventures in Wonderland* (1865) and *Through the Looking Glass* (1872), who was based on his child friend Alice Liddell, daughter of the Dean of Christ Church, Oxford. The spelling ≫**Alys** is now also found.

Alicia F Modern Latinate form of ≫**Alice**.

Alina F Of uncertain origin. It is probably a variant of ≫**Aline**, but could alternatively be of Arabic origin, from a word meaning 'noble' or 'illustrious'. In Scotland it is used as a feminine form of ≫**Alistair**.

Alinda F In the English-speaking world this name is of recent origin, apparently a blend of ≫**Alina** and ≫**Linda**.

It is also found in German-speaking countries, where it is a shortened form of the old Germanic personal name *Adelinde*, from *adal* 'noble' + *lind* 'soft', 'tender'.

Aline F This originated in the Middle Ages as a contracted form of **»Adeline**. In modern use it is either a revival of this or a respelling of **»Aileen**. In Scotland and Ireland it also represents a modern coinage based on the Gaelic word *àlainn* (Scottish), *álainn* (Irish), meaning 'lovely'.

Alison F From a very common medieval name, a Norman French diminutive of **»Alice**. It virtually died out in England in the 15th century, but survived in Scotland, with the result that until its revival in England in the 20th century it had a strongly Scottish flavour. The usual spelling in North America is **Allison**.

Alissa F Variant of **»Alicia**.

Alistair M Scottish: altered spelling of **»Alasdair**, the Gaelic form of **»Alexander**. Alexander has long been a popular name in Scotland, and was borne by three medieval kings of the country. Alternative spellings include **Alisdair**, **Alastair**, **Alister**, and **Al(l)aster**.

Alix F Variant of **»Alex**, used only as a girl's name. The spelling has probably been influenced by **»Alice**.

Allan M Variant spelling of **»Alan**, common mainly in Scotland and North America.

Allaster M Scottish: variant spelling of **»Alistair**. It is borne, for example, by a minstrel in Sir Walter Scott's *Rob Roy* (1818), which ensured its popularity in the 19th century.

Allegra F From the feminine form of the Italian adjective *allegro* 'gay', 'jaunty' (familiar in English as a musical tempo). As a given name it was an original coinage when it was given to Byron's illegitimate daughter (1817–22), but since then it has been taken up by parents in many English-speaking countries.

a **Allen** M Variant spelling of ≫**Alan**. Generally found only as a surname in Britain, this is the most common form of the given name in North America.

Allison F Variant spelling of ≫**Alison**.

Alma F Ostensibly an adoption as a given name of a Latin vocabulary word meaning 'nourishing' or 'kind'. However, it first came into vogue in Britain following the Battle of Alma (1854), which is named from the river in the Crimea by which it took place, and has nothing to do with the Latin adjective. In Tennessee Williams's play *Summer and Smoke* (1948) a bearer of the name explains that it is 'Spanish for soul', but this seems to be no more than coincidental.

Aloysius M Of unknown origin, possibly a Latinized form of a Provençal version of ≫**Louis**. It was relatively common in Italy in the Middle Ages, and was subsequently enjoyed some popularity among Roman Catholics in honour of St Aloysius Gonzaga (1568–91).

Althea F From Greek mythology. Although often considered to be a contracted form of ≫**Alethea**, it is actually a distinct name (Greek *Althaia*), of uncertain origin. It was borne in classical legend by the mother of Meleager, who was given a brand plucked from the fire at the instant of her son's birth, with the promise that his life would last as long as the brand did; some twenty years later she destroyed it in a rage. The name was used by the 17th-century poet Richard Lovelace as a poetic pseudonym for his beloved.

Alun M Welsh: ostensibly a cognate of ≫**Alan**. It is borne in the *Mabinogi* by Alun of Dyfed, a character mentioned in passing several times. It is also a river-name and a regional name in Wales, sometimes spelled *Alyn*. Alun was adopted as a bardic name by the poet John Blackwell (1797–1840).

Alva F Anglicized form of the traditional Irish Gaelic name **Ailbhe**, which is derived from Old Irish *albho* 'white'. In medieval times this was a boy's name, but it **a** has been revived mainly as a girl's name

Alvar M As a medieval name this represents the Old English personal name *Ælfhere*, composed of words meaning 'elf warrior'. In modern use it may be a revival of this, a transferred use of the surname derived from it, or an Anglicized form of Spanish *Álvaro*, a Visigothic personal name meaning 'guardian of all things'.

Alvin M From an Old English personal name meaning 'elf friend', revived in the 19th century and now popular in the United States.

Alys F Variant spelling of »**Alice**.

Alyssa F Variant spelling of »**Alissa**.

Amanda F A 17th-century literary coinage from the Latin gerundive (feminine) *amanda* meaning 'lovable' or 'fit to be loved'. This is evidently modelled on »**Miranda**.

Amber F One of the 19th-century coinages as girls' names that were derived from words denoting gemstones. The vocabulary word *amber* is derived via Old French and Latin from Arabic *ambar*. As a given name, it owed much of its popularity in the 1940s and 1950s to Kathleen Winsor's novel *Forever Amber* (1944).

Ambrose M English form of the Late Latin name *Ambrosius*, which is from post-classical Greek *Ambrosios* 'immortal'. This was borne by various early saints, most notably a 4th-century bishop of Milan. It has long been a popular name among Roman Catholics, especially in Ireland.

Amelia F A blend of two medieval names: *Emilia* (which is of Latin origin: see »**Emily**) and *Amalia* (Latinized short form of various Germanic female names containing the word *amal* 'work'). It was used by Henry Fielding for the heroine of his novel *Amelia* (1751).

a **Amos** M Biblical name borne by a Hebrew prophet of the 8th century BC, whose sayings are collected in the book of the Bible that bears his name. The Hebrew name is of uncertain derivation, but may be connected with the verb *amos* 'to carry': in some traditions it is assigned the meaning 'borne by God'.

Amy F Anglicized form of Old French *Amee* 'beloved'.

Anastasia F Russian: feminine form of the Greek boy's name *Anastasios* (a derivative of *anastasis* 'resurrection'). This is a popular name in Eastern Europe, bestowed in honour of a 4th-century saint who was martyred at Sirmium in Dalmatia. One of the daughters of the last tsar of Russia bore this name. She was murdered along with the rest of the family by the Bolsheviks in 1918, but in 1920 a woman claiming to be the Romanov Princess Anastasia came to public notice in Germany, and a film was based on her story (1956).

André M French form of **»Andrew**.

Andrea F Of disputed origin. It is now generally taken as the feminine equivalent of **»Andrew**, but it may also be a learned coinage from the Greek vocabulary word *andreia* meaning 'virility'.

Andreas M The original New Testament Greek form of **»Andrew**, adopted in the English-speaking world as a learned variant and now increasingly popular.

Andrew M English form of the Greek name *Andreas*, a short form of any of various compound names derived from *andr-* 'man', 'warrior'. St Andrew was the first disciple to be called by Jesus; after the Resurrection, he preached in Asia Minor and Greece, and tradition has it that he was crucified at Patras in Achaia. He was one of the most popular saints of the Middle Ages and was adopted as the patron of Scotland, Russia, and Greece.

Aneirin M Welsh: of uncertain derivation, possibly from
a word related to Irish Gaelic *nár* 'noble', 'modest'. The
original form of the name was *Neirin*; the initial *A*- was
added in the 13th century. This was the name of the
first known Welsh poet, who lived in about AD 600. The
Book of Aneirin is a 13th-century manuscript which
purports to preserve his work, including the *Gododdin*,
an epic recounting the defeat of the Welsh by the
Saxons. The modern spelling **Aneurin** is now the more
common form.

Angela F 18th-century coinage from the feminine of
Church Latin *angelus* 'angel', from *angelos* 'messenger'.
In New Testament Greek this word developed the
specialized meaning 'messenger of God', i.e. an angel.

Angelica F From Church Latin, from the feminine form
of the Latin adjective *angelicus* 'angelic'.

Angelina F Latinate elaboration of >>**Angela**. The
French form *Angeline* is also found.

Angharad F Welsh: traditional name composed of
intensive prefix *an-* + *câr* 'love' + the noun suffix *-ad*.
This was the name of the mother of the 12th-century
chronicler Giraldus Cambrensis ('Gerald the Welshman'). In the *Mabinogi* Angharad Golden Hand at first
rejects Peredur's suit, but later falls in love with him
when he comes back as the unknown Mute Knight.
The name has been strongly revived in Wales since the
1940s, and is well known as that of the actress
Angharad Rees (b. 1949).

Angus M Scottish: Anglicized form of the Gaelic name
Aonghus or >>**Aonghas** (pronounced 'een-yis'), from
Celtic words meaning 'one' and 'choice', the name of an
ancient Celtic god. It is first recorded as a personal
name in Adomnan's 'Life of St Columba', where it
occurs, in the form *Oinogussius*, as the name of a man
for whom the saint prophesied a long life and a peaceful
death. It is also the name of an 8th-century Pictish

a king. The usual Irish Gaelic forms are *Óengus*, *Áengus*, and *Aonghus*. Aonghus Óg was the ancient Irish god of love.

Anita F Originally a Spanish pet form of *Ana*, the Spanish form of **»Anne**. It is now widely used in English-speaking countries with little awareness of its Spanish origin. In the 1950s it came to prominence as the name of the Swedish film actress Anita Ekberg (b. 1931).

Ann F Variant spelling of **»Anne**. *Ann* was the usual spelling in the 19th century.

Anna F Latinate variant of **»Anne**.

Annabel F Sometimes taken as an elaboration of **»Anna**, but more probably an altered form of *Amabel*, an obsolete French name derived from Latin *amābilis* 'lovable', which also lies behind the name **»Mabel**. It has been common in Scotland since the 12th century and in the rest of the English-speaking world since the 1940s. The Latinized form **Annabella** and the Frenchified spelling **Annabelle** are also found, influenced by Latin *bella* and French *belle* 'beautiful'.

Anne F English form (via Old French, Latin, and Greek) of the Hebrew girl's name *Hanna*, which means 'He (i.e. God) has favoured me (i.e. with a child)'. This is the name borne in the Bible by the mother of Samuel (see **»Hannah**), and according to non-biblical tradition also by the mother of the Virgin Mary. It was the widespread folk cult of the latter that led to the great popularity of the name in various forms throughout Europe. The simpler spelling **»Ann** was more common in the 19th century, but the form with final -*e* has grown in popularity during the 20th century.

Annette F French pet form of **»Anne**, now also widely used in the English-speaking world as a name in its own right.

a

Anthea F Latinized spelling of Greek *Antheia*, a personal name derived from the feminine of the adjective *antheios* 'flowery'. This was used in the classical period, for example as a byname of the goddess Hera at Argos, but as a modern given name it was reinvented in the 17th century by the English pastoral poet Robert Herrick.

Anthony M From the Latin name *Antōnius*, a Roman family name of uncertain origin, probably Etruscan. The spelling with -*th*- (not normally heard in the pronunciation) represents a learned but erroneous attempt to associate it with Greek *anthos* 'flower'. In the post-classical period it was a common Christian name, borne by various early saints, most notably a 3rd-century Egyptian hermit who is regarded as the founder of Christian monasticism.

Antoinette F Feminine diminutive of the male name *Antoine*, French form of »**Anthony**. It has become popular in the English-speaking world.

Anton M German and Russian form of »**Anthony**, now also used in the English-speaking world.

Antonia F Latin feminine form of »**Anthony**, unaltered since classical times, when it was a common Roman girl's name.

Antony M Variant spelling of »**Anthony**, historically more correct but now much less common.

Aodh M Irish and Scottish Gaelic (pronounced 'ee'): modern form of the Old Gaelic name *Áed*, from a vocabulary word meaning 'fire'. This was the name of the Celtic sun god and was a common personal name from the earliest times. From the later Middle Ages onwards it was commonly Anglicized as *Hugh*, and more recently as *Eugene*, but the Gaelic form is now coming back into use.

Aoibheann F Traditional Irish Gaelic name (pronounced 'ee-ven'), meaning 'beautiful'. It was a

a

fairly common name among the ancient royal families of Ireland, and has recently been revived. It is also spelled **Aoibhinn**. The usual Anglicized form is **»Eavan**.

Aoife F Irish and Scottish Gaelic name, pronounced 'ee-fya'. It is probably a derivative of *aoibh* 'beauty' (cf. **»Aoibheann**), but has also been associated with *Esuvia*, a Gaulish goddess. It was borne by several different heroines in ancient Irish legend, and in historical times by a daughter of King Dermot of Leinster, who married Richard de Clare, Earl of Pembroke, leader of the Anglo-Norman incursion into Ireland of 1169. The usual Anglicized form is **»Eva**.

Aonghas M The modern Scottish Gaelic form of **»Angus**, also spelled **Aonghus**.

Apollonia F Latin feminine form of the Greek masculine name *Apollonios*, an adjectival derivative of the name of the sun god, *Apollo*. This is of uncertain origin, and may be pre-Greek. St Apollonia was an elderly deaconess martyred at Alexandria under the Emperor Decius in the mid 3rd century.

April F From the month (Latin *(mensis) aprīlis* 'opening month', i.e. the month when buds open and flowers appear). It forms part of a series with **»May** and **»June**, all names taken from months associated with the spring and early summer, a time of new birth and growth.

Arabella F Of uncertain origin. It occurs in Scotland and northern England from the 1600s, and probably represents an alteration of *An(n)abella* (see **»Annabel**).

Aranrhod F Welsh: name borne in the *Mabinogi* by the mother of Dylan and Lleu Llaw Gyffes. It is apparently derived from words meaning 'round' or 'humped' + 'wheel'; the legendary heroine may originally have been the Celtic moon goddess. See also **»Arianrhod**.

Archibald M Of Norman French origin, from a Germanic (Frankish) personal name derived from *ercan* 'genuine' + *bald* 'bold', 'brave'. It has long been

associated with Scotland, where it is in regular use as **a**
the English equivalent of Gaelic *Gilleasbaig* (see
»Gillespie).

Archie　M　Pet form of **»Archibald**, also used
independently.

Ariadne　F　From classical mythology: name of a
daughter of the Cretan king Minos. She gave the
Athenian hero Theseus a ball of wool to enable him to
find his way out of the Labyrinth after killing the
Minotaur. He took her with him when he sailed from
Crete, but abandoned her on the island of Naxos on
the way back to Athens. Greek lexicographers of the
Hellenistic period claimed that the name meant 'very
holy' (from *adnos* 'holy'), and the name survived in the
Christian era partly because of this and partly because
of the cult of the Phrygian martyr St Ariadne (d. *c*.130).

Arianrhod　F　Welsh: altered form of **»Aranrhod**, made
up of the modern Welsh words *arian* 'silver' + *rhod*
'wheel'.

Arianwen　F　Welsh: from *arian* 'silver' + *(g)wen*,
feminine of *gwyn* 'white', 'fair', 'blessed', 'holy'. This
name was borne in the 5th century by one of the
daughters of Brychan, a semi-legendary Welsh
chieftain.

Ariel　M, F　This is a biblical name, but in the Bible it is
actually a placename, mentioned at Ezra (8:16) and
Isaiah (29:1–2), and said to mean 'lion of God' in
Hebrew. It is relatively common as a boy's given name
in modern Israel, but in the United States it is more
frequently used as a girl's name.

Arielle　F　Recent coinage, a distinctively feminine form
of **»Ariel**. The Latinate form **Ariella** is also found.

Arlene　F　Modern coinage of unknown origin, probably
a fanciful coinage based on **»Marlene** or **»Charlene**
or both. It became famous in the 1950s as the name of

a   the American actress and beauty columnist Arlene Dahl (b. 1924).

Arlette F Of ancient but uncertain origin. It is apparently a Norman French double diminutive from Germanic *arn* 'eagle'. It was the name of the mistress of Duke Robert of Normandy in the 11th century; their son was William the Conqueror.

Armani M, F Modern coinage, inspired no doubt by the celebrated Italian fashion designer Giorgio Armani (b. *c.*1934), whose surname is derived from the medieval personal name *Armanno*, a Lombardic name, from Germanic *hariman* 'freeman'.

Arnold M From an Old French name, *Arnald*, *Arnaud*, which is of Germanic (Frankish) origin, from *arn* 'eagle' + *wald* 'ruler'. It was adopted by the Normans and introduced to Britain by them. An early saint of this name, whose cult contributed to its popularity, was a musician at the court of Charlemagne. The name died out in England in the 14th century, and was one of the medieval names revived in the 19th century.

Art M Traditional Irish Gaelic name, from a vocabulary word meaning 'bear', also 'champion'. In Irish legend Art Óenfer ('Art the lonely') is a son of Conn Cétchathach ('Conn of the Hundred Battles'), who overcomes a series of dangers and challenges in order to win his bride, Delbchaem. *Art* is also now used as a short form of **»Arthur**, which is of more recent origin.

Arthur M Of Celtic origin. The historical King Arthur was a British king of the 5th or 6th century, about whom very few facts are known. He ruled in Britain after the collapse of the Roman Empire, at the time of the first invasions of the Angles and Saxons, to which he led the resistance. A vast body of legends and romances grew up around him in the literatures of medieval Western Europe. His name is first found in the Latinized form *Artorius*; the origin is unknown. The

spelling with -th- is a 16th-century development. The
name became particularly popular in Britain in the 19th
century, partly in honour of Arthur Wellesley (1769–
1852), Duke of Wellington, the victor of Waterloo,
partly because of the popularity of Tennyson's *Idylls of
the King* (1859–85), and partly because of the enormous
Victorian interest in things medieval in general and in
Arthurian legend in particular.

Asa M Biblical name borne by one of the early kings of
Judah, who reigned for forty years, according to 1 Kings
and 2 Chronicles. It was originally a byname meaning
'doctor' or 'healer' in Hebrew, and is still a common
Jewish name. It was first used among English-speaking
Christians by the Puritans in the 17th century.

Ashley F, M Now a popular given name for girls, this is
a transferred use of the surname, which comes from
any of numerous places in England named in Old
English as 'ash wood' or 'ash clearing'. Its use as a given
name for boys in the 19th century was probably
inspired, at least in part, by Anthony Ashley Cooper
(1801–85), Earl of Shaftesbury, the philanthropist and
social reformer. It has a large number of fanciful
alternative spellings, including **Ashly**, **Ashlea**, **Ashleigh**,
Ashlee, and **Ashlie**.

Ashling F Irish: Anglicized form of »**Aisling**.

Ashlyn F Altered form of »**Ashling**, influenced by the
common suffix of girls' names -*lyn*.

Ashton M, F Transferred use of the surname, which is
a local name from any of the numerous places in
England named with Old English *æsc* 'ash-tree' + *tūn*
'enclosure', 'settlement'. Formerly a boy's name, it is
now used also for girls, perhaps under the influence of
»**Ashley**.

Astrid F Scandinavian name derived from Old Norse
áss 'god' + *fríthr* 'fair', 'beautiful'. It came into use in
the English-speaking world during the 20th century,

a

influenced to some extent by Queen Astrid of the Belgians (1905–35).

Auberon M From an Old French name of Germanic (Frankish) origin. There is some doubt about its origin; it may be connected with **»Aubrey** or be derived from *adal* 'noble' + *ber(n)* 'bear'. The spelling **»Oberon** is also used.

Aubrey M, F Norman French form of the Germanic name *Alberic* 'elf power'. This was the name, according to Germanic mythology, of the king of the elves. The native Old English form, *Ælfrīc*, borne by a 10th-century archbishop of Canterbury, was superseded at the Norman Conquest by the Continental form. It was a relatively common given name during the Middle Ages, but later fell out of use. Its revival in the 19th century in part represents a transferred use of the surname (which is derived from the Norman given name), as well as a revival of the medieval form. In the United States this is mainly a girl's name, perhaps under the influence of **»Audrey**.

Audrey F Much altered form of the Old English female name *Æthelthryth*, derived from *æthel* 'noble' + *thryth* 'strength'. This was the name of a 6th-century saint (normally known by the Latinized form of her name, *Etheldreda*), who was a particular favourite in the Middle Ages. According to tradition she died from a tumour of the neck, which she bore stoically as a divine punishment for her youthful delight in fine necklaces. The name fell out of favour in the Tudor period, being associated with *tawdry*, that is, lace and other goods sold at St Audrey's fairs, the medieval equivalent of flea markets. Shakespeare bestowed it on Touchstone's comic sweetheart in *As You Like It*. In the 20th century the name has been revived, partly due to the popularity of the actress Audrey Hepburn (1929–93).

Audrina F Fanciful elaboration of **»Audrey**, of recent origin.

Augusta F Latin feminine form of **»Augustus**.

Augustine M English form of the Latin name
Augustīnus (a derivative of **»Augustus**). Its most
famous bearer is St Augustine of Hippo (354–430), one
of the Fathers of the Church. He formulated the
principles followed by the numerous medieval
communities named after him as 'Augustinians' or
'Austin friars'. Also important in England was St
Augustine of Canterbury, who brought Christianity to
Kent in the 6th century. See also **»Austin**.

Augustus M Roman name, from the Latin adjective
augustus 'great', 'magnificent'. This vocabulary word
was adopted as a title by Roman emperors from
Octavian onwards. The latter was the adopted son of
Julius Caesar; he assumed the title *Augustus*, by which
he is now generally known, in 27 BC.

Aurelia F Feminine form of Latin *Aurēlius*, a family
name derived from *aureus* 'golden'. The name was
borne by several minor early saints.

Aurora F From Latin *aurōra* 'dawn', also used in the
classical period as the name of the personified goddess
of the dawn. It was not used as a given name in the
post-classical or medieval period, but is a reinvention
of the Renaissance, and has generally been bestowed
as a learned equivalent of **»Dawn**.

Austin M Medieval contracted form of the Latin name
Augustīnus (see **»Augustine**). The present-day use of
this form as a given name is a reintroduction from its
survival as a surname.

Ava F This is found as a medieval Germanic name, a
short form of any of the various compound female names
beginning with *Av-* (an element of uncertain meaning,
found for example in **»Avis**). St Ava or Avia was a 9th-
century abbess of Dinart in Hainault and a member of
the Frankish royal family. Evidence for the existence
of the name between the early Middle Ages and the

a mid 20th century is lacking; the modern name may well be an independent coinage. Its popularity since the 1950s is largely due to the film actress Ava Gardner (1922–90).

Avelina F Latinate form of the Norman name **≫Evelyn**.

Avery M Transferred use of the surname, which originated in the Middle Ages from a Norman French pronunciation of **≫Alfred**.

Avis F From a Norman French form of the ancient Germanic name *Aveza*, derived from a short form of one or more compound names containing the first element *av* (as in **≫Ava**; the meaning is uncertain). The correspondence in form to the Latin word *avis* 'bird' is coincidental. The spelling **Avice** is also found.

Avril F Although generally taken as the French form of the name of the fourth month (see **≫April**), the development of this name was also influenced by an Old English female personal name derived from *eofor* 'boar' + *hild* 'battle'.

Azalea F Modern coinage, from the name of the flowering shrub, one of the most recent of the names taken from terms denoting flora from the 19th century onwards. The shrub was named in the 18th century with the feminine form of Greek *azaleos* 'dry', because it flourishes in dry soil.

Azalia F Modern coinage, probably simply an altered spelling of **≫Azalea**. However, *Azaliah* is found in the Bible (2 Kings 22:3), but as a male name (meaning 'reserved by God' in Hebrew), borne by a minor character.

Azania F Modern coinage. *Azaniah* is a male name (meaning 'heard by God' in Hebrew) borne by a minor biblical character, but it seems more likely that this name is bestowed with reference to the old African nationalist name for South Africa.

Azaria F Although this is now used as a girl's name, it
is apparently derived from the male biblical name
Azariah (meaning 'helped by God' in Hebrew). He was
a prophet who recalled King Asa to a proper observance
of religion (2 Chronicles 15:1–8). The name is borne
by a number of other minor characters in the Bible, all
of them male.

Azelia F Modern coinage, apparently a variant of
≫Azalia, possibly influenced by the Greek word *azēlos*
'not jealous'.

B

Bailey M, F Transferred use of the surname, which has various origins. Most commonly it was an occupational name for a bailiff or administrative official; in other cases it was a local name for someone who lived near a 'bailey' (a city fortification); in others it may be a local name from *Bailey* in Lancashire, which gets its name from Old English *bēg* 'berry' + *lēah* 'wood' or 'clearing'. In the United States this is now more common as a girl's name, often in fanciful spellings such as **Baylee** and **Bayleigh**.

Baldwin M Transferred use of the modern surname, which comes from a Norman and Old French personal name, *Baldwine* 'brave friend' or 'friend of the brave', of Germanic origin. It was the name of the Norman crusader Baldwin of Boulogne, who in 1100 was elected first king of Jerusalem, and of four further crusader kings of Jerusalem.

Barbara F From a Latin and Greek name meaning 'foreign woman' (feminine form of Greek *barbaros* 'foreign'), borne by an early Christian saint. St Barbara has always been one of the most popular saints in the calendar, although there is some doubt whether she ever actually existed. According to legend, she was imprisoned in a tower and subsequently murdered by her father, who was then struck down by a bolt of lightning. Accordingly, she is regarded as the patron of architects, stonemasons, firework makers, and artillerymen. The name is now occasionally spelled **Barbra**, as in the case of Barbra Streisand (b. 1942).

Barclay M Transferred use of the Scottish surname, which was taken to Scotland in the 12th century by Walter de *Berchelai*, who became chamberlain of Scotland in 1165. His descendants became one of the most powerful families in Scotland. The surname is from *Berkeley* in Gloucestershire, which is named with Old English *beorc* 'birch-tree' + *lēah* 'wood' or 'clearing'.

Barnabas M From the New Testament, where *Barnabas* is the Greek form of an Aramaic name meaning 'son of consolation'. St Barnabas was a companion of St Paul and one of the earliest Christian missionaries.

Barnaby M Vernacular English form of **>>Barnabas**.

Barry M Anglicized form of the Irish Gaelic name **Barra** (Old Irish *Bairre*), a pet form of *Fionnbarr* (see **>>Finbar**). In the 20th century this name has become very popular throughout the English-speaking world, especially in Australia, influenced in part by the existence of a common surname derived from the same source.

Bartholomew M Of New Testament origin, the name of an apostle mentioned in the gospels and in the Acts of the Apostles. It is from Aramaic *Bar-Talmai*, meaning 'son of Talmai'; Talmai is a Hebrew name meaning 'abounding in furrows'. Scholars think that St Bartholomew may in fact be identical with the apostle **>>Nathaniel**.

Barton M Transferred use of the surname, originally a local name from any of the many places in England named in Old English as *bere tūn* 'barley settlement'.

Basil M From the Greek name *Basileios* 'royal' (a derivative of *basileus* 'king'). This was borne by St Basil the Great (c.330–379), bishop of Caesarea, a theologian regarded as one of the Fathers of the Eastern Church. It was also the name of several early saints martyred in the East.

b

Baxter M Transferred use of the surname, which originated in the Middle Ages as an occupational name for a baker, Old English *bæcestre*.

Baylie F Variant spelling of **»Bailey**.

Beatrice F Italian and French form of **»Beatrix**, occasionally used in England during the Middle Ages and revived in the 19th century. It is most famous as the name of Dante's beloved.

Beatrix F From a Late Latin personal name, which was borne by a saint martyred in Rome in the early 4th century. The original form of the name was probably *Viātrix*, a feminine version of *Viātor* 'voyager (through life)', which was a favourite name among early Christians. This was altered by association with Latin *Beātus* 'blessed'. See also **»Beatrice**.

Beattie F Pet form of **»Beatrice** or **»Beatrix**.

Beau M, F Recent coinage as a given name, originally a nickname meaning 'handsome', as borne by Beau Brummell (1778–1840), the dandy who was for a time a friend of the Prince Regent. The word was also used in the 19th century with the meaning 'admirer' or 'sweetheart'. Its adoption as a given name seems to have been due either to the hero of P. C. Wren's novel *Beau Geste* (1924) or to the character of Beau Wilks in Margaret Mitchell's *Gone with the Wind* (1936), which was made into an exceptionally popular film in 1939.

Becca F Modern shortened form of **»Rebecca**.

Becky F Traditional pet form of **»Rebecca**. It was especially popular in the 18th and 19th centuries.

Béibhinn F Traditional Irish Gaelic name, pronounced 'bay-vin, meaning 'white lady' or 'fair lady'. It is sometimes Anglicized as **»Bevin**.

Belinda F Of uncertain origin. It was used by Sir John Vanbrugh for a character in his comedy *The Provok'd Wife* (1697), was taken up by Alexander Pope in *The*

Rape of the Lock (1712), and has enjoyed a steady popularity ever since. It is not known where Vanbrugh got the name from. In Italian literature it is the name of the wife of Orlando, vassal of Charlemagne. It may be an Italian coinage based on *bella* 'beautiful' (see **»Bella**) + *-inda*, as in **»Lucinda**).

Bella F Shortened form of *Isabella*, the Italian version of **»Isabel**, but also associated with the Italian adjective *bella* 'beautiful'.

Belle F Variant of **»Bella**, based on French *belle* 'beautiful'.

Benedict M From Church Latin *Benedictus* 'blessed'. Saint Benedict (*c.*480–*c.*550) composed the Benedictine rule, which governs Christian monastic life. In *c.*529 he founded the great monastery at Monte Cassino that is still the centre of the Benedictine order. The name is used mainly by Roman Catholics. See also **»Bennett**.

Benjamin M Biblical name borne by the youngest of the twelve sons of Jacob (Genesis 35:16–18; 42:4). His mother, Rachel, died in giving birth to him; in her last moments she named him *Benoni* 'son of my sorrow'. His father, however, did not wish him to bear such an ill-omened name, and renamed him *Benyamin*. The meaning of this is uncertain: it could be 'son of my right hand', 'son born in the south', or 'son of (my) old age'.

Bennett M Transferred use of the surname, which is derived from a medieval English vernacular form of the given name **»Benedict**.

Benson M Transferred use of the surname, which originated as a patronymic from *Ben*, a short form of **»Benedict**, or as a local name from Benson, Oxfordshire.

Bentley M Transferred use of the surname, a local name from any of the dozen or so places in England so called from Old English *beonet* 'bent grass' + *lēah* 'wood' or 'clearing'.

Berenice F From the Greek female name *Berenīkē*, which apparently originated in the royal house of Macedon. It is probably a Macedonian dialectal form of the Greek name *Pherenīkē* 'victory bringer'. It was introduced to the Egyptian royal house by the widow of one of Alexander the Great's officers, who married Ptolemy I. It was also borne by an early Christian woman mentioned in Acts 25. See also **»Bernice**.

Bernadette F French feminine diminutive of **»Bernard**. In Britain and Ireland it is used mainly by Roman Catholics, who take it in honour of St Bernadette Soubirous of Lourdes (1844–79), a French peasant girl who had visions of the Virgin Mary and uncovered a spring where miraculous cures are still sought.

Bernard M Norman and Old French name of Germanic (Frankish) origin, meaning 'bear-hardy'. This was borne by three famous medieval churchmen: St Bernard of Menthon (923–1008), founder of a hospice on each of the Alpine passes named after him; the monastic reformer St Bernard of Clairvaux (1090–1153); and the scholastic philosopher Bernard of Chartres.

Bernice F Contracted form of **»Berenice**.

Bert M Short form of any of the various names beginning or ending with this syllable, for example **»Albert** and **»Bertrand**.

Bertha F Latinized version of a Germanic name, a short form of any of a number of names derived from the word *berht* meaning 'bright' or 'famous'. It died out as a medieval name, and was reintroduced into the English-speaking world from Germany in the 19th century.

Bertram M From a Norman and Old French name of Germanic (Frankish) origin, *Berhtramn*, meaning 'bright raven'. Ravens were traditional symbols of wisdom in Germanic mythology; the god Odin was regularly accompanied by ravens called Hugin and Munin. See also **Bertrand**.

Bertrand M Medieval French variant of **Bertram**, imported to Britain by the Normans. In modern times it was famous in particular as the given name of the philosopher Bertrand Russell (1872–1970).

Beryl F One of the numerous girl's names taken from gemstones which came into use at the end of the 19th century. Beryl is a pale green semiprecious stone (of which emerald is a variety). Other colours are also found. The word is from Greek, and is ultimately of Indian origin.

Bess F Short form of **Elizabeth**, in common use since the days of Queen Elizabeth I, who was known as 'Good Queen Bess'.

Beth F Short form of **Elizabeth**. It was not used before the 19th century, when it became popular in America and elsewhere after publication of Louisa M. Alcott's novel *Little Women* (1868), in which Beth March is one of the four sisters who are the central characters.

Bethan F Originally a pet form of **Beth** used in Wales, now also popular elsewhere in the English-speaking world.

Bethany F Of New Testament origin. In the New Testament it is a placename, that of the village just outside Jerusalem where Jesus stayed during Holy Week, before going on to Jerusalem and crucifixion (Matthew 21:17; Mark 11:1; Luke 19:29; John 12:1). Its Hebrew name probably means 'house of figs' (*beth te'ena* or *beth te'enim*). The given name is favoured by Roman Catholics, being bestowed in honour of Mary of Bethany, sister of Martha and Lazarus.

Betsy F Pet form of **Elizabeth**, a blend of **Betty** and **Bessie**, which is also used independently.

b

Bette F Variant of »**Betty**, associated particularly with the film actress Bette Davis (1908–89), born Ruth Elizabeth Davis.

Bettina F Latinate elaboration of »**Betty**.

Betty F Pet form of »**Elizabeth**, dating from the 18th century.

Beulah F Biblical name: from the name (meaning 'married' in Hebrew) applied to the land of Israel by the prophet Isaiah (Isaiah 62:4). 'The land of Beulah' was sometimes taken as a reference to heaven. It was taken up as a given name in England at the time of the Reformation and was popular among the Puritans in the 17th century.

Beverley mainly F Transferred use of the surname, which is from a place in East Yorkshire. **Beverly** is the usual spelling in America. It is not clear why it should have become such a popular girl's name. Association with Beverly Hills near Los Angeles, California, the district where many film stars live, is probably a factor.

Bevin F Anglicized form of the Gaelic name »**Béibhinn**.

Bianca F Italian: from *bianca* 'white' (i.e. 'pure', but cf. »**Blanche**). The name was used by Shakespeare for characters in two of his plays set in an Italian context: the mild-mannered sister of Katharina, the 'shrew' in *The Taming of the Shrew*, and a courtesan in *Othello*.

Bill M Altered short form of »**William**; see »**Billy**.

Billie F, M Variant of »**Billy**, now mainly used for girls, and sometimes bestowed at baptism as a female equivalent of »**William**.

Billy M, F Pet form of »**William**. The change of *W-* to *B-* probably took place in Ireland: English words beginning with *w-* are regularly changed to *b-* when borrowed into Gaelic. The nickname 'King Billy' for William of Orange is an early example.

Binnie F Pet form of **≫Bernice**.

Blaine M Anglicized form of the Gaelic personal name
Bládán, originally a byname from a diminutive of *blá*
'yellow'. It was the name of an early Celtic saint who
lived in the 6th century. The spellings **Blain** and **Blane**
are also found.

Blair M, F Transferred use of the Scottish surname, in
origin a local name from any of various places named
with Gaelic *blàr* 'plain', 'field'. In North America this is
now widely used as a girl's name. The spelling **Blaire**
is also found.

Blaise M French, from the Latin name *Blasius*, probably
meaning 'lisping'. This was the name of a saint who
enjoyed great popularity throughout Europe in the
Middle Ages. He was a bishop of Sebaste in Armenia,
and was martyred in the early years of the 4th century;
these bare facts were elaborated in a great number of
legends that reached Europe from the East at the time
of the Crusades. He was supposedly endowed with
miraculous healing power, and while imprisoned and
awaiting torture and execution he miraculously saved
a boy from choking to death. He is the patron of
sufferers from sore throats.

Blake M Transferred use of the common English
surname, which has two quite distinct origins. It is both
from Old English *blæc* 'black' and from Old English *blāc*
'pale', 'white'. It was thus originally a nickname given
to someone with hair and complexion that was either
remarkably dark or remarkably light.

Blanche F Originally a nickname for a blonde, from
blanche, feminine of Old French *blanc* 'white'. It came
to be associated with the notion of whiteness as
indicating purity, and was introduced into England as
a given name by the Normans. A pale complexion
combined with light hair was long considered an ideal
of beauty in Europe.

Bláthnat F Traditional Irish Gaelic name, pronounced 'blah-nat', from a diminutive of *blath* 'flower'. This was the name of a queen of West Munster, who fell in love with Cú Chulainn, who abducted her, killing her husband Cú Roí. She was, however, killed by Cú Roí's minstrel, who seized her and leapt off a cliff to the rocks below.

Blodwedd F Welsh: name borne by a character in the *Mabinogi*. She was conjured up out of flowers as a bride for Lleu Llaw Gyffes, and was originally called *Blodeuedd*, a derivative of *blawd* 'flowers'. After she had treacherously had her husband killed she was transformed into an owl, and her name was changed to *Blodeuwedd* 'flower face', an allusion to the markings round the eyes of the owl.

Blodwen F Welsh traditional name, derived from *blawd* 'flowers' + (*g*)*wen* 'white', feminine of *gwyn* 'white', 'fair', 'blessed', 'holy'. The name was relatively common in the Middle Ages and has recently been revived.

Blossom F 19th-century coinage as a girl's name, from the vocabulary word for flowers on a fruit tree or ornamental tree (Old English *blōstm*). It has long been used as an affectionate pet name for a young girl.

Bobbie F, M Variant of *Bobby*, now mainly used for girls, as a pet form of »**Roberta** or »**Robin**. The modish variant **Bobbi** is also popular.

Bobby M, F Pet form of »**Robert** or »**Roberta**; see also »**Bobbie**.

Bonita F Apparently coined in the United States in the 1940s, from the feminine of Spanish *bonito* 'pretty'. This is not normally used as a given name in Spanish-speaking countries. *Bonita* would be the feminine form of a medieval Latin male name, *Bonītus* (from *bonus* 'good'), but no records of the female name prior to the 1940s in America are known.

Bonnie F Originally an affectionate nickname from the Scottish word *bonnie* meaning 'fine', 'attractive', or 'pretty'. However, until recently it was not used as a given name in Scotland. Its popularity may be attributed to the character of Scarlett O'Hara's infant daughter Bonnie in the film *Gone With the Wind* (1939), based on Margaret Mitchell's novel of the same name. (Bonnie's name was really Eugenie Victoria, but she had 'eyes as blue as the bonnie blue flag'.) A famous American bearer was Bonnie Parker, accomplice of the bank robber Clyde Barrow; their life together was the subject of the film *Bonnie and Clyde* (1967). The name has enjoyed a vogue in the second part of the 20th century, and has also been used as a pet form of ▶▶**Bonita**.

Boris M Russian: introduced into the English-speaking world in the 20th century. It is from the Tartar nickname *Bogoris* 'small'. Later, however, it was taken to be a shortened form of the Russian name *Borislav*, from *bor* 'battle' + *slav* 'glory'. The name was borne in the 9th century by a ruler of Bulgaria who converted his kingdom to Christianity and sheltered disciples of Saints Cyril and Methodius when they were expelled from Moravia. It was also borne by a 10th-century Russian saint, son of Prince Vladimir of Kiev.

Braden M Transferred use of the Irish surname, Gaelic *Ó Bradáin* 'descendant of Bradán', a personal name meaning 'salmon'.

Bradford M Mainly U.S.: transferred use of the English surname, in origin a local name from any of the numerous places in England named in Old English as 'the broad ford'. The surname was borne most famously by William Bradford (1590–1657), leader of the Pilgrim Fathers from 1621 and governor of Plymouth Colony for some 30 years.

Bradley M Transferred use of the surname, which originated as a local name from any of the numerous

b

places in England named in Old English as the 'broad wood' or 'broad clearing'.

Brady M, F Mainly North American: transferred use of the surname, which is of Irish origin, from Gaelic Ó Brádaigh 'descendant of Brádach', an old Irish byname of uncertain origin, possibly a contracted form of brághadhach 'large-chested', from brágha 'chest'.

Brandon M Transferred use of the surname, in origin a local name from any of various places in England so called. The given name may also be an altered form of ≫**Brendan**.

Brandy F Mainly U.S.: probably invented as a feminine form of ≫**Brandon**.

Branwen F Welsh traditional name, apparently from brân 'raven' + (g)wen, feminine of gwyn 'white', 'fair', 'blessed', 'holy', but more probably a variant of ≫**Bronwen**. The story of Branwen, daughter of Llŷr, forms the second chapter or 'branch' of the Mabinogi: it tells of her beauty and of the conflict on her account between her brother Bran, King of the 'Island of the Mighty' (i.e. Britain), and her husband Matholwch, King of Ireland.

Breda F Irish: Anglicized or Latinized form of Gaelic Bríd (see ≫**Bride**, ≫**Bridget**).

Brenda F A very popular name, of uncertain origin. Until the 20th century it was confined mainly to Scotland and Ireland; it is often taken as a feminine form of ≫**Brendan**. It is more probably of Scandinavian origin: a short form of any of the various compound names derived from Old Norse brand 'sword', for example Hildebrand.

Brendan M From the old Irish personal name Bréanainn, probably derived from an Old Celtic word meaning 'prince'. This was the name of two 6th-century Irish saints, Brendan the Voyager and Brendan of Birr. According to legend, the former was the first European

to set foot on North American soil, in the course of a
seven-year voyage. The modern Irish Gaelic form
Breandán and the Anglicized *Brendan* are based on the   **b**
medieval Latin form *Brendanus*.

Brenna   F   Mainly U.S.: modern coinage, apparently
created as a feminine form of »**Brennan**, but perhaps
also influenced by »**Brianna**.

Brennan   F   Mainly U.S.: transferred use of the Irish
surname, Gaelic *Ó Braonáin* 'descendant of Braonán', a
personal name derived from a diminutive of *braon*
'moisture', 'drop'. It may also be taken as a contracted
form of »**Brendan**.

Brent   M   Mainly U.S.: transferred use of the surname,
which is derived from any of several places in Devon
and Somerset which are on or near prominent hills, and
were named with a Celtic or Old English term for a
hill.

Brett   M   Transferred use of the surname, which
originated in the Middle Ages as an ethnic name for a
Breton. Quite a large number of Bretons arrived in
England in the wake of the Norman Conquest, and the
surname is most common in East Anglia, where Breton
settlement was particularly concentrated.

Brian   M   Originally Irish, but now extremely popular
throughout the English-speaking world. It may be from
an Old Celtic word meaning 'high' or 'noble'. The name
has been perennially popular in Ireland, in particular
on account of the fame of Brian Boru (Gaelic *Brian
Bóroimhe*, d. 1014), a Munster warrior of the 10th
century who eventually became high king of all Ireland.

Brianna   F   Recent coinage to create a female equivalent
of »**Brian**.

Briar   F   20th-century coinage from the vocabulary word
briar or *brier* (Old English *brær*), denoting a thorny
bush of wild roses ('sweet briars') or brambles.

Brice M This was the name of a saint who was a disciple and successor of St Martin of Tours. His name is found in the Latinized forms *Bri(c)tius* and *Bricius* and is probably of Gaulish origin, possibly derived from a word meaning 'speckled' (cf. Welsh *brych*).

Bride F Irish: Anglicized form of **Bríd**, a modern Gaelic form of *Brighid* (see **»Bridget**). The pet form **Bridie** is very common in Ireland.

Bridget F Anglicized form of the Irish name **Brighid**, pronounced 'breed'. St Brighid of Kildare (c.450–c.525) is one of the patron saints of Ireland. Very few facts are known about her life: she founded a religious house for women at Kildare and is said to be buried at Downpatrick, where St Patrick and St Columba are also buried. The name itself dates back to well before the Christian era: Brighid (probably derived from a vocabulary word meaning 'exalted') was the ancient Irish goddess of poetry, prophecy, and divination. Many of the stories of miracles told about St Brighid seem to be Christianized versions of pagan legends concerning a pre-Christian goddess. Another St Bridget (c.1303–73), mystic, visionary, and benefactress, is the patron saint of Sweden; she was of Irish birth.

Brigham M Mainly U.S.: name adopted in honour of the Mormon leader Brigham Young (1801–77). It was originally a surname, a local name from places in Cumbria and North Yorkshire named in Old English *brycg hām* 'homestead by the bridge'. Brigham Young was the son of John and Abigail Young of Whitingham, Vermont.

Brigid F Mainly Irish variant of **»Bridget**.

Brigitte F French form of **»Bridget**, associated particularly with the French film star of the 1950s Brigitte Bardot (b. 1934 as Camille Javal).

Briony F Variant spelling of **»Bryony**.

Brittany F Mainly North American: modern coinage, from the regional name denoting the traditionally Celtic-speaking province of north-west France. This was known in medieval Latin as *Britannia*, as it was settled by refugees from Cornwall and Devon in the 5th and 6th centuries AD, following the Anglo-Saxon conquest of Wessex. The spelling **Britney** is very fashionable.

Brock M Mainly U.S.: transferred use of the surname, originally a nickname for someone resembling a badger (Middle English *broc(k)*, Old English *brocc*, a word of Celtic origin).

Brodie M, F Transferred use of the Scottish surname, which is taken from Brodie Castle in Moray, probably so named from Gaelic *brothhach* 'muddy place'. The spelling **Brody** is also found.

Brogan M, F Either an Anglicized form of the Irish male personal name *Brógán*, which is probably from a diminutive of Gaelic *bróg* 'shoe', or a transferred use of the surname derived from the personal name, used for both boys and girls.

Brónach F Traditional Irish Gaelic name meaning 'sorrowful'.

Bronwen F Welsh: from *bron* 'breast' + *(g)wen*, feminine of *gwyn* 'white', 'fair', 'blessed', 'holy'.

Brooke F Transferred use of the surname, which was originally a local name for someone who lived near a brook or stream (Old English *bróc*). It has been borne by two well-known American film actresses: Brooke Adams (b. 1949) and Brooke Shields (b. 1965).

Brooklyn M, F Modern coinage, apparently an adoption of the American placename, a district of New York city, originally named by Dutch settlers as *Breukelen*. The choice of the name by David and Victoria Beckham for their eldest son (b. 1999) will no doubt have added to its popularity.

Bruce M Transferred use of the Scottish surname, now used as a given name throughout the English-speaking world. In the earlier part of the 20th century it was particularly popular in Australia. The Bruces were an extremely powerful and influential Norman family in Scottish affairs in the early Middle Ages; its most famous member was Robert the Bruce (1274–1329). He ruled Scotland as King Robert I from 1306 to 1329.

Bruno M Latinized form of the Old German word *brun* 'brown', which was used as a name among the ruling families of Germany during the Middle Ages. St Bruno was a 10th-century saint, son of the Emperor Henry the Fowler. A Saxon Duke Bruno gave his name to Brunswick (German *Braunschweig*, which means 'Bruno's settlement'). It was brought to the English-speaking world in the 19th century by settlers of German ancestry in the United States.

Bryan M Variant of ➤➤**Brian**.

Bryce M, occasionally F Variant of ➤➤**Brice**, now fairly commonly used as a given name, originating as a transferred use of the Scottish surname derived from the medieval given name.

Bryn M Welsh: 20th-century coinage from the Welsh topographical term *bryn* 'hill', in part as a short form of ➤➤**Brynmor**. Compare ➤➤**Brynn**.

Brynmor M Welsh: 20th-century coinage from the name of a place in Gwynedd, named with *bryn* 'hill' + *mawr* 'large'.

Brynn M, F Variant spelling of ➤➤**Bryn**. In the United States this is now predominantly a girl's name, no doubt by association with names such as ➤➤**Lynn**.

Bryony F From the name of the plant (Greek *bryonia*). This is one of several names coined in the early 20th century from vocabulary words denoting flowers.

Bryson M Mainly U.S.: transferred use of the surname, which has a double origin. In part it is a patronymic

from the given name **»Brice** or **»Bryce**, in part an
Anglicized form of the Irish Gaelic surname Ó *Briosáin*,
an altered form of Ó *Muirgheasáin* 'descendant of
Muirgheasán', a personal name perhaps from *muir gus*
'sea vigour'. The Ó Muirgheasáins were hereditary poets
(and keepers of the relics of St Columba) in Donegal
and Scotland.

Burgess M Transferred use of the surname, which is a
status name from the Old French word *burgeis* 'freeman
of a borough'.

Burt M Mainly U.S.: of various origins. In the case of
the film actor Burt Lancaster (1913–94) it is a short
form of **»Burton**, but it is also found as a variant
spelling of **»Bert**: the pianist and composer Burt
Bacharach (b. 1928) is the son of one Bert Bacharach.

Burton M Transferred use of the surname, in origin a
local name from any of the numerous places in England
so called. In most cases the placename is a compound
of Old English *burh* + *tūn*, meaning 'fortified
settlement'.

Byron M Transferred use of the surname, first bestowed
as a given name in honour of the poet Lord Byron
(George Gordon, 6th Baron Byron, 1784–1824). The
surname is a locative name derived from Old English
æt thæm bӯrum 'at the byres (cattlesheds)'.

Cade M Transferred use of the surname, originally a nickname from a word denoting something round and lumpish. It is one of several given names that owe their origin to Margaret Mitchell's novel *Gone with the Wind* (1936).

Cadell M Welsh traditional name, derived from *cad* 'battle' + the diminutive suffix *-ell*.

Cadogan M Anglicized form of the Old Welsh personal name *Cadwgan* or *Cadwgawn*, meaning 'battle glory'. This was borne by several Welsh princes in the early Middle Ages and is mentioned as the name of two characters in the *Mabinogi*. It was revived in the 19th century, in part as a transferred use of the surname derived from it.

Caesar M Mainly U.S.: Anglicized form of Italian *Cesare* or French *César*, or a direct adoption of the Roman imperial family name *Caesar*, which may be of Etruscan origin. Its most notable bearer was Gaius Julius Caesar (?102–44 BC) and it was also borne by his adopted son Augustus. Subsequently it was used as an imperial title and eventually became a vocabulary word for an emperor (leading to German *Kaiser* and Russian *tsar*).

Cahan M Irish: see ≫**Kane**.

Caileigh F See ≫**Kayley**.

Caitlín F Irish Gaelic form of ≫**Katherine**, pronounced 'kat-leen'. It is being increasingly widely used in the English-speaking world, generally without the accent and with the pronunciation 'kate-lin'.

Caitrín F Irish Gaelic form of ≫**Katherine**.

Caleb M Biblical name, borne by an early Israelite, one of only two of those who set out with Moses from Egypt to live long enough to enter the promised land (Numbers 26:65). The name, which is apparently derived from the word for 'dog' in Hebrew, is said in some Jewish traditions to symbolize dog-like devotion to God. It was popular among the Puritans and was introduced by them to America.

Caleigh F See ≫**Kayley**.

Callie F Mainly U.S.: probably originally a variant of ≫**Kelly** or ≫**Kayley**. It is also spelled **Cally**.

Callum M Scottish Gaelic form of the Late Latin personal name *Columba* 'dove', popular among early Christians because the dove symbolized gentleness, purity, peace, and the Holy Spirit. St Columba was one of the most influential of all the early Celtic saints. He was born in Donegal in 521 into a noble family, founded monastery schools at Durrow, Derry, and Kells, and then, in 563, sailed with twelve companions to Scotland. He established a monastery on the island of Iona, and from there converted the Pictish and Irish inhabitants of Scotland to Christianity. He died in 597 and was buried at Downpatrick. The traditional Scottish spelling of his name is **Calum**; its Irish form is ≫**Colm**.

Calvin M From the French surname, used as a given name mainly among Low-Church Protestants and Nonconformists in honour of the French Protestant theologian Jean Calvin (1509–64). The surname, meaning 'little bald one', is derived from a diminutive of *calve*, Picard form of French *chauve* 'bald'. (The theologian was born in Picardy.)

Cameron M, F Transferred use of the Scottish surname, which is borne by an important Highland clan. Their name is popularly derived from an ancestor with a crooked nose (Gaelic *cam sròn*). There were also

c

Camerons in the Lowlands, apparently the result of an assimilation to this name of a Norman baronial name derived from *Cambernon* in Normandy. It is common throughout the English-speaking world, and is now used on both sides of the Atlantic as a girl's name.

Camilla F Feminine form of the Roman family name *Camillus*, of obscure, probably non-Roman origin. According to tradition, as recorded by the Roman poet Virgil, Camilla was the name of a warrior maiden, Queen of the Volscians, who fought in the army of Aeneas (*Aeneid* 7:803–17).

Campbell M Transferred use of the Scottish surname, borne by one of the great Highland clans, whose head is the Duke of Argyll. The name is derived from an ancestor with a crooked mouth (Gaelic *cam beul*).

Candace F The hereditary name of a long line of queens of Ethiopia. One of them is mentioned in the Bible (Acts 8:27), where the apostle Philip baptizes 'a man of Ethiopia, an eunuch of great authority under Candace queen of the Ethiopians, who had the charge of all her treasure'.

Candice F Apparently a respelling of **»Candace**, perhaps influenced by **»Clarice** or by a folk etymology deriving the name from Late Latin *canditia* 'whiteness'. The name is best known as that of the American actress Candice Bergen (b. 1946).

Candida F From Late Latin, meaning 'white'. White is associated in Christian imagery with purity and salvation (cf. Revelation 3:4 'thou hast a few names even in Sardis which have not defiled their garments; and they shall walk with me in white: for they are worthy'). This was the name of several early saints, including a woman whose illness was supposedly cured by St Peter himself.

Candy F Mainly North American: from an affectionate nickname derived from the vocabulary word *candy* 'confectionery'. The word *candy* is from French *sucre* *candi* 'candied sugar', i.e. sugar boiled to make a crystalline sweet. The French word is derived from Arabic *qandi*, which is in turn of Indian origin. *Candy* is also found as a short form of **»Candice**.

Caoimhe F Irish Gaelic name, pronounced '**kee-va**', from a vocabulary word meaning 'gentleness', 'loveliness', or 'grace'.

Cara F 20th-century coinage, from the Italian term of endearment *cara* 'beloved' or the Irish Gaelic vocabulary word *cara* 'friend'. There may also have been some influence from the traditional Irish Gaelic name **Ceara**, said to mean 'red-headed'.

Caradoc M Welsh: respelling of *Caradog*, an ancient Celtic name apparently derived from the root *câr* 'love'. A form of this name was borne by the British chieftain recorded under the Latinized version *Caractacus*, son of Cunobelinos. He rebelled against Roman rule in the 1st century AD, and although the rebellion was swiftly put down he is recorded by the Roman historian Tacitus as having impressed the Emperor Claudius by his proud bearing in captivity.

Careen F Of recent origin and uncertain derivation. Its first appearance seems to have been in Margaret Mitchell's novel *Gone with the Wind* (1936), where it is borne by one of the sisters of Scarlett O'Hara. The name may represent a combination of **»Cara** with the diminutive suffix *-een* (of Irish origin; cf. **»Maureen**), or it may be an altered form of **»Corinna** or **»Carina**.

Carey F Variant spelling of **»Cary**, used mainly as a girl's name, under the influence of **»Carrie**.

Carina F Late 19th-century coinage, apparently representing a Latinate elaboration of the feminine adjective *cara* 'beloved'; in part it may also have been inspired by **»Karin**.

Carissa F Recent coinage, either a simplified spelling of **»Charissa** or an elaborated form of **»Carys**.

c

Carl M From an old-fashioned German spelling variant of *Karl*, the German version of **»Charles**. It is now increasingly used in the English-speaking world, and for some reason is particularly popular in Wales.

Carla F Feminine form of **»Carl**.

Carlotta F Italian form of **»Charlotte**, occasionally used in the English-speaking world.

Carlton M Transferred use of the surname, a local name from any of the many places in England named in Old English as *carlatūn* 'settlement of the (free) peasants'. This is the same name in origin as **»Charlton**.

Carly F Pet form or variant of **»Carla**.

Carmel F A name of early Christian origin, referring to 'Our Lady of Carmel', a title of the Virgin Mary. *Carmel* is the name (meaning 'garden' or 'orchard' in Hebrew) of a mountain in the Holy Land, which was populated from very early Christian times by hermits. They were later organized into the Carmelite order of monks. The name is used mainly by Roman Catholics.

Carmen F Spanish variant of **»Carmel**, altered by folk etymology to the form of the Latin word *carmen* 'song'. It is now found as a given name in the English-speaking world, in spite of, or perhaps because of, its association with the tragic romantic heroine of Bizet's opera *Carmen* (1875), based on a short story by Prosper Mérimée.

Carol F, originally M Anglicized derivative of *Carolus* (Latin form of **»Charles**) and of its feminine form **Carola**. This was never common as a boy's name, and has become even less so since its growth in popularity as a girl's name. This began in the 19th century, probably as a short form of **»Caroline**.

Carole F French form of **»Carol**. In the 1930s it was associated particularly with the film star Carole Lombard (1908–42).

Caroline F From the French form of Latin or Italian **Carolina**, a feminine derivative of *Carolus* (see ≫**Charles**).

Carolyn F Altered form of ≫**Caroline**.

Carrie F Pet form of ≫**Caroline** and occasionally of other girls' names beginning with the syllable *Car-*.

Carson M, occasionally F Transferred use of the Scottish surname, of uncertain derivation. The first known bearer is a certain Robert *de Carsan* (or *de Acarson*), recorded in 1276; the 'de' suggests derivation from a placename, but if this is right the place in question has not been identified. Among Protestants in Northern Ireland, it is sometimes bestowed in honour of Edward Carson (1854–1935), the Dublin barrister and politician who was a violent opponent of Home Rule for Ireland.

Carter M Transferred use of the surname, which originated as an occupational name for someone who transported goods in a cart.

Cary M, sometimes F Transferred use of the surname, which comes from one of the places in Devon or Somerset so called from an old Celtic river name. *Cary* became popular due to the fame of the film actor Cary Grant (1904–89), who was born in Bristol and made his first theatrical appearances under his baptismal name of Archie Leach.

Caryl F, occasionally M Of uncertain origin, probably a variant of ≫**Carol**.

Carys F Welsh: modern creation, from *câr* 'love' + the ending *-ys*, coined by analogy with names such as ≫**Gladys**.

Casey F, M Originally a North American name, bestowed in honour of the engine driver and folk hero 'Casey' Jones (1863–1900), who acquired the nickname from his place of birth, Cayce, Kentucky. Recently the name has become equally popular in Britain, particularly for girls. In part, this may reflect a transferred use of the Irish surname, a reduced Anglicized form of *Ó Cahasaigh* 'descendant of Cathasach'.

Caspar M Dutch form of **»Jasper**, also found occasionally in English. According to legend, this was the name of one of the three Magi or 'wise men' who brought gifts to the infant Christ. The magi are not named in the Bible, but early Christian tradition assigned them the names *Caspar*, *Balthasar*, and *Melchior*.

Cass F Medieval and modern short form of **»Cassandra**.

Cassandra F From Greek legend. Cassandra was a Trojan princess blessed with the gift of prophecy but cursed with the fate that she was never believed. She was brought back to Greece as a captive concubine by Agamemnon and met her death at the hands of his jealous wife Clytemnestra. Despite the omens, this is now a popular girl's name, revived by parents looking to classical mythology for distinctive names.

Cassidy F, M Transferred use of the Anglicized form of the Irish Gaelic surname *Ó Caiside*. Its use as a girl's name may be due to the *-y* ending, coupled with the fact that it could be taken as an elaborated form of **»Cass**.

Cassie F Pet form of **»Cassandra**.

Cathal M Traditional Irish Gaelic name (pronounced 'ko-hal'), derived from the Old Celtic words *cath* 'battle' + *val* 'rule'. It was borne by a 7th-century saint who served as head of the monastic school at Lismore, Co. Waterford, before being appointed bishop of Taranto in south Italy.

Catherine F Alternative (and equally common) spelling of **»Katherine**, due in part to the Old French spelling *Caterine*. The spelling **Catharine** is also found.

Cathleen F Variant spelling of **≫Kathleen**.

Catrin F Welsh form of **≫Katherine**.

Catrina F Simplified spelling of **≫Catriona**.

Catriona F Anglicized form of the Gaelic names **Ca(i)triona** (Scottish) and **Caitríona** (Irish), which are themselves forms of **≫Katherine**. This name is now used throughout the English-speaking world, as well as being especially popular among people of Scottish ancestry. It attracted wide attention as the name of the heroine of Robert Louis Stevenson's novel *Catriona* (1893).

Cayleigh F See **≫Kayley**.

Ceallach M, F Traditional Irish Gaelic name, pronounced 'kell-ach', said to mean 'bright-headed'. See **≫Kelly**.

Cecil M Transferred use of the surname of a great noble family, which rose to prominence in England during the 16th century. The Cecils were of Welsh origin; their surname represents an Anglicized form of *Seissylt*, an Old Welsh form of the Latin name *Sextilius*, from *Sextus* 'sixth'. It has also sometimes been taken as an English form of Latin *Caecilius* (see **≫Cecilia**).

Cecilia F From the Latin name *Caecilia*, feminine of *Caecilius*, a Roman family name borne by a 3rd-century saint, derived from the byname *Caecus* 'blind'. The girl's name was a good deal more common than the masculine form, largely due to the cult of the 2nd- or 3rd-century virgin martyr whose name is still mentioned daily in the Roman Catholic Canon of the Mass. She is the patron saint of music and has inspired works such as Purcell's 'Ode on St Cecilia's Day'.

Cecily F The medieval vernacular English form of **≫Cecilia**, also found in the spelling **≫Cicely**.

Cedric M Coined by Sir Walter Scott for the character Cedric of Rotherwood in *Ivanhoe* (1819); probably an altered form of *Cerdic*, the name of the traditional founder of the kingdom of Wessex. The name is presumably Old English, but the formation is not clear.

Ceinwen F Welsh traditional name, from *cain* 'fair', 'lovely' + *(g)wen* 'white', 'blessed', 'holy'. It was borne by a 5th-century saint, daughter of the chieftain Brychan.

Céleste F French, now also quite common in the English-speaking world (usually without the accent): from Latin *Caelestis* 'heavenly', a popular name among early Christians.

Celia F From Latin *Caelia*, feminine form of the Roman family name *Caelius* (probably a derivative of *caelum* 'heaven'). The name was introduced to the English-speaking world as the name of a character in Shakespeare's *As You Like It*. It is sometimes taken as a short form of ≫**Cecilia**.

Ceri F Welsh, pronounced '**kerry**'. It is now very popular in Wales, but is of uncertain origin, probably a short form of ≫**Ceridwen**.

Ceridwen F Welsh: name in Celtic mythology of the goddess of poetic inspiration. This is apparently derived from *cerdd* 'poetry' + *(g)wen* feminine of *gwyn* 'white', 'fair', 'blessed', 'holy'. According to legend, it was the name of the mother of the 6th-century Welsh hero Taliesin.

Chad M Modern spelling of the Old English name *Ceadda*, the name of a 7th-century saint who was Archbishop of York. His name is of unknown origin.

Chadwick M Mainly U.S.: transferred use of the surname, a local name from any of the various places in England named as the 'dairy farm (Old English *wīc*) of Ceadda or Ceadel'. In modern use, this name is sometimes taken, wrongly, as a full form of *Chad*.

Chance M Mainly U.S.: transferred use of the surname, in origin a nickname for a gambler, or perhaps for someone who had survived an accident by good luck, from Anglo-Norman *chea(u)nce* (good) fortune.

Chandler M, occasionally F Transferred use of the surname, which originated as an occupational name for someone who made and sold candles (an agent noun from Old French *chandele* 'candle'). The extended sense 'retail dealer' arose in the 16th century.

Chanel F Transferred use of the French surname *Chanel*, borne most notably by Gabrielle 'Coco' Chanel (1883–1971), who founded a famous Parisian fashion house. The spelling **Chanelle** is also found.

Chantal F French name sometimes used in the English-speaking world. It was originally bestowed as a given name in honour of St Jeanne-Françoise Frémiot (1572–1641), Baroness de Chantal (a place in Saône-et-Loire). After the death of her husband she became a nun and, with the support of St Francis of Sales, founded a new religious order.

Chapman M Transferred use of the surname, which originated as an occupational name for a merchant or pedlar, Old English *cēapmann*, from *cēapan* 'to buy and sell', 'trade'.

Charis F From Greek *kharis* 'grace', a key word in early Christian thought, denoting a gift or ability freely bestowed on a person by God. As a given name it is a 17th-century innovation, perhaps influenced by the Latin *caritās* (see **»Charity**).

Charissa F Recent coinage, apparently an elaboration of **»Charis**, perhaps in part a blend with **»Clarissa**.

Charity F From the vocabulary word, denoting Christian love for one's fellow man (Latin *caritās*, from *carus* 'dear'). In spite of St Paul's words 'and now abideth faith, hope, charity, these three; but the greatest of these is charity' (1 Corinthians 13:13), *Charity* is now much less common as a given name than **>>Faith** and **>>Hope**.

Charlene F Chiefly Australian and North American: 20th-century coinage, from **>>Charles** + the feminine suffix *-ene*.

Charles M Ultimately from a Germanic word meaning 'free man', cognate with Old English *ceorl* 'man'. The name owed its original popularity in Europe to the Frankish leader Charlemagne (?742–814), who in 800 established himself as Holy Roman Emperor. His name (Latin *Carolus Magnus*) means 'Charles the Great'. *Charles* or *Karl* (the German form) was a common name among Frankish leaders. It was introduced to Britain by Mary Queen of Scots (1542–87), who had been brought up in France. She chose the names *Charles James* for her son (1566–1625), who became King James VI of Scotland and, from 1603, James I of England. His son and grandson both reigned as King Charles, and the name thus became established in the 17th century in the Stuart royal house and in particular among Scottish supporters of the Stuart monarchy. After the enforced abdication of King James II in 1688, *Charles* was a popular name among Jacobites (the supporters of 'the King over the Water'). In the 19th century its popularity was further increased by romanticization of the story of 'Bonnie Prince Charlie', leader of the 1745 Jacobite rebellion.

Charlie M, F Pet form of **>>Charles** and **>>Charlotte**, now also used as an independent given name for both boys and girls.

Charlotte F French feminine diminutive of **>>Charles**, used in England since the 17th century. It was very popular in the 18th and 19th centuries, due in part to Queen Charlotte (1744–1818), wife of George III, and in part to the novelist Charlotte Brontë (1816–55), and returned to prominence in the 1980s.

Charlton   M   Transferred use of the surname. Use as a given name is largely due to the fame of the film actor Charlton Heston (b. 1924 as John Charles Carter; *Charlton* was his mother's maiden name). The surname is a local name from any of numerous places, mainly in southern England, named in Old English as the 'settlement of the free peasants'.

Charmaine   F   Possibly a variant of ≫**Charmian**, influenced by names such as ≫**Germaine**, but more probably a coinage based on the vocabulary word *charm* + *-aine* as in ≫**Lorraine**.

Charmian   F   From the Late Greek name *Kharmion* (a diminutive of *kharma* 'delight'). The name was used by Shakespeare in *Antony and Cleopatra* for one of the attendants of the Egyptian queen; he took it from Sir Thomas North's translation of Plutarch's *Parallel Lives*.

Chastity   F   Mainly U.S.: from the vocabulary word (from Late Latin *castitās*, a derivative of *castus* 'pure', 'undefiled'). It was given by the singer and actress Cher to her daughter.

Chelle   F   Short form of ≫**Michelle**, ≫**Rochelle**, and other names with this ending.

Chelsea   F   A 20th-century coinage, from the name of a district in south-west London which became known as the hub of the Swinging Sixties. It is also the name of several places in North America, and happens to be the name of the daughter of former President Clinton.

Cherelle   F   Respelling of ≫**Cheryl**, influenced by the popular feminine ending of names *-elle*.

Cherene   F   Chiefly U.S.: modern coinage, a combination of *Cher-* (cf. the many names following) with the feminine ending *-ene*.

Cherida   F   Modern coinage, a blend of ≫**Cheryl** and ≫**Phillida**, also influenced by the Spanish vocabulary word *querida* 'darling' (cf. ≫**Cherie**).

Chérie F Modern coinage from the French vocabulary word *chérie* 'darling'.

Cherry F 19th-century coinage, apparently taken from the vocabulary word denoting the fruit (Middle English *cheri(e)*, from Old French *cherise*). However, Dickens used it as a pet form of **»Charity**: in *Martin Chuzzlewit* (1844) Mr Pecksniff's daughters Charity and Mercy are known as Cherry and Merry. In modern usage it is perhaps also to be regarded as an Anglicization of **»Chérie**.

Cheryl F Blend of **»Cherry** with *-yl* as in **»Beryl**. It is not found before the 1920s and not common until the 1940s, but increasingly popular since.

Cheryth F Evidently a blend of **»Cherry** with **»Gwyneth**, influenced by the biblical placename *Cherith*. 'The brook Cherith' was a dry riverbed in which the prophet Elijah took refuge from the wrath of Ahab and Jezebel (1 Kings 17: 3–5).

Chester M Transferred use of the surname, in origin a local name from the town of *Chester*, named with the Old English form of Latin *castra* 'legionary camp'.

Chevonne F Anglicized (or rather, Frenchified) spelling of the Irish name **»Siobhán**.

Chloe F From the Late Greek name *Khloē*, originally used in the classical period as an epithet of the fertility goddess Demeter. A person of this name receives a fleeting mention in the New Testament (1 Corinthians 1:11); modern use as a given name almost certainly derives from this reference, since it was adopted in the 17th century among the Puritans, who were always raking the Bible for Christian names uncontaminated by association with the Roman Catholic Church.

Chloris F Literary name derived from a character in Greek mythology. *Khlōris* was a minor goddess of vegetation; her name derives from Greek *khlōros* 'green'. Her name was used by the Roman poet Horace as a pseudonym for one of his loves (cf. **»Lalage**), and hence it was taken up by Augustan poets of the 17th and 18th centuries.

Chris M, F Short form of **»Christopher** or **»Christine**. C

Chriselda F Elaboration of **»Chris**, apparently on the model of **»Griselda**.

Christa F Latinate short form of **»Christine** and **»Christina**. This seems to have originated in Germany, but is now also well established in the English-speaking world.

Christabel F 19th-century coinage, from the first syllable of **»Christine** with the suffix -bel (see **»Belle**). The combination was apparently first made by Samuel Taylor Coleridge (1772–1834) in a poem called *Christabel* (1816). The name was borne by the suffragette Christabel Pankhurst (1880–1958), in whose honour it is sometimes bestowed. The spellings **Christabelle** and **Christabella** are also found.

Christelle F French altered form of **»Christine**, derived by replacement of the feminine diminutive suffix -ine with the equally feminine suffix -elle. The name is now also used in the English-speaking world, where its popularity has been enhanced by its resemblance to **»Crystal**, of which it may in some cases be a variant.

Christian M, F From Latin *Christiānus* 'follower of Christ', in use as a given name during the Middle Ages and sporadically ever since.

Christie F, M Pet form of **»Christine** or, particularly in Scotland and Ireland, of **»Christopher**. The spelling **Christy** is also found.

Christina F Simplified form of Latin *Christiāna*, feminine of *Christiānus* (see **»Christian**).

Christine F French form of **»Christina**. Until fairly recently it was associated mainly with Scotland, but now it is very popular in all parts of the English-speaking world. It has a large number of pet forms, including **Chrissie**, **>>Christie**, and **>>Kirstie**.

Christopher M From the Greek name *Khristophoros*, literally 'bearer of Christ'. This was popular among early Christians, conscious of the fact that they were metaphorically bearing Christ in their hearts. A later interpretation gave rise to the legend of a saint who actually bore the Christ-child over a stream; he is regarded as the patron of travellers.

Cian M Traditional Irish Gaelic name, pronounced 'kee-an', derived from the Irish vocabulary word meaning 'ancient'. It was borne by a son-in-law of Brian Boru, who played a leading role in the battle of Clontarf (1014).

Ciara F Irish name, pronounced 'kee-a-ra', from *ciar* 'black'. It is thus a feminine form of **>>Ciarán**. It is sometimes Anglicized as **>>Kiera**.

Ciarán M Traditional Irish Gaelic name, pronounced 'kee-a-rawn' and often Anglicized as **>>Kieran**. It was originally a byname, a pet form of *ciar* 'black'. It was borne by two Irish saints, a hermit of the 5th century and the founder of the monastery at Clonmacnoise (d. 547).

Cicely F Variant of **>>Cecily**.

Cillian M Irish Gaelic name, often Anglicized as **>>Killian**. Originally a byname representing a pet form of Gaelic *ceallach* 'strife', or possibly derived from Gaelic *cill* 'monastery', 'church' (cf. **>>Kelly**), it was borne by various early Irish saints, including the 7th-century author of a life of St Bridget, a missionary to Artois, and a missionary to Franconia.

Cindy F Pet form of **>>Cynthia** or **>>Lucinda**, now commonly used as a given name in its own right, especially in North America. It is sometimes taken as a short form of the name of the fairy-tale heroine

Cinderella, which is in fact unrelated (being from French *Cendrillon*, a derivative of *cendre* 'cinders').

Claire F French form of ≫**Clara**. It was introduced to Britain by the Normans, but subsequently abandoned. This spelling was revived in the 19th century as a variant of ≫**Clare**.

Clancy M Mainly U.S.: transferred use of the Irish surname, Gaelic *Mac Fhlannchaidh* 'son of Flannchadh'. The latter is an ancient Irish personal name, probably derived from *flann* 'red'.

Clara F Post-classical Latin name, from the feminine form of the adjective *clārus* 'famous'. In the modern English-speaking world it represents a re-Latinization of the regular English form ≫**Clare**. It was made famous in the 1920s by the silent film actress Clara Bow (1905–65), known as 'the It girl' (because, whatever 'it' was, she had it).

Clare F The normal English vernacular form of ≫**Clara** during the Middle Ages and since.

Clarence M 19th-century coinage, used in honour of the popular elder son of Edward VII, who was created Duke of Clarence in 1890, but died in 1892. His title (*Dux Clarentiae* in Latin) originated with a son of Edward III, who in the 14th century was married to the heiress of Clare in Suffolk (which is derived from a Celtic river name and has no connection with the given name ≫**Clare**). The title has been held by various British royal princes at different periods in history.

Clarice F Medieval English and French form of the Latin name *Claritia*, an elaboration of ≫**Clara**. It was borne by a character who features in some versions of the medieval romances of Roland and the other paladins of Charlemagne.

Clarinda F Literary elaboration of ≫**Clara** (cf. ≫**Belinda** and ≫**Lucinda**). *Clarinda* first appears in Spenser's *Faerie Queene* (1596). The formation was influenced by the Italian name *Clorinda*, which is itself an arbitrary elaboration of **Chloris**. Robert Burns (1759–96) wrote four poems *To Clarinda*.

c **Clarissa** F Latin form of **Clarice**, occasionally found in medieval documents. It was revived by Samuel Richardson as the name of the central character in his novel *Clarissa* (1748).

Clark M Transferred use of the surname, which originated as an occupational name denoting a clerk (Latin *clēricus*), in the Middle Ages a man in minor holy orders who earned his living by his ability to read and write. It was associated particularly with the film star Clark Gable (1901–60). The spelling **Clarke** is also found.

Claud M Anglicized spelling of **Claude**.

Claude M From French, from the Latin name *Claudius*, a Roman family name derived from the byname *Claudus* 'lame'. It was borne by various early saints; its popularity in France is largely due to the fame of the 7th-century St Claude of Besançon. In France, *Claude* is also found as a girl's name.

Claudette F French: feminine diminutive form of **Claude**, now also used in the English-speaking world. It gained considerable prominence in the 1930s as the name of the French film star Claudette Colbert (1903–96), a Hollywood favourite for many years.

Claudia F Latin female name, a feminine form of *Claudius* (see **Claude**). It is mentioned in one of St Paul's letters to Timothy (2, 4:21 'Eubulus greeteth thee, and Pudens, and Linus, and Claudia, and all the brethren'), as a result of which it was taken up by the Puritans in the 16th century.

Claudine F French: feminine diminutive form of **Claude**. It was made popular at the beginning of the 20th century as the name of the heroine of a series of novels by the French writer Colette (1873–1954), and is now also occasionally used in the English-speaking world.

Clay M Either a shortened form of >>**Clayton** or a transferred use of the surname *Clay*, a local name for someone who lived on a patch of land whose soil was predominantly clay (Old English *clæg*).

Clayton M Especially U.S.: transferred use of the surname, originally a local name from any of the several places in England (for example, in Lancs., Staffs., Sussex, and W. Yorks.) named in Old English as *clæg tūn* 'settlement on the clay'.

Cledwyn M Welsh traditional name, apparently derived from *caled* 'hard', 'rough' + *(g)wyn* 'white', 'fair', 'blessed', 'holy'.

Clematis F From the name of the flower (so named in the 16th century from Greek *klēmatis* 'climbing plant'), perhaps under the influence of names such as >>**Clemence**, with the ending -*is* found in names such as >>**Phyllis**.

Clemence F Medieval French and English form of Latin *Clēmentia*, a derivative of *Clēmens* (see >>**Clement**) or an abstract noun meaning 'mercy'.

Clement M From the Late Latin name *Clēmens* (genitive *Clēmentis*) meaning 'merciful'. This was borne by several early saints, notably the fourth pope and the early Christian theologian Clement of Alexandria (Titus Flavius Clemens, AD ?150–?215).

Clementine F Feminine form of >>**Clement**. The name was first used in the 19th century, and for a time it was very popular. It is now largely associated with the popular song with this title. The Latinate form **Clementina** is also found.

Cleo F Short form of >>**Cleopatra**, but see also >>**Clio**.

Cleopatra F From the Greek name *Kleopatra*, derived from *kleos* 'glory' + *patēr* 'father'. This was borne by a large number of women in the Ptolemaic royal family of Egypt. The most famous (?69–30 BC) was the lover of Mark Antony, and has always figured largely in both literature and the popular imagination as a model of a passionate woman of unsurpassed beauty, who 'gave all for love' and in the process destroyed the man she loved.

Cliff M Short form of »**Clifford**, now also sometimes of »**Clifton**. Its use as a given name dates mainly from the advent in the 1950s of the pop singer Cliff Richard (b. 1940 as Harry Roger Webb).

Clifford M Well-established transferred use of the surname, which originated as a local name from any of several places named in Old English as 'ford by the slope (*clif*)'.

Clifton M Transferred use of the surname, a local name from any of the numerous places named in Old English as 'settlement on the slope (*clif*)'.

Clint M Short form of »**Clinton**, made famous by the actor Clint Eastwood (b. 1930).

Clinton M Mainly North American: transferred use of the English surname, a local name from *Glympton* in Oxfordshire or *Glinton* in Northants. It was originally used as a given name in America in honour of the Clinton family, whose members included the statesman George Clinton (1739–1812), governor of New York.

Clio F From Greek *Kleio*, the name borne in classical mythology both by one of the nymphs and by one of the Muses. It is probably ultimately connected with the vocabulary word *kleos* 'glory'; cf. »**Cleopatra**.

Cliona F Anglicized form of the traditional Irish Gaelic name *Clíodhna*, which is of unknown origin. In Irish legend, Clíodhna was one of three beautiful daughters of the poet Libra; she eloped with Ciabhán, a prince of Ulster, but was drowned by a great wave shortly afterwards, while he was away hunting.

Clive M Long-established transferred use of the surname, which is a local name from any of the various places (e.g. in Cheshire and Shropshire) so named. As a given name it seems to have been originally chosen in honour of 'Clive of India' (Robert Clive, created Baron Clive of Plassey in 1760).

Clodagh F A recent Irish coinage. It is the name of a river in Tipperary, which seems to have been arbitrarily transferred to use as a given name. There may be some literary association with the Latin name *Clōdia* (borne by the mistress of the Roman poet Catullus), a variant of **»Claudia**.

Clyde M Mainly North American: from the name of a river in south-west Scotland that runs through Glasgow, perhaps by way of a surname derived from the river name, although it may be relevant that for many Scottish emigrants the River Clyde was the point of departure from Scotland. The bank robber Clyde Barrow became something of a cult figure after the film *Bonnie and Clyde* (1967), in which he was played by Warren Beatty.

Cody M, F Transferred use of the Irish surname, an Anglicized form of Gaelic *Ó Cuidighthigh* 'descendant of Cuidightheach', a byname meaning 'helpful', or of *Mac Óda* 'son of Óda', a personal name of uncertain origin. Use as a given name in the United States especially has been at least in part inspired by William Frederick Cody (1846–1917), better known as 'Buffalo Bill', the showman of the Wild West.

Colbert M Transferred use of the surname, which is from an Old French given name of Germanic (Frankish) origin, from *col* (of uncertain meaning) + *berht* 'bright', 'famous'. This was introduced to Britain by the Normans.

Colby M Especially U.S.: transferred use of the surname, a local name from places in Norfolk and

Cumbria, named in Anglo-Scandinavian as 'Koli's settlement (Old Norse *býr*)'. Use as a given name seems to have been influenced by the 1980s television serial *The Colbys*, a spinoff from *Dynasty*.

Cole M Transferred use of the surname, which is from a medieval given name of uncertain origin. It may represent a survival into Middle English of the Old English byname *Cola* 'swarthy', 'coal-black', from *col* 'charcoal'. As a given name it is associated with the songwriter Cole Porter (1893–1964).

Coleman M Variant of ➤➤**Colman**. In part it also represents a transferred use of the surname spelled thus.

Colette F French feminine diminutive form of the medieval name *Col(le)*, a short form of ➤➤**Nicholas**. It was famous as the name of the French novelist Colette (1873–1954).

Colin M Diminutive form of the medieval name *Col(le)*, a short form of ➤➤**Nicholas**. In Scotland it is used as an Anglicized form of the Gaelic name *Cailean*. The Irish equivalent, *Cóilin*, is likewise a derivative of ➤➤**Nicholas**.

Coll M From a medieval short form of ➤➤**Nicholas**. Its use as a modern given name in part represents a transferred use of the surname derived from the given name in the Middle Ages. In Scotland it has been used as an Anglicized form of the Gaelic name *Colla*, perhaps from an Old Celtic root meaning 'high'.

Colleen F Mainly North American and Australian: from the Anglo-Irish vocabulary word *colleen* 'girl', 'wench' (Gaelic *cailín*). It became established as a name in the 1920s in North America, and was associated with the star of the silent screen Colleen Moore (1901–88), whose real name was Kathleen Morrison. It is not used as a given name in Ireland. It is sometimes used as a feminine of ➤➤**Colin**.

Collette F Variant spelling of **»Colette**.

Colm M Irish Gaelic form of Latin *Columba*; see
»Callum. The spelling **Col(l)um** is also used.

Colman M Irish: Anglicized form of the Gaelic name
Colmán, from Late Latin *Columbānus*, a derivative of
Columba (see **»Callum**). The name was borne by a
number of early Irish saints, including Colmán of
Armagh, a 5th-century disciple of St Patrick.

Comhghall M Irish Gaelic name, pronounced 'cow-all',
meaning 'fellow hostage'. This was borne by several
early Irish saints, including the 6th-century founder of
the great monastery at Bangor. The name is Anglicized
as **»Cowall**.

Conall M Irish and Scottish Gaelic traditional name,
composed of Old Celtic words meaning 'wolf' and
'strong'. This name was borne by many early chieftains
and warriors of Ireland, including the Ulster hero
Conall Cearnach, one of the two sons of Niall of the
Nine Hostages. (The other was Eoghan.) Conall gave
his name to *Tirconell*, otherwise known as Donegal.

Conan M Irish: Anglicized form of the Gaelic name
Conán, a pet form of *cú* 'hound' or 'wolf'. In Irish
legend, Conán was a foul-mouthed and abusive member
of the Fianna, the band of followers of the legendary
hero Finn mac Cumhaill (Finn McCool). After
undergoing many trials and tribulations, Conán is
awarded the 'fourteen best women in the Land of
Promise' as compensation for his troubles. In historical
times, the name was borne by a 7th-century saint,
bishop of the Isle of Man. Sir Arthur Conan Doyle
(1859–1930), creator of Sherlock Holmes, was born in
Edinburgh, and of Irish stock. The science-fiction creation
Conan the Destroyer owes more to the villain of legend
than to the bishop or the writer.

Conley M Irish: Anglicized form of the Gaelic name
Conlaodh, which is probably from *connla* 'pure', 'chaste',

'sensible' + the personal name **»Aodh**. St Conlaodh or Conláed, a contemporary of St Brighid (see **»Bridget**), was the first bishop of Kildare.

c Conn M Irish Gaelic name meaning 'chief'. It is now also used as a short form of **»Connor** and of various non-Irish names beginning with the syllable *Con-*.

Connor M Irish: Anglicized form of the Gaelic name **Conchobhar**, which probably meant 'lover of hounds'. Conchobhar was a legendary Irish king of Ulster who lived at the time of Christ.

Conrad M Germanic personal name derived from *kuon rad*, literally 'bold counsel'. It was used occasionally in Britain in the Middle Ages, but modern use is a reimportation from Germany dating mainly from the 19th century.

Constance F Medieval form of the Late Latin name *Constantia*, which is either a feminine derivative of *Constans* (see **»Constant**) or an abstract noun meaning 'constancy'. This was a popular name among the Normans; it was borne by the formidable Constance of Sicily (1158–98), wife of the Emperor Henry VI.

Constant M Medieval form of the Late Latin name *Constans* 'steadfast' (genitive *Constantis*). It was taken up as a religious name by the Puritans because of its transparent meaning, expressing a determination to 'resist steadfast in the faith' (1 Peter 5:9).

Constantine M From the Late Latin name *Constantīnus*, a derivative of *Constans*; see **»Constant**. The Roman emperor Constantine the Great (?288–337) is specially honoured in the Christian church as the first Christian emperor. The name was also borne by three kings of medieval Scotland, where it represents an Anglicized form of the Gaelic name **»Conn**.

Cora F Used by James Fenimore Cooper for one of the characters in *The Last of the Mohicans* (1826), apparently as an original coinage. It could also represent a Latinized form of Greek *korē* 'maiden'. However, in classical mythology this was a euphemistic name of the goddess of the underworld, Persephone, and would not have been a well-omened name to take.

Coral F One of the group of late 19th-century girls' names taken from vocabulary words denoting gemstones. Coral, the pink calcareous material found in warm seas, has long been used to make semi-precious jewellery.

Coralie F Elaboration of »**Cora** or »**Coral**, on the model of »**Rosalie**.

Corbin M Mainly U.S.: of uncertain derivation, perhaps a short form of »**Corbinian** or a transferred use of the surname, which originated as a nickname from a diminutive of Anglo-Norman *corb* 'crow'.

Corbinian M The name of a Frankish saint (?670–770) who evangelized Bavaria from a base at Freising, near Munich. His name was presumably originally Frankish, but in the form in which it has been handed down it appears to be an adjectival derivative of Late Latin *corbus* 'crow', 'raven'. This may represent a translation of the Germanic personal name *Hraban*.

Cordelia F The name used by Shakespeare for King Lear's virtuous daughter. It is not clear where he got it from; it does not seem to have a genuine Celtic origin. It may be a fanciful elaboration of Latin *cor* 'heart' (genitive *cordis*).

Cordula F Late Latin pet form of *cor* 'heart' (genitive *cordis*). A saint of this name was, according to legend, one of Ursula's eleven thousand companions.

Coretta F Elaborated form of »**Cora**. This is the name of the widow of the American civil rights campaigner Martin Luther King.

Corey M Especially common as a Black name in Britain and North America. It is probably a transferred use of the English surname *Corey*, which is derived from the

Old Norse personal name *Kori*. The spellings **»Cory** and **Corie** are also found.

Corin M From Latin *Quirīnus*, the name of an ancient Roman divinity associated with the legendary figure of Romulus. In the early Christian period this name was borne by several saints martyred for their faith. In the English-speaking world it is often taken as a male equivalent of **»Corinna**.

Corinna F Latin form of the Greek name *Korinnē* (probably a derivative of *Korē*; cf. **»Cora**). It was used by the poet Ovid for the woman addressed in his love poetry. The French form **Corinne** is also widely used in the English-speaking world.

Cormac M Irish Gaelic traditional name, of uncertain origin. It has been a very popular name in Ireland from the earliest times.

Cornelia F From the Latin feminine form of the old Roman family name **»Cornelius**. It was borne in the 2nd century BC by the mother of the revolutionaries Tiberius and Gaius Sempronius Gracchus and is still occasionally bestowed in her honour.

Cornelius M From an old Roman family name, *Cornēlius*, which is of uncertain origin, possibly a derivative of Latin *cornu* 'horn'. It was the name of a 3rd-century pope, who is venerated as a saint.

Cornell M Medieval vernacular form of **»Cornelius**. In modern use it normally represents a transferred use of the surname, which is of very varied origin.

Cory M Variant spelling of **»Corey**.

Cosima F Feminine form of **»Cosmo**, occasionally used in the English-speaking world. The name was borne by Cosima Wagner (1837–1930), daughter of Franz Liszt and devoted wife of Richard Wagner.

Cosmo M Italian form (also found as **Cosimo**) of the Greek name *Kosmas* (a short form of various names containing the word *kosmos* 'order', 'beauty'). This was borne by a Christian saint martyred, together with his brother Damian, at Aegea in Cilicia in the early 4th century. It was brought to Britain in the 18th century by the Scottish Dukes of Gordon, who had connections with the ducal house of Tuscany. The name was traditional in that family, having been borne most famously by Cosimo de' Medici (1389–1464), one of the chief patrons of the Italian Renaissance.

Courtney F, M Transferred use of the surname, which was originally a Norman baronial name from any of several places in Northern France called *Courtenay* 'domain of Curtius'. From an early period it was wrongly taken as a nickname derived from Old French *court nez* 'short nose'.

Cowall M Anglicized form of Irish **»Comhghall**.

Craig M Transferred use of the Scottish surname, a local name derived from the Gaelic word *creag* 'rock', or in some cases a nickname based on this word. The given name is now fashionable throughout the English-speaking world, and is chosen by many people who have no connection with Scotland.

Creighton M Transferred use of the Scottish surname, a local name from *Crichton* in Midlothian, which is named with a combination of Gaelic *crioch* 'border', 'boundary' + Middle English *tune* 'settlement' (Old English *tūn*).

Cressa F Modern name, a short form of **»Cressida**.

Cressida F From a medieval legend, told by Chaucer and Shakespeare among others, set in ancient Troy. Cressida is a Trojan princess, daughter of Calchas, a priest who has defected to the Greeks. When she is restored to her father, she abandons her Trojan lover Troilus in favour of the Greek Diomedes. The story is not found in classical sources. Chaucer used the name in the form *Criseyde*, getting it from Boccaccio's

Criseida. This in turn is ultimately based on Greek *Khryseis* (a derivative of *khrysos* 'gold'), the name of a Trojan girl who is mentioned briefly as a prisoner of the Greeks at the beginning of Homer's *Iliad*. Chaucer's version of the name was Latinized by Shakespeare as *Cressida*. In spite of the unhappy associations of the story, the name has enjoyed some popularity since the latter part of the 20th century.

Crichton M Variant of >>**Creighton**.

Crispin M From Latin *Crispīnus*, a derivative of the Roman family name *Crispus* 'curly(-headed)'. St Crispin was martyred, together with his brother Crispinian, in *c*.285, and the pair were popular saints in the Middle Ages.

Cristina F Italian, Spanish, and Portuguese form of >>**Christina**, sometimes also used in the English-speaking world.

Crystal F 19th-century coinage: one of the group of names taken from words denoting gemstones and other precious objects. The word *crystal*, denoting high-quality cut glass, is derived from Greek *krystallos* 'ice'.

Curt M Originally an old spelling of the German name *Kurt* (a contracted form of *Konrad*; see >>**Conrad**). It is now also used as a short form of >>**Curtis**.

Curtis M Transferred use of the surname, which originated in the Middle Ages as a nickname for someone who was 'courteous' (Old French *curteis*). At an early date, however, it came to be associated with Middle English *curt* 'short' + *hose* 'leggings'; cf. >>**Courtney**.

Cuthbert M An Old English personal name derived from *cūth* 'known' + *beorht* 'bright', 'famous'. This was borne by two pre-Conquest English saints: a 7th-century bishop of Lindisfarne and an 8th-century archbishop of Canterbury.

Cynthia F From Greek *Kynthia*, an epithet applied to the goddess Artemis, who was said to have been born on Mount *Kynthos* on the island of Delos. *Cynthia* was later used by the Roman poet Propertius as the name of the woman to whom he addressed his love poetry. The English given name dates from the classical revival **c** of the 17th and 18th centuries.

Cyprian M From the Late Latin family name *Cypriānus* 'native of Cyprus'. This was borne by one of the leading figures in the history of the Western Church, a 3rd-century bishop of Carthage.

Cyril M From the post-classical Greek name *Kyrillos*, a derivative of *kyrios* 'lord'. It was borne by a large number of early saints, notably two theologians, Cyril of Alexandria and Cyril of Jerusalem. It was also the name of one of the two Greek evangelists (the other was Methodius) who brought Christianity to the Slavonic peoples of Eastern Europe; in order to provide written translations of the gospels for their converts, they devised the alphabet known as Cyrillic, which is still used for Russian, Bulgarian, and Serbian.

Cyrus M From the Greek form (*Kyros*) of the name of several kings of Persia, notably Cyrus the Great (d. 529 BC). The origin of the name is not known, but in the early Christian period it was associated with Greek *kyrios* 'lord' and borne by various saints, including an Egyptian martyr and a bishop of Carthage.

D

Dafydd M Welsh form of **»David**; see also **»Dewi** and **»Dai**. This form of the name was in use during the Middle Ages and revived in the late 19th century.

Dagmar F Scandinavian: of uncertain origin. It is apparently from Old Norse *dag* 'day' + *mār* 'maid'. *Dag* is a boy's name in its own right in Swedish and Norwegian. Alternatively, *Dagmar* may represent a reworking of the Slavonic name *Dragomira*, which is from *dorog* 'dear' + *meri* 'great', 'famous'.

Dahlia F From the name of the flower, which was named in the 19th century in honour of the pioneering Swedish botanist Anders Dahl (1751–89).

Dai M Welsh: now used as a pet form of **»Dafydd** or **»Dewi**, but originally of distinct origin, probably from an Old Celtic word *dei* 'to shine'.

Daisy F One of the 19th-century girls' names taken from words denoting flowers. The daisy was named in Old English as *dægesēage* 'day's eye', because it uncovers the yellow disc of its centre in the morning and closes its petals over it again at the end of the day.

Dale M, F Transferred use of the surname, originally a local name for someone who lived in a *dale* or valley.

Daley M Transferred use of the Irish surname, the Gaelic form of which is Ó *Dálaigh* 'descendant of Dálach', a personal name derived from *dál* 'assembly', 'gathering'. The spelling **Daly** is also found.

Dalia F In part an alternative spelling of **»Dahlia**, in part a Jewish name derived from Modern Hebrew *dalia* 'flowering branch'. The spelling **Daliah** is associated particularly with the actress Daliah Lavi (b. 1940).

Damaris F New Testament name, borne by a woman converted to Christianity by St Paul (Acts 17:34). The name is probably Greek in origin, perhaps from *damalis* 'calf'. It was taken up by the Puritans in the 17th century.

Damhnait F Irish Gaelic name, pronounced 'dav-nit', a feminine diminutive, meaning 'fawn', from *damh* 'stag'. A 6th-century saint of this name founded a convent in Co. Monaghan. It is sometimes Anglicized as **Davnat**. See also **»Dymphna**.

Damian M From Greek *Damianos*, name of the brother of Cosmas (see **»Cosmo**). The two brothers were martyred together at Aegea in Cilicia in the early 4th century. The origin of the name is probably akin to **»Damon**. The French form **Damien** is also used in the English-speaking world.

Damon M From a classical Greek name, a derivative of *damān* 'to tame, subdue, or kill'. This was famous in antiquity from the story of Damon and Pythias. In the early 4th century BC Pythias was condemned to death by Dionysius, ruler of Syracuse. His friend Damon offered to stand surety for him, and took his place in the condemned cell while Pythias put his affairs in order. When Pythias duly returned to be executed (rather than absconding and leaving his friend to his fate), Dionysius was so impressed by the trust and friendship of the two young men that he pardoned them both. The name was not used in the early centuries of the Christian era or during the Middle Ages. Its modern use dates from the 1930s and is associated in particular with the American writer Damon Runyon (1884–1946). It is sometimes taken as a variant of **»Damian**.

Dan M In modern use this is taken as a short form of **»Daniel**, but it is also an independent biblical name, meaning 'he judged' in Hebrew, borne by one of Jacob's twelve sons (Genesis 30:6).

Dana F, M Mainly North American: transferred use of a surname that is fairly common in the United States. Its origin is unknown; it may be Irish. *Dana* or *Ana* was the name of an ancient Irish fertility goddess, and this was also used in medieval times as a girl's name. However, it is not clear whether there is any connection between this ancient Irish name and the modern given name, which is now sometimes also used as a feminine form of »**Dan** or »**Daniel**. Modern use as a boy's given name began in honour of Richard Dana (1815–82), author of *Two Years before the Mast*. A lawyer by profession as well as a writer and traveller, he supported the rights of fugitive slaves before and during the Civil War. The popularity of the given name was increased by the fame of the film star Dana Andrews (1909–92).

Dane M Transferred use of the surname. This originated as a local name, a dialect variant of »**Dean**, which was common in south-east England, not as an ethnic name for someone from Denmark. However, the latter may be the sense of the given name in some cases.

Daniel M Biblical name (meaning 'God is my judge' in Hebrew), borne by the prophet whose story is told in the Book of Daniel. He was an Israelite slave of the Assyrian king Nebuchadnezzar, with whom he obtained great favour through his skill in interpreting dreams. Most famously, he interpreted the message of doom in the 'writing on the wall' that appeared at a feast held by Nebuchadnezzar's son Belshazzar. His enemies had him cast into a lions' den, from which he was saved by God.

Daniela F Latinate feminine form of »**Daniel**.

Danielle F French feminine form of »**Daniel**.

Daphne F Name borne in Greek mythology by a nymph who was changed into a laurel by her father, a river god, to enable her to escape the attentions of Apollo. The name means 'laurel' in Greek. According to the myth the nymph gave her name to the shrub, but in fact of course it was the other way about. The name came into use in England at the end of the 19th century, when it was adopted as part of the vogue for flower names at that time.

d

Darby M Transferred use of the surname, a local name from the city of *Derby* or the district of West Derby near Liverpool. These were named in Old Norse as *diur býr* 'deer settlement'. In Ireland this name has been used as an Anglicized form of Gaelic **»Diarmaid** (see also **»Dermot**).

Darcy F, M Transferred use of the Irish surname, originally a Norman baronial name (*d'Arcy*) borne by a family who came from *Arcy* in northern France. It is the surname of the hero of Jane Austen's novel *Pride and Prejudice*. The girl's name is also spelled **Darcey**.

Daria F Of ancient Greek origin: feminine form of **»Darius**. St Daria (d. 283) was a Greek woman married to an Egyptian Christian called Chrysanthus; they lived at Rome and were martyred under the emperors Numerian and Carinus.

Darin M Mainly U.S.: variant of **»Darren**, associated with the singer Bobby Darin (1936–73), who was originally called Walden Robert Cassotto. He chose the name that he made famous from a list of surnames in a telephone directory. The spelling **Darrin** is also found.

Darina F Anglicized form of the Irish Gaelic name **Dáirine**, meaning 'fertile', a feminine diminutive of *Dáire* (see **»Darragh**).

Darius M From Greek *Dareios*, the name of various Persian kings. The original form of the name was *Darayavalush*, from *daraya* 'possess' or 'maintain' + *vahu* 'good'. A saint of this name was martyred at Nicaea with three companions at an uncertain date.

d

Darlene F Mainly Australian and North American: modern coinage, an alteration of the affectionate term of address *darling*, influenced by *-lene*, a productive feminine name ending in recent years, as in **»Marlene** and **»Charlene**. The spelling **Darleen** is also found.

Darnell M Of uncertain derivation. It may be a transferred use of the surname, or it may be a variant of **»Darrell**, influenced by the plant name *darnel*.

Darragh M Irish and Scottish name, of Gaelic origin. It is popularly associated with the Scottish Gaelic vocabulary word *darach* 'oak' (Irish *dair*, genitive *darach*). As an Irish name it also functions as an Anglicized form of the Gaelic name **Dáire**, from a vocabulary word meaning 'fertile'. This was the name of an ancient Irish fertility god associated with a bull cult. The Brown Bull of Cooley (subject of the legendary cattle raid) was originally owned by a certain Dáire mac Fiachna.

Darrell M Transferred use of a surname, originally a Norman baronial name (*d'Airelle*) borne by a family who came from *Airelle* in Calvados. It was first used as a given name towards the end of the 19th century.

Darren M 20th-century coinage, of uncertain derivation. It may be a transferred used of a surname (itself of obscure origin). It was borne by the American actor Darren McGavin (b. 1922), and is the name of a character in the American television comedy series *Bewitched*, made in the 1960s.

Darrene F Feminine form of **»Darren**, formed with the feminine name ending *-ene*, as in **»Charlene**.

Darryl M, occasionally F Variant of **»Darrell**. Like its variant **Daryl**, it is occasionally borne by women, no doubt by analogy with names such as **»Cheryl**.

David M Biblical name, borne by the greatest of all the kings of Israel, whose history is recounted with great vividness in the first and second books of Samuel and elsewhere. As a boy he killed the giant Philistine Goliath with his slingshot. As king of Judah, and later of all Israel, he expanded the power of the Israelites and established the security of their kingdom. He was also noted as a poet, many of the Psalms being attributed to him. The Hebrew derivation of the name is uncertain; it is said by some to represent a nursery word meaning 'darling'. It is the name of the patron saint of Wales (see **»Dewi**) and was borne by two medieval kings of Scotland.

Davina F Latinate feminine form of **»David**. This name evidently originated in Scotland. It is occasionally elaborated to **Davinia**, on the model of **»Lavinia**.

Dawn F From the vocabulary word denoting daybreak, originally bestowed as a given name in the 1920s, no doubt because of the connotations of freshness and purity of this time of day. It may have originated as a translation of **»Aurora**.

Dean M Transferred use of the surname, which has a double origin. In part it is a local name for someone who lived in a valley (Old English *denu*), in part an occupational name for an ecclesiastical dean (Latin *decanus*). The given name is also used as an Anglicized form of Italian *Dino*, for example in the case of the actor and singer Dean Martin (1917–95).

Deanna F Variant of **»Diana**, coined in 1936 by the film star and singer Deanna Durbin (b. 1921), whose actual given names were *Edna May*. It is sometimes used as a feminine form of **»Dean**.

Deborah F Biblical name (meaning 'bee' in Hebrew), borne by the nurse of Rebecca (Genesis 35:8) and by a woman judge and prophet (Judges 4–5), who led the Israelites to victory over the Canaanites. It has always been popular as a Jewish name, and was taken up among Christians by the Puritans in the 17th century, influenced by the fact that the bee was a symbol of industriousness. Among other famous bearers is the actress Deborah Kerr (b. 1921). In recent years a variety of modish spellings have appeared, such as **Debora**, **Debra**, and the pet forms **Debbie**, **Debbi**, and **Debi**.

Declan M Irish: Anglicized form of the Gaelic name *Deaglán*, which is of uncertain origin. It was borne by a 5th-century bishop of Ardmore, a disciple of St Colmán.

Dee F, occasionally M Originally a pet form of any of several girls' given names beginning with the letter *D*- (cf. ≫**Kay**), especially ≫**Dorothy**. It is now also used as an independent name in its own right.

Deiniol M Welsh: taken as a form of ≫**Daniel** but possibly of Celtic origin. It was the name of a 6th-century Welsh saint.

Deirdre F Name borne in Irish legend by a tragic heroine, known as 'Deirdre of the Sorrows'. The story goes that she was betrothed to Conchobhar, King of Ulster, but instead eloped to Scotland with her beloved Naoise. Eventually, the jilted king murdered Naoise, and Deirdre herself died of a broken heart or, according to some versions, threw herself out of a chariot. She is sometimes taken as symbolic of the fate of Ireland under English rule. The name is widely popular, partly due to the retellings of the legend by the poet W. B. Yeats (1907) and the playwright J. M. Synge (1910). The name itself is of uncertain derivation, the early forms being very variable.

Delia F From a classical Greek epithet of the goddess Artemis, referring to her birth on the island of *Delos* (cf. ≫**Cynthia**). It was taken up by the pastoral poets of the 17th century.

Delicia F Feminine form of the Late Latin name *Delicius*, a derivative of *deliciae* 'delight'. Use as a given name seems to be a modern phenomenon; it is not found in the Middle Ages.

Delilah F Biblical name (of uncertain origin), borne by Samson's mistress, who wheedled him into revealing that the secret of his strength was in his hair and then cut it off while he was asleep, before betraying him to the Philistines (Judges 16:4–20). Although the biblical Delilah was deceitful and treacherous, the name was taken up enthusiastically by the Puritans in the 17th century, perhaps because she was also beautiful and clever.

Dell M Transferred use of the surname, originally a local name for someone who lived in a *dell* or hollow.

Della F This name first appeared in the 1870s and has continued to grow steadily in popularity ever since. Its derivation is not clear; if it is not simply an arbitrary creation, it may be an altered form of »Delia or »Delilah or a short form of »Adela. In modern use it is sometimes taken as a feminine form of »Dell.

Delphine F French: from Latin *Delphīna* 'woman from Delphi'. The Blessed Delphina (1283–1358) was a Provençal nun, who was probably named in honour of the 4th-century St Delphinus of Bordeaux.

Delwyn F Welsh: modern name composed of the words *del* 'pretty', 'neat' + *(g)wyn* 'white', 'fair', 'blessed', 'holy'.

Delyth F Welsh: recent coinage composed of the vocabulary word *del* 'pretty', 'neat' + the ending *-yth*, formed on the analogy of names such as »Gwenyth.

Demelza F Modern Cornish name, which has no history as a Celtic personal name but is derived from a placename in the parish of St Columb Major. The given name began to be used in the 1950s; its popularity was increased by the serialization on British television of the 'Poldark' novels by Winston Graham, in which it is the name of the heroine.

Dena F Modern coinage, representing either a respelling of **»Dina** or a coinage as a feminine version of **»Dean**.

Denice F Altered form of **»Denise**.

Denis M Variant spelling (and the usual French form) of **»Dennis**.

Denise F French feminine form of **»Denis**, now also widely used in the English-speaking world.

Dennis M Medieval vernacular form of the Greek name *Dionysios*, which was borne by several early Christian saints, including St Denis, a 3rd-century evangelist who converted the Gauls and became a patron saint of Paris. It was on his account that the name was popular in France and was adopted by the Normans. In classical times, the word originally denoted a devotee of the god *Dionysos*. This deity was a relatively late introduction to the classical pantheon; his orgiastic cult seems to have originated in Persia or elsewhere in Asia. His name is of uncertain derivation.

Denton M Transferred use of the surname, originally a local name from any of the numerous places named in Old English as *denu tūn* 'valley settlement'.

Denzel M From the Cornish surname *Denzell*, a local name from a place in Cornwall. It came to be used as a given name in the Hollis family in the 16th century, when the Hollis family and the Denzell family became connected by marriage, and spread from there into more general use. The spelling **Denzil** is also found.

Derek M From a Low German form of *Theodoric* (see **»Terry**), introduced to Britain during the Middle Ages by Flemish weavers. The spellings **Dereck** and **Der(r)ick** are also found.

Dermot M Anglicized form of the Gaelic name **»Diarmaid**.

Derrick M The usual North American spelling of
»Derek.

Derry M Of uncertain origin, perhaps a blend of **»Derek**
and **»Terry**.

Dervila F Irish: Anglicized form of the Gaelic name
Deirbhile (pronounced '**djair**-veel-a'), from *der*
'daughter' + *file* 'poet'. This was the name of an Irish
saint who founded a convent at Fallmore, Co. Mayo, in
the 6th century. It has absorbed the ancient Irish name
Dearbháil 'daughter of Fál', Fál being a poetic name
for Ireland. The latter is more correctly Anglicized as
Derval.

Desdemona F Name occasionally chosen by parents
in search of an unusual name, who are no doubt
attracted by the sweet nature and innocence of
Shakespeare's character and not deterred by her tragic
fate. She was murdered by her husband Othello in an
ill-founded jealous rage. Her name is particularly
appropriate to her destiny, as it probably represents a
Latinized form of Greek *dysdaimōn* 'ill-starred'.

Desirée F French (now also used in the English-
speaking world, often without the accent), from Latin
Desiderāta 'desired'. This name was given by early
Christians to a longed-for child, but the French form is
now sometimes taken as suggesting that the bearer will
grow up into a desirable woman.

Desmond M Of Irish origin: transferred use of an
Irish surname derived from the Gaelic by-name
Deasmumhnach, literally 'man from Muman', a district
of south Munster around Cork. This was a byname in
the MacCarthy family (formerly kings of south Munster)
and the Fitzgeralds, earls of Desmond.

Devon M, F Mainly North American: from the name of
the English county, probably a transferred use of this as
a surname. It derives from a British tribal name, said to

mean 'worshippers of the god Dumnōnos'. As a girl's name the variant **Devonne** is also found.

Dewi M A Welsh form (earlier **Dewydd**) of **»David**. This form of the name was borne by the patron saint of Wales, who was born in South Wales in the 5th century and became the first bishop of Menevia, the tiny cathedral city now known as St Davids. Otherwise, this form of the given name was little used during the Middle Ages, but during the 20th century it has become quite common in Wales.

Dexter M Mainly U.S.: transferred use of the surname, which is from Old English *dēagestre* 'dyer'. The modern form of this occupational name coincides in form with Latin *dexter* 'right-handed', 'auspicious', and it may sometimes have been chosen as a given name because of this.

Diana F Name borne in Roman mythology by the goddess of the moon and of hunting, equivalent to the Greek Artemis, who is characterized as both beautiful and chaste. Her name is of ancient and uncertain derivation; it may be connected with that of the Greek god *Dionysos* (see **»Dennis**). It was adopted in Britain during the Tudor period as a learned name, a borrowing from Latin influenced by the French form **»Diane**. Although it was much used by Elizabethan poets celebrating the virgin goddess and alluding to the virgin queen, it was not particularly popular as a given name until the end of the 19th century. In earlier centuries some clergymen were reluctant to baptize girls with this pagan name, mindful of the riots against St Paul stirred up by worshippers of Diana of the Ephesians (Acts 19:24–41). In the late 20th century it has enjoyed great popularity because of its association with the late Diana, Princess of Wales (1961–97), who was renowned for her beauty, glamour, and compassion.

Diane F French form of **»Diana**, now also popular in the English-speaking world. It was especially popular among the Renaissance aristocracy, who loved hunting and were therefore proud to name their daughters after the classical goddess of the chase. The spelling **Dianne** is also found (originating by association with **»Anne**), and in the U.S. **Dyan**.

Diarmaid M Irish and Scottish Gaelic name normally Anglicized as **Dermot**. In Irish legend, Diarmaid was the lover of Gráinne, who had been promised to the aging hero Finn mac Cumhaill, leader of the Fianna. The lovers eloped, but were pursued for sixteen years by Finn; according to one version of the story, Diarmaid was eventually killed by a wild boar and Gráinne died of grief. The derivation of the name is uncertain; it has been suggested that it may be from the phrase *dí airmait* 'without envy'. It is also spelled **Diarmait**.

Digby M Transferred use of the surname, in origin a local name from a place in Lincolnshire, named in Old Norse as *díki býr* 'settlement at the dyke'.

Dillon M Variant spelling of **»Dylan**, based on an English surname of different origin. The surname *Dillon* or *Dyllon* derives in part from a now extinct Norman French personal name of Germanic origin; in part it is a local name from *Dilwyn* in Herefordshire.

Dilly F Pet form of **»Dilys**, **»Dilwen**, and **»Dolores**.

Dilwen F Welsh: recent coinage, from *Dil*- (see **»Dilys**) + *(g)wen*, feminine form of *gwyn* 'white', 'fair', 'blessed', 'holy'.

Dilys F Welsh: recent coinage, from the vocabulary word *dilys* 'genuine', 'steadfast', 'true'.

Dina F In part a variant spelling of **»Dinah**, with which it normally shares the pronunciation 'dye-na'. In part, it also derives from the Italian name *Dina* (pronounced 'dee-na'), which is a short form of diminutives such as *Bernardina*.

Dinah F Biblical name (a feminine form derived from Hebrew *din* 'judgement'), borne by a daughter of Jacob.

She was raped by Shechem but avenged by her brothers Simeon and Levi (Genesis 34). In modern times it is often taken as a variant of the more common **»Diana**.

Dion M French name, from Latin *Dio* (genitive *Diōnis*), a short form of any of the various names of Greek origin derived from *Dio-* 'Zeus'. Examples include *Diodoros* 'gift of Zeus' and *Diogenēs* 'born of Zeus'. It is also popular in the English-speaking world, especially as a Black name.

Dionne F Feminine form of **»Dion**.

Dirk M Flemish and Dutch form of **»Derek**. Its use in the English-speaking world since the 1960s is largely due to the fame of the actor Dirk Bogarde (b. 1921 in Scotland, of Dutch parentage; originally called Derek Niven van den Bogaerde). The manly image of the name has been reinforced by its coincidence in form with the Scottish vocabulary word *dirk* 'dagger' (from Gaelic *durc*).

Dolly F Originally (from the 16th century onwards) a pet form of **»Dorothy**; now also a pet form of **»Dolores**. It is also found as an independent given name (taken as being from the vocabulary word *doll*, which was in fact derived in the 17th century from the pet name for *Dorothy*).

Dolores F Spanish: from *Maria de los Dolores* 'Mary of the Sorrows', a reference to the Seven Sorrows of the Virgin Mary. The feast of Our Lady's Dolours was established in 1423. The name is now also borne in the English-speaking world, mainly by Roman Catholics. In part, it was popularized by the film star Dolores Del Rio (1905–83).

Dominic M From the Late Latin name *Dominicus*, a derivative of *dominus* 'lord'. It is used mainly by Roman Catholics, in honour of St Dominic (1170–1221), founder of the Dominican order of monks. The old spelling **Dominick** is still in occasional use.

Dominique F Feminine form of **»Dominic**, from a French form used as both a girl's and a boy's name.

Donagh M Irish: Anglicized form of the Gaelic name *Donnchadh*; see **»Duncan**.

Donal M Irish: Anglicized form of the Gaelic name *Dónal*, earlier *Domhnall*, from Old Celtic *dubno* 'world' + *val* 'rule'. This was very popular in ancient Ireland, being borne by five High Kings of Ireland and three saints. The spelling **»Donall** is also common.

Donald M Scottish: Anglicized form of the Gaelic name *Domhnall* (see **»Donal**). The final *-d* of the Anglicized form derives partly from misinterpretation by English speakers of the Gaelic pronunciation, and partly from association with the Norse name **»Ronald**. This name is strongly associated with clan Macdonald, the clan of the medieval Lords of the Isles, but it is now also used by families with no Scottish connections.

Donall M Variant spelling of **»Donal**.

Donna F Of recent origin (not found before the 1920s); from the Italian vocabulary word *donna* 'lady' (cf. **»Madonna**), although it is also used as a feminine form of **»Donald**.

Donnchadh M Gaelic form of **»Duncan**.

Donovan M Transferred use of the Irish surname, Gaelic *Ó Donndubháin* 'descendant of Donndubhán', a personal name from *donn* 'brown-haired man' or 'chieftain' + *dubh* 'black', 'dark' + the diminutive suffix *-án*. Its use as a given name dates from the early 1900s. The folk-rock singer Donovan probably had some influence on its increase in popularity in the 1960s.

Dora F 19th-century coinage, a short form of **»Isidora**, **»Theodora**, **»Dorothy**, and any other name containing the Greek word *doron* 'gift'. Wordsworth's daughter (b. 1804), christened Dorothy in honour of his sister, was known in adult life as Dora.

Dorcas F From Greek *dorkas* 'doe', 'gazelle'. It was not used as a personal name by the ancient Greeks, but is offered in the Bible as an interpretation of the Aramaic name **»Tabitha** (Acts 9:36), and was taken up by the early Christians. It was much used among the Puritans in the 16th century.

Dorean F Irish: Anglicized form of the Gaelic name **Dáireann** or **Doirind**, which is of uncertain origin. Gaelic *der Fhinn* 'daughter of Finn' has been suggested. It has been revived as a given name in the 20th century. It is probably the source of the English name **»Doreen**, which is one of its Anglicized forms; others are **Dorren** and **Derinn**.

Doreen F Anglicization of the Irish name **»Dorean**. It may also be a derivative of **»Dora** with the addition of the productive suffix *-een*, representing an Irish pet form.

Doria F Probably a back-formation from **»Dorian** or else an elaboration of **»Dora** on the model of the numerous women's given names ending in *-ia*.

Dorian M Late 19th-century coinage, apparently invented by Oscar Wilde, as no evidence has been found of its existence before he used it for the central character in *The Portrait of Dorian Gray* (1891). Dorian Gray is a dissolute rake who retains unblemished youthful good looks; in the attic of his home is a portrait which does his ageing for him, gradually acquiring all the outward marks of his depravity. Wilde may have taken the name from Late Latin *Dōriānus*, from Greek *Dōrieus* 'Dorian', i.e. a member of the Greek-speaking people who settled in the Peloponnese in pre-classical times.

Dorinda F 18th-century coinage, an elaboration of **»Dora** with the suffix *-inda* (as in **»Clarinda** and **»Lucinda**).

Doris F From a classical Greek ethnic name meaning 'Dorian woman'. The Dorians were Greeks who settled mainly in the Peloponnese. In Greek mythology, Doris was a minor goddess of the sea, the consort of Nereus and the mother of his daughters, the Nereids or sea-nymphs, who numbered fifty (in some versions, more). The name enjoyed a great vogue from about 1880 to about 1930, being borne by the film star Doris Day (b. 1924 as Doris Kappelhoff), among others.

Dorothea F Latin form of a post-classical Greek name, from *dōron* 'gift' + *theos* 'god' (the same words as in **»Theodora**, but in reverse order). The masculine form *Dōrotheus* was borne by several early Christian saints, the feminine only by two minor ones, but only the female name has survived. In modern use in the English-speaking world it represents either a 19th-century Latinization of **»Dorothy** or a learned reborrowing.

Dorothy F Usual English form of **»Dorothea**. The name was not used in the Middle Ages, but was taken up in the 16th century and became common thereafter. It was borne by the American film star Dorothy Lamour (1914–96, born Dorothy Kaumeyer).

Dougal M Scottish: Anglicized form of the Gaelic name **Dubhghall** or **Dùghall**, from *dubh* 'black', 'dark' + *gall* 'stranger'. This was a byname applied to Danes, in contrast to the fairer Norwegians and Icelanders (see **»Fingal**).

Douglas M Transferred use of the surname borne by one of the most powerful families in Scotland, the earls of Douglas and of Angus, also notorious in earlier times as Border reivers. Their surname is derived from the place in the Southern Uplands of Scotland where they had their stronghold, named with the Gaelic words *dubh* 'black' + *glas* 'stream'.

Dreda F Shortened form of **»Etheldreda**, used as an independent given name in the 19th century, when the longer form was also briefly in fashion.

Drew M, F Scottish short form of **»Andrew**, often used as an independent name in Scotland, and in recent years increasingly popular elsewhere in the English-speaking world, also as a girl's name.

Drusilla F From a Late Latin name, a feminine diminutive of the old Roman family name *Dr(a)usus*, which was first taken by a certain Livius, who had killed in single combat a Gaul of this name and, according to a custom of the time, took his victim's name as a cognomen. Of the several women in the Roman imperial family who were called Livia Drusilla, the most notorious was Caligula's sister and mistress. The name is borne in the Bible by a Jewish woman, wife of the Roman citizen Felix, who was converted to Christianity by St Paul (Acts 24:24). In England it was taken up as a given name in the 17th century as a result of the biblical mention.

Drystan M Welsh variant of **»Tristan**. Drystan son of Tallwch is fleetingly mentioned in the *Mabinogi* as one of the members of King Arthur's council of advisers.

Duald M Irish: Anglicized form of the Gaelic name **Dubhaltach** (pronounced 'doo-al-tah'), which probably means 'black-haired' (Gaelic *dubhfholtach*). The Anglicized form **Dualta** is also found.

Duane M Irish: Anglicized form of the Gaelic name **Dubhán** (pronounced 'doo-wain'). This was originally a byname, a diminutive of Gaelic *dubh* 'dark', 'black'. In modern use it may be derived from the surname Ó *Dubháin* 'descendant of Dubhán'. Its popularity in the mid-1950s was influenced by the guitarist Duane Eddy. The spellings **Dwane**, **»Dwayne**, and **Dwain** are also found.

Dudley M Transferred use of the surname of a noble family, who took it from Dudley in the West Midlands, which was named in Old English as 'Dudda's wood or clearing'. Their most famous member was Robert Dudley, Earl of Leicester (?1532–88), who was at one time expected to marry Queen Elizabeth I.

d

Duff M Scottish: from the Gaelic nickname *dubh* 'black', i.e. 'dark-haired one'. In modern use it is in part a transferred use of the surname *Duff*, which is derived from the nickname.

Dugald M Anglicized form of the Gaelic name *Dubhghall* (see **»Dougal**). The final *-d* is due to a mishearing of the Gaelic form, in which the final *-ll* sounds like *-ld* to English ears.

Duke M In modern use this normally represents a coinage parallel to **»Earl** and **»King**, but it is also a short form of **»Marmaduke**.

Dulcie F 19th-century coinage: a learned re-creation of the Middle English girl's name *Dulce* or *Dowse*, Late Latin *Dulcia*, a derivative of *dulcis* 'sweet'.

Duncan M Scottish: Anglicized form of the Gaelic name **Donnchadh**, from *donn* 'brown' + *chadh* 'chief' or 'noble'. This was the name of a 7th-century Scottish saint (abbot of Iona), a 10th-century Irish saint (abbot of Clonmacnoise), and two medieval kings of Scotland. The final *n* in the Anglicized form seems to be the result of confusion with the Gaelic word *ceann* 'head' and is also found in the Latinized form *Duncanus*. In Ireland, *Donnchadh* is now often spelled *Donncha*; it was formerly sometimes Anglicized as **»Dennis**.

Dunstan M From an Old English personal name derived from *dūn* 'dark' + *stān* 'stone', borne by a 10th-century saint who restored monastic life at Glastonbury and later became archbishop of Canterbury. The name is now used mainly by Roman Catholics.

Dustin M Transferred use of the surname, which is of uncertain origin, probably a Norman form of the Old Norse personal name *Thorsteinn*, composed of words meaning 'Thor's stone'. It is now used fairly regularly as a given name, largely due to the fame of the film actor Dustin Hoffman (b. 1937), who is said to have been named in honour of the silent film actor Dustin Farnam (1870–1929).

Dwayne M Variant spelling of **»Duane**.

Dwight M Transferred use of the English surname, which probably comes from the medieval English female name *Diot*, a pet form of *Dionysia* (see **»Dennis**). It is found mainly in North America, where its increase in popularity after the Second World War was due to the fame of the American general and president Dwight D. Eisenhower (1890–1969). He was named in honour of the New England philosopher Timothy Dwight (1752–1817) and his brother Theodore Dwight (1764–1846).

Dylan M Welsh: of uncertain origin, probably connected with a Celtic word meaning 'sea'. In the *Mabinogi* it is the name of the miraculously born son of Arianrhod, who became a minor sea god. Since the second half of the 20th century the name has become popular outside Wales, partly as a result of the fame of the Welsh poet Dylan Thomas (1914–53) and the American singer Bob Dylan (b. 1941), who changed his surname from Zimmerman as a tribute to the poet.

Dymphna F This is the name, sometimes spelled **Dympna**, of a medieval Flemish saint about whom little is known beyond the fact that she is regarded as the protector of lunatics and epileptics. According to legend, she was an Irish girl who had been abused by her father and killed by him when she opposed his wishes. Her relics are preserved at Gheel, near Antwerp in Belgium, where an important mental hospital of medieval foundation still bears her name. Her name has been identified, rightly or wrongly, with Irish **»Damhnait**.

d

E

Eamon M Irish name, pronounced 'ay-mon', the Gaelic form of >>**Edmund**. The normal Gaelic spellings are *Éamon(n)* and *Éaman(n)*. Éamonn de Valera (1882–1973) was president of Ireland 1959–73. The name was popularized throughout Britain in the 1950s due to the fame of the broadcaster Eamon Andrews (1922–87).

Earl M North American name: from the vocabulary word denoting a rank of the peerage. Before being used as a boy's given name, it was used as a nickname, parallel to >>**Duke**, >>**King**, etc. The title is from Old English *eorl* meaning 'warrior', 'nobleman', or 'prince', and was used in England in Norman times as an equivalent of the French *comte* 'count'.

Earla F Mainly U.S.: recent coinage, a feminine form of *Earl*. A large number of elaborated forms are also found, for example **Earlina**, **Earline**, **Earlene**, and **Earleen**.

Eavan F Anglicized form of the Gaelic name >>**Aoibheann**.

Ebenezer M Biblical term, meaning 'stone of help' in Hebrew. This was a placename, the site of a battle in which the Israelites were defeated by the Philistines (1 Samuel 4:1). After they took their revenge, Samuel set up a memorial stone bearing this name (1 Samuel 7:12). It was taken up as a boy's given name by the Puritans in the 17th century.

Ebony F From the name of the deeply black wood (Late Latin *ebenius*, from Greek *ebenos*, ultimately of Egyptian origin). This name has been enthusiastically adopted since the 1970s by Black people as a symbol of pride in their colour.

Edan M Scottish and Irish: variant of **»Aidan**. St Edan was an Irish disciple of St David of Wales, who later became bishop of Ferns.

Eden F, M Of uncertain origin. The reference is probably to the biblical Garden of Eden, so named from Hebrew *'eden* 'place of pleasure'. As a boy's name it may also represent a variant of **»Edan** or a transferred use of the English surname *Eden*, which was derived in the Middle Ages from the Old English given name *Edun* or *Edon*, derived from *ēad* 'prosperity', 'riches' + *hūn* 'bear cub'.

Edgar M From an Old English personal name derived from *ēad* 'prosperity', 'riches' + *gār* 'spear'. This was the name of an English king and saint, Edgar the Peaceful (d. 975), and of Edgar Atheling (?1060–?1125), the young prince who was chosen by the English to succeed Harold as king in 1066, but who was supplanted by the Normans.

Edith F From an Old English female personal name, derived from *ēad* 'prosperity', 'riches' + *gȳth* 'strife'. This was borne by an illegitimate daughter (961–84) of Edgar the Peaceful. Her mother took her as a baby to the convent at Wilton in Wiltshire, where she spent all her short life. She was noted for her great humility and is regarded as a saint.

Edmund M From an Old English personal name derived from *ēad* 'prosperity', 'riches' + *mund* 'protector'. This was borne by several early royal and saintly figures, including a 9th-century king of East Anglia killed by invading Danes, allegedly for his adherence to

Christianity. The French spelling **Edmond** is also widely used.

Edna F Generally, this is an Anglicized form of the Irish name **»Eithne**. However, *Edna* also occurs in the Bible, in the apocryphal Book of Tobit, where it is borne by the mother of Sarah and stepmother of Tobias. This is probably from Hebrew *'ednah* 'pleasure', 'delight', and thus is the same word as the Garden of Eden. The earliest known uses of the given name in England are in the 17th century, when it was probably imported from Ireland, rather than taken from the Bible.

Edsel M In Germanic mythology this name is a variant of *Etzel*, which is either from *adal* 'noble' or from the nickname *Atta* 'father'. In modern times its best-known bearer was Edsel Ford, son of Henry Ford, founder of the Ford Motor Corporation. The family was partly of Dutch or Flemish descent, but the reason for the choice of given name is not known.

Edward M From an Old English personal name derived from *ēad* 'prosperity', 'riches' + *weard* 'guard'. This has been one of the most popular of all Old English names, surviving from before the Conquest to the present day and spreading into other European languages. It was the name of three Anglo-Saxon kings and eight English kings of England since the Norman Conquest. The most influential early bearer was King Edward the Confessor (?1002–66; ruled 1042–66). He died childless, and his death sparked off conflicting claims to the throne, which were resolved by the victory of William the Conqueror at the Battle of Hastings. Edward was revered by Normans and English alike for his fairness and his piety. He was canonized in the 12th century and came to be venerated throughout Europe as a model of a Christian king.

Edwin M 19th-century revival of an Old English personal name derived from *ēad* 'prosperity', 'riches' + *wine* 'friend'. It was borne by a 7th-century king of

Northumbria, who was converted to Christianity by St Paulinus and killed in battle against pagan forces, a combination of circumstances which led to his being venerated as a martyr.

Edwina F 19th-century coinage, a Latinate feminine form of >>**Edwin** or >>**Edward**. Edwina Ashley, the wife of Earl Mountbatten, was named in honour of King Edward VII, who had originally wished her to be called *Edwardina*.

Effie F Pet form of >>**Euphemia**, also used for the biblical name >>**Hephzibah**. It was popular in the 19th century.

Egan M Irish: Anglicized form of the Gaelic name **Aogán**, earlier *Aodhagán*, a double diminutive of >>**Aodh**.

Egbert M Old English personal name derived from *ecg* 'edge (of a sword)' + *beorht* 'bright', 'famous'. This was borne by two English saints of the 8th century and by a 9th-century king of Wessex. It survived for a while after the Conquest, but fell out of use by the 14th century, and was briefly revived in the 19th century.

Eiddwen F Welsh: modern coinage, apparently derived from *eiddun* 'fond', with the feminine names suffix *(g)wen*, from *gwyn* 'white', 'fair', 'blessed', 'holy'.

Eileen F Anglicized form of the Irish Gaelic name spelt **Eibhlín**, **Eilín**, or **Aibhilín**. This was derived from Norman French *Aveline*, a derivative of >>**Ava**. *bh* is normally pronounced as 'v' in Gaelic but is sometimes silent, whence the Anglicized form. This name became extremely popular in many parts of the English-speaking world in the early part of the 20th century. The spelling >>**Aileen** is also found, especially in Scotland.

Eilidh F Scottish Gaelic name, pronounced 'ay-lee', a comparatively recent coinage on the basis of English >>**Ellie**. The Anglicized spelling >>**Ailie** is also found.

Eira F Welsh: modern given name, coined from the vocabulary word *eira* 'snow'.

Eireen F Of recent origin, a respelling of **»Irene** under the influence of **»Eileen**.

Eirlys F Welsh: modern given name, coined from the vocabulary word for the snowdrop.

Eirwen F Welsh: modern coinage, from *eira* 'snow' + (*g*)*wen*, feminine form of *gwyn* 'white', 'fair', 'blessed', 'holy'.

Eithne F Irish Gaelic: traditional name, pronounced 'ee-na', apparently from the vocabulary word *eithne* 'kernel', which was used as a term of praise in bardic poetry. This is found in Irish literature as the name of various kings' wives and saints' mothers. It has been Anglicized variously as **»Edna**, **»Ena**, **Et(h)na**, and **Ethenia**. St Eithne was a daughter of King Laoghaire and one of St Patrick's first converts, together with her sister Fidelma.

Elaine F Originally an Old French form of **»Helen**, but now generally regarded as an independent name. The Greek and Latin forms of the name had a long vowel in the second syllable, which in Old French produced this form (as opposed to **»Ellen**). In Arthurian legend Elaine is one of the women who fell in love with Lancelot. Most Arthurian characters have names that are Celtic in origin, although subjected to heavy French influence, and it has therefore been suggested that *Elaine* may actually be derived from a Welsh word meaning 'hind' or 'fawn'.

Eldon M Transferred use of the surname, a local name from a place in Co. Durham, named in Old English as *Ella dūn* 'Ella's hill'.

Eleanor F From an Old French respelling of the Old Provençal name *Alienor*. This has sometimes been taken as a derivative of **»Helen**, but it is more probably of Germanic origin, from *ali* 'other', 'foreign'. It was introduced to England by Eleanor of Aquitaine (1122–1204), who came from south-west France to be the wife of King Henry II. It was also borne by Eleanor of Provence, the wife of Henry III, and Eleanor of Castile, wife of Edward I.

Elen F Welsh form of **»Helen**. It is identical with the Welsh vocabulary word *elen* 'nymph', but this is probably no more than coincidence. It is found in Welsh texts from an early period as an equivalent of *Helen*, for example as the name of the mother of Constantine, finder of the True Cross. The spelling **»Elin** is also found.

Elena F Italian and Spanish form of **»Helen**.

Eleonora F Italian form of **»Eleanor**.

Eleri F Welsh: ancient name of uncertain origin. It was borne in the 5th century by a daughter of the semi-legendary chieftain Brychan. *Eleri* is also a Welsh river name, probably derived from *alar* 'surfeit'. It is not clear whether there is a connection between the personal name and the river name.

Elfreda F 19th-century revival of a Latinized form of the Old English female personal name *Ælfthryth*, meaning 'elf strength'. This form probably absorbed the Old English name *Æthelthryth*, which was originally distinct (see **»Audrey**).

Eli M Biblical name, from a Hebrew word meaning 'height'. This was borne by the priest and judge who brought up the prophet Samuel (1 Samuel 4). It was especially popular among Puritans and Dissenters from the 17th to the 19th century.

Elias M Biblical name, from the Greek form (used in the New Testament) of the name of the prophet **»Elijah**. See also **»Ellis**.

Elijah M Biblical name (meaning 'Yahweh is God' in Hebrew), borne by an Israelite prophet whose exploits are recounted in the First and Second Book of Kings.

Elijah's victory over the prophets of Baal on Mount
Carmel played an important part in maintaining the
Jewish religion, recognizing a single God. This story
and other stories in which he figures, including his
conflicts with Ahab's queen, Jezebel, and his prophecies
of doom, are among the most vivid in the Bible.

Elin F Welsh: variant of **»Elen**.

Elinor F Variant spelling of **»Eleanor**.

Eliot M Variant spelling of **»Elliot**.

Elisabeth F The spelling of **»Elizabeth** used in the
Authorized Version of the New Testament and in most
modern European languages. This was the name of the
mother of John the Baptist (Luke 1:60). Etymologically,
the name means 'God is my oath' and it is therefore
identical with *Elisheba*, the name of the wife of Aaron,
according to the genealogy at Exodus 6:23. The final
element was probably altered by association with
Hebrew *shabbāth* 'Sabbath'.

Elise F From French *Élise*, a short form of **»Elisabeth**.

Eliza F Short form of **»Elizabeth**, first used in the 16th
century and increasingly popular in the 18th and 19th
centuries. It was used by George Bernard Shaw for the
main female character, Eliza Dolittle, in his play
Pygmalion (1913), which was the basis for the musical
and film *My Fair Lady*.

Elizabeth F The usual spelling of **»Elisabeth** in
English. It first became popular because of its
association with Queen Elizabeth I of England (1533–
1603). Throughout the 20th century it has been
extremely fashionable, partly because it was the name
of Elizabeth Bowes-Lyon (b. 1900), who in 1936
became Queen Elizabeth as the wife of King George VI;
even more influentially, it is the name of their daughter
Queen Elizabeth II (b. 1926). There are numerous short
forms, pet forms, and derivatives, including **»Eliza**,
»Liza, **»Lisa**, **»Elsa**, **Liz**, **»Beth**, **Bet**, **»Bess**, **»Elsie**,

Bessy, **»Betty**, **»Betsy**, **»Libby**, and **Lizzie**. See also
»Elspeth and **»Isabel**.

Ella   F   Of Germanic origin, introduced to Britain by the
Normans. It was originally a short form of various
compound names derived from *ali* 'other', 'foreign' (cf.
»Eleanor). It is now often taken as a variant or pet
form of **»Ellen**.

Ellen   F   Originally a variant of **»Helen**, although now
no longer associated with that name. Initial *H-* tended
to be added and dropped rather capriciously, leading to
many doublets (cf. e.g. **»Esther** and **»Hester**). A
common pet form is **»Nell**.

Ellenor   F   Variant spelling of **»Eleanor**, a blend with
»Ellen.

Ellie   F   Pet form of any of the numerous girl's names
beginning with the syllable *El-*, in particular **»Eleanor**,
now used independently.

Elliot   M   Transferred use of the English surname, which
is derived from a medieval (Norman French) boy's
given name, an Old French diminutive of **»Elias**. The
modern given name is also spelled **Elliott** and **Eliot**.

Ellis   M, F   Transferred use of the surname, which
represents the usual medieval vernacular form of **»Elias**.
In Wales it is now sometimes taken as an Anglicized
form of the Old Welsh name *Elisud*, a derivative of *elus*
'kind', 'benevolent'.

Elmer   M   Transferred use of the English surname, which
is from an Old English personal name derived from
æthel 'noble' + *mær* 'famous'. This has been used as a
given name in United States since the 19th century, in
honour of the brothers Ebenezer and Jonathan Elmer,
leading activists in the American Revolution. It is also
found in Canada.

Elroy   M   Variant of **»Leroy**. The initial syllable seems to
be a simple transposition of the first two letters, perhaps
influenced by the Spanish definite article *el*.

Elsa F Shortened form of **»Elisabeth** or **»Elizabeth**. The name was borne by the English-born film actress Elsa Lanchester (1902–86). Elsa Belton was a character in Angela Thirkell's once widely read *Barsetshire Chronicles*. The name is now also associated with the lioness named Elsa, featured in the book *Born Free* by Joy Adamson, which was made into a film.

Elsdon M Mainly U.S.: transferred use of the surname, a local name from a place in Northumberland. The place is named as 'Elli's valley' (Old English *denu*).

Elsie F Scottish: simplified form of *Elspie*, a pet form of **»Elspeth**. This came to be used as an independent name, and in the early 20th century proved more popular than *Elspeth*.

Elspeth F Scottish contracted form of **»Elizabeth**.

Elton M Transferred use of the surname, in origin a local name from any of numerous places in England so called (mostly from the Old English masculine personal name *Ella* + Old English *tūn* 'enclosure', 'settlement'). In England it is largely associated with the singer-songwriter Elton John; born Reginald Dwight, he adopted the given name in honour of the saxophonist Elton Dean.

Eluned F Welsh: apparently a revival of the older Welsh name *Luned* or *Lunet*, of unknown origin. *Lunete* is the form of the name used by the medieval French writer Chrétien de Troyes. Cf. **»Lynette**.

Elvira F Spanish name of Germanic (Visigothic) origin, very common in the Middle Ages and in select use today. The original form and meaning of the elements of which it is composed are uncertain (perhaps *ali* 'other', 'foreign' + *wēr* 'true'). The name was not used in the English-speaking world until the 19th century, when it was made familiar as the name of the long-suffering wife of Don Juan, both in Mozart's opera *Don Giovanni* (1789) and Byron's satirical epic poem *Don*

Juan (1819–24). It is the name of the heroine of the Swedish film *Elvira Madigan* (1967), directed by Bo Widerberg, a romantic tragedy about a pair of lovers who would rather die than be separated.

Elvis M Of obscure derivation, made famous by the American rock singer Elvis Presley (1935–77). It may be a transferred use of a surname, or it may have been made up, but it was certainly not chosen for the singer in anticipation of a career in show business, as he inherited it from his father, whose name was Vernon Elvis Presley. A shadowy Irish St Elvis, of the 6th century, is also referred to as *Elwyn*, *Elwin*, *Elian*, and *Allan*.

Elwyn M Welsh and Irish: of uncertain origin. In the modern Welsh name the influence of the word *(g)wyn* 'white', 'fair', 'blessed', 'holy' is apparent (see ≫**Delwyn**). However, this is also one of the forms used for the name of a 6th-century Irish saint; it may be no more than a variant of ≫**Alan**.

Elyse F Altered spelling of ≫**Elise**.

Emanuel M See ≫**Emmanuel**.

Emer F Anglicized form of Irish Gaelic **Eimer** or **Émer**: a traditional name of uncertain derivation. This was the name of Cú Chulainn's beloved, a woman of many talents who was blessed with the gifts of beauty, voice, sweet speech, needlework, wisdom, and chastity. It has been revived as a given name in the 20th century.

Emerald F Recent coinage, from the word for the gemstone.

Emily F From a medieval form of the Latin name *Aemilia*, the feminine version of the old Roman family name *Aemilius* (probably from *aemulus* 'rival'). It was not common in the Middle Ages, but was revived in the 19th century and is very popular today. Its best-known 19th-century bearer was probably the novelist and poet Emily Brontë (1818–48).

Emlyn M Welsh: of uncertain origin, possibly from Latin *Aemiliānus* (a derivative of the old Roman family name *Aemilius*; see ≫**Emily**). On the other hand, it may have a Celtic origin; there are Breton and Irish saints recorded as *Aemilianus*, which may be a Latinized form of a lost Celtic name.

Emma F Old French name, of Germanic (Frankish) origin, originally a short form of compound names such as *Ermintrude*, containing the word *erm(en)*, *irm(en)* 'entire'. It was adopted by the Normans and introduced by them to Britain. Its popularity in medieval England was greatly enhanced by the fact that it had been borne by the mother of Edward the Confessor, herself a Norman.

Emmanuel M Biblical name (meaning 'God is with us' in Hebrew) used for the promised Messiah, as prophesied by Isaiah (7:14; referred to in Matthew 1:23). The Authorized Version of the Bible uses the Hebrew form ≫**Immanuel** in the Old Testament, *Emmanuel* in the New. The spelling ≫**Emanuel** is also found.

Emmeline F Old French name of Germanic (Frankish) origin, introduced to Britain by the Normans. It probably originated as a derivative of ≫**Emma**, but when it was revived in the 19th century it became confused with ≫**Emily**. A famous bearer was the suffragette Emmeline Pankhurst (1858–1928), mother of Christabel and Sylvia.

Emrys M Welsh form of ≫**Ambrose**, very popular in Welsh families in the 20th century.

Emyr M Welsh: originally a byname meaning 'ruler, king, lord', borne by a 6th-century Breton saint who settled in Cornwall.

Ena F One of several Anglicized forms of the Gaelic name ≫**Eithne**. In the case of Queen Victoria's granddaughter Princess Ena (Victoria Eugénie Julia

Ena, 1887–1969) it had a different origin: it was a misreading by the minister who baptized her of a handwritten note of the intended name **»Eva**.

Enid F Celtic name of uncertain derivation, borne by a virtuous character in the Arthurian romances, the long-suffering wife of Geraint. The name was revived in the second half of the 19th century, following Tennyson's *Idylls of the King* (1859), which contains the story of Geraint and Enid, in which Enid recovers her husband's trust by patience and loyalty after he has suspected her, wrongly, of infidelity.

Enoch M Biblical name (possibly meaning 'experienced' in Hebrew), borne by the son of Cain (Genesis 4:16–22) and father of Methuselah (Genesis 5:18–24). The apocryphal 'Books of Enoch' are attributed to him.

Enola F 20th-century coinage of uncertain derivation. One theory is that it originated as a reversal in spelling of the word *alone*, but this may be no more than coincidental.

Enos M Biblical name (meaning 'mankind' in Hebrew), borne by a son of Seth and grandson of Adam (Genesis 4:26), said to have lived for 905 years.

Eóghan M Traditional Gaelic name, said to be derived from *iúr* 'yew' and to mean 'born of yew'. In Irish legend, this was the name of one of the two sons of Niall of the Nine Hostages (the other was Conall); he gave his name to Co. Tyrone (Tír Eoghain). **»Owen** and, occasionally, **»Eugene** are used as English equivalents.

Eoin M Irish Gaelic form of **»John**.

Ephraim M Biblical name, borne by one of the sons of Joseph and hence one of the tribes of Israel. The name probably means 'fruitful' in Hebrew; it is so explained in the Bible (Genesis 41:52 'and the name of the second called he Ephraim: For God hath caused me to be fruitful in the land of my affliction'). Unlike many Old

Testament names, this was not particularly popular with the Puritans, and was used more in the 18th and 19th centuries than the 17th. It is still a common Jewish given name.

Erasmus M Latinized form of Greek *Erasmos*, a derivative of *erān* 'to love'. St Erasmus (d. 303) was a bishop of Formiae in Campania, martyred under Diocletian; he is numbered among the Fourteen Holy Helpers and is a patron of sailors. This is a rare given name in the English-speaking world. It is sometimes bestowed in honour of the great Dutch humanist scholar and teacher Erasmus Rotterodamus (?1466–1536).

Eric M Of Old Norse origin, from *ei* 'ever', 'always' (or *einn* 'one', 'alone') or *ríkr* 'ruler'. It was introduced into Britain by Scandinavian settlers before the Norman Conquest. As a modern given name, it was revived in the mid 19th century and has remained in use since.

Erica F Latinate feminine form of **»Eric**, coined towards the end of the 18th century. It has also been reinforced by the fact that *erica* is the Latin word for 'heather'.

Erin F From Irish Gaelic *Éirinn*, dative case of *Éire* 'Ireland'. *Erin* has been used as a poetic name for Ireland for centuries, and in recent years this has become a popular given name throughout the English-speaking world.

Erna F Simplified version of *Ernesta*, created as a feminine form of **»Ernest**.

Ernan M Irish: Anglicized form of the Gaelic name *Earnán*, possibly a derivative of *iarn* 'iron'. St Earnán is the patron saint of Tory Island.

Ernest M Of Germanic origin, derived from the Old High German vocabulary word *eornost* 'serious business', 'battle to the death'. The name was introduced into England in the 18th century by followers of King George I, who was also the Elector of Hanover. The adjective *earnest* is not directly connected with the name.

Ernestine F Elaborated feminine form of **≫Ernest**, created in the 19th century.

Errol M Transferred use of the Scottish surname, which derives from a placename. It was made famous by the actor Errol Flynn (1909–59), noted for his swash-buckling film roles. He was born in Australia, but spent most of his career in Hollywood. It is now very popular as a Black name, often in the spelling **Erroll**, influenced by such figures as the jazz pianist Errol Garner (1921–77).

Erskine M Transferred use of the Scottish surname, which is from the name of a place near Glasgow. The surname has also been taken to Ireland by Scottish settlers, and became known as the given name of the Irish writer and political activist Erskine Childers (1870–1922).

Esmeralda F From the Spanish vocabulary word *esmeralda* 'emerald'. Its use as a given name dates from Victor Hugo's *Notre Dame de Paris* (1831), in which it is the nickname of the gypsy girl loved by the hunchback Quasimodo; she was given the name because she wore an amulet containing an artificial emerald.

Esmond M From an Old English personal name derived from *ēast* 'grace', 'beauty' + *mund* 'protection'. This is found in Norman French, reflecting a Continental Germanic original. However, it was not used in Britain as a given name between the 14th century and the 19th century, when it was revived.

Estelle F Old French name meaning 'star' (Latin **≫Stella**), comparatively rarely used during the Middle Ages. It was revived in the 19th century, together with the Latinate form **Estella**, which was used by Dickens for the ward of Miss Havisham in *Great Expectations* (1861).

Esther F Biblical name, borne by a Jewish captive who became the wife of the Persian king Ahasuerus. According to the book of the Bible that bears her name, she managed, by persuasion and ingenuity, to save large numbers of her people from the evil machinations of the royal counsellor Haman. Her Hebrew name was *Hadassah* 'myrtle', and the form *Esther* is said to be a Persian translation of this, although others derive it from Persian *stara* 'star'. It may alternatively be a Hebrew form of the name of the Persian goddess *Ishtar*.

Esyllt F Welsh: traditional name, probably meaning 'of fair aspect'. It is the Welsh form of ≫**Isolde**.

Étaín F Traditional Irish Gaelic name, sometimes identified as that of the ancient Celtic sun goddess, said to be derived from *ét* 'jealousy'.

Ethan M Biblical name (meaning 'firmness' or 'long-lived' in Hebrew) of an obscure figure, Ethan the Ezrahite, mentioned as a wise man whom Solomon surpassed in wisdom (1 Kings 4:31). The name became famous in the United States since it was borne by Ethan Allen (1738–89), leader of the 'Green Mountain Boys', a group of Vermont patriots who fought in the American Revolution.

Ethel F 19th-century revival of an Old English name, a short form of various female personal names containing *ethel* 'noble' as a first element, for example ≫**Etheldreda**.

Etheldreda F Latinized form of the Old English female personal name *Æthelthryth* (see ≫**Audrey**), taken up in the 19th century.

Ethna F Irish: Anglicized or Latinized form of ≫**Eithne**.

Etta F Short form of names such as *Rosetta* and *Henrietta*. -*etta* was originally no more than an Italian feminine diminutive suffix.

Euan M Scottish: Anglicized form of the Gaelic name
»Eóghan.

Eudora F Ostensibly a Greek name, from *eu* 'well',
'good' + a derivative of *dōron* 'gift'. However, there is
no saint of this name, and it is probably a 19th-century
coinage.

Eugene M From the Old French form of the Greek
name *Eugenios* (from *eugenēs* 'well-born', 'noble'). This
name was borne by various early saints, notably a 5th-
century bishop of Carthage, a 7th-century bishop of
Toledo, and four popes. It is sometimes used as an
Anglicized form of Irish **»Eóghan**. The short form
»Gene is often found, especially in North America.

Eugenia F Feminine form of Greek *Eugenios* or Latin
Eugenius; see **»Eugene**.

Eugénie F French form of **»Eugenia**. The name was
introduced to England as the name of the Empress
Eugénie (Eugenia María de Montijo de Guzmán, 1826–
1920), wife of Napoleon III, and has since been
occasionally used (with or without the accent) in the
English-speaking world.

Euna F Scottish: Anglicized form of the Gaelic name
Ùna (see **»Una**).

Eunan M Irish and Scottish: Anglicized form of the
Gaelic name **Ádhamhnán**, traditionally said to be a
diminutive form of **Ádhamh**, the Gaelic version of
»Adam. However, it is more likely to have originated
as a byname, a diminutive of *adomnae* 'great fear', i.e.
'little horror'. The name was borne by a 7th-century
saint, abbot of Iona and biographer of St Columba.

Eunice F From a Late Greek name, derived from *eu*
'well', 'good' + *nikē* 'victory'. This is mentioned in the
New Testament as the name of the mother of Timothy,
who introduced him to Christianity (2 Timothy 1:5).
This reference led to the name being taken up by the
Puritans in the 17th century.

Euphemia F Latin form of a Late Greek name derived from *eu* 'well', 'good' + *phēmi* 'I speak'. This was the name of various early saints, notably a virgin martyr believed to have been burnt at the stake at Chalcedon in 307. It was particularly popular in England in the Victorian period, especially in the pet form **»Effie**.

e **Eustace** M From the Old French form of the Late Greek names *Eustakhios* and *Eustathios*. These are of separate origin, the former derived from *eu* 'well', 'good' + *stakhys* 'grapes', the latter from *eu* 'well' + *stēnai* 'to stand'. However, the tradition is very confused. The name was introduced to Britain by the Normans, among whom it was popular due to the fame of St Eustace, who was said to have been converted to Christianity by the vision of a crucifix between the antlers of the stag that he was hunting.

Eva F Latinate form of **»Eve**, now very popular in its own right. It is also found as an Anglicization of the Gaelic name **»Aoife**.

Evadne F From a Greek personal name derived from *eu* 'well', 'good' + another element, of uncertain meaning. The name was borne by a minor figure in classical legend, who threw herself on to the funeral pyre of her husband, and was therefore regarded as an example of wifely piety.

Evan M As a Welsh name this represents an Anglicized form of *Iefan*, a later development of **»Ieuan**. As a Scottish name it is a variant of **»Euan**.

Evander M Classical name, used in the Scottish Highlands as an Anglicized form of Gaelic Ìomhair (see **»Ivor**). In classical legend, *Evander* is the name of an Arcadian hero who founded a city in Italy where Rome was later built. It is a Latin form of Greek *Euandros*, derived from *eu* 'good' + *anēr* 'man' (genitive *andros*).

Evangeline F Fanciful name derived from Latin *evangelium* 'gospel' (Greek *euangelion*, from *eu* 'good'

+ *angelma* 'tidings') + the suffix *-ine* (in origin a French feminine diminutive). *Evangeline* is the title of a narrative poem (1848) by the American poet Henry Wadsworth Longfellow, in which the central character is called Evangeline Bellefontaine.

Eve F English vernacular form of the name borne in the Bible by the first woman, created from one of Adam's ribs (Genesis 2: 22). It derives, via Latin *Ēva*, from Hebrew *Havva*, which is considered to be a variant of the vocabulary word *hayya* 'living' or 'animal'. Adam gave names to all the animals (Genesis 2: 19–20) and then to his wife, who was 'the mother of all living' (Genesis 3:20).

Evelina F Latinate form of ≫**Evelyn** as a girl's name, or combination of ≫**Eve** with the suffix *-lina*.

Evelyn F, M Modern use of this as a given name for both boys and girls derives from a transferred use of an English surname, from the Norman female name *Aveline*, an elaborated form of ≫**Ava**. It is also found as a variant Anglicization of Irish *Éibhleann* (see ≫**Evlin**). As a girl's name it can also be spelled **Evelyne** and **Eveline**. As a boy's name it is now infrequent.

Everard M From an Old English personal name derived from *eofor* 'boar' + *heard* 'hardy', 'brave', 'strong'. This was reinforced at the time of the Norman Conquest by an Old French cognate of Germanic origin, introduced by the Normans. The modern given name may be a transferred use of the surname, but it was in regular use as a given name in the Digby family of Rutland from the 15th to the 17th centuries, probably as a survival of the Norman name.

Everett M Transferred use of the surname, which is a variant of ≫**Everard**.

Evette F Altered form of ≫**Yvette**, influenced by ≫**Eve**.

Evlin F Anglicized form of the Irish Gaelic name **Éibhleann**, said to be a derivative of the Old Irish vocabulary word *óiph* 'radiance', 'beauty', and sometimes found in the form **Éibhliu**. It is sometimes confused with **Eibhlín**, the Gaelic form of **»Evelyn**.

Evonne F Altered form of **»Yvonne**, influenced by **»Eve**.

Ewan M The usual Anglicized form in Scotland of Gaelic *Eóghan* (see **»Euan**).

Ewart M Transferred use of the Scottish surname, probably first used as a boy's name in honour of the Victorian statesman William Ewart Gladstone (1809–98). The surname has several possible origins: it may represent a Norman form of **»Edward**, an occupational name for a ewe-herd, or a local name from a place in Northumberland.

Ezekiel M Biblical name (meaning 'God strengthens' in Hebrew), borne by one of the major prophets. The book of the Bible that bears his name is known for its vision of a field of dry bones, which Ezekiel prophesies will live again (chapter 37). His prophecies were addressed to the Jews in Babylonian exile, after Nebuchadnezzar had seized Jerusalem in 597 BC. In the U.S. the short form **»Zeke** is sometimes found.

Ezra M Biblical name (meaning 'help' in Hebrew), borne by an Old Testament prophet, author of the book of the Bible that bears his name. This was one of the Old Testament names taken up by the Puritans in the 17th century.

F

Fabia F Latin: feminine form of the old Roman family name *Fabius*; see **»Fabian**, of which this is now used occasionally as a feminine form.

Fabian M From the Late Latin name *Fabiānus*, a derivative of the old Roman family name *Fabius* (said to be a derivative of *faba* 'bean'). St Fabian was an early pope (236–50) who was martyred under the Emperor Decius. The name was introduced into Britain by the Normans, but it has never been much used in the English-speaking world.

Fabiola F Late Latin feminine diminutive form of the old Roman family name *Fabius* (see **»Fabian**). St Fabiola (d. *c.*400) was a Roman widow who founded the first Western hospital, originally a hostel to accommodate the flood of pilgrims who flocked to Rome, in which she tended the sick as well as accommodating the healthy.

Fae F Variant spelling of **»Fay**.

Faith F From the abstract noun denoting the quality of believing and trusting in God. As a girl's name this came into use in the 16th century, and was very popular among the Puritans of the 17th.

Fanny F Pet form of **»Frances**, very popular in the 18th and 19th centuries, but now much rarer.

Fay F Late 19th-century coinage, from the archaic word *fay* 'fairy'. It was to some extent influenced by the revival of interest in Arthurian legend, in which Morgan le Fay is King Arthur's half-sister, a mysterious sorceress who both attempts to destroy Arthur and tends his wounds in Avalon after his last battle. She is sometimes identified with the 'Lady of the Lake'.

Faye F Alternative spelling of **»Fay**, associated particularly with the American actress Faye Dunaway (b. 1941).

Felicia F Latinate feminine form of **»Felix**, of medieval origin as a girl's name.

Felicity F From the abstract noun denoting luck or good fortune (via Old French from Latin *felicitās*; cf. **»Felix**). The English vocabulary word was first used as a given name in the 17th century. It also represents the English form of the Late Latin personal name *Felicitas*, which was borne by several early saints, notably a slave martyred in 203 together with her mistress Perpetua and other companions.

Felim M Anglicized form of the Irish Gaelic name **Feidhlimidh**, said to mean 'eternally virtuous'. It was borne by several early Irish saints and kings and, more recently, by Sir Felim O'Neill, leader of opposition to the plantations of the 17th century, who was executed as a traitor by the British in 1653.

Felix M Latin name, originally a byname meaning 'lucky' applied to the dictator Sulla (138–78 BC). It was a popular given name among the early Christians and was borne by a number of early saints.

Fenella F Mainly Scottish: Anglicized form of the Gaelic name **»Fionnuala**. The spellings **»Finella** and **»Fi(o)nola** are also found, the latter mainly in Ireland.

Ferdinand M From a Spanish name (originally *Ferdinando*, now *Hernán*), of Germanic (Visigothic) origin, derived from *farth* 'journey' (or possibly an altered form of *frith* 'peace') + *nand* 'ready', 'prepared'. This was a traditional name in the royal families of Spain from an early date. It became popular in Britain in the 16th century among Roman Catholic supporters of Queen Mary I, who married Philip II of Spain in 1554.

Fergal M Irish: Anglicized form of the Gaelic name **Fearghal**, which is derived from *fear* 'man' + *gal* 'valour'. This was the name of an 8th-century king of Ireland, Fearghal mac Máeldúin, famous for his murderous exploits.

Fergus M Scottish and Irish: Anglicized form of the Gaelic name *Fearghas*, derived from *fear* 'man' + *gus* 'vigour'. This was the name of a shadowy hero in Irish mythology, also of several early saints, including the grandfather of St Columba.

Fern F One of several words denoting flowers and plants that have been pressed into service as names during the past hundred years.

Fiachra M Traditional Irish Gaelic name derived from *fiach* 'hunt' + *rí* 'king'. This was the name in Irish legend of one of the children of Lir, who were turned into swans by their stepmother. In historical times, it was borne by an Irish saint and missionary in France (died 670 at Meaux). By way of the name of an inn named after him, he gave his name to the *fiacre*, a type of horse-drawn four-wheeled hackney cab.

Fidelma F Latinized form of the traditional Irish Gaelic name **Feidhelm**, the origin of which is unknown. In Irish legend it is borne by a daughter of Conchobhar mac Nessa, a female warrior renowned for her beauty. It was also the name of one of St Patrick's first converts, a daughter of King Laoghaire and sister of St Eithne.

Fife M Transferred use of the Scottish surname, which originated as a local name for someone from the kingdom (now region) of Fife. In Gaelic legend this is said to be named from the legendary Pictish hero *Fib*, one of the seven sons of Cruithne. The name is also spelled ≫**Fyfe**.

Fifi F French nursery form of **»Joséphine**, used occasionally in the English-speaking world in spite of its connotations of frivolity.

Fillan M Scottish: Anglicized form of the Gaelic name **Faolán**, which means 'wolf'. St Fillan was an early medieval missionary to Scotland.

Finbar M Irish: Anglicized form of Gaelic **Fionnb(h)arr**, from *fionn* 'white', 'fair' + *barr* 'head'. This was the name of at least three early Irish saints, one of whom became the first bishop of Cork in the 6th century. He is the subject of many legends, for example that he crossed the Irish Sea on horseback. The pet form of his name is **Bairre** (see **»Barry**), and the Isle of Barra in the Hebrides is said to be named after him.

Finella F Anglicized form in Scotland of the Gaelic name **»Fionnuala**; see also **»Fenella**.

Fingal M Scottish: Anglicized form of the Gaelic name **Fionnghall**, derived from *fionn* 'white', 'fair' + *gall* 'stranger'. It was originally a byname applied to Norse settlers (cf. **»Dougal**), and was used by James Macpherson (1736–96), author of the Ossianic poems, to render the name of the Gaelic hero Fionn mac Cumhaill (see **»Finn**). The spelling **Fingall** is also found.

Finlay M, occasionally F Anglicized form of the Scottish Gaelic name **Fionnlagh**, derived from *fionn* 'white', 'fair' + *laogh* 'warrior', 'hero'.

Finn M Either a transferred use of the surname derived in the Middle Ages from the Old Norse personal name *Finnr* 'Finn', used both as a byname and as a short form of various compound names with this first element, or a traditional Irish Gaelic name meaning 'white', 'fair' (the modern Gaelic form is **Fionn**). In Irish legend the Fenians or *Fianna* were led by Finn MacCool (*Finn mac Cumhaill*).

Finnian M Irish: Anglicized form of Gaelic **Finnén**, a derivative of *finn* 'white', 'fair'. This name was borne by several early Irish saints, including two famous 6th-century bishops. The spelling **Finian** is also found.

Finola F Irish: Anglicized form of **»Fionnuala**, also found in the spellings **»Fionola** and **Finnuala**. See also **»Fenella** and **»Finella**.

Fintan M Irish: Anglicized form of the traditional Irish Gaelic name **Fiontan**, a derivative of *finn* 'white', 'fair' + *tine* 'fire'. This name was borne by numerous early Irish saints.

Fiona F Scottish: Latinate derivative of the Gaelic word *fionn* 'white', 'fair'. It was first used by James Macpherson (1736–96), author of the Ossianic poems, which were supposedly translations from Gaelic. 'Fiona MacLeod' was adopted as a pen-name by William Sharp (1855–1905), author of many romantic novels.

Fionnuala F Popular Gaelic name, pronounced 'fyun-noo-a-la': the modern form of *Fionnguala*, a traditional name derived from *fionn* 'white', 'fair' + *guala* 'shoulder'. In Ireland it is Anglicized as **Finuala** or **»Fi(o)nola**, and in Scotland as **»Fenella** or **»Finella**. The short form **»Nuala** is also popular.

Fionola F One of several Anglicized forms of the Gaelic name **»Fionnuala**. See also **»Fenella** and **»Finola**.

Flann M Irish Gaelic: from a nickname meaning 'red' or 'ruddy'. It is a traditional name, borne by several early Irish heroes, and was at one time also used as a girl's name.

Flannan M Irish: Anglicized form of the Gaelic name **Flannán**, originally a diminutive of Gaelic *flann* 'red', 'ruddy'. St Flannan is the patron of the diocese of Killaloe in Co. Clare, and this is still a popular given name in that area.

Flavia F Feminine form of the old Roman family name *Flāvius*, from Latin *flāvus* 'yellow(-haired)'. This was the name of at least five early saints.

Fletcher M Transferred use of the surname, an occupational name for a maker of arrows, from Old French *flech(i)er*. An early bearer of this as a given name was Fletcher Christian, leader of the mutiny on the *Bounty* in 1789.

Fleur F From an Old French name meaning 'flower', occasionally used in the Middle Ages. Modern use, however, seems to derive mainly from the character of this name in John Galsworthy's *The Forsyte Saga* (1922).

Floella F Recent coinage, in Britain especially popular as a Black name. It is evidently a compound of **Flo** (a short form of **»Flora** or **»Florence**) and **»Ella**.

Flora F Name borne in Roman mythology by the goddess of flowers and the spring (a derivative of Latin *flōs* 'flower', genitive *flōris*). It is also the feminine form of the old Roman family name *Flōrus*, likewise derived from *flōs*. *Flora* was little used in England before the 18th century, when it was imported from Scotland. Flora Macdonald (1722–90) helped Bonnie Prince Charlie to escape to the Isle of Skye, disguised as a woman, after his defeat at Culloden in 1746. This was an act of considerable heroism in view of the relentless ferocity with which the troops of 'Butcher' Cumberland were pursuing the followers of the defeated Pretender. *Flora* was an Anglicized form of her Gaelic name, *Fionnaghal*; see **»Fionnuala**. Her fame made the name *Flora* popular in the Highlands and elsewhere.

Florence F, formerly also M Medieval form of the Latin boy's name *Florentius* (a derivative of *florens* 'blossoming' or 'flourishing') and its feminine form *Florentia*. In the Middle Ages the name was commonly given to boys (as, for example, the historian Florence of Worcester), but it is now exclusively a girl's name. This was revived in the second half of the 19th century, being given in honour of Florence Nightingale (1820–1910), the founder of modern nursing, who organized a group of nurses to serve in the Crimean War. She herself received the name because she was born in the Italian city of Florence.

Floyd M Transferred use of the Welsh surname, which originated as a variant of **»Lloyd**, attempting to represent the sound of the Welsh initial *Ll-* using traditional English pronunciation and orthography.

Forbes M Transferred use of the Scottish surname, in origin a local name from the lands of Forbes in Aberdeenshire, named in Gaelic from *forba* 'field', 'district' + *-ais* 'at'. The name was traditionally pronounced as two syllables.

Ford M Transferred use of the surname, originally a local name for someone who lived by a ford.

Francene F Variant spelling of **»Francine**.

Frances F Feminine form of **»Francis**. In the 16th century the two spellings were used indiscriminately for both sexes; the distinction between *Frances* for girls and *Francis* for boys was established in the 17th century.

Francesca F Italian form of **»Frances**. Originally a vocabulary word meaning 'French', it was bestowed from the 13th century onwards in honour of St Francis of Assisi. Its most famous bearer was Francesca di Rimini, daughter of Giovanni da Polenta, Count of Ravenna. A legendary beauty, she was betrothed by her father to the misshapen Giovanni Malatesta, Lord of Rimini, in return for military support. Malatesta's handsome younger brother Paolo acted as his proxy in the betrothal, but unfortunately Francesca and he fell in love. They were discovered and put to death by Malatesta in 1289. Their tragedy is enshrined in the

f

Fifth Canto of Dante's *Inferno*, as well as in several other works of literature and in a symphonic fantasy by Tchaikovsky.

Francine F From a French pet form of *Françoise*, the French form of **»Frances**.

Francis M English form of Italian *Francesco*, originally a vocabulary word meaning 'French' or 'Frenchman' (Late Latin *Franciscus*; cf. **»Frank**). The name is often bestowed in honour of St Francis of Assisi (1181–1226), who acquired it originally as a nickname because of his wealthy father's business connections with France. St Francis had an unremarkable childhood, but after two serious illnesses, a period of military service, and a year as a prisoner of war in Perugia, he turned from the world and devoted himself to a religious life, caring for the poor and sick and respecting all living creatures. He was joined by groups of disciples, calling themselves 'minor friars'. The main features of the Franciscan rule are humility, poverty, and love for all God's creatures. The given name was introduced into England in the early 16th century, when there was a surge of admiration for, and imitation of, Italian Renaissance culture.

Frank M Of Germanic origin, originally an ethnic name for a member of the Frankish people, who are said to have been named from the characteristic type of spear that they used. When the Franks migrated into Gaul in the 4th century, the country received its modern name of France (Late Latin *Francia*) and the tribal term Frank came to mean 'Frenchman'. The name is now used also as a short form of **»Francis** or **»Franklin**.

Frankie M, F Pet form of **»Frank**, also sometimes of **»Frances**, **»Francesca**, or **»Francine**. As a girl's name, it is perhaps most familiar as the name of the heroine of *The Ballad of Frankie and Johnny*, who ended up in the electric chair, 'with the sweat running through her hair'.

Franklin M Transferred use of the surname, derived from Middle English *frankeleyn* 'freeman', denoting a member of a class of men who were not of noble birth but who were nevertheless freeholders. The vocabulary word is derived from Old French *franc*, meaning both 'free' and 'Frankish'. In the United States, this is often given as a boy's name in honour of the statesman and scientist Benjamin Franklin (1706–90). A more recent influence was President Franklin D. Roosevelt (1882–1945).

Fraser M Transferred use of the surname of a leading Scottish family. The surname seems to be of Norman origin, but its exact derivation is uncertain. The earliest forms recorded are *de Frisselle* and *de Fresel(iere)*, but it was altered, possibly by association with Old French *fraise* 'strawberry'. The spelling **Frazer** is also found, especially in Northern Ireland.

Freda F Short form of names such as ≫**Elfreda** and ≫**Winifred**, also occasionally of ≫**Frederica**. It is now used as a girl's name in its own right, and in some cases may have been adopted as an English equivalent of the popular German name *Frieda*, a short form of such old German compound names as *Friedegund* and *Friedelind*. The common element of all these names is Germanic *frid-* 'peace'.

Frederica F Latinate feminine form of ≫**Frederick**.

Frederick M From an Old French name of Germanic origin, from *frid* 'peace' + *rīc* 'power', 'ruler'. It was adopted by the Normans and introduced into Britain by them, but did not survive long. Modern use in Britain dates from its reintroduction in the 18th century by followers of the Elector of Hanover, who in 1714 became George I of England. It was reinforced by the vogue for Germanic names in Victorian times.

Freya F Scottish: of Old Norse origin. *Freya* or *Fröja* was the goddess of love in Scandinavian mythology, and her name seems to be derived from a cognate of Old High German *frouwa* 'lady', 'mistress'. The name has for long been a traditional one in Shetland, and it is still popular in Scotland. A notable modern bearer is the explorer and writer Freya Stark.

Fulk M Of Germanic origin, introduced to Britain by the Normans. The name originally represented a short form of various compound names containing the word *volk* 'people', 'tribe' (cf. modern English *folk* and the German boy's name *Volker*, anciently *Volkheer* 'people army'). The spelling **Fulke** is also found, used in certain families, such as the Grevilles: Fulke Greville, 1st Baron Brooke, was a leading figure at the court of Queen Elizabeth I.

Fulton M Transferred use of the Scottish surname, which probably originated as a local name from a lost place in Ayrshire. Robert Fulton (1765–1815) was the American engineer who designed the first commercially successful steamboat.

Fulvia F Latin name, the feminine form of the old Roman family name *Fulvius*, a derivative of Latin *fulvus* 'dusky', 'tawny'. The name was not much used among early Christians, and no saints Fulvia or Fulvius are known. In classical times its most famous bearer was the wife of Mark Antony, who opposed Octavian by force on her husband's behalf while he was in Egypt. Its modern use began with the classical revival of the 18th century.

Fyfe M Variant of ≫**Fife**.

G

Gabriel M, F Biblical name (meaning 'man of God' in Hebrew), borne by one of the archangels. Gabriel appeared to Daniel in the Old Testament (Daniel 8:16; 9:21), and in the New Testament to Zacharias (Luke 1:19; 26:27) and, most famously, to Mary to announce the impending birth of Christ (Luke 1:2). Used only fairly infrequently during the 20th century, *Gabriel* has recently found favour as a given name in the English-speaking world and is now also found as a girl's name.

Gabriela F Latinate feminine form of **»Gabriel**.

Gabrielle F French feminine form of **»Gabriel**.

Gae F From the English vocabulary word *gay* in its original meaning 'blithe' or 'cheerful'. This came to be used as a given name in the early 20th century because of its well-omened meaning, but fell out of favour again in the 1960s, when the vocabulary word acquired the meaning 'homosexual'. The name survives in occasional use in the spelling *Gae*.

Gaenor F Welsh: variant of **»Gaynor** adapted to Welsh orthography, but also influenced by the name of the saint commemorated at *Llangeinwyr* in Glamorgan, known popularly as *Llangeinor*, literally 'church of the beautiful maiden'. Welsh *cain wyr* means 'beautiful maiden'.

Gaia F From Greek *Gaia*, name of the primeval earth goddess in Greek mythology.

Gail F Shortened form of **»Abigail**. It is now well known as an independent given name, but was rare until the middle of the 20th century. The spelling **»Gayle** is also found.

Gala F Of Russian origin, a short form of **Galina**, which is said to be from the Greek name *Galēnē* meaning 'calm', although it may instead be a vernacular form of **»Helen**.

Gareth M Probably of Celtic origin, although the derivation is uncertain. The name first occurs in Malory's *Morte D'Arthur* as the name of the lover of Eluned, and seems to have been heavily altered from its original form, whatever that may have been (possibly the same as **»Geraint**). It is now very popular in Wales. **»Gary**, which is actually an independent name, is often taken to be a pet form of this name.

Garfield M Transferred use of the surname, a local name for someone who lived near a triangular piece of land, from Old English *gār* 'triangular piece of land' + *feld* 'open country'. Its best-known bearer is the West Indian cricketer Sir Garfield Sobers.

Garret M Irish: Anglicization of **Gearóid**, the Gaelic form of **»Gerald**. It is also found as a transferred use of the surname, which is derived from the given names **»Gerald** and **»Gerard**. The spelling **Garrett** is also found.

Garrick M Mainly U.S.: transferred use of the surname, in some cases perhaps adopted in honour of the English actor-manager David Garrick (1717–79). He was of Huguenot descent, the grandson of a certain David *de la Garrigue*. *Garrigue* is a Languedoc placename, from the southern French word *garrigue*, denoting a stretch of open limestone country.

Garrison M Mainly U.S.: transferred use of the surname, generally a patronymic for the son of someone called **»Garret**. William Lloyd Garrison (1805–79) was a prominent American anti-slavery campaigner: the given name may originally have been

bestowed in honour of him. It is now sometimes given
to the sons of fathers who are called **»Gary** or **»Garry**.

Garry M Variant spelling of **»Gary**, influenced by
»Barry.

Garth M Transferred use of a surname, but often
believed to be a contracted form of **»Gareth**. The
surname originated in the north of England as a local
name for someone who lived by or in an enclosure
(Old Norse *garthr*). In modern times its popularity is
enhanced by the virile superhero of this name, main
character in a long-running strip cartoon in the *Daily
Mirror*.

Gary M As a given name, this is of quite recent origin,
although it derives from a well-established surname. The
latter is most probably from a Norman personal
name of Germanic origin, a short form of any of a
number of compound names with *gar* 'spear' as their
first element. One bearer of this surname was the
American industrialist Elbert Henry Gary (1846–1927),
who gave his name to the steel town of Gary, Indiana.
In this town was born the theatrical agent Nan Collins,
who suggested *Gary* as a stage name for her client
Frank J. Cooper, who thus became the film star Gary
Cooper (1901–61). The spelling **»Garry** is also found.

Gavin M Of Celtic origin, but uncertain derivation. It is
borne in the Arthurian romances by one of the knights
of the Round Table, more familiar in English versions
as *Sir Gawain*. The name died out in the 16th century
except in Scotland, whence it has spread widely in the
past forty years.

Gayle F Variant spelling of **»Gail**. Its popularity is partly
due to the American film actress Gayle Hunnicutt (b.
1942).

Gaynor F A medieval English form of the name of King
Arthur's queen, **»Guinevere**. See also **»Gaenor**.

Gearóid M Irish Gaelic form of >>**Gerald**.

Ged M Short form of >>**Gerard** or >>**Gerald**.

Gemma F From a medieval Italian nickname meaning 'gem', 'jewel'. It has been chosen in modern times mainly because of its transparent etymology. Among Roman Catholics it is sometimes chosen in honour of St Gemma Galgani (1878–1903), who was the subject of many extraordinary signs of grace, such as ecstasies and the appearance of the stigmata.

g

Gene M, F Short form of >>**Eugene**, now also used independently as a boy's name, especially in North America. It has been made familiar by film actors such as Gene Autry, Gene Hackman, Gene Kelly, and Gene Wilder. It is also occasionally used as a girl's name, in which case it represents a respelling of >>**Jean**.

Genette F Variant spelling of >>**Jeannette**.

Genevieve F The name of the patron saint of Paris, **Geneviève** in French. She was a 5th-century Gallo-Roman nun who encouraged the people of Paris under Frankish occupation and the threat of attacks by the Huns. Her name is said to be derived from Celtic words meaning 'tribe' and 'woman', but if so it has been heavily altered. It was introduced to Britain from France in the 19th century.

Geoffrey M Norman boy's name, of Germanic (Frankish and Lombard) origin. It was in regular use among the counts of Anjou, ancestors of the English royal house of Plantagenet, who were descended from Geoffrey Plantagenet, Count of Anjou (1113–51). It was a particularly popular name in England and France in the later Middle Ages; notable bearers in England include the poet Geoffrey Chaucer (c.1340–1400) and in Wales the chronicler Geoffrey of Monmouth (d. 1155). The original form and meaning of the name are uncertain. It may be a variant of >>**Godfrey**, or it may represent a blend of several different early Germanic names. It is now also commonly spelled **»Jeffrey**.

George M Via Old French and Latin from Greek *Georgios*. The Greek name is a derivative of *geōrgos* 'farmer', from *gē* 'earth' + *ergein* 'to work'. This was the name of several early saints, including the legendary figure who is now the patron of England (as well as of Germany and Portugal). If the saint existed at all, he was perhaps martyred in Palestine in the persecutions instigated by the Emperor Diocletian at the beginning of the 4th century. The popular legend in which he is a hero who slays a dragon is a medieval Italian invention. He was for a long time a more important saint in the Orthodox Church than in the West, and the name was not much used in England during the Middle Ages, even after St George came to be regarded as the patron of England in the 14th century. The real impulse for its popularity was the accession of the first king of England of this name, who came from Germany in 1714 and brought many German retainers 'with him. It has been one of the most popular English male names ever since.

Georgette F French feminine diminutive of *Georges*, the French form of **»George**.

Georgia F Latinate feminine form of **»George**. It was borne by a 5th-century saint who became a recluse near Clermont in the Auvergne.

Georgiana F Elaborated Latinate form of **»Georgia** or **»Georgina**.

Georgie F, M Originally a pet form of the boy's name **»George**, but now more commonly used as a girl's name, a female equivalent of **»George** or a pet form of **»Georgia** or **»Georgina**.

Georgina F Latinate feminine derivative of **»George**. This feminine form originated in Scotland in the 18th century, when *George* itself became common among anti-Jacobites.

Geraint M Welsh: of uncertain origin, derived from a British name that first appears in a Greek inscription in the form *Gerontios*, possibly influenced by the Greek vocabulary word *gerōn* 'old man' (genitive *gerontos*). The story of Geraint (or *Gereint*), son of Erbin of Cornwall, is told in the *Mabinogi*. Geraint, one of the knights of Arthur's Round Table, wins the love of Enid at a tournament, and marries her. He is infatuated with her to the point of neglecting all else, but comes to suspect her, wrongly, of infidelity. By her submissiveness and loyalty, she regains his trust. The story of Geraint and Enid was used by Tennyson in the *Idylls of the King* (1859). In recent years the name has become extremely popular in Wales.

Gerald M From an Old French name of Germanic (Frankish) origin, derived from *gēr* 'spear' + *wald* 'rule'. It was adopted by the Normans and introduced by them to Britain, where it soon became confused with ≫**Gerard**. It died out in England at the end of the 13th century. However, it continued in Ireland, where it had been introduced in the 12th century following Strongbow's invasion. It was revived in England in the 19th century, along with several other long-extinct names of Norman, Old English, and Celtic origin, and is now more common than *Gerard*, which survived all along as an English 'gentry' name.

Geraldine F Feminine derivative of ≫**Gerald**, invented in the 16th century by the English poet Henry Howard, Earl of Surrey (?1517–47), in a poem praising Lady Fitzgerald. It enjoyed a sudden increase in popularity in the 18th century.

Gerard M Old French name of Germanic (Frankish) origin, introduced to Britain by the Normans. It is derived from *gēr* 'spear' + *hard* 'brave', 'hardy', 'strong'. In the later Middle Ages this was a much more common name than ≫**Gerald**, with which it was sometimes confused. Nowadays it is less common, surviving mainly among Roman Catholics, in honour of the many saints of this name.

Germaine F, M Feminine form of the rarer French male name **Germain** (Late Latin *Germānus* 'brother'; the original reference may have been to the concept of Christian brotherhood). Germaine Cousin (*c.*1579–1601) was a Provençal saint, canonized in 1867. The name is now also sometimes bestowed in honour of the Australian feminist Germaine Greer (b. 1939). The name in this spelling is now also sometimes used as a boy's name in the United States; see also **»Jermaine**.

Gerrard M Variant spelling of **»Gerard**, in part a transferred use of the surname which was derived from the given name in the Middle Ages.

Gertrude F From a Germanic girl's name, derived from *gēr* 'spear' + *thrūth* 'strength'. The name is not found in England immediately after the Conquest, but only in the later Middle English period: it was probably introduced by migrants from the Low Countries, who came to England in connection with the cloth trade.

Gervaise M Norman name, probably of Germanic origin, although the derivation is unclear. It is bestowed, mainly by Roman Catholics, in honour of a certain St Gervasius, whose remains, together with those of Protasius, were discovered in Milan in the year 386. Nothing is known about their lives, but St Ambrose, who had ordered the search for their remains, declared that they were martyrs, and a cult soon grew up. See also **»Jarvis**. The spelling **Gervase** is also found.

Ghislain F A recent introduction to the English-speaking world, a revival of the Old French name **»Giselle** in a spelling that suggests Dutch or Flemish influence. It is also spelled **Ghislaine**.

Gideon M Biblical name (meaning 'he who cuts down' in Hebrew), borne by an Israelite leader appointed to deliver his people from the Midianites (Judges 6:14).

He did this by getting his army to creep up on them with their torches hidden in pitchers. The name was popular among the 17th-century Puritans and has remained in select use.

Gigi F French pet form of >>**Giselle**, popularized in the English-speaking world by Lerner and Loewe's musical *Gigi* (1958).

Gilbert M Old French name introduced to Britain by the Normans. It is of Germanic (Frankish) origin, derived from *gisil* 'pledge' + *berht* 'bright', 'famous'. It was borne by the founder of the only native British religious order (abolished at the Dissolution of the Monasteries), St Gilbert of Sempringham (?1083–1189), in whose honour it is still sometimes bestowed, especially among Roman Catholics.

Giles M Much altered English vernacular form of the Late Latin name *Aegidius*, from Greek *Aigidios* (a derivative of *aigidion* 'kid', 'young goat'). This was bestowed in honour of the 8th-century St Giles. According to tradition, he was an Athenian citizen who fled to Provence because he could not cope with the adulation resulting from his ability to work miracles, in particular by healing the lame and crippled.

Gill F Short form of >>**Gillian**, rather less frequent than >>**Jill**.

Gillespie M Scottish: Anglicized form of Gaelic *Gille Easbaig* 'bishop's servant'. Gille Easbaig Cambeul ('wrymouth') was the founder of Clan Campbell.

Gillian F Variant of >>**Julian**, from which it was differentiated in spelling in the 17th century. The spelling >>**Jillian** is also found, while the short forms >>**Gill** and >>**Jill** are sometimes used as names in their own right.

Gilroy M Transferred use of the Irish and Scottish surname, perhaps influenced to some extent by >>**Elroy**

and **»Leroy**. The surname is of Gaelic origin, from *an giolla ruadh*, meaning 'the red-haired lad'.

Gina F   Shortened form of **»Georgina**. As an Italian name it also represents a short form of *Giorgina* or *Luigina*, and was made famous by the actress Gina Lollobrigida (b. 1927, baptized *Luigina*).

Giselle F   French name of Frankish origin, from the Germanic word *gisil* 'pledge'. It was a common practice in medieval Europe to leave children as pledges for an alliance, to be brought up at a foreign court, and the name may be derived as a byname from this practice. This was the name by which the wife of Duke Rollo of Normandy (*c*.860–*c*.930) was known. On her account the name enjoyed considerable popularity in France from an early period. Use of the name in English-speaking countries is much more recent, and is due mainly to the ballet *Giselle* (first performed in 1841).

g

Gladstone M   Transferred use of the Scottish surname, in origin a local name from *Gledstanes* in Biggar. As a given name it has sometimes been bestowed in honour of the Victorian Liberal statesman William Ewart Gladstone (1809–98). It is now favoured especially among West Indians.

Gladwin M   Transferred use of the surname, itself from a medieval given name derived from Old English *glæd* 'bright' + *wine* 'friend'.

Gladys F   From the Welsh name *Gwladus*, which is of uncertain derivation. It has been quite widely used outside Wales since the early 20th century.

Glen M   Modern coinage from the Scottish word *glen* 'valley' (Gaelic *gleann*), in some cases perhaps representing a transferred use of the surname derived from this word. In recent years it has become used far beyond Scotland as a given name. It has become confused with the Welsh name **»Glyn**, which has the same meaning. The spelling **»Glenn** is also common.

Glenda F Welsh: modern coinage, composed of the vocabulary words *glân* 'clean', 'pure', 'holy' + *da* 'good'. It is associated particularly with the actress and politician Glenda Jackson (b. 1936).

Glenn M, F Variant spelling of **»Glen**, borne as a girl's name by the American actress Glenn Close.

Glenys F Welsh: modern coinage from *glân* 'pure', 'holy' + the ending *-ys* by analogy with names such as **»Dilys** and **»Gladys**.

Gloria F From the Latin word meaning 'glory', not used as a given name before the 20th century. It first occurs as the name of a character in George Bernard Shaw's play *You Never Can Tell* (1898) and was fairly popular in the 1940s and 1950s.

Glory F Anglicized form of **»Gloria**, now occasionally used as a given name.

Glyn M Welsh: from the Welsh word *glyn* 'valley'. This was adopted as a given name in the 20th century, as the result of a desire to bestow on Welsh children specifically Welsh names. It is sometimes also spelled **»Glynn**.

Glyndwr M Welsh: adopted in the 20th century in honour of the medieval Welsh patriot Owain Glyndŵr (c.1359–1416; known in English as Owen Glendower). In his case it was a byname referring to the fact that he came from a place named with Welsh *glyn* 'valley' + *dŵr* 'water'.

Glynis F Altered form of **»Glenys**.

Glynn M Welsh: variant spelling of **»Glyn**.

Gobbán M Traditional Irish Gaelic name, from *gobha* 'smith'. In Irish legend Gobbán was a master craftsman who could fashion a sword or spear with just three blows of his hammer.

Gobnat F Traditional Irish Gaelic name, feminine of **»Gobbán**. St Gobnat was the foundress of the

monastery at Ballyvourney, Co. Cork, at a place where
she encountered nine white deer.

Godfrey M From the Old French name *Godefroy*, which
is of Germanic (Frankish) origin, from *god* 'god' (or *gōd*
'good') + *fred*, *frid* 'peace'. This was adopted by the
Normans, and introduced by them to Britain. It was a
very popular name in the Middle Ages, and was borne
by, among others, a Norman saint (c.1066–1115) who
became bishop of Amiens. There has been some
confusion with ≫**Geoffrey**.

Godwin M From the Old English personal name
Godwine, derived from *god* 'god' + *wine* 'friend'. This
was borne in the 11th century by the Earl of Wessex,
the most important man in England after the king. He
was an influential adviser to successive kings of England
and father of the King Harold who was defeated at
Hastings in 1066. The personal name continued in use
after the Norman Conquest long enough to give rise to
a surname. Modern use as a given name is probably a
transferred use of the surname, rather than a revival
of the Old English name.

Goodwin M Transferred use of the surname, which is
derived from the Old English personal name *Gōdwine*,
from *gōd* 'good' + *wine* 'friend'. There has been some
confusion with ≫**Godwin**.

Gordon M Transferred use of the Scottish surname,
which is derived from a placename. It is a matter of
dispute whether it referred originally to the Gordon in
Berwickshire or to a similarly named place in
Normandy. As a given name it seems to have been taken
up in the 19th century in honour of Charles George
Gordon (1833–85), the British general who died at
Khartoum.

Goronwy M Welsh: of uncertain derivation, borne in
the *Mabinogi* by Goronwy the Staunch, Lord of Penllyn.
He became the lover of the flower-maiden Blodeuedd

and murdered her husband Lleu Llaw Gyffes, but Lleu was later restored to life and definitively dispatched Goronwy.

Grace F From the abstract noun (via Old French, from Latin *grātia*), first used as a given name by the Puritans in the 17th century. It has always been particularly popular in Scotland and northern England (borne, for example, by Grace Darling, the lighthouse keeper's daughter whose heroism in 1838, saving sailors in a storm, caught the popular imagination). In more recent times it was famous as the name of the actress Grace Kelly (1928–82), who became Princess Grace of Monaco. In Ireland it is used as an Anglicized form of **»Gráinne**.

Graham M Transferred use of a Scottish surname, in origin a local name from *Grantham* in Lincolnshire. The surname was taken to Scotland in the 12th century by Sir William de Graham, founder of a famous clan, among whose descendants were the earls of Montrose. Alternative spellings of the given name include **Grahame** and **Graeme**.

Gráinne F Irish Gaelic name, pronounced '**gron**-nya'. It is of uncertain origin, possibly connected with *grán* 'grain', as the name of an ancient corn goddess. In Irish legend Gráinne is the daughter of King Cormac, who was beloved by the aging hero Finn Mac Cumhaill, but eloped with Finn's nephew Diarmait. Finn pursued them over great distances for sixteen years, and (according to one version of the story) eventually brought about the death of Diarmait, after which Gráinne killed herself. Gráinne Uí Mháille, known in English as Grace O'Malley, was a semi-legendary commander of war galleys on the Mayo coast in the late 16th century, 'for forty years the stay of all rebellions in the west'.

Grania F Latinized form of the Irish Gaelic name **»Gráinne**.

Grant M Transferred use of the surname, common in Scotland, where it is the name of a famous clan. It is derived from a descriptive nickname meaning 'large' (from French *grand*). In the United States the name is sometimes bestowed in honour of the Civil War general and 18th president, Ulysses S. Grant (1822–85).

Granville M From one of the Norman baronial names that subsequently became aristocratic English surnames and are now used intermittently as boys' names. This one derives from any of several places in Normandy named with Old French as *grand ville* 'large settlement'.

g

Granya F Variant spelling of ≫**Grania**, influenced by the English spelling of Russian names such as ≫**Sonya** and ≫**Tanya**.

Greer F Transferred use of the Scottish surname, which originated in the Middle Ages from a contracted form of ≫**Gregor**. Its use as a girl's name in the English-speaking world is due to the actress Greer Garson (1903–96), whose mother's maiden name it was.

Gregor M Scottish form of ≫**Gregory**. In part it represents an Anglicized form of Gaelic *Griogair*.

Gregory M Via Latin *Gregorius* from the post-classical Greek name *Gregórios* 'watchful' (a derivative of *gregórein* 'watch', 'be vigilant'). The name was very popular among the early Christians, who were mindful of the injunction 'be sober, be vigilant' (1 Peter 5:8). It was borne by a number of early saints, the most important of whom were Gregory of Nazianzen (*c.*329–90), Gregory of Nyssa (d. *c.*395), Gregory of Tours (538–94), and Pope Gregory the Great (*c.*540–604). Its modern popularity is partly due to the film star Gregory Peck (1916–2003).

Greta F Short form of *Margareta*, a Latinate form of ≫**Margaret**. It became fairly popular in the English-speaking world as a result of the fame of the Swedish-born film actress Greta Garbo (1905–92).

Greville M Transferred use of the surname, a Norman baronial name from *Gréville* in La Manche. The Greville family were earls of Warwick and held Warwick Castle from the time of Queen Elizabeth I, who granted it to her favourite Fulke Greville (1554–1628).

Griffin M Welsh: from a medieval Latinized form, *Griffinus*, of >>**Griffith**.

Griffith M Welsh: Anglicized form of *Gruffudd* or *Griffudd*, Old Welsh *Grip(p)iud*. The second element of this means 'lord', prince'; the first is of uncertain origin. Gruffydd ap Llewellyn (d. 1063) was one of the most able rulers of Wales in the Middle Ages, scoring some notable victories over the English until he was eventually defeated by King Harold in 1063.

Griselda F Of uncertain origin, possibly from a Germanic name derived from *gris* 'grey' + *hild* 'battle'. Its popularity in the Middle Age was due to the tale of 'patient Griselda' (told by Boccaccio and Chaucer), who was taken as a model of the patient, long-suffering wife.

Guaire M Traditional Irish Gaelic name, of uncertain origin. It is said to be from a word meaning 'noble' or 'proud'.

Guinevere F From the Old French form of the Welsh name *Gwenhwyfar*, from *gwen* 'white', 'fair', 'blessed', 'holy' + *hwyfar* 'smooth', 'soft'. It is famous as the name of King Arthur's wife, who in most versions of the Arthurian legends is unfaithful to him, having fallen in love with Sir Lancelot. See also >>**Gaynor** and >>**Jennifer**.

Guy M From an Old French name, of Germanic (Frankish) origin, originally a short form of a compound name starting with *witu* 'wood' or *wit* 'wide'. This was adopted by the Normans and introduced by them to England. In Old French initial *w-* regularly became *gu-*. The usual Norman forms of the name were *Gy* or *Guido*. In medieval Latin the same name is found as *Wido*. It was a popular name among the Normans, enhanced no doubt by the romance of Guy of Warwick, recounting the exploits of a folk hero of the Crusades.

Gwen F Welsh: short form of **»Gwendolen** or **»Gwenllian**, or an independent name from Welsh *gwen*, the feminine form of *gwyn* 'white', 'fair', 'blessed', 'holy' (see **»Gwyn**). It was borne by a 5th-century saint, aunt of St David and mother of the minor saints Cybi and Cadfan.

g

Gwenda F Welsh: of modern origin, composed of the vocabulary words *gwen* 'white', 'fair', 'blessed', 'holy' (see **»Gwen**) + *da* 'good'.

Gwendolen F Welsh: from *gwen* 'white', 'fair', 'blessed', 'holy' (see **»Gwyn**) + *dolen* 'ring', 'bow'. According to Geoffrey of Monmouth, this was the name of the wife of a mythical Welsh king Locrine, who abandoned her for a German princess called Estrildis. Gwendolen in revenge had Estrildis and her daughter Sabrina drowned in the River Severn. The name is borne by one of the principal characters in Oscar Wilde's play *The Importance of Being Earnest*, first performed in 1895. Alternative spellings include **Gwendolin**, **Gwendolyn**, and **Gwendoline**.

Gwenllian F Welsh traditional name, derived from *gwen* 'white', 'fair', 'blessed', 'holy' (see **»Gwyn**) + *lliant* 'flood', 'flow' (probably in the transferred sense 'foamy' or 'white', referring to a pale complexion).

Gwenyth F Welsh: probably a variant of **»Gwyneth**, but it may alternatively be based on Welsh *gwenith* 'wheat', a word used in poetry to mean 'the favourite' or 'the pick of the bunch'.

Gwilym M Welsh form of **»William**, in use since the Middle Ages.

Gwyn M Welsh: originally a byname from Welsh *gwyn* 'white', 'fair', 'blessed', 'holy'. See also **»Wyn**.

Gwynedd M Welsh boy's name taken from the name of a region of medieval North Wales (now resurrected as the name of a new composite county in Wales).

Gwyneth F Welsh: altered form of **»Gwynedd**, used as a girl's name. Its popularity from the late 19th century, at first in Wales and then more widely in the English-speaking world, seems to have been due to the influence of the popular novelist Annie Harriet Hughes (1852–1910), who adopted the pen-name Gwyneth Vaughan.

Gwynfor M Welsh: coined in the 20th century from *gwyn* 'white', 'fair', 'blessed', 'holy' + *fawr*, the mutated form of *mawr* 'great', 'large' (found in this form in a number of placenames).

H

Haidee F As the name of a character in Byron's poem *Don Juan* (1819–24), this may have been intended to be connected with the classical Greek adjective *aidoios* 'modest'. In modern use it is taken as a variant of **»Heidi**.

Hailey F Variant spelling of **»Hayley**.

Hal M Short form of **»Harry**, of medieval origin. It was used by Shakespeare in *King Henry IV* as the name of the king's son, the future Henry V.

Hale M Transferred use of the surname, in origin a local name for someone living in a nook or recess (Old English *halh*).

Haley F Variant spelling of **»Hayley**.

Hamilton M Mainly North American: transferred use of an illustrious Scottish surname. This was brought to Scotland before the 13th century from a village (now deserted) called *Hamilton* or *Hameldune*, near Barkby in Leicestershire (named in Old English as *hamel dūn* 'flat-topped hill'). It is the surname of a very influential family, who acquired many titles, including the dukedom of Hamilton. The town near Glasgow so called is named after the family. Use as a given name in the United States owes something to Alexander Hamilton (?1757–1804), Secretary of the Treasury under George Washington. He was killed in a duel with the irascible Aaron Burr.

Hamish M Scottish: Anglicized spelling of the vocative case, *Sheumais*, of *Seumas*, the Gaelic form of **»James**.

It is now also chosen by families with no Scottish connections.

Hannah F Biblical name, borne by the mother of the prophet Samuel (1 Samuel 1:2), Hebrew *Hanna*. It is derived from a Hebrew word meaning 'He (i.e. God) has favoured me (i.e. with a child)'. See also **»Anne**. This form of the name was very popular among the Puritans in the 16th and 17th centuries.

Hardy M Especially U.S.: transferred use of the surname, which originated as a nickname for a stout-hearted man (from Middle English, Old French *hardi* 'brave', 'hardy', a word of Germanic origin).

Harlan M Mainly U.S.: transferred use of the surname, in origin a local name from any of various places in England called *Harland*, from Old English *hār* 'grey' or *hara* 'hare' + *land* 'cleared land'. Use as a given name honours the American judge John Marshall Harlan (1833–1911), a conservative Republican who was nevertheless a pioneering supporter of civil rights in the Supreme Court. He was a descendant of the Quaker George Harland from Durham, England, who emigrated to Delaware in 1687, and became governor there in 1695. The spelling **Harland** is also found, both as a surname and a given name.

Harley M, F Transferred use of the surname, in origin a local name from places so called in Shropshire and West Yorkshire, from Old English *hær* 'rock', 'tumulus' + *lēah* 'wood', 'clearing'. Among bikers it has been used with the Harley Davidson motorcycle in mind.

Harold M From an Old English personal name derived from *here* 'army' + *weald* 'ruler'. This was reinforced before the Norman Conquest by the Scandinavian cognate *Haraldr*, introduced by Norse settlers. The name was not common in the later Middle Ages, probably because it was associated with the unfortunate King Harold, killed at the Battle of Hastings

in 1066. It was revived in the 19th century, along with
a number of other Old English names.

Harper M, F Mainly U.S.: transferred use of the
surname, in origin an occupational name for someone
who played the harp. As a girl's name it is associated in
particular with the southern American writer Harper
Lee, author of *To Kill a Mockingbird* (1960).

Harriet F Anglicized form of French *Henriette*, a
feminine pet form of **»Henry** (French *Henri*), coined
in the 17th century.

Harriette F Variant of **»Harriet**, probably coined to
look more feminine. It could also be a blend of **»Harriet**
with its source *Henriette*.

Harrison M Transferred use of the surname, which
originated as a patronymic meaning 'son of Harry'. Use
as a given name may have been influenced by the U.S.
presidents William Henry Harrison (1773–1841) and
his grandson Benjamin Harrison (1833–1901). A more
recent influence is the actor Harrison Ford (b. 1942).

Harry M Pet form of **»Henry**. It was the usual English
vernacular form of **»Henry** up to the Tudor period. It
was used by Shakespeare, for example, as the familiar
name of the mature King Henry V (compare **»Hal**).

Hartley M Transferred use of the surname, in origin a
local name from any of the numerous places so called.
Most (for example, those in Berkshire, Dorset,
Hampshire, and Kent) are so called from Old English
heorot 'hart', 'male deer' + *lēah* 'wood', 'clearing'. One
in Northumberland is from *heorot* + *hlāw* 'hill', and
one in Cumbria is probably from *heard* 'hard' + *clā*
'claw', i.e. hard ridge or fork of land.

Harvey M Transferred use of the surname, which is
derived from a Breton personal name, derived from
haer 'battle' + *vy* 'worthy'. It was introduced to Britain
by Bretons who settled in East Anglia and elsewhere in
the wake of the Norman Conquest.

h

Haydn M From the surname of the composer, adopted in his honour particularly by the music-loving Welsh. Josef Haydn (1732–1809) spent most of his working life at the Esterhazy palace near Vienna, where he was Kapellmeister. His German surname is a variant spelling of *Heiden* meaning 'heathen'. **Hayden** and **Haydon** are also found as English given names, transferred uses of English surnames.

Hayley F Transferred use of the surname, which derives from a placename, probably *Hailey* in Oxfordshire. Use as a given name began in the 1960s, inspired perhaps by the actress Hayley Mills (b. 1946), daughter of Sir John Mills and Mary Hayley Bell. It then enjoyed a period of great popularity, in a variety of spellings, including **»Hailey**, **Haylee**, **Hailee**, **»Haley**, and **Haleigh**.

Hazel F From the vocabulary word denoting the tree (Old English *hæsel*) or its light reddish-brown nuts. This is one of the most successful of the names coined in the 19th century from words denoting plants. The fact that it also denotes an eye colour may have contributed to its continuing popularity.

Heather F From the vocabulary word denoting the hardy, brightly coloured plant. The Middle English word was *hather*; the spelling was altered in the 18th century as a result of folk etymological association with *heath*.

Hebe F Pronounced 'hee-bee': from a Greek name, a feminine form of the adjective *hēbos* 'young'. This was borne in Greek mythology by a minor goddess who was a personification of youth. She was a daughter of Zeus and the wife of Hephaistos; it was her duty to act as cup-bearer to the gods.

Heber M Irish: Anglicized form of the Gaelic name *Éibhear* (pronounced '**ay**-ver'). This was borne in Irish legend by the son of Míl, leader of the Gaelic race that first conquered Ireland. Its origins are lost in the mists of time.

Hector M Name borne in classical legend by the Trojan champion, killed in battle by Achilles. His name is probably from a Greek word meaning 'restrainer'. It is also a Scottish surname, from the Gaelic personal name *Eachdonn* 'brown horse', and this may have been a factor affecting the choice of the name in Scotland.

Heddwyn M Welsh: modern coinage, from *hedd* 'peace' + *(g)wyn* 'white', 'fair', 'blessed', 'holy'. Use as a given name was popularized by the fame of the poet Ellis Humphrey Evans, who posthumously won the bardic chair at the National Eisteddfod in 1917, having been killed in the First World War; his bardic name was *Hedd Wyn*.

Hedley M Transferred use of the surname, in origin a local name from one of the places so called, for example in Durham and Northumberland.

Heidi F Swiss pet form of *Adelheid*, the German form of ≫**Adelaide**. The name is now popular in the English-speaking world, largely due to Johanna Spyri's children's classic *Heidi* (1881).

Heilyn M Welsh traditional name, originally an occupational byname for a steward or wine-pourer, composed of the stem of the verb *heilio* 'to prepare', 'wait on' + the diminutive suffix *-yn*. The name is borne in the *Mabinogi* by two characters: Heilyn the son of Gwynn the Old, and Heilyn the Red, son of Cadgwawn.

Heledd F Welsh traditional name of uncertain derivation. It was borne by a semi-legendary princess of the 7th century, in whose name a lament for her brother's death was composed in the 9th century.

Helen F English vernacular form of the name (Greek *Hēlēnē*, Latin *Helena*) borne in classical legend by the famous beauty, wife of Menelaus, whose seizure by the Trojan prince Paris sparked off the Trojan War. Her

name is of uncertain origin; it may be derived from a
word meaning 'ray' or 'sunbeam'; cf. Greek *hēlios* 'sun'.
It has sometimes been associated with the Greek word
meaning 'Greek', *Hellēn*, but the connection is very
doubtful.

Helena F Latin form of **»Helen**. In the early Christian
period this name was borne by the mother of the
Emperor Constantine, who is venerated as a saint and
was credited with having found the True Cross in
Jerusalem. She was born in about 248, probably in
Bithynia, but in medieval England (due to a misreading
of *Bithynia*) the belief arose that she had been born in
Britain, which greatly increased the popularity of the
name there.

Helga F From an Old Norse female personal name, a
derivative of the adjective *heilagr* 'prosperous',
'successful' (from *heill* 'hale', 'hearty', 'happy'). It was
introduced to England before the Conquest, but did
not survive long. It has been reintroduced to the
English-speaking world in the 20th century from
Scandinavia and Germany. See also **»Olga**.

Henrietta F Latinate form of French *Henriette*, a
feminine diminutive of *Henri*, the French form of
»Henry. See also **»Harriet**.

Henry M A perennially popular given name, of Old
French origin, introduced by the Normans to Britain and
borne by eight kings of England. The Old French name
is of Germanic (Frankish) origin, from *haim* 'home' +
rīc 'power', 'ruler'. Not until the 17th century did the
form *Henry* (as opposed to **»Harry**) became the
standard vernacular form, mainly due to the influence
of the Latin form *Henricus* and French *Henri*. The pet
forms **»Hal**, **Hank**, and **»Harry** are also found as
independent given names.

Hephzibah F Biblical name (meaning 'my delight is in
her' (i.e. a new-born daughter)), borne by the wife of

Hezekiah, King of Judah; she was the mother of
Manasseh (2 Kings 21). It is also used in the prophecies
of Isaiah as an allusive name for the land of Israel (cf.
>>Beulah). It is sometimes spelled **Hepzibah**.

Herbert M From an Old French name of Germanic
(Frankish) origin, introduced to Britain by the
Normans. It is derived from *heri, hari* 'army' + *berht*
'bright', 'famous'. An Old English form, *Herebeorht*,
existed in England before the Conquest, but was
superseded by the Norman form, which gave rise to an
important surname. The family in question were earls
of Pembroke in the 16th and 17th centuries; the poet
George Herbert was a member of the family. By the end
of the Middle Ages *Herbert* was little used as a given
name, and its greater frequency in Britain from the 19th
century onwards is due partly to the trend for the
revival of medieval names and partly to the trend for
the transferred use of surnames.

Herman M English form of *Hermann*, from a Germanic
personal name derived from *heri, hari* 'army' + *man*
'man'. The name was in use among the Normans, but
had died out by the 14th century. It enjoyed a limited
revival in Britain in the 19th century, when it also
became common in America, most probably as a result
of the influence of German immigrants.

Hermione F Name borne in classical mythology by a
daughter of Helen and Menelaus, who grew up to
marry her cousin Orestes. It is evidently a derivative of
Hermes, name of the messenger god, but the formation
is not clear. The name was used by Shakespeare for one
of the main characters in *A Winter's Tale*.

Hesketh M Transferred use of the surname, a local
name from any of the various places in northern
England named with Old Norse *hestr* 'horse' + *skeithr*
'course'. Horse racing and horse fighting were favourite
sports among the Scandinavian settlers in England.

Hester F Variant of **»Esther**, of medieval origin. For a long while the two forms were interchangeable, the addition or dropping of *h*- being commonplace in many words, but now they are generally regarded as two distinct names.

Hilary F, M From the medieval form of the (post-classical) Latin masculine name *Hilarius* (a derivative of *hilaris* 'cheerful') and its feminine form *Hilaria*. From the Middle Ages onwards, the name was borne principally by men (in honour of the 4th-century theologian St Hilarius of Poitiers). Now, however, it is given almost exclusively to girls.

Hilda F Of Germanic origin, a Latinized short form of any of several female names derived from *hild* 'battle'. Many of these are found in both Continental Germanic and Old English forms. St Hilda (614–80) was a Northumbrian princess who founded the abbey at Whitby and became its abbess. *Hilda* was a popular name in England both before and after the Norman Conquest. Its popularity waned in Tudor times, but it never quite died out, and was strongly revived in the 19th century. It is also found in the spelling **Hylda**.

Hillary F Variant spelling of **»Hilary**, found mainly in North America.

Hiram M Biblical name, borne by a king of Tyre who is mentioned several times in the Bible (2 Samuel 2:11; 1 Kings 5; 9:11; 10:11; 1 Chronicles 14:1; 2 Chronicles 2:11) as supplying wood, craftsmen, and money to enable David and Solomon to construct various buildings. It was also the name of a craftsman of Tyre who worked in brass for Solomon (1 Kings 7:13). The name is presumably of Semitic origin, but is probably a Phoenician name; if it is Hebrew, it could be a shortened form of *Ahiram* 'brother of the exalted'. In England, the name was taken up briefly by the Puritans in the 17th century. It is still used in the United States.

Holly   F   From the vocabulary word denoting the evergreen shrub or tree (Middle English *holi(n)*, Old English *holegn*). The name was first used at the beginning of the 20th century, and has been particularly popular since the 1990s. It is bestowed especially on girls born around Christmas, when sprigs of holly are traditionally taken indoors to decorate rooms. It is frequently spelled **Hollie**.

Homer   M   English form of the name of the Greek epic poet *Homēros*, now regularly used as a given name in the United States (cf. **»Virgil**). Many theories have been put forward to explain the name of the poet, but none is conclusive. It is identical in form with the Greek vocabulary word *homēros* 'hostage'.

Honesty   F   Originally from the vocabulary word denoting the moral quality (via Old French, from Latin *honestās*), but as a modern revival probably partly influenced by the flowering plant named with this word.

Honey   F   From the vocabulary word (Old English *huneg*). Honey was used throughout the Middle Ages as a sweetener, until it was partly replaced by cane sugar, which was introduced from the New World in the 16th century. The word has long been used as a term of endearment. Modern use as a given name was partly prompted by a character in Margaret Mitchell's novel *Gone with the Wind* (1936), made into a film in 1939.

Honor   F   Variant spelling of **»Honour**; the dominant spelling of both the vocabulary word and the given name in the United States today. This is now the more frequent spelling of the name in Britain also, used for example by the actress Honor Blackman (b. 1926).

Honora   F   Latinate elaboration of **»Honor**, used mainly in Ireland.

Honour F From the vocabulary word denoting the quality (via Old French, from Latin *honor*). The name first became popular among the Puritans in the 17th century.

Hope F From the vocabulary word (Old English *hopa*) denoting the quality, in particular the Christian quality of expectation in the resurrection and in eternal life. The name was created by the Puritans.

Hopkin M Transferred use of the surname, now found mainly in Wales. It is derived from a medieval given name, a pet form (with the diminutive suffix *-kin*) of *Hob*, a short form of **»Robert** that probably had its origin through English mishearing of the Norman pronunciation of *R-*.

Horace M From the old Roman family name **»Horatius**. The name was once widely used among admirers of the Roman poet Horace (Quintus Horatius Flaccus). See also **»Horatio**.

Horatia F Feminine form of Latin **»Horatius**. It has never been common in the English-speaking world, but was borne, for example, by the daughter of Horatio Nelson.

Horatio M Variant of **»Horace**, influenced by the Latin form **»Horatius** and the Italian form *Orazio*. It is chiefly known as having been borne by Admiral Horatio Nelson (1758–1805), victor of many sea battles against the French during the Napoleonic Wars, culminating in the Battle of Trafalgar, in which he was killed.

Horatius M An old Roman family name, which is of obscure, possibly Etruscan, origin. Its most famous bearer was the Roman poet Quintus Horatius Flaccus (65–8 BC), generally known in English as **»Horace**. From the mid 19th century the original Latin form of the name has been in occasional use among English speakers, although this may owe more to a Roman hero in Macaulay's *Lays of Ancient Rome* (1842) than to the poet. Macaulay relates, in verse that was once enormously popular, 'How Horatius kept the bridge'.

Hortense F French form of Latin *Hortensia*, the feminine version of the old Roman family name *Hortensius*. This is of uncertain origin, but may be derived from Latin *hortus* 'garden'. The given name began to be used in the English-speaking world in the 19th century, but is not common today.

Howard M Transferred use of the surname of an English noble family. The surname has several possible origins, but in the case of the noble family early forms often have the spelling *Haward*, probably from a Scandinavian personal name derived from *hā* 'high' + *ward* 'guardian'.

Howell M Anglicized form of the Welsh name **»Hywel**, or a transferred use of the surname derived from that name.

Hubert M Old French name of Germanic (Frankish) origin, derived from *hug* 'heart', 'mind', 'spirit' + *berht* 'bright', 'famous'. It was popular among the Normans, who introduced it to Britain, where it was later reinforced by settlers from the Low Countries. An 8th-century St Hubert succeeded St Lambert as bishop of Maastricht and is regarded as the patron of hunters, since, like St Eustace, he is supposed to have seen a vision of Christ crucified between the antlers of a stag.

Hugh M From an Old French name, *Hugues*, **»Hugo**, of Germanic (Frankish) origin, derived from *hug* 'heart', 'mind', 'spirit'. It was originally a short form of various compound names containing this element. This was borne by the aristocracy of medieval France, adopted by the Normans, and introduced by them to Britain.

Hugo M Latinized form of *Hugh*, used throughout the Middle Ages in official documents, and revived as a modern given name.

Humbert M From an Old French name of Germanic (Frankish) origin, derived from *hun* 'bear-cub', 'warrior' + *berht* 'bright', 'famous'. It was adopted by the Normans and introduced by them to Britain. However, it was not common in Britain in the Middle Ages, and has always had a Continental flavour. It was used by Vladimir Nabokov for the name of the demented pederast, Humbert Humbert, who is the narrator in his novel *Lolita* (1955). This may have contributed to its demise as a given name in the English-speaking world.

h **Humphrey** M From a Norman name, *Hunfrid*, of Germanic origin, derived from *hun* 'bear-cub', 'warrior' + *fred*, *frid* 'peace'. The Norman form absorbed the native Old English form, *Hunfrith*, which existed in England before the Conquest. The spelling with -*ph*- reflects classicizing influence. It has always enjoyed a modest popularity in England, and was borne by a Duke of Gloucester (1391–1447), 'Duke Humphrey', the youngest son of King Henry IV. He was noted as a patron of literature, and founded what became the Bodleian Library at Oxford. In modern times, probably the most famous bearer has been the film star Humphrey Bogart (1899–1957). The spellings **Humphry** and **Humfr(e)y** are also found.

Hunter M Especially U.S.: transferred use of the surname, in origin an occupational name. The term was used not only of hunters on horseback of game such as stags and wild boars, which was in the Middle Ages a pursuit restricted to the ranks of the nobility, but also of much humbler bird catchers and poachers seeking food.

Huw M Welsh form of ≫**Hugh**, now sometimes also used in other parts of the English-speaking world.

Hyacinth F English form of the name (Greek *Hyakinthos*) borne in classical mythology by a beautiful youth who was accidentally killed by Apollo and from whose blood sprang a flower bearing his name (not the

modern hyacinth, but a type of dark lily). The name
was later borne by various early saints, principally one
martyred in the 3rd century with his brother Protus.
This encouraged its use as a boy's name in Christian
Europe, including, occasionally, Britain. However, in
Britain at the end of the 19th century there was a vogue
for coining new girl's names from vocabulary words
denoting plants and flowers. *Hyacinth* accordingly
came to be regarded exclusively as a girl's name. It has
never been common.

Hyam M Jewish: from the Hebrew word *hayyim* 'life'.
This is sometimes added in apposition to the existing
given name of a seriously ill person during prayers for
his recovery, and this practice no doubt encouraged its
use as a given name.

h

Hywel M Welsh traditional name, originally a byname
from a vocabulary word meaning 'eminent, conspicu-
ous'. This name was common in the Middle Ages and
gave rise to the surname **»Howell**, which is now also
used as a first name.

I

Iain M Scottish: the normal Gaelic spelling of »**Ian**.

Ian M Scottish form of »**John**, now also extensively used in the wider English-speaking world.

Ida F Norman name, ultimately derived from the ancient Germanic word *īd* 'work'. This was introduced to Britain by the Normans in the 11th century. It died out during the later Middle Ages, but was revived in the 19th century, when it was used for the central character in Tennyson's *Princess* (1847), who devotes herself to the cause of women's rights and women's education. There are also associations with Mount Ida in Crete, which was connected in classical times with the worship of Zeus, king of the gods, who was supposed to have been born there.

Idris M Welsh traditional name, derived from *iud* 'lord' + *rīs* 'ardent', 'impulsive'.

Idwal M Welsh traditional name, derived from *iud* 'lord', 'master' + *(g)wal* 'wall', 'rampart'.

Ieuan M The original Welsh form (pronounced '**yai**-an') of »**John**, from Latin *Johannes*.

Ifor M Welsh: traditional name of uncertain derivation. It is often Anglicized as »**Ivor**, and the pronunciation is the same. But in fact the two names are distinct, for the English name is of Scandinavian origin, while the Welsh one is Celtic.

Ignatius M Derivative of the old Roman family name *Egnatius*, which is of uncertain origin, possibly Etruscan. This was altered in the early Christian period by association with Latin *ignis* 'fire'. It was borne by various early saints, and more recently by St Ignatius Loyola (1491–1556), who founded the Society of Jesus (Jesuits). It is used mainly among Roman Catholics.

Igor M Russian name of Scandinavian origin, from *Ingvar* 'Ing's warrior'; Ing was the ancient Norse fertility god. The name was taken to Russia at the time of the earliest Scandinavian settlements at Kiev in the 9th century. In the English-speaking world it is a 20th-century borrowing.

Illtud M Welsh traditional name, derived from *il*, *el* 'multitude' + *tud* 'land' or 'people'. This was borne by a Welsh saint (d. *c*.505) who founded the abbey of Llantwit (originally *Llan-Illtut* 'church of Illtud'). It is now also found in the spelling **Illtyd**.

Ilona F Hungarian form of **»Helen**.

Immanuel M Variant of **»Emmanuel**. This is the spelling used in the Old Testament.

Imogen F This name owes its existence to a character in Shakespeare's *Cymbeline* (1609). In his sources this character is called *Innogen*, so the modern name is due either to a misreading by Shakespeare or to misprinting in the play's text by his printer. The name *Innogen* is of Celtic origin; cf. Gaelic *inghean* 'girl', 'maiden'.

Ina F Short form of any of the various girls' names ending in this as a Latinate feminine suffix, for example *Christina* and *Georgina*. See also **»Ena**.

India F From the name of the subcontinent, Greek *India*, a derivative of *Indus*, the name of the great river on its eastern side. This was used as the name of a character in Margaret Mitchell's novel *Gone with the Wind* (1936). In some cases the name has been chosen because of family association with the subcontinent.

Inga F Respelled version of the German and Scandinavian name *Inge*, a short form of **»Ingrid** or any of various other names (for example *Ingeborg*) based on the name of the fertility god *Ing*.

Ingrid F From an Old Norse female personal name composed of the name of the fertility god *Ing* + *fríthr* 'fair', 'beautiful'. It was introduced into the English-speaking world from Scandinavia in the 20th century and became very popular, largely because of the fame of the Swedish film actress Ingrid Bergman (1915–82).

Inigo M From the medieval Spanish given name *Íñigo*, a vernacular derivative of »**Ignatius**. It is now rarely used as a given name in Spain. In the English-speaking world it is mainly associated with the architect and stage designer Inigo Jones (1573–1652).

Innes M, F Scottish: as a boy's name, this is an Anglicized form of Gaelic *Aonghas* (see »**Angus**) or a transferred use of the surname *Innes*. As a girl's name, it is either from the surname or a borrowing of the Spanish girl's name **Inés**.

Iolo M Welsh: pet form of »**Iorwerth**.

Íomhar M Scottish Gaelic form of »**Ivor**.

Iona F From the name of the tiny sacred island in the Hebrides, off the west coast of Mull. In 563 St Columba came from Ireland to found a monastery here, which became the most important centre of Christianity in northern Britain, from which missionaries went out all over Scotland and northern England, and from which the monastery at Lindisfarne was founded. The name of the island is said to be the result of a misreading of Latin *Ioua*, representing its Gaelic name *Ì*, from Old Norse *ey* 'island'.

Ione F 19th-century coinage, apparently with reference to the glories of Ionian Greece in the 5th century BC. No such name exists in classical Greek.

Iorwerth M Welsh traditional name, derived from *iôr* 'lord' + a mutated form of *berth* 'handsome'. It is borne in the *Mabinogi* by the jealous brother of Madawg, son of Maredudd. It came to be regarded as a Welsh form of **»Edward**, with which it is in fact unconnected. It is sometimes used in the Anglicized spelling **»Yorath**.

Ira M Biblical name (meaning 'watchful' in Hebrew), borne by a character mentioned briefly in the Bible, one of the chief officers of King David (2 Samuel 20:26). It was taken up by the Puritans in the 17th century, possibly under the influence of the Latin vocabulary word *ira* 'anger', with reference to the righteous wrath of God directed at sinners. Nowadays it is found mainly in the United States.

Irene F From Greek *eirēnē* 'peace'. In Greek mythology Irene was a minor goddess who personified peace. The name was taken up in the English-speaking world at the end of the 19th century and became popular in the 20th, partly as a result of being used for one of the main characters in Galsworthy's *Forsyte Saga* (1922). It was formerly pronounced as three syllables, but is now often heard as two.

Iris F From Greek *iris* 'rainbow'. In Greek mythology Iris, the goddess of the rainbow, was one of the messengers of the gods, the rainbow being thought to be a sign from the gods to men. In English the name was used from the 16th century onwards to denote both the flower and the coloured part of the eye, in both cases on account of their variegated colours.

Irma F Pet form of various German girls' names, for example *Irmgard* and *Irmtraud*, introduced to the English-speaking world at the end of the 19th century.

Irvine M Transferred use of the Scottish surname, in origin a local name from a place in Ayrshire. The placename is probably derived from a Celtic river name meaning 'fresh water' (Welsh *yr afon*).

Irving M Transferred use of the Scottish surname, which is from a place near Dumfries. In the case of the songwriter Irving Berlin (1888–1989), it represents the

Jewish name *Israel* (his original name was Israel Baline).

Irwin M Transferred use of the English surname, from the medieval given name *Irwyn*, derived from Old English *eofor wine* 'boar friend'.

Isaac M Biblical name borne by the son of Abraham. The story in the Bible (Genesis 22:1–13) tells how he was about to be sacrificed by his father at God's command, but was saved at the last moment when Abraham was commanded instead to sacrifice a ram, conveniently caught in a nearby thicket. Isaac married Rebecca and became the father of Esau and Jacob. The traditional derivation is from a Hebrew verb meaning 'to laugh', but this is uncertain. In the Middle Ages it was borne only by Jews, but it was taken up more widely by the Puritans in the 17th century.

Isabel F Originally a Spanish version of »**Elizabeth**, imported into France in the early Middle Ages, and thence into England. It was a royal name, borne by, among others, the wife of King Edward II, daughter of Philip IV of France. She led a turbulent life and eventually had her husband murdered, but this did little to diminish the popularity of the name. The spelling »**Isobel** is also common.

Isabella F Latinate form of »**Isabel**, which became very popular in England in the 18th century.

Isabelle F French elaborated form of »**Isabel**.

Isadora F Variant spelling of »**Isidora**, borne by the American dancer Isadora Duncan (1878–1927).

Isaiah M Biblical name (meaning 'God is salvation' in Hebrew), borne by the most important of the major prophets. Surprisingly, the name has never been common in the English-speaking world, although it was occasionally used among the Puritans in the 17th century. It is well established as a Jewish name.

Isbel F Scottish variant of **»Isabel**.

Iseult F French form of **»Isolde**.

Isidora F Feminine form of **»Isidore**.

Isidore M English form of Greek *Isidōros*, literally 'gift of Isis'. In spite of its pagan connotations the name was common among early Christians. It was borne by the encyclopedist St Isidore of Seville (*c*.560–636). By the late Middle Ages, it had come to be considered a typically Jewish name, even though it was originally adopted as a Christianized version of **»Isaiah**.

Isla F Scottish, pronounced 'ai-la': 20th-century coinage, from *Islay*, name of an island in the Hebrides pronounced thus.

Islwyn M Welsh: taken from the name of a mountain in the county of Gwent, which is named with Welsh *is* 'below' + *llwyn* 'grove'.

Isobel F Variant of **»Isabel**, formerly used mainly in Scotland. The Gaelic form is **Iseabail**.

Isolde F Probably of Celtic origin; cf. Welsh **»Esyllt**. This was the name of the tragic mistress of Tristan in the Arthurian romances. There are several versions of her story. The main features are that the beautiful Isolde, an Irish princess, is betrothed to the aged King Mark of Cornwall. Through accidentally drinking a magic potion, she and the young Cornish knight Tristan fall in love, with tragic consequences. The story exercised a powerful hold on the European imagination. The Latinized form **Isolda** is also used.

Israel M Biblical name: originally the byname (meaning 'he who strives with God' in Hebrew) given to Jacob after he had wrestled with an angel: 'Thy name shall be called no more Jacob, but Israel: for as a prince hast thou power with God and with men, and hast prevailed' (Genesis 32:28). The name was later applied to his descendants, the Children of Israel, and was chosen as the name of the modern Jewish state. The given name was used by the Puritans in the 17th century, but is now once again almost exclusively a Jewish name.

Ivan M Russian equivalent of »**John**, also widely used in the English-speaking world since the 20th century.

Ivo M Form of »**Yves** used in Germany and occasionally in the English-speaking world.

Ivon M Variant of »**Ivo**.

Ivor M Of Scandinavian origin, from an Old Norse personal name derived from *ýr* 'yew', 'bow' + *herr* 'army'. In the 1920s and 30s it came to prominence as the name of the songwriter and actor Ivor Novello (1893–1951). The Gaelic spelling »**Iomhar** has been revived in Scotland, and **Iobhar** in Ireland.

Ivy F From the vocabulary word denoting the plant (Old English *ífig*). This was adopted as a given name at the end of the 19th century together with a large number of other girls' names derived from words denoting flowers and plants.

J

Jabez M Biblical name, said to mean 'sorrowful' in Hebrew: 'and his mother called his name Jabez, saying Because I bare him with sorrow' (I Chronicles 4:9). It is now out of fashion, but it was popular among the Puritans in the 17th century, as the mention of Jabez in the Bible lent support to the Protestant work ethic. Jabez was 'more honourable than his brethren'; he called on the Lord for protection and wealth, and the Lord duly obliged.

Jacinta F Spanish name, equivalent of ≫**Hyacinth**.

Jack M Originally a pet form of ≫**John**, but now a very popular given name in its own right. It is derived from Middle English *Jankin*, later altered to *Jackin*, from *Jan* (a contracted form of *Jehan* 'John') + the diminutive suffix *-kin*. It is sometimes also used as an informal pet form of ≫**James**, no doubt influenced by the French form *Jacques*.

Jackson M Transferred use of the surname, meaning originally 'son of Jack' and in modern times sometimes bestowed with precisely this meaning. In the United States it has also been used in honour of President Andrew Jackson (1767–1845) and the Confederate general Thomas 'Stonewall' Jackson (1824–63).

Jaclyn F Simplified spelling of ≫**Jacquelyn**.

Jacob M English form of the biblical Hebrew name *Yaakov*. This was borne by one of the most important of the patriarchs in the Book of Genesis. Jacob was the father of twelve sons, who gave their names to the

Jacques of Israel. He was the son of Isaac and
According to the story in Genesis, he was the
younger twin who persuaded his older brother
au to part with his right to his inheritance for an
exchange for a bowl of soup ('a mess of pottage'). Later,
he tricked his blind and dying father into blessing him
in place of Esau. The derivation of the name has been
much discussed. It is traditionally explained as being
from Hebrew *akev* 'heel' and to mean 'heel
grabber', because when Jacob was born 'his hand took
hold of Esau's heel' (Genesis 25:26). This is interpreted
later in the Bible as 'supplanter'; Esau himself remarks,
'Is he not rightly named Jacob? for he has supplanted
me these two times' (Genesis 27:36). *Jacob* is especially
common as a Jewish name, although it is also used by
Christians. Compare **»James**.

Jacqueline F Feminine diminutive form of *Jacques*, the
French version of **»James**. In the 1960s it became very
popular in the United States and elsewhere, influenced
in part by the fame and stylish image of Jacqueline
Bouvier Kennedy Onassis, whose family was of French
extraction. The pet forms **Jackie**, **Jacky**, and **»Jacqui**
are all now common.

Jacquelyn F Respelled form of **»Jacqueline**, influenced by the productive suffix *-lyn* (see **»Lynn**). The
spelling **»Jaclyn** is also found.

Jacquetta F Respelling (influenced by **»Jacqueline**)
of the Italian name *Giachetta*, a feminine diminutive of
Giacomo 'James'.

Jacqui F Pet form of **»Jacqueline**, once a modish
spelling of *Jackie*, now also established in its own right.

Jade F From the name of the precious stone, a word
that reached English from Spanish *(piedra de) ijada*,
which literally means '(stone of the) bowels'. It was so
called because it was believed to have the magical
power of providing protection against disorders of the

intestines. The name was famously chosen in the 1970s for the daughter of the English rock singer Mick Jagger, though it came to prominence in the 1990s.

Jago M Cornish form of **»James**.

Jaime F, M This is the Spanish form of **»James**, but among English-speakers it has come to be used also as a girl's name, apparently a respelling of **»Jamie**.

Jaimie F Variant spelling of **»Jamie** as a girl's name.

Jake M Variant of **»Jack**, of Middle English origin, which has now come back into fashion as an independent given name. It is also sometimes used as a short form of **»Jacob**.

James M English form of the name borne in the New Testament by two of Christ's disciples, James son of Zebedee and James son of Alphaeus. It is derived from Late Latin *Iacomus*, a variant of *Iacobus* (Greek *Iakobos*) and is the same name as Old Testament **»Jacob** (Hebrew *Yaakov*). In Britain, *James* is a royal name that from the beginning of the 15th century onwards has been associated particularly with the Scottish house of Stuart: James I of Scotland (1394–1437; ruled 1424–37) was a patron of the arts and a noted poet, as well as an energetic ruler. King James VI of Scotland (1566–1625; reigned 1567–1625) succeeded to the English throne as James I of England in 1603. His grandson, James II of England (1633–1701; reigned 1685–8) was a Roman Catholic, deposed in 1688 in favour of his Protestant daughter Mary and her husband William of Orange. From then on he, his son (also called James), and his grandson Charles ('Bonnie Prince Charlie') made unsuccessful attempts to recover the English throne, notably the Scottish risings of 1715 and 1745. Their supporters were known as Jacobites (from Latin *Iacobus*), and the name James became for a while particularly associated with Roman Catholicism on the one hand and Highland opposition to the English government on the other.

Jamie M, F Originally a boy's name, a pet form of **»James** and still so used, especially in Scotland and Northumberland. It is now found also as a female equivalent of *James*, particularly in North America.

Jan M, F As a male name this represents either a revival of Middle English *Jan*, a byform of **»John**, or an adoption of the common European form with this spelling. As a girl's name it is a short form of names such as **»Janet** and **»Janice**.

Jana F Distinctively feminine variant of **»Jan**: in the English-speaking world a 20th-century importation from eastern Europe.

Jancis F Modern blend of **»Jan** and **»Frances**, first used in the novel *Precious Bane* by Mary Webb, published in 1924.

Jane F Originally a feminine form of **»John**, the Old French feminine being *Jehanne*. It has proved the most popular of the feminine forms of *John*, ahead of **»Joan** and **»Jean**. It was borne by the tragic Lady Jane Grey (1537–54), who was unwillingly proclaimed queen in 1553, deposed nine days later, and executed the following year. Seventy years earlier, the name had come into prominence as that of Jane Shore, mistress of King Edward IV and subsequently of Thomas Grey, 1st Marquess of Dorset, Lady Jane's grandfather. Jane Shore's tribulations in 1483 at the hands of Richard III, Edward's brother and successor, became the subject of popular ballads and plays. A 19th-century influence was its use as the name of the central character in Charlotte Brontë's novel *Jane Eyre* (1847). In the 1940s it was borne by the statuesque American film star Jane Russell (b. 1921). The spelling **»Jayne** became fashionable in the 1950s.

Janelle F Modern elaborated form of »**Jane**, with the feminine ending -*elle* abstracted from names such as »**Danielle**. In the United States this form is now commoner than *Jane*. The Latinate form **Janella** (based on names such as »**Prunella**) is also found.

Janet F Originally a medieval diminutive of »**Jane**. At the end of the Middle Ages the name died out except in Scotland. It was revived at the end of the 19th century and became extremely popular throughout the English-speaking world.

Janette F Either an elaborated version of »**Janet** or a simplified form of »**Jeannette**.

Janice F Derivative of »**Jane**, which was first used as the name of the heroine of the novel *Janice Meredith* by Paul Leicester Ford, published in 1899. The spelling »**Janis** is also found.

Janine F Simplified form of »**Jeannine**.

Janis F Variant spelling of »**Janice** which became quite popular in the United States in the 1960s and 70s by association with the rock singer Janis Joplin (1943–70).

Janna F Recent coinage, an elaboration of »**Jan**.

Jared M Biblical name (probably meaning 'descent' in Hebrew), borne by a descendant of Adam (Genesis 5:15). According to the Book of Genesis, he became the father of Enoch at the age of 162, and lived for a further eight hundred years. This name was occasionally used by the Puritans and has since been revived periodically.

Jarlath M Anglicized form of Irish Gaelic **Iarlaithe**, the name of a 5th-century Irish saint associated with Tuam.

Jarrett M Transferred use of the surname, which is a variant of »**Garrett**.

Jarvis M Transferred use of the surname, which is from the Norman given name »**Gervaise**.

Jasmine F From the vocabulary word denoting the climbing plant with its delicate, fragrant flowers (from Old French, ultimately from Persian *yasmin*). The variants **Jasmin** and **»Yasmin** are also found.

Jason M From Greek *Iasōn*, possibly meaning 'healer'. In Greek mythology, Jason was the leader of the Argonauts, who sailed to Colchis in search of the Golden Fleece. It owes its popularity in Christendom to two brief mentions in the New Testament of an early Christian in Thessalonica, at whose house St Paul stayed (Acts 17:5–9; Romans 16:21). It was popular among the Puritans in the 17th century, and was revived in the mid 20th century. The film actor Jason Robards (1920–2000) is the son of another actor called Jason Robards. A more recent influence is the Australian actor Jason Donovan (b. 1968).

Jasper M The usual English form of the name assigned in Christian folklore to one of the three Magi or 'wise men', who brought gifts to the infant Christ at his birth (Matthew 2:1). The name does not appear in the Bible, and is first found in medieval tradition. It seems to be ultimately of Persian origin, from a word meaning 'treasurer'. There is no connection with the English vocabulary word *jasper* denoting a gemstone.

Jay M, F Pet form of any of the given names beginning with the letter J- (cf. **»Dee** and **»Kay**); now also used as an independent given name.

Jayne F Elaborated spelling of **»Jane**.

Jean F, M Like **»Jane** and **»Joan**, a medieval variant of Old French *Je(h)anne*. Towards the end of the Middle Ages this form was almost entirely confined to Scotland. By the 20th century it was more widely used, but still retains a Scottish flavour. It is also used as a boy's name, a respelling of **»Gene**.

Jeane F Variant spelling of ≫**Jean**.

Jeanette F Variant spelling of ≫**Jeannette**, in the 1920s and 30s associated particularly with the singer and film star Jeanette MacDonald (1902–65).

Jeanine F Variant spelling of ≫**Jeannine**.

Jeannette F French diminutive form of *Jeanne*, feminine form of *Jean* 'John'.

Jeannine F French diminutive form of *Jeanne*, feminine form of *Jean* 'John'.

Jed M Now used as an independent given name, this was originally a short form of **Jedidiah**, meaning 'beloved of God' in Hebrew, an alternative name of King Solomon (2 Samuel 12:25). It was a favourite with the Puritans, who considered themselves, too, to be loved by God. See also ≫**Ged**.

j

Jeff M Short form of ≫**Jeffrey**, now also used as an independent given name, especially in North America.

Jefferson M Transferred use of the surname, originally meaning 'son of Jeffrey'. In the United States it has often been bestowed in honour of the statesman and writer Thomas Jefferson (1743–1826), principal author of the Declaration of Independence, who became the third president of the Union.

Jeffrey M Variant spelling of ≫**Geoffrey**. This is now the usual spelling of the name in North America and Britain. The spelling **Jeffery** is also found.

Jem M From a medieval vernacular form of ≫**James**. In modern use, however, it is often used as a short form of ≫**Jeremy**.

Jemima F Biblical name (meaning 'dove' or 'bright as day' in Hebrew), borne by the eldest of the daughters of Job. The name was common in the first part of the 19th century.

Jemma F Variant spelling of ≫**Gemma**.

Jenessa F Recent coinage, a blend of ≫**Jennifer** and ≫**Vanessa**.

Jenkin M Transferred use of the surname, which is derived from the medieval given name *Jankin*. This was a pet form of the male name ≫**Jan**, with the diminutive suffix *-kin*.

Jenna F Fanciful alteration of ≫**Jenny**, with the Latinate feminine ending *-a*.

Jenni F Variant spelling of ≫**Jenny**, now commonly used for the sake of variety or stylishness.

Jennifer F Of Celtic (Arthurian) origin: a Cornish form of ≫**Guinevere**. A mere Cornish curiosity at the beginning of the 20th century, it has since become enormously popular all over the English-speaking world, partly due to the influence of the film star Jennifer Jones (b. 1919 as Phyllis Isley).

Jenny F Now universally taken as a short form of ≫**Jennifer**, although in fact this name existed during the Middle Ages as a pet form of ≫**Jean**. The variants ≫**Jenni** and ≫**Jenna** are also found.

Jeremiah M Biblical name (meaning 'appointed by God' in Hebrew), borne by a Hebrew prophet of the 7th–6th centuries BC, whose story, prophecies of judgement, and lamentations are recorded in the book of the Bible that bears his name. The Book of Lamentations is also attributed to him; it bewails the destruction of Jerusalem and the temple by the Babylonians in 587 BC. Despite the gloomy subject-matter of these texts, the name enjoyed some popularity among Puritans and Christian fundamentalists, partly perhaps because Jeremiah also preached reconciliation with God after his wrath was assuaged.

Jeremy M Anglicized form, used in the Authorized Version of the New Testament (Matthew 2:17; 27:9), of the biblical name **»Jeremiah**. The short form **»Jem** and the pet form **»Jerry** are now also popular.

Jermaine M Variant spelling of **»Germaine**, now the more common form of the male name in the United States.

Jerome M Anglicized form of the Greek name *Hieronymos*, derived from *hieros* 'holy' + *onoma* 'name'. St Jerome (*c.*342–420) was chiefly responsible for the translation into Latin of the Bible, the Vulgate, on which he also wrote many works of commentary and exposition.

Jerry M, F As a male name this is a pet form of **»Jeremy** or **»Gerald**, or occasionally of **»Gerard** and **»Jerome**. As a girl's name it is a variant of **»Gerry**.

Jervaise M Variant spelling of **»Gervaise**.

Jess F, M Usually a girl's name, a short form of **»Jessie** or **»Jessica**. As a male name, it is a short form of **»Jesse** or **»Jessie**.

Jesse M, F Biblical name (meaning 'gift' in Hebrew), borne by the father of King David (1 Samuel 16), from whose line (according to the New Testament) Jesus was ultimately descended. It was popular among the Puritans. As a girl's name it is a respelling of **»Jessie**.

Jessica F Apparently of Shakespearian origin. This was the name of the daughter of Shylock in *The Merchant of Venice* (1596). Shakespeare's source has not been established, but he presumably intended it to pass as a typically Jewish name. It may be from a biblical name that appeared, in the translations available in Shakespeare's day, as *Jesca* (Genesis 11:29; *Iscah* in the Authorized Version).

Jessie F, M Usually a girl's name, a pet form of **»Jessica**, also long used in Scotland as a pet form of **»Jean**, although the derivation is not clear. The Gaelic form is *Teasag*. It is now used as a given name in its own right. As a boy's name it is a respelling of **»Jesse**.

Jethro M Biblical name, borne by the father of Moses's wife Zipporah (Exodus 3:1; 4:18). It seems to be a variant of the Hebrew name *Ithra*, said to mean 'excellence', which is found at 2 Samuel 17:25. It was popular among the Puritans, but then fell out of general use. Since the appearance in 1968 of a British 'progressive rock' group called Jethro Tull (after an 18th-century agricultural reformer), the given name *Jethro* has enjoyed a modest revival of popularity.

Jetta F Comparatively recent coinage, a Latinate derivative of the vocabulary word denoting the mineral *jet*. This word is derived from Old French *jaiet*, from Latin *(lapis) gagātēs* 'stone from Gagai' (a town in Lycia, Asia Minor).

Jewel F A recent adoption of the vocabulary word meaning 'gemstone' (from Old French *jouel*, diminutive of *jou* 'plaything', 'delight'). The given name may derive from its use as a term of affection, or may have been suggested by the vogue in the 19th century for creating given names from words denoting particular gemstones, e.g. **»Beryl**, **»Ruby**.

Jill F Short form (respelled) of **»Gillian**, also used as a given name in its own right.

Jillian F Variant spelling of **»Gillian**.

Jo F, M In this spelling, usually a girl's name, a short form of **»Joanna**, **»Joanne**, **»Jody**, or **»Josephine**, sometimes used independently or in combination with other names, for example *Nancy Jo* and *Jo Anne* (see **»Joanne**). Occasionally it is used as a boy's name, a variant of **»Joe**.

Joachim M Biblical name, *Johoiachin* in Hebrew, meaning 'established by God'. This was borne by a king of Judah who was defeated by Nebuchadnezzar and carried off into Babylonian exile (2 Kings 24). His father's name was *Jehoiakim*, and there has clearly been some confusion between the two forms in the derivation of the modern name. The reason for its great popularity in Christian Europe is that in medieval tradition it was the name commonly ascribed to the father of the Virgin Mary. His name is not recorded in the Bible, but with the growth of the cult of Mary many legends grew up about her early life, and her parents came to be venerated as saints under the names Joachim and Anne.

Joan F Contracted form of Old French *Johanne*, from Latin *Iohanna* (see **»Joanna**). In England this was the usual feminine form of **»John** from the Middle English period onwards, but in the 16th and 17th centuries it was largely superseded by **»Jane**. It was strongly revived in the first part of the 20th century, partly under the influence of George Bernard Shaw's play *St Joan* (1923), based on the life of Joan of Arc (1412–31).

j

Joanna F From the Latin form, *Iohanna*, of Greek *Iōanna*, the feminine equivalent of *Iōannēs* (see **»John**). In the New Testament this name is borne by a woman who was one of Jesus's followers (Luke 8:3; 24:10). She was the wife of the steward of the household of King Herod Antipas. The name was regularly used throughout the Middle Ages in most parts of Europe as a feminine equivalent of **»John**, but in England it has only been in common use as a vernacular given name since the 19th century. The short form **»Jo** is now common.

Joanne F From Old French *Jo(h)anne*, and so a doublet of **»Joan**. This too was revived as a given name in its own right in the first half of the 20th century. It has to some extent been influenced by the independently formed combination *Jo Anne*.

Job M Biblical name (meaning 'persecuted' in Hebrew), borne by the eponymous hero of the Book of Job, a man of exemplary patience, whose faith was severely tested by God's apparently unprovoked maltreatment of him. The name was used among Puritans and Christian fundamentalists.

Jocasta F Name borne in classical legend by the mother of Oedipus, King of Thebes. As the result of a series of misunderstandings, she also became his wife and the mother of his children. The derivation of the name is not known.

Jocelyn F, M Now normally a girl's name, but in earlier times more often given to boys. It is a transferred use of the English surname, which is derived from an Old French masculine personal name introduced to Britain by the Normans in the form *Joscelin*. The spelling **Josceline** is also found for the girl's name.

Jock M Scottish: variant of ≫Jack.

Jodene F Recent fanciful coinage, formed from ≫Jody plus the productive suffix *-ene*.

Jody F, M Of uncertain origin. It may have originated as a pet form of ≫Judith and ≫Jude; alternatively, it may be a playful elaboration of ≫Jo and ≫Joe. The spelling **Jodie** is associated particularly with the actress Jodie Foster (b. 1962 as Alicia Christian Foster); the spelling **Jodi** is also found.

Joel M Biblical name, composed of two different Hebrew elements, *Yah(weh)* and *El*, both of which mean 'God'; the implication of the name is that the Hebrew God, *Yahweh*, is the only true god. This is a common name in the Bible, being borne by, among others, one of King David's 'mighty men' (1 Chronicles 11:38), and a minor prophet who lived in the 8th century BC. It has been perennially popular as a Jewish name; it was also taken up by the Puritans and other Christian fundamentalists.

Joelle F Borrowing of the fashionable French name *Joëlle*, a feminine form of ≫Joel.

Johanna F Latinate feminine form of *Johannes* (see ≫John), a variant of ≫Joanna.

John M English form of Latin *Io(h)annes*, New Testament Greek *Iōannēs*, a contracted form of the Hebrew name *Johanan* 'God is gracious' (the name of several different characters in the Old Testament, including one of King David's 'mighty men'). *John* is the spelling used in the Authorized Version of the New Testament. The name is of great importance in early Christianity. It was borne by three seminal figures: John the Baptist (the precursor of Christ, who baptized sinners in the River Jordan), John the Apostle (one of Christ's disciples, a fisherman, brother of James), and John the Evangelist (the author of the fourth gospel, identified in Christian tradition with the apostle, but more probably a Greek-speaking Jewish Christian living over half a century later). The name was also borne by numerous saints and by twenty-three popes, including John XXIII (Giuseppe Roncalli, 1881–1963), whose popularity was yet another factor influencing people to choose this given name. It was also a royal name, being borne by eight Byzantine emperors and by kings of Hungary, Poland, Portugal, France, and elsewhere. In its various forms in different languages, it has been the most perennially popular of all Christian names.

j

Johnathan M Respelled form of »**Jonathan**, as if a combination of »**John** and »**Nathan**.

Jolene F Mainly U.S.: modern coinage, combining the short form »**Jo** with the productive suffix *-lene*, extracted from names such as »**Marlene**. It seems to have originated in the United States in the 1930s. It was made famous by a hit song with this title, recorded by Dolly Parton in 1979.

Jolyon M Medieval variant spelling of »**Julian**. Its occasional use in modern Britain derives from the name of a character in John Galsworthy's sequence of novels *The Forsyte Saga* (1922), which was serialized on television in the late 1960s.

Jon M Simplified spelling of **»John** or short form of **»Jonathan**.

Jonah M Biblical name (meaning 'dove' in Hebrew), borne by a prophet whose adventures are recounted in the Book of Jonah. God appears to Jonah and orders him to go and preach in Nineveh. When Jonah disobeys, God causes a storm to threaten the ship in which Jonah is travelling. His shipmates, realizing that Jonah is the cause of their peril, throw him overboard. A 'great fish' swallows Jonah and delivers him, willy-nilly, to the coasts of Nineveh. This story was immensely popular in the Middle Ages, and a favourite subject of miracle plays.

Jonas M New Testament form of **»Jonah**.

Jonathan M Biblical name, meaning 'God has given'. This is the name of several characters in the Bible, most notably a son of King Saul, who was a devoted friend and supporter of the young David, even when David and Saul were at loggerheads (1 Samuel 31; 2 Samuel 1:19–26). The name is often taken as symbolic of steadfast friendship and loyalty. The spellings **Jonathon**, **Jonothon**, and **»Johnathan** are also found.

Joni F Modern respelling of *Joanie*, pet form of **»Joan**. It is particularly associated with the Canadian folk singer Joni Mitchell (b. 1943 as Roberta Joan Anderson).

Jonquil F From the word denoting the flower, which was taken into English from French *jonquille*.

Jordan M, F Originally a name given to a child of either sex baptized in holy water that was, purportedly at least, brought from the River Jordan, whose Hebrew name, *ha-yarden*, means 'flowing down'. It was in this river that Christ was baptized by John the Baptist. The modern given name is either a revival of this, or else a transferred use of the surname that was derived from it.

Josceline F Variant of **»Jocelyn** as a girl's name.

Joseph M English form of the biblical Hebrew name *Yosef*, meaning '(God) shall add (another son)'. In the Bible this is borne by the favourite son of Jacob, whose brothers become jealous of him and sell him into slavery (Genesis 37). He is taken to Egypt, where he rises to become chief steward to Pharaoh, eventually being reconciled to his brothers when they come to buy corn during a seven-year famine (Genesis 43–7). In the New Testament *Joseph* is the name of the husband of the Virgin Mary. It is also borne by a rich Jew, Joseph of Arimathea (Matthew 27:57; Mark 15:43; Luke 23:50; John 19:38), who took Jesus down from the Cross, wrapped him in a shroud, and buried him in a rock tomb. According to medieval legend, Joseph of Arimathea brought the Holy Grail to Britain.

Josephine F From French *Joséphine*, a feminine equivalent of **»Joseph** formed with the diminutive suffix *-ine*. It is now widely used in the English-speaking world.

Josette F Modern French pet form of *Joséphine*, now sometimes also used in the English-speaking world.

Joshua M Biblical name (meaning 'God is salvation' in Hebrew), borne by the Israelite leader who took command of the children of Israel after the death of Moses and led them to take possession of the promised land. The name, long favoured by Jews and also by Nonconformist Christians, enjoyed a great surge in popularity in the 1990s.

Josiah M Biblical name (meaning 'God heals' in Hebrew), borne by a king of Judah, whose story is recounted in 2 Kings 22–3. This was fairly frequently used as a given name in the English-speaking world, especially among Dissenters, from the 18th to the early 20th century. The most famous English bearer is the potter Josiah Wedgwood (1730–95). In North America it was a recurrent name in the Quincy family of Massachusetts; the best-known Josiah Quincy (1744–75) was a pre-Revolutionary patriot, who died while returning from arguing the cause of the American colonists in London.

Josie F Pet form of »**Josephine**, now widely used as an independent given name.

Joss M, F Short form of »**Jocelyn**, occasionally used as an independent given name. In part it may also be a revival of a medieval male name (see »**Joyce**).

Joy F From the vocabulary word (Old French *joie*, Late Latin *gaudia*). Being 'joyful in the Lord' was a duty that the Puritans took seriously, so the name became popular in the 17th century under their influence.

Joyce F, formerly M Apparently from the Norman male name *Josce* (Middle English *Josse*), which in turn is from *Jodocus*, a Latinized form of a Breton name, *Iodoc*, meaning 'lord', borne by a 7th-century Breton saint. Although this was fairly common as a male given name in the Middle Ages, it had virtually died out by the 14th century. There is some evidence of its use as a girl's name in the 17th and 18th centuries, perhaps as a variant of »**Joy**. It was strongly revived in the 19th century under the influence of popular fiction. It is borne by characters in Mrs Henry Wood's *East Lynne* (1861) and Edna Lyall's *In the Golden Days* (1885). Modern use may well have been influenced also by the common Irish surname, which is derived from the medieval Norman male name. See also »**Joss**.

Judah M Biblical name (said to mean 'praised' in Hebrew), borne by the fourth son of Jacob (Genesis 29:35), who gave his name to one of the twelve tribes of Israel and to one of its two kingdoms.

Judd M Medieval pet form of »**Jordan**, now restored to use as a given name from the derived surname.

Jude M, F Short form of **Judas**, itself a Greek form of
≫Judah. This form is occasionally used in the New
Testament and elsewhere to distinguish the apostle Jude
(Judas Thaddaeus) from the traitor Judas Iscariot. It is
also borne by the central character in Thomas Hardy's
novel *Jude the Obscure* (1895). As a girl's name it is a
short form of **≫Judith** or **≫Judy**, and is sometimes used
independently.

Judith F Biblical name, meaning 'Jewess' or 'woman
from Judea', borne by a Jewish heroine whose story is
recorded in the Book of Judith in the Apocrypha. Judith,
a beautiful widow, delivers her people from the
invading Assyrians by gaining the confidence of their
commander, Holofernes, and cutting off his head while
he is asleep; without their commander, the Assyrians
are duly routed. The name is also borne by one of the
Hittite wives of Esau (Genesis 26:34). This has been a
perennially popular Jewish name. In the English-
speaking world it was taken up among Nonconformists
in the 18th century, and enjoyed great popularity in
the 20th century.

Judy F Pet form of **≫Judith**. This was the name adopted
by the singer and film star Judy Garland (1922–69).

Jules M, now sometimes also F French form of **≫Julius**.
It is a very common given name in France and is
occasionally used in the English-speaking world, where
it is also fairly common as an informal pet form of
≫Julian and **≫Julie**.

Julia F Feminine form of the old Roman family name
≫Julius. A woman called Julia is mentioned in Paul's
Epistle to the Romans (Romans 16:15), and the name
was borne by numerous early saints. Its frequency
increased with the vogue for classical names in the 18th
century.

Julian M, occasionally F From the common Late Latin
name *Juliānus*, a derivative of **≫Julius**. In classical

times *Juliānus* was a name borne not only by various minor early saints, but also by the Roman emperor Julian 'the Apostate', who attempted to return the Roman Empire from institutionalized Christianity to paganism. For many centuries the English name *Julian* was borne by women as well as men, for example by the Blessed Julian of Norwich (c.1342–after 1413). The differentiation in form between *Julian* and **≫Gillian** did not develop until the 16th century. *Julian* is still occasionally used as a girl's name.

Juliana F Latin feminine form of *Juliānus* (see **≫Julian**), which was revived in England in the 18th century and has been used occasionally ever since.

Julianne F Modern combination of the given names **≫Julie** and **≫Anne**, perhaps sometimes intended as a Frenchified form of **≫Juliana**.

Julie F French form of **≫Julia**. It was imported to the English-speaking world in the 1920s, and soon became enormously popular, boosted no doubt by the fame in the 1960s of the actresses Julie Harris (b. 1925), Julie Andrews (b. 1935 as Julia Wells), and Julie Christie (b. 1940).

Juliet F Anglicized form of French *Juliette* or Italian *Giulietta*, diminutive forms of **≫Julia**. The name is most famous as that of the 'star-crossed' heroine of Shakespeare's tragedy *Romeo and Juliet*.

Julitta F Of uncertain origin, probably a Late Latin form of **≫Judith**, influenced by **≫Julia**. This was the name borne by the mother of the infant saint Quiricus; she was martyred with him at Tarsus in 304.

Julius M Roman family name, of obscure derivation, borne most notably by Gaius Julius Caesar (?102–44 BC). It was in use among the early Christians, and was the name of an early and influential pope (337–52), as well as of a later pope (1443–1513) who attempted to combat corruption in the papacy during the Renaissance.

June F One of the names coined in the early 20th century from the names of months of the year (cf. **»April** and **»May**).

Juniper F From the name of the plant (derived in the Middle Ages from Late Latin *iunipērus*).

Justin M English form of the Latin name *Justīnus*, a derivative of **»Justus**. The name was borne by various early saints, notably a 2nd-century Christian apologist and a (possibly spurious) boy martyr of the 3rd century. *Justin* has enjoyed considerable popularity since the second part of the 20th century.

Justina F Feminine form of **»Justin**, from Latin *Justīna*. This was the name of a virgin martyr executed at Padua under Diocletian.

Justine F Feminine form of **»Justin**, from a French version of **»Justina**. Its regular use in Britain since the 1960s has been partly due to the influence of Lawrence Durrell's novel of this name.

Justus M Mainly U.S.: Latin name meaning 'just' or 'fair'. Because of its transparently well-omened meaning, it has been used occasionally as a given name in several countries, including Germany and the Netherlands.

K

Kailey F Variant spelling of **≫Kayley**.

Kale M Of uncertain origin, perhaps an Anglicized form of the Irish Gaelic name **≫Cathal**. It may have been invented as a masculine equivalent of **≫Kayley**.

Kaley F Variant spelling of **≫Kayley**.

Kane M Irish: Anglicized form of the traditional Gaelic name *Cathán*, meaning 'little battler', a derivative of *cath* 'battle', now also used outside Ireland.

Kara F Variant spelling of **≫Cara**.

Karen F Danish form of **≫Katherine**, first introduced to the English-speaking world by Scandinavian settlers in America. It has been used in Britain only since the 1940s, but soon became very popular.

Karin F Swedish form of **≫Katherine**, found as a less common variant of **≫Karen** in both America and Britain.

Karl M German and Scandinavian form of **≫Charles**, also used by English speakers. See also **≫Carl**.

Katarina F Swedish form of **≫Katherine**, also occasionally used in the English-speaking world.

Kate F Short form of **≫Katherine**, reflecting the French pronunciation with *-t-* for *-th-*, which was also usual in medieval England. It has been continuously popular since the Middle Ages and was used by Shakespeare for two important characters: the daughter of the King of France who is wooed and won by King Henry V, and the 'shrew' in *The Taming of the Shrew*.

Katelyn F Elaboration of **»Kate** with the suffix *-lyn* (see **»Lynn**), or a respelling of **»Caitlín**.

Katerina F From a Russian popular form of **»Katherine**, now occasionally used in the English-speaking world.

Katha F Altered form of **Kathy** or elaborated form of **Kath**, with the Latinate feminine suffix *-a*.

Katharine F Variant of **»Katherine**, associated by folk etymology with Greek *katharos* 'pure'. This is the preferred spelling in Germany. It is the one used in the name of the film star Katharine Hepburn (1909–2003).

Katherine F English form of the name of a saint martyred at Alexandria in 307. The story has it that she was condemned to be broken on the wheel for her Christian belief. However, the wheel miraculously fell apart, so she was beheaded instead. The earliest sources that mention her are in Greek and give the name in the form *Aikaterinē*. The name is of unknown etymology, but from an early date it was associated with the Greek adjective *katharos* 'pure'. This led to spellings with *-th-* and to a change in the middle vowel (see **»Katharine**). Several later saints also bore the name, including the mystic St Katherine of Siena (1347–80), who both led a contemplative life and played a role in the affairs of state. *Katherine* is also a royal name: in England it was borne by Katherine of Aragon (1485–1536), first wife of Henry VIII, as well as by the wives of Henry V and Charles II. The spellings **»Katharine**, **»Catherine**, **Catharine**, **»Kath(e)ryn**, and **Cathryn** are also found.

k

Katheryn F Altered spelling of **»Katherine**, influenced by the productive name suffix *-yn*.

Kathleen F Of Irish origin: Anglicized form of Gaelic **»Caitlín**. The spelling **»Cathleen** is also found.

Kathryn F Variant of **»Katherine**.

Katlyn F Variant of **»Katelyn**.

Katrina F Variant spelling of **»Catrina**.

Katrine F German and Danish form of **»Katherine**, occasionally now also used in the English-speaking world.

Katya F Russian pet form of *Yekaterina* 'Katherine', now sometimes used as a given name in the English-speaking world.

Kay F, M Pet form of any of the various names beginning with the letter *K*-, most notably **»Katherine** and its many variants. As a male name it may also in part represent the name of the Arthurian knight Sir Kay, whose name is probably a Celticized form of the ancient Roman given name *Gaius*. As a girl's name it was famous as that of the actress Kay Kendall (1926–59).

Kaye F Variant spelling of **»Kay** as a girl's name.

Kayla F Altered form of **»Kayley**, a recent coinage which is very popular in North America. It is also spelled **Kaylah**.

Kayley F Of recent origin and uncertain derivation. It is perhaps a transferred use of the Irish surname *Kayley*, an Anglicized form of Gaelic *Ó Caollaidhe* 'descendant of Caolladhe'. The latter is a male personal name derived from *caol* 'slender'. Its adoption as a modern given name has probably also been influenced by the popularity of **»Keeley**, **»Kelly**, and **»Kylie**, not to mention **»Cally**. It occurs in a remarkably large number of different spellings, including **Kayly**, **Kayli(e)**, **Kaylee**, **Kayleigh**, **»Kail(e)y**, **Kailee**, **Kaileigh**, **»Kaley**, **Kalie**, **Kalee**, **Kaleigh**; **»Cayleigh**; **»Caileigh**; **»Caleigh**.

Kean M Irish: Anglicized form of the Gaelic name **»Cian**. The spelling **Keane** is also found.

Keanu M Hawaiian name meaning 'cool breeze', recently made popular by the film actor Keanu Reeves (b. 1965).

Keegan M Transferred use of the Irish surname, an Anglicized form of Gaelic *Mac Aodhagáin*, a patronymic from the personal name *Aodhagán*, double diminutive of ≫**Aodh**.

Keeley F Of recent origin and uncertain etymology, possibly an alteration of ≫**Keelin** to fit in with the pattern of girls' names ending in *-(e)y* or *-ie*. The spellings **Keely**, **Keelie**, **Keeleigh**, and ≫**Keighley** are also found.

Keelin F Irish: Anglicized form of the Gaelic name *Caoilfhionn*, derived from *caol* 'slender' + *fionn* 'white'.

Keenan M Transferred used of the Irish surname, Gaelic *Ó Cianáin* 'descendant of Cianán'. The latter is a personal name representing a diminutive of ≫**Cian**.

Keeva F Irish: Anglicized form of the Gaelic name ≫**Caoimhe**.

Keighley F Fanciful respelling of ≫**Keeley**, inspired by the Yorkshire town of *Keighley*, which is pronounced 'keeth-lee'.

Keir M Transferred use of the Scottish surname, in origin a variant of ≫**Kerr**. The name has sometimes been chosen in honour of the first Labour MP, James Keir Hardie (1856–1915), whose mother's maiden name was Keir.

Keith M Transferred use of a Scottish surname, originally a local name derived from lands so called in East Lothian, probably from a Celtic (Brythonic) word meaning 'wood'. The principal family bearing this surname were hereditary Earls Marischal of Scotland from 1455 to 1715. This is one of a number of Scottish aristocratic surnames that have become well established since the 19th century as male given names throughout the English-speaking world. Others include **»Bruce**, **»Douglas**, and **»Graham**.

Kelan M Irish: Anglicized form of Gaelic *Caolán* originally a byname representing a diminutive form of *caol* 'slender'.

Kellen M Of uncertain derivation, perhaps an altered form of **»Kelan**, or from the Scottish surname *McKellen* (Gaelic *Mac Ailein* 'son of Alan' or *Mac Cailein* 'son of Colin').

Kelly F, M As a male name, this is an Anglicized form of Irish Gaelic *Ceallach*, a traditional name of disputed origin. It is said to mean 'bright-headed', or possibly also 'strife', but could equally well be from *ceall*, genitive plural of *cill* 'monastery', 'church'. It is now very widely used, mainly as a girl's name, in the English-speaking world. This use probably derives from the Irish surname (Gaelic *Ó Ceallaigh* 'descendant of Ceallach'). The spellings **Kelley** and **Kellie** are also found.

Kelsey F, M Transferred use of the surname, which is from an Old English masculine personal name *Cēolsige*, derived from *cēol* 'ship' + *sige* 'victory'. Its use as a girl's name may have been influenced by names such as **»Elsie**. The girl's name is also spelled **Kelsie** and **Kelsi**.

Kelvin M Modern given name, first used in the 1920s. It is taken from the name of a river which runs through Glasgow into the Clyde (cf. **»Clyde**). Its use as a given name may also have been influenced by names such as **»Kevin** and **»Melvin** and the fame of the scientist Lord Kelvin (1824–1907).

Kemp M Transferred use of the surname, which originated in the Middle Ages as an occupational name or nickname from Middle English *kempe* 'athlete', 'wrestler' (from Old English *kempa* 'warrior', 'champion').

Kendall F, M Transferred use of the surname, which is at least in part a local name, either from *Kendal* in

Cumbria, or from *Kendale* in Driffield, East Yorkshire. The surname may in some cases be derived from the Welsh personal name *Cynddelw*, which is of uncertain origin. The spellings **Kendal**, **Kendel(l)**, and **Kendle** are also found.

Kendra F Recently coined name, probably as a feminine form of ≫**Kendrick**.

Kendrick M In modern use a transferred use of the surname, the origins of which are complex. The source in many cases is the Old Welsh personal name *Cynwrig*, which is of uncertain origin. The Scottish surname *Ken(d)rick* is a shortened form of *MacKen(d)rick* (Gaelic *Mac Eanraig* 'son of Henry'). As an English surname, *Ken(d)rick* is derived, at least in part, from the Middle English given name *Cenric*, in which two Old English personal names have fallen together: *Cēnrīc* (from *cēne* 'keen' + *rīc* 'power') and *Cyneric* (from *cyne* 'royal' + *rīc* 'power'). *Cenric* survived as a Christian name into the 17th century. The spelling ≫**Kenrick** is also found.

Kenelm M From an Old English personal name derived from *cēne* 'keen', 'bold' + *helm* 'helmet', 'protection'. The name was popular in England during the Middle Ages, when a 9th-century Mercian prince of this name was widely revered as a saint and martyr, although his death seems to have been rather the result of personal and political motives. It has remained in occasional use ever since.

Kennard M Transferred use of the surname, which is derived from a Middle English personal name in which several Old English names had fallen together. The first element may be either *cēne* 'keen' or *cyne* 'royal'; the second is either *weard* 'guardian' or *heard* 'hardy', 'brave', 'strong'.

Kennedy F, M Anglicized form of Irish Gaelic *Cinnéidigh*, a traditional name derived from *ceann* 'head' + *éidigh* 'ugly'. In recent years it has sometimes been used as a given name in the English-speaking world in honour of the assassinated American president John F. Kennedy (1917–63) and his brother Robert (1925–68).

Kenneth M Scottish: Anglicized form of two different Gaelic names, *Cinaed* and *Cainnech*. The former is a derivative of *Aed* (see **»Aodh**), meaning 'born of the fire god'. It was the Gaelic name of Kenneth mac Alpin (d. 858), first king of the united Picts and Scots. The latter is a byname meaning 'handsome', and survives today in Scotland as the common Gaelic name *Coinneach* (cf. **»Mackenzie**). Since early in the 20th century *Kenneth* has enjoyed great popularity as a given name well beyond the boundaries of Scotland.

k **Kenrick** M Variant of **»Kendrick**.

Kent M Transferred use of the surname, in origin a local name from the English county. Use as a given name is of recent origin; it may in part be a short form of **»Kenton**.

Kenton M Transferred use of the surname, in origin a local name from any of various places so called.

Keren F Shortened form of the Biblical name *Keren-happuch*, borne by the third of Job's daughters (Job 42:14). The name means 'horn of eye-paint' in Hebrew.

Kerena F Latinate elaboration of **»Keren**.

Kermit M Mainly U.S.: transferred use of the surname *Kermit*, Anglicized form of Gaelic *Mac Dhiarmaid* 'son of Diarmad' (see **»Dermot**). The name was borne by a son of President Theodore Roosevelt, and more recently by a frog puppet on Jim Henson's *Muppet Show*.

Kerr M Transferred use of the surname, which is a northern English local name for someone who lived by a patch of wet ground overgrown with brushwood (Old Norse *kjarr*).

Kerry F, M As a given name this is of Australian origin, probably from the name of the Irish county. It is also quite common in Britain and elsewhere in the English-speaking world, especially as a girl's name; as such it is also spelled **Kerrie**, **Kerri**, and **Keri**. See also **»Ceri**.

Kester M Medieval Scottish form of **»Christopher**, occasionally revived as a modern given name.

Kestrel F One of the rarer girls' names derived from vocabulary words denoting birds that have come into use in the 20th century. The word itself derives from Old French *cresserelle*, apparently a derivative of *cressele* 'rattle'.

Keturah F Biblical name (meaning 'incense' in Hebrew), borne by the woman Abraham married after Sarah's death (Genesis 25:1).

Kevin M Of Irish origin: Anglicized form of the Gaelic name *Caoimhín*, originally a byname representing a diminutive of *caomh* 'comely', 'beloved'. This was the name of a 7th-century saint who is one of the patrons of Dublin.

Keziah F Biblical name, borne by one of Job's daughters, born to him towards the end of his life, after his prosperity had been restored (Job 42:14). It represents the Hebrew word for the cassia tree (the English name of which is derived, via Latin and Greek, from Hebrew or a related Semitic source). The spelling **Kezia** and pet forms **Kizzie** and **»Kizzy** are also found.

Kiera F Recently coined feminine form of **»Kieran**; cf. **»Ciara**.

Kieran M Irish: Anglicized form of Gaelic **»Ciarán**. Also found are the variants **»Kyran** and **Kieron**, the latter being borne, for example, by the Irish actor Kieron Moore (b. 1925).

Killian M Irish: Anglicized form of Gaelic **»Cillian**. This name was borne by various early Irish saints, including the 7th-century author of a 'Life of St Bridget', and

k

missionaries to Artois and Franconia. It is also found in the spelling **Kilian**.

Kim F, M Originally a short form of **»Kimberley**, now established as an independent given name. The hero of Rudyard Kipling's novel *Kim* (1901) bore the name as a short form of *Kimball* (a surname used as a given name). As a girl's name it has been borne by a number of well-known people, including the film stars Kim Novak (b. 1933) and Kim Basinger (b. 1953).

Kimberley F, M The immediate source of the given name is the town in South Africa, the scene of fighting during the Boer War, which brought it to public notice at the end of the 19th century. The town was named in 1871 after John Wodehouse, Lord Kimberley (1826–1902), the British colonial secretary at the time, who took his title from a place in Norfolk called Kimberley. As a girl's name it is also spelled **Kimberly** (the more common North American spelling), **Kimberli(e)**, **Kimberlee**, and **Kimberleigh**.

King M From the vocabulary word for a male monarch, bestowed with a hint of the notion that the bearer would have kingly qualities. In some cases it may be a transferred use of the surname (originally a nickname or an occupational name given to someone who was employed in a royal household). Its frequency has increased recently as a Black name, no doubt partly in honour of the civil rights leader Martin Luther King (1929–68).

Kingsley M, occasionally F Transferred use of the surname, originally a local name derived from various places (in Cheshire, Hampshire, Staffordshire) so named. It is not clear what was the initial impulse towards its use as a given name; the usual pattern in such cases is for a mother's maiden name to be chosen as a given name, but in this case the choice may have been made in honour of the author Charles Kingsley

(1819–75). For the girl's name, the spelling **Kingslie** is also found.

Kirk M Transferred use of the surname, originally a northern English and Scottish local name for someone who lived near a church (from Old Norse *kirkja*). Recent use has probably been influenced to some extent by the film actor Kirk Douglas (b. 1916).

Kirsten F Danish and Norwegian form of >>**Christine**, now well established also in the English-speaking world.

Kirstie F Scottish pet form of >>**Kirstin**, now used as an independent given name throughout the English-speaking world.

Kirstin F Scottish vernacular form of >>**Christine**, now also used outside Scotland.

Kirsty F Variant spelling of >>**Kirstie**.

Kit M, F Pet form of >>**Christopher**; also of >>**Katherine** and its variants.

Kitty F Pet form of >>**Katherine**.

Kizzy F Pet form of >>**Keziah**. It is also found in the spelling **Kizzie**.

Krista F Variant spelling of >>**Christa**.

Kristeen F Fanciful respelling of >>**Christine**. The variants >>**Kristene** and **Kristine** are also found.

Kristene F Fanciful respelling of >>**Christine**.

Kristie F Variant of the girl's name >>**Christie**, under the influence of the Scottish form >>**Kirstie**.

Kristina F This coincides with the Swedish and Czech form of the name. Respelling of >>**Christina**.

Kristine F Variant spelling of >>**Christine**, under the influence of >>**Kristina**.

Kristy F Variant spelling of **»Kristie**.

Kyla F Recently coined name, created as a feminine form of **»Kyle** or else a variant of **»Kylie**.

Kyle M, occasionally F From a Scottish topographic term denoting a narrow strait or channel, from Gaelic *caol* 'narrow'. In part it is a transferred use of the surname, a local name from the region in Ayrshire named with this word.

Kylie F Of Australian origin, said to represent an Aboriginal term for the boomerang. However, it seems more likely that the name is an invention, influenced by **»Kyle** and **»Kelly**. It is popular in Australia and, in part due to the Australian actress Kylie Minogue (b. 1968), it has also acquired currency in Britain and elsewhere. Alternative spellings include **Kyley**, **Kylee**, **Kyleigh**.

Kyra F Apparently a variant spelling of *Cyra*, feminine form of **»Cyrus**, or else a feminine name formed directly from **»Kyran**.

Kyran M Variant spelling of **»Kieran**.

L

Lacey F, occasionally M Transferred use of the surname, originally a Norman baronial name from *Lassy*, Calvados. The Lacey family was powerful in Ireland during the early Middle Ages. The spelling **Lacy** is also found.

Lachlan M Scottish (Gaelic *Lachlann*, earlier *Lochlann*): said to refer originally to a migrant from Norway, the 'land of the lochs'. Formerly used only in families with some Highland connection, it has now acquired wide popular appeal, especially in Australia.

Laetitia F Original Latin form of ≫**Lettice**.

Laila F Variant spelling of ≫**Leila**.

Lalage F Classical name, pronounced 'lal-a-dgee' or 'lal-a-ghee'. It was used by Horace in his *Odes* as the name of his beloved of the moment. This was a literary pseudonym derived from Greek *lalagein* 'to chatter' or 'babble'. It has enjoyed a modest popularity since the 19th century. It occurs in John Fowles's *The French Lieutenant's Woman* (1969).

Lambert M Transferred use of the surname, which is from an Old French given name of Germanic origin, from *land* 'land', 'territory' + *beorht* 'famous'. This was introduced to Britain by the Normans, but its frequency in Britain in the later Middle Ages was mainly due to its popularity among immigrants from the Low Countries; St Lambert of Maastricht was a 7th-century saint who aided St Willibrord in his evangelical work.

Lamont M Mainly U.S.: transferred use of the Irish and Scottish surname, derived from the medieval given name *Lagman*, from Old Norse *Logmathr*, from *log* 'law' + *mathr* 'man'.

Lana F Of uncertain origin. If not simply an invention, it may have been devised as a feminine equivalent of »**Alan** (of which it is an anagram), or a shortened form of »**Alana**. It seems to have been first used by the American film actress Lana Turner (1920–95), whose original name was Julia.

Lance M Old French form of the Germanic personal name *Lanzo*, a pet form of various compound names with the first element *land* 'land', 'territory', but associated from an early date with Old French *lance* 'lance' (the weapon, from Latin *lancea*). The modern use as a given name most probably arose as a transferred use of the surname derived from the medieval given name, although it is also commonly taken as a short form of »**Lancelot**.

Lancelot M The name borne by one of King Arthur's best and most valued knights, who eventually betrayed his trust by becoming the lover of Queen Guinevere. The name is of uncertain origin. It is probably, like other Arthurian names, of Celtic derivation, but has been heavily distorted by mediation through French sources.

Landon M Mainly U.S.: transferred use of the surname, in origin a local name from any of various places in England called *Langdon* 'long hill'.

Lane M, occasionally F Mainly U.S.: apparently a transferred use of the surname, in origin a local name for someone who lived in or by a lane (Old English *lane*, originally denoting a narrow pathway between hedges or banks).

Lanna F Shortened form of »**Alanna**.

Laoise F Irish Gaelic name, pronounced 'lee-sha', of uncertain origin. It may be identical with the old Gaelic name *Luigsech* 'radiance', a derivative of *Lug*, name of the goddess of light.

Lara F Russian short form of **»Larissa**, introduced in the early 20th century to the English-speaking world. It gained some favour as the name of one of the principal characters in Boris Pasternak's novel *Dr Zhivago* (1957), which was made into a film in 1965.

Laraine F Mainly U.S., especially African American: of uncertain origin, perhaps a variant spelling of **»Lorraine** or derived from the French phrase *la reine* 'the queen' (cf. **»Raine**). Alternative spellings are **Lareine** and **Lareina**.

Larch F Mainly U.S.: from the name of the tree (adopted in the 16th century from German *larche*, ultimately from Latin *larix*).

Larissa F Russian name, of uncertain origin. It is the name of a Greek martyr venerated in the Eastern Church, and may perhaps be derived from the ancient Thessalian town of Larissa.

Lark F Mainly North American and Australian: from the name of the bird (Old English *lāwerce*). This is one of a small set of girls' names derived from vocabulary words denoting birds, which achieved some currency in the mid-20th century. The lark is traditionally associated with early rising and cheerfulness, and is noted for its sweet song.

Larry M Pet form of **»Laurence** or **»Lawrence**.

Lassarina M Irish: Anglicized form of the Gaelic name *Lasairíona*, derived from *lasair* 'flame' + *fíon* 'wine'. The spelling **Lasrina** is also found.

Latasha F Mainly U.S., especially African American: recent blending of **»Latisha** and **»Natasha**.

Latisha F Recent coinage, probably a respelling of **»Laetitia**.

Laura F Feminine form of the Late Latin male name *Laurus* 'Laurel'. St Laura was a 9th-century Spanish martyr, a nun who met her death in a cauldron of molten lead. Laura is the name of the woman addressed in the love poetry of the Italian poet Petrarch (1304–74), and it owes much of its subsequent popularity to this. The popularity of the given name in the English-speaking world dates from the 19th century, when it was probably imported from Italy.

Laurel F 19th-century adoption of the vocabulary word for the evergreen tree (Middle English *lorel*), probably influenced by **»Laura** and perhaps taken as a pet form of the latter.

Laurelle F Elaborated form of **»Laurel**.

Lauren F Apparently modelled on **»Laurence**, this was first brought to public attention by the film actress Lauren Bacall (b. 1924), famous for her partnership with Humphrey Bogart. See also **»Loren**.

Laurence M From a French form of Latin *Laurentius* 'man from Laurentum', a town in Latium. The given name was popular in the Middle Ages, under the influence of a 3rd-century saint who was one of the seven deacons of Rome. He was martyred in 258. The legend is that, having been required to hand over the Church's treasures to the civil authorities, he assembled the poor and sick and presented them. For this act of Christian defiance, he was roasted to death on a gridiron. In England the name is also associated with St Laurence of Canterbury (d. 619). A more recent influence has been the actor Sir Laurence Olivier (1907–89). See also **»Lawrence**.

Lauretta F Italian diminutive form of **»Laura**, also sometimes used in the English-speaking world.

Laurie F, M Pet form of **»Laura**, **»Laurel**, and **»Laurence**.

Lavender F From the vocabulary word denoting the herb with sweet-smelling flowers (Old French *lavendre*, from Late Latin *lavendula*).

Lavery M Irish: Anglicization of the Gaelic name *Labhraidh*; see **»Lowry**.

Lavinia F In Roman mythology, the name of the wife of Aeneas, and thus the mother of the Roman people. Legend had it that she gave her name to the Latin town of *Lavinium*, but in fact she is more likely to have been invented to explain the placename, which is of pre-Roman origin. She was said to be the daughter of King Latinus, who was similarly invented to account for the name of *Latium*.

Lawrence M Anglicized spelling of **»Laurence**. This is the usual spelling of the surname and is becoming increasingly common as a given name, especially in North America.

Layla F Variant of **»Leila**.

Lea F Variant spelling of **»Leah** or **»Lia**, or possibly sometimes a shortened form of **»Azalea**. Occasionally it is a variant of the girl's name **»Lee**, from an alternative form of the surname, pronounced as a single syllable.

Leaf M From the vocabulary word (Old English *lēaf*). This was one of the names taken from the world of nature in the 1960s under hippy influence. Choice as a given name may also have been influenced by the Scandinavian name *Leif*, from Old Norse *Leifr*, meaning 'heir'.

Leah F Biblical name (meaning 'languid' in Hebrew), borne by the elder sister of Rachel (Genesis 29:23). Jacob served her father Laban for seven years in return for the hand of Rachel, but was deceived into marrying Leah first. He was then given Rachel as well, but had to labour seven more years afterwards. The name was favoured by Jews and by the Puritans in the

17th century. In the 1990s it acquired broad popular appeal.

Leander M Latin form of the Greek name *Leandros*, derived from *leōn* 'lion' + *anēr* 'man' (genitive *andros*). In Greek legend, Leander swam across the Hellespont every night to visit his beloved Hero and back again every morning; he was eventually drowned during a storm. In Christian times, the name was borne by a 6th-century saint; the brother of Sts Fulgentius, Isidore, and Florentina, he was a leading ecclesiastical figure of his day and became archbishop of Seville. In modern times, the name has occasionally been used as an elaboration of the male name **»Lee**.

Leanne F Modern coinage. It may be a combination of **»Lee** and **»Anne**, or a respelling of **»Liane**. On the other hand, its popularity in Scotland suggests the possible influence of the Gaelic vocabulary word *leannan* 'sweetheart' (see **»Lennan**). The variant **Leanna** is also found.

Leary M Irish: Anglicized form of the Gaelic name **Laoghaire**, which is said to mean 'calf herd'. This was borne by several early Irish saints, princes, and kings, including the High King of Ireland at the time of St Patrick (5th century). It is found as a surname, also in the form *O'Leary*, and modern use as a given name may be due to transferred use of the surname.

Leda F Name borne in classical mythology by a queen of Sparta, who was ravished by Zeus in the shape of a swan. She gave birth to two eggs which, when hatched, revealed the two sets of twins: Castor and Pollux, and Helen and Hermione.

Lee M, occasionally F Transferred use of the surname, in origin a local name from any of numerous places so called. It is popular in the United States, where it is sometimes chosen in honour of the great Confederate general Robert E. Lee (1807–70).

Leesa F Respelled version of **»Lisa**, influenced by **»Lee**.

Leigh F, M Variant of **»Lee**, from an alternative spelling of the surname and placename. Use as a girl's name may have been influenced by the British actress Vivien Leigh (1913–67).

Leighton M Transferred use of the surname, in origin a local name from any of several places named with this word, for example Leighton Buzzard in Bedfordshire.

Leila F Of Arabic origin, now fairly common in the English-speaking world, having been used as a name for an oriental beauty by Byron, in *The Giaour* (1813) and *Don Juan* (1819–24), and by Lord Lytton for the heroine of his novel *Leila* (1838). In Arabic it means 'night', apparently alluding to a dark complexion. The popularity of the spelling **»Layla** was enhanced by its use for a song by Eric Clapton (1972). The spellings **»Laila** and **»Lila** are also found.

Leland M Mainly U.S.: transferred use of the surname, in origin a local name for someone who lived by a patch of fallow land, from Middle English *lay*, *ley* 'fallow' + *land* 'land'. The surname is well established in the United States. It was borne by the humorous writer Charles Leland (1824–1903), and it is the name of a town in Mississippi.

Len M Short form of **»Leonard** and possibly also of the rarer given name **»Lennox**. It has also been used as a short form of **»Lionel**.

Lena F Abstracted from names ending in these syllables, such as *Helena* and *Magdalena*. In America it is famous as the name of the singer Lena Horne (b. 1917).

Lenda F 20th century coinage, an arbitrary alteration of **»Linda**.

Lennan M Anglicized form of the Irish Gaelic name **Leannán** 'darling', 'sweetheart', a word also used to denote a fairy lover. This was a common given name in medieval times, especially in Co. Clare, though its revival no doubt has also something to do with the transparent meaning of the vocabulary word.

Lennard M Variant spelling of »**Leonard**, perhaps in part a transferred use of the surname, which was derived from the given name in the Middle Ages.

Lennox M Transferred use of the Scottish surname, which is also the name of an earldom. It originated as a local name from a district north of Glasgow formerly known as *The Levenach*. This was the first name of the British composer Sir Lennox Berkeley (1903–89).

Lenora F Originally a contracted form of »**Leonora**, although sometimes chosen as an expanded version of »**Lena**.

Leo M From a Late Latin personal name, meaning 'lion', which was borne by a large number of early Christian saints, most notably Pope Leo the Great (?390–461). The variant form **Leon** (taken from the oblique case) is also found.

Leona F Latinate feminine form of »**Leo**.

Leonard M From an Old French personal name of Germanic origin, derived from *leon* 'lion' + *hard* 'hardy', 'brave', 'strong'. This was the name of a 5th-century Frankish saint, the patron of peasants and horses. Although it was introduced into Britain by the Normans, *Leonard* was not a particularly common name during the Middle Ages. It was revived in the 19th century and became very popular. The spelling »**Lennard** is also found.

Léonie F French: from Latin *Leonia*, feminine form of *Leonius*, derived from *leo* 'lion'. It is now also widely used (normally without the accent) in the English-speaking world.

Leonora F Shortened form of >>**Eleonora**.

Leopold M From an Old French name of Germanic
(Frankish) origin, from *liut* 'people' + *bold* 'bold',
'brave'. The first element was altered by association
with Latin *leo* 'lion'. A name of this origin may have
been introduced into Britain by the Normans, but if so
it did not survive long. It was reintroduced from the
Continent towards the end of the 19th century in
honour of Queen Victoria's uncle Leopold, King of the
Belgians (1790–1865), after whom she named one of
her sons.

Leroy M Now considered a typical African-American
given name, but formerly also extensively borne by
White Americans. It is from a French nickname meaning
'the king'.

Lesley F, M Originally a variant of >>**Leslie**, but now
specialized as the usual girl's form. Its first recorded
use as a girl's name is in a poem by Robert Burns.

Leslie M, F Transferred use of the Scottish surname
derived from the lands of *Lesslyn* in Aberdeenshire.
Surnames and clan names have been used as given
names more readily and from an earlier date in
Scotland than elsewhere, and this is the name of an
ancient family, who in the 14th and 15th centuries
were close associates of the Scottish royal house of
Stewart and who have held the earldom of Rothes since
1457. The British film actor Leslie Howard (1890–1943)
was an influence on the popularity of the name,
especially in the United States, where he appeared in
Gone with the Wind (1939). A famous female bearer is
the French film actress Leslie Caron (b. 1930).

Lester M Transferred use of the surname, in origin a
local name from the city of *Leicester*, recorded in the
10th century as *Ligora cæster* 'Roman fort of the Ligore
tribe'.

Leticia F Simplified spelling of ≫**Laetitia**.

Lettice F From the medieval vernacular form of the Latin name ≫**Laetitia**. It was popular among the Victorians.

Levi M Biblical name (meaning 'associated' in Hebrew), given by Jacob's wife Leah to her third son as an expression of her hope, 'Now this time will my husband be joined unto me, because I have born him three sons: therefore was his name called Levi' (Genesis 29:34). The Levites (a Jewish priestly caste) are descended from Levi. In the New Testament, Levi is a byname of the apostle and evangelist Matthew. In modern times the name is mainly Jewish.

Lewis M Common English form, since the Middle Ages, of the French name ≫**Louis**. In modern use it is also in part a transferred use of the surname derived from this given name.

Lexine F Scottish: elaboration of ≫**Lexy** with the addition of the feminine diminutive suffix -*ine*.

Lexy F Pet form of ≫**Alexandra**, found particularly in Scotland.

Lia F Italian: of uncertain derivation, probably a short form of *Rosalia* (see ≫**Rosalie**).

Liadan F Anglicized form of the Irish Gaelic name **Líadan**, probably a derivative of *liath* 'grey'. In Irish legend, Líadan forsook her lover Cuirithir in order to enter a nunnery; both of them died of grief.

Liam M Irish: short form of **Uilliam**, Gaelic form of ≫**William**, also used throughout the English-speaking world as an independent given name.

Liane F Of uncertain origin, probably a short form of French *Éliane*, from Latin *Aeliāna*, the name of an early martyr at Amasea in Pontus. *Aeliānus* was an old Roman family name. The spelling **Lianne** is also found.

Libby F Pet form of **»Elizabeth**, based originally on a child's unsuccessful attempts to pronounce the name.

Lila F Variant spelling of **»Leila**.

Lilac F From the vocabulary word denoting the shrub with large sprays of heavily scented purple or white flowers. The word is from French, which derived it via Spanish from Arabic *līlak*, from Persian *nīlak* 'bluish'.

Lilian F Of uncertain origin, first recorded in the late 16th century, and probably derived from a nursery form of **»Elizabeth**. It is now sometimes regarded as a derivative of the flower name **»Lily**, but this was not used as a given name in England until the 19th century. The spelling **Lillian** is also found.

Lilith F The name borne, according to medieval tradition, by a wife of Adam prior to Eve. She is said to have been turned into an ugly demon for refusing to obey him. *Lilith* occurs in the Bible as a vocabulary word meaning 'night monster' or 'screech owl' (Isaiah 34:14), and in Jewish folklore is the name of an ugly demon. In spite of its unpleasant connotations, it has occasionally been used as a given name in modern times, perhaps in part being taken as an elaborated form of **»Lily**.

Lily F From the vocabulary word for the flower (via Old French, from Latin *lilium*), regarded in Christian imagery as a symbol of purity. The spelling **Lillie** is also found; in this form the name was borne by the actress Lillie Langtry (1853–1929), friend of King Edward VII.

Lincoln M Transferred use of the surname, in origin a local name from the name of the city of Lincoln. As a given name it has sometimes been bestowed in honour of Abraham Lincoln (1809–65), 16th president of the United States, who led the Union to victory in the Civil War and enforced the emancipation of slaves.

Linda F Of relatively recent origin and uncertain etymology. It is first recorded in the 19th century. It may be a shortened form of **»Belinda**, an adoption of Spanish *linda* 'pretty', or a Latinate derivative of any of various Germanic female names ending in *-lind* meaning 'weak', 'tender', 'soft'. It was popular in the 20th century, especially in the 1950s.

Linden F Ostensibly from the vocabulary word denoting the lime tree (originally the adjectival form, derived from Old English *linde*). However, the given name is of recent origin and is more likely to be an elaboration of **»Linda**, along the lines of **»Lauren** from **»Laura**.

Lindon M Variant spelling of **»Lyndon**.

Lindsay F, M Transferred use of the Scottish surname, originally borne by Sir Walter de Lindesay, one of the retainers of King David I of Scotland (1084–1153), who took the name to Scotland from Lindsey in Lincolnshire. It was at first used as a male name, and it is still occasionally used for boys in Scotland, but elsewhere it is now used for girls. Variant spellings include **Lindsey**, **»Lins(e)y**, and **»Linzi**.

Linford M Transferred use of the surname, a local name from any of various places in England so named. As a given name it is associated in particular with the British athlete Linford Christie (b. 1960).

Linnet F Simplified spelling of **»Linnette**, strongly influenced in popularity by the vocabulary word for the small bird (Old French *linotte*, a derivative of *lin* 'flax', on the seeds of which it feeds).

Linnette F Variant spelling of **»Lynette**.

Linsey F Simplified spelling of *Lindsey* (see **»Lindsay**).

Linton M Transferred use of the surname, originally a local name from any of numerous places in England so called.

Linus M Latin form of the Greek name *Linos*, which is of uncertain origin. In Greek mythology, Linus is a famous musician who taught music to Hercules; it is also the name of an infant son of Apollo who was exposed to die on a mountainside in Argos. In the Christian era, *Linus* was the name of the second pope, St Peter's successor, who was martyred in *c*.76. Nowadays, the given name is associated with a character in the popular *Peanuts* strip cartoon series, a little boy inseparable from his security blanket.

Linzi F Fanciful respelling of **»Lindsay**.

Liona F Altered form of **»Leona**, influenced by **»Lionel**.

Lionel M From a medieval diminutive of the Old French name *Léon* (see **»Leo**) or the Middle English nickname *Lion*.

Lisa F Variant of **»Liza**, influenced by French *Lise* and German *Liese*.

Lisette F French diminutive form of *Lise*, which is itself a shortened form of **»Elisabeth**.

Lisha F Modern coinage, a shortened and respelled form of names such as **»Delicia** and **»Felicia**, on the model of *Trisha* from **»Patricia**.

Lissa F Short form of **»Melissa**. See also **»Lyssa**.

Livia F In modern use often taken as a short form of **»Olivia**, but originally a distinct name, a feminine form of the Roman family name *Livius*. This is of uncertain derivation, perhaps connected with *lividus* 'bluish'.

Liza F Shortened form of **»Eliza**, also spelled **»Lisa**.

Lleu M Welsh: traditional name, meaning 'bright, shining', cognate with the name of the Celtic god known in Old Irish as *Lugh*, in Gaulish as *Lugus*. This name was borne in the *Mabinogi* by Lleu Llaw Gyffes 'Lleu Skilful Hand', the son of Aranrhod. It has been revived in modern times.

Llew M Welsh: traditional name meaning 'lion'. It is also used as a short form of **»Llewelyn**.

Llewelyn M Very popular traditional Welsh name: an altered form (influenced by the vocabulary word *llew* 'lion') of *Llywelyn*, an ancient name of uncertain derivation. It probably goes back to the Old Celtic name *Lugobelinos*, the first element of which is *Lugu-* (the name of a god; see »**Lleu**); the second is a name-forming element. In historical times the name was borne in particular by Llywelyn ap Iorwerth (1173–1240) and his grandson Llywelyn ap Gruffydd (d. 1282), Welsh princes who for a time united their countrymen in North Wales and led opposition to the power of the Norman barons in South Wales and the Marches.

Lloyd M Transferred use of the Welsh surname, originally a nickname meaning 'grey(-haired)' (Welsh *llwyd*). See also »**Floyd**.

Logan M, F Transferred use of the Scottish surname, in origin a local name from a place so called in Ayrshire.

Lois F New Testament name, of unknown derivation, borne by the grandmother of the Timothy to whom St Paul wrote two epistles (see 2 Timothy 1:5).

Lola F Spanish pet form (originally a nursery form) of »**Dolores**, now established as an independent given name in the English-speaking world. It owes some of its popularity to the fame of Lola Montez (1818–1861), stage name of Marie Gilbert, an Irish dancer and courtesan who from 1846–8 so captivated the elderly Ludwig I of Bavaria that she became the virtual ruler of the country, precipitating riots, a constitutional crisis, and the abdication of the king. She arrived in New York in 1851, and spent the last years of her life working to help prostitutes.

Lolicia F Mainly U.S.: elaborated form of »**Lola**, with the addition of a suffix derived from names such as »**Delicia**.

Lolita F Spanish diminutive form of »**Lola**. This was once quite common as a given name in its own right in

America, with its large Hispanic population, but has since been overshadowed by its association with Vladimir Nabokov's novel *Lolita* (1955). The Lolita of the title is the pubescent object of the narrator's desires, and the name is now used as a generic term for any under-age sex kitten.

Lonnie M Of uncertain origin, possibly an Anglicized or pet form of the Spanish name *Alonso* or a variant of **»Lenny**. It is associated in Britain with the skiffle singer Lonnie Donegan, famous in the 1950s and 60s.

Lora F German form of **»Laura**, occasionally also used in the English-speaking world.

Lorcan M Irish: Anglicized form of the Gaelic name **Lorcán**, from a diminutive of Gaelic *lorc* 'fierce'. This was borne most famously by St Lorcán Ó Tuathail (1128–80), archbishop of Dublin, known in English as Laurence O'Toole.

Loreen F Elaboration of **»Lora**, with the addition of the suffix *-een* (originally an Irish diminutive, Gaelic *-ín*). The spelling **Lorene** is also found.

Lorelle F Elaboration of **»Lora**, with the addition of the suffix *-elle* (originally a French feminine diminutive).

Loren F, occasionally M Variant spelling of **»Lauren**.

Lorena F Latinate elaboration of the girl's name **»Loren**.

Loreto F Religious name borne by Roman Catholics, referring to the town in central Italy to which in the 13th century the Holy House of the Virgin is supposed to have been miraculously transported from Nazareth by angels.

Loretta F Variant of **»Lauretta**, normally borne by Roman Catholics, among whom it is associated with **»Loreto**.

Lori F Pet form of **»Lorraine** or variant of **»Laurie**.

Lorin M Mainly U.S.: variant spelling of the male name **»Loren**. The spelling **»Lorrin** is also found.

Lorinda F Elaboration of **»Lora**, with the addition of the productive feminine suffix -inda.

Lorna F Invented by R. D. Blackmore for the heroine of his novel *Lorna Doone* (1869), child captive of the outlawed Doones on Exmoor, who is eventually discovered to be Lady Lorna Dugal, daughter of the Earl of Dugal. Blackmore seems to have derived the name from the Scottish placename *Lorn(e)* (Gaelic *Latharna*), a territory in Argyll. The given name is popular in Scotland.

Lorne M Mainly Canadian: of uncertain derivation, presumably from the territory of *Lorne* in Argyll (cf. **»Lorna**). One of the earliest bearers was the Canadian actor Lorne Greene (1915–87).

Lorraine F Transferred use of the surname, in origin denoting a migrant from the province of Lorraine in eastern France. *Lorraine* began to be used as a girl's name in Scotland in the 19th century, and during the 1950s and 60s was very popular. The alternative spellings **Loraine** and **Lorane** are also found.

Lorri F Pet form of **»Lorraine** or fanciful spelling of **»Laurie**.

Lorrin M Mainly U.S.: variant spelling of the male name **»Loren**.

Lottie F Pet form of **»Charlotte**. It was common in the 19th century, and is enjoying a modest revival at the present time. The spelling **Lotty** is also found.

Louella F Modern coinage from the first syllable of **»Louise** + the productive suffix -ella (an Italian or Latinate feminine diminutive). It is particularly associated with the Hollywood gossip columnist

Louella Parsons (1880–1972). The spelling **Luella** is also found.

Louis M French name, of Germanic (Frankish) origin, from *hlud* 'fame' + *wīg* 'warrior' (modern German **Ludwig**). It was very common in French royal and noble families. Louis I (778–840) was the son of Charlemagne, who ruled both as King of France and Holy Roman Emperor. Altogether, the name was borne by sixteen kings of France up to the French Revolution, in which Louis XVI perished. Louis XIV, 'the Sun King' (1638–1715), reigned for seventy-two years (1643–1715), presiding in the middle part of his reign over a period of unparalleled French power and prosperity. In modern times *Louis* is also found in the English-speaking world (usually pronounced 'loo-ee'). In Britain the Anglicized form **Lewis** is rather more common, whereas in America the reverse is true.

Louisa F Latinate feminine form of **Louis**, commonly used as an English given name since the 18th century.

Louise F French feminine form of **Louis**, introduced to England in the 17th century.

Lourdes F Religious name borne by Roman Catholics, referring to the place in southern France where a shrine was established after a young peasant girl, Bernadette Soubirous, had visions of the Virgin Mary and uncovered a healing spring in 1858. In recent times, Lourdes has become a major centre for pilgrimage, especially by the sick or handicapped.

Lovell M Transferred use of the surname, which originated in the Middle Ages from the Old (Norman) French nickname *Louvel* 'wolf-cub'.

Lowell M Mainly U.S.: transferred use of the surname of a well-known New England family, whose members included the poet Robert Lowell (1917–77). The surname is a variant of **Lovell**.

Lowry M This is generally a transferred use of the surname, which has two origins. As a Scottish and Northern English name it is from a pet form of **»Laurence**. In Ireland it is an Anglicization of the Gaelic name **Labhraidh** 'spokesman', also Anglicized as **»Lavery**.

Loyal M Mainly U.S.: name derived from the modern English adjective.

Luana F First used in King Vidor's 1932 film *The Bird of Paradise* as the name of a Polynesian maiden, and taken up since. It is apparently an arbitrary combination of the syllables *Lu-* and *-ana*. The variants **Luanna** and **Luanne** are also found.

Lucas M In part a learned form of **»Luke**, in part a transferred use of the surname derived from it in the Middle Ages. The Latin form *Lucas* was often used in the Middle Ages in written documents in place of the spoken vernacular form *Luke*, hence the common surname. It is also the spelling preferred in the Authorized Version of the New Testament, which has had some influence on its selection as a given name.

Lucetta F Fanciful elaboration of **»Lucia** or **»Lucy**, formed with the productive suffix *-etta*, originally an Italian feminine diminutive suffix. The name is found in Shakespeare, where it is borne by Julia's waiting woman in *Two Gentlemen of Verona*, but it is not much used in Italy and was unusual in England before the 19th century.

Lucia F Feminine form of the old Roman given name *Lucius*, which is probably a derivative of Latin *lux* 'light'. The girl's name is common in Italy and elsewhere, and is found as a learned, Latinate doublet of *Lucy* in England. St Lucia of Syracuse, who was martyred in 304, was a very popular saint in the Middle Ages.

Lucilla F Latin pet form of **»Lucia**, with the diminutive feminine suffix *-illa*. This name was borne by various minor early saints, including one martyred at Rome in c.258.

Lucille F French form of **»Lucilla**, used also in the English-speaking world, especially in the United States. A well-known bearer of the name was the American comedy actress Lucille Ball (1910–89).

Lucinda F Derivative of **»Lucia**, with the addition of the productive suffix -inda. The formation is first found in Cervantes's *Don Quixote* (1605), but was not much used in the 17th century except as a literary name. It enjoyed considerable popularity in England in the 18th century, and has been in use ever since.

Lucretia F Feminine form of the Roman family name *Lucretius*, which is of unknown derivation. In Roman legend, this is the name of a Roman maiden of the 5th century BC who killed herself after being raped by the King of Rome. It was also borne by a Spanish martyr who perished under Diocletian, but is now chiefly remembered as the name of Lucretia Borgia (1480–1519), regarded in legend as a demon poisoner who had incestuous relations with her father, Pope Alexander VI, and her brother Cesare. Although these allegations cannot be disproved, history records her, after her marriage in 1501 to Alfonso d'Este, Duke of Ferrara, as being a beautiful, intelligent, and fair-minded woman, and a generous patron of the arts.

Lucy F From Old French *Lucie*, the vernacular form of **»Lucia**. It is sometimes assumed that *Lucy* is a pet form of **»Lucinda**, but there is no etymological justification for this assumption. It was in fairly widespread use in the Middle Ages, and increased greatly in popularity in the 18th century.

Ludmila F Russian and Czech: from a Slavonic personal name derived from *lud* 'people', 'tribe' + *mil* 'grace', 'favour'. St Ludmila (d. 921) was a duchess of Bohemia and grandmother of St Wenceslas; she was murdered on the orders of her mother-in-law and came to be regarded as a martyr. In the English-speaking world, the spelling **Ludmilla** is also found.

Ludovic M From Latin *Ludovicus*, the form used in medieval documents to represent the Germanic name *Hludwig* (see **»Louis**). In the west of Scotland it came to be used as an Anglicized form of the Gaelic name *Maol Dòmhnaich* 'devotee of the Lord', probably because both contain the same succession of sounds: l-d-o-v-c(h).

Luella F Variant spelling of **»Louella**.

Luke M Middle English vernacular form of **»Lucas**, Latin form of the Greek name *Loukas* 'man from Lucania'. This owes its perennial popularity throughout Christian Europe to the fact that, since the 2nd century, the third gospel in the New Testament has been ascribed to the Lucas or Luke mentioned at various places in Acts and in the Epistles. Little is known about him beyond the facts that he was a doctor, a Gentile, and a friend and convert of St Paul.

Lulu F Pet form, originally a reduplicated nursery form, of *Luise*, the German form of **»Louise**. It is now also used in the English-speaking world, both as a pet form of *Louise* and as an independent given name.

Luther M From the German surname, which is from a Germanic personal name derived from *liut* 'people' + *heri, hari* 'army'. It is commonly bestowed among evangelical Protestants, in honour of the ecclesiastical reformer and theologian Martin Luther (1483–1546). In recent times it has also been bestowed in honour of the assassinated civil rights leader Martin Luther King (1929–68).

Lyall M Transferred use of the Scottish surname, which is probably derived from the Old Norse personal name *Liulfr*, of which the second element is *úlfr* 'wolf'. See also **»Lyle**.

Lydia F Of Greek origin, meaning 'woman from Lydia', an area of Asia Minor. The name is borne in the Bible by a woman of Thyatira who was converted by St Paul and who entertained him in her house (Acts 16:14–15, 40). It has enjoyed steady popularity in the English-speaking world since the 17th century.

Lyle M Transferred use of the mainly Scottish surname, in origin a local name for someone who came 'from the island' (Anglo-Norman *de l'isle*). (The island in question would in many cases have been an area of higher, dry ground in a marsh or fen, rather than in a sea or river.) There may have been some confusion with **≫Lyall**.

Lyn F Variant spelling of **≫Lynn**.

Lynda F Variant spelling of **≫Linda**.

Lyndon M Transferred use of the surname, in origin a local name from a place so called in the former county of Rutland (now part of Leicestershire). In the United States, use as a given name has been influenced by the American president Lyndon Baines Johnson (1908–73). The spelling **≫Lindon** is also found.

Lynette F In modern use a derivative of **≫Lynn**, formed with the French feminine diminutive suffix *-ette*. However, this is not the origin for the name as used in Tennyson's *Idylls of the King* (1859–85), through which it first came to public attention. There, it represents an altered form of some Celtic original; cf. Welsh **≫Eluned**. The spelling variants **Lynnette**, **≫Lin(n)ette**, and **≫Linnet** are also found.

Lynn F Of uncertain origin: possibly an altered short form of **≫Linda**, or a derivative of the French name *Line*, which originated as a short form of various girls' names ending in this syllable, for example *Caroline*. The element *-lyn(n)* has been a productive suffix of English girls' given names since at least the middle of the 20th century. *Lynn* itself has enjoyed considerable popularity in recent times.

Lynsey F Variant spelling of **≫Lindsay**.

Lysette F Variant spelling of **≫Lisette**.

Lyssa F Short form of **≫Alyssa**. In form it coincides
with the name, in Greek mythology, of the personification of madness or frenzy. See also **≫Lissa**.

M

Mabel F Originally a nickname from the Old French vocabulary word *amabel*, *amable* 'lovely' (related to modern English *amiable* 'friendly', 'good-humoured'). The initial vowel began to be lost as early as the 12th century, but a short vowel in the resulting first syllable was standard, giving a rhyme with *babble*, until the 19th century, when people began to pronounced the name to rhyme with *table*.

Mabelle F Elaborated form of **»Mabel**, under the influence of the French phrase *ma belle* 'my beautiful one'.

Mable F Variant spelling of **»Mabel**.

Mackenzie M, F Transferred use of the Scottish surname, which is from Gaelic *Mac Coinnich*, a patronymic from *Coinneach* 'comely'. In North America this is more commonly a girl's name than a boy's one. The spelling **Makenzie** is also found.

Maddison F, M Variant spelling of **»Madison**.

Madelaine F Variant spelling of **»Madeleine**.

Madeleine F The French form of the byname of a character in the New Testament, Mary *Magdalene* 'Mary of Magdala' (Magdala was a village on Lake Galilee). The woman 'which had been healed of evil spirits and infirmities' (Luke 8:2) was given this name in the Bible to distinguish her from other bearers of the name **»Mary**. Variants include **»Madelaine**, **»Madeline**, **»Mad(e)lyn**, **»Madoline**, and **»Magdalen**.

Madeline F Variant of **»Madeleine**, common especially in the United States.

Madelyn F Variant of **»Madeleine**, influenced by the suffix *-lyn* (see **»Lynn**).

Madison F, M Transferred use of the surname, in origin a metronymic from the medieval female given name *Madde*, a pet form of **»Madeleine**. Use as a given name in the United States seems to have been influenced by James Madison (1751–1836), who was president during the War of 1812 and took part in drafting the U.S. constitution and Bill of Rights. It has recently enjoyed something of a vogue as a girl's name. The spelling **»Maddison** is also found.

Madlyn F Contracted spelling of **»Madelyn**.

Madoc M Welsh (also **Madog**): traditional name, probably derived from the vocabulary word **mad** 'good', 'fortunate', which survives in various surnames (principally *Maddox*). It has recently been revived as a given name in Wales, and is also found in Ireland in the Gaelic spelling **Maedhóg**.

Madoline F Variant of **»Madeline** (see **»Madeleine**).

Madonna F From an Italian title of the Virgin Mary (literally 'my lady'), applied to countless Renaissance paintings of a young woman (with and without an infant), representing the mother of Christ. Its use as a given name is a fairly recent phenomenon, arising among Americans of Italian descent. The name is now particularly associated with the American pop star and actress Madonna Ciccone (b. 1959).

Mae F Variant spelling of **»May**, possibly influenced by **»Maeve**. It has been most notably borne by the American film actress Mae West (1892–1980), whose prominent bust led to her name being given to a type of inflatable life jacket used in the Second World War.

Maeve F Irish: Anglicized form of Gaelic **Meadhbh**, an ancient name meaning 'intoxicating', 'she who makes drunk'. It is borne by the Queen of Connacht in the Irish epic *Táin Bó Cuailnge*. In this, Meadhbh leads a raid on Ulster in order to seize the Brown Bull of Cooley, although she is repulsed by the hero Cú Chulainn. Shakespeare's Queen Mab, 'the fairy's midwife' (*Romeo and Juliet* I. iv. 53), owes her name, if nothing else, to the legendary Queen of Connacht. The spellings **»Mave** and **»Meave** are also found.

Magdalen F English vernacular form of **»Madeleine**, the usual form of the given name in the Middle Ages.

Magnus M Originally a Latin byname meaning 'great', this was first extracted from the name of *Charlemagne* (recorded in Latin chronicles as *Carolus Magnus* 'Charles the Great') and used as a given name by the Scandinavians. It was borne by seven medieval kings of Norway, including Magnus I (1024–47), known as Magnus the Good, and Magnus VI (1238–80), known as Magnus the Law Mender. There are several early Scandinavian saints called Magnus, including an earl of Orkney (d. 1116), to whom Kirkwall cathedral is dedicated. The name was imported to Scotland and Ireland during the Middle Ages.

Maidie F From a pet form of the vocabulary word *maid* 'young woman', originally used as an affectionate nickname.

Mair F Welsh form of **»Mary**, derived from Latin *Maria* via Old Welsh *Meir*. See also **»Mari**.

Máire F Irish Gaelic form of **»Mary**.

Mairéad F Irish Gaelic form of **»Margaret**, pronounced 'my-raid' (in Munster) or 'ma-**raid**' (in Connacht). The name is also used in Scotland, where it is spelled **Mairead** or **Maighread**.

Mairenn F Irish: traditional Gaelic name, said to be derived from *muir* 'sea' + *fhionn* 'fair'. It is also spelled **»Muireann**.

Màiri F Scottish Gaelic form of **»Mary**.

Maisie F Scottish: pet form derived from *Mairead*, the Gaelic form of **»Margaret**, with the Scottish and northern English diminutive suffix *-ie*.

Malachy M Traditional name in Ireland, representing an adaptation of more than one medieval Gaelic name to a biblical name. St Malachy (1095–1148), born Máel Maedhog (see **»Madoc**) Ó Morgair, was a famous bishop of Armagh, who did much to promote greater contact between the Church in Ireland and the papacy in Rome. His biography was written by St Bernard of Clairvaux. Earlier, *Malachy* had been used to refer to an Irish king who defeated the Norse invaders. His Gaelic baptismal name was *Maoileachlainn* 'devotee of St Seachnall or Secundinus', but in medieval sources this has already been altered to coincide with that of the biblical prophet **Malachi**. Malachi was the last of the twelve minor prophets of the Old Testament; he foretold the coming of Christ and his name means, appropriately, 'my messenger' in Hebrew.

Malcolm M Anglicized form of the medieval Gaelic name *Mael Coluim* 'devotee of St Columba'. Columba, whose name means 'dove' in Latin, was a 6th-century monk of Irish origin who played a leading part in the conversion to Christianity of Scotland and northern England; see also **»Calum** and **»Colm**. He has always been one of the most popular saints in Scotland, but in the Middle Ages it was felt to be presumptuous to give the names of saints directly to children; instead their blessing was invoked by prefixing the name with *mael* 'devotee of' or *gille* 'servant of'.

Mallory F, M Especially North American: transferred use of the surname, which originated as a Norman French nickname for an unfortunate person, from Old French *malheure* 'unhappy' or 'unlucky'. It is now used mainly as a girl's name. The variant spelling **Mallery** is also found.

Malvina F Semi-fictional name, based on Gaelic *mala mhìn* 'smooth brow', invented by James Macpherson (1736–96), the Scottish poet who published works allegedly translated from the ancient Gaelic bard Ossian. The name became popular in Scandinavia because of the admiration of the Emperor Napoleon for the Ossianic poems: he was godfather to several of the children of his marshal Jean Baptiste Bernadotte (who ruled Norway and Sweden (1818–44) as Karl XIV Johan) and imposed his own taste in names on them, hence the frequency of Ossianic given names in Scandinavia.

Mamie F Short form of ≫**Margaret** or ≫**Mary**, originating as a nursery form. It has occasionally been used as an independent given name, especially in America, where it was the name by which the wife of President Eisenhower was usually known.

Mandy F Pet form of ≫**Amanda**, now sometimes used as an independent given name.

Manfred M From an old Germanic personal name, usually said to be from *man* 'man' + *fred, frid* 'peace'. However, it is more likely that the first element was *magin* 'strength' (the usual Norman form being *Mainfred*) or *manag* 'much'. This name was introduced to Britain by the Normans, but it did not become part of the common stock of English given names, and was reintroduced from Germany in the 19th century. It was a traditional name among the Hohenstaufens, and was borne by the last Hohenstaufen king of Sicily (1258–66). The name was also used by Byron for the central character in his poetic drama *Manfred* (1817), a brooding outcast, tormented by incestuous love for his half-sister.

Manley M Transferred use of the surname, which in most cases originated as a local name from places so named in Devon and Cheshire. Its choice as a first name may well have been influenced by association with the

vocabulary word *manly* and the hope that the qualities
denoted by the adjective would be attributes of the
bearer. The vocabulary word may also lie behind some
cases of the surname, as a nickname for a 'manly'
person.

Mara   F   Of biblical origin, from Hebrew *Mara* 'bitter', a
name referred to by Naomi when she went back to
Bethlehem because of the famine in the land of Moab
and the deaths of her husband and two sons: 'call me
not Naomi, call me Mara: for the Almighty hath dealt
very bitterly with me' (Ruth 1:20).

Marc   M   French form of **»Mark**, now also quite popular
in the English-speaking world. It was given some
currency in England in the 1960s by the pop singer
Marc Bolan.

Marcel   M   French: from the Latin name *Marcellus*,
originally a pet form of **»Marcus**. The name has always
been popular in France as it was borne by a 3rd-century
missionary to Gaul, martyred at Bourges with his
companion Anastasius. It is occasionally also used in
the English-speaking world.

Marcella   F   Feminine form of *Marcellus*; see **»Marcel**.
St Marcella was a Roman noblewoman of the late 4th
century who lodged St Jerome for three years.

Marcia   F   Often used as a feminine equivalent of
»Mark, but in fact a feminine form of *Marcius*, itself a
derivative of **»Marcus**. It was the name of three minor
saints. The variant spelling **»Marsha** is also found.

Marcus   M   The original Latin form of **»Mark**, of
unknown derivation; it may be connected with *Mars*,
the name of the Roman god of war, or the adjective *mas*
'male', 'virile' (genitive *maris*). This was one of the few
Roman given names of the classical period: there were
only about a dozen such names in general use, with
perhaps another dozen confined to particular families.
Marcus was rarely used as a given name in the English-

speaking world until recent years, when it has been seized on by parents looking for a distinctive form of a popular name. As an African-American name it is sometimes bestowed in honour of the Black Consciousness leader Marcus Garvey (1887–1940).

Marea   F   Altered spelling of ➤➤**Maria**.

Mared   F   Welsh form of ➤➤**Margaret**, a simplified form of *Marged*.

Maretta   F   Scottish: Anglicized form of *Mairead*, the Gaelic version of ➤➤**Margaret**. See also ➤➤**Marietta**.

Marga   F   Short form of ➤➤**Margaret** or any of the large number of related names beginning with these two syllables.

Margaret   F   An extremely common medieval given name, derived via Old French *Marguerite* and Latin *Margarīta* from Greek *Margarītēs*, from *margaron* 'pearl'. The first St Margaret was martyred at Antioch in Pisidia during the persecution instigated by the Emperor Diocletian in the early 4th century. However, there is some doubt about her name, as the same saint is venerated in the Orthodox Church as ➤➤**Marina**. There were several other saintly bearers of the name, including St Margaret of Scotland (d. 1093), wife of King Malcolm Canmore and daughter of Edmund Ironside of England. It was also the name of the wife of Henry VI of England, Margaret of Anjou (1430–82), and of Margaret Tudor (1489–1541), sister of Henry VIII, who married James IV of Scotland and ruled as regent there after his death. See also ➤➤**Margery**, ➤➤**Marjorie**. There are numerous short forms, pet forms, and derivatives, including ➤➤**Meg**, **Peg**, **Madge**, **Marge**, ➤➤**Maggie**, **Meggie**, ➤➤**Peggy**, **Margie**, and ➤➤**May**. See also ➤➤**Daisy**.

Margery   F   The usual medieval vernacular form of ➤➤**Margaret** (now also commonly spelled ➤➤**Marjorie**).

m

Margot   F   French pet form of >>**Marguerite**, now used as an independent given name. In England it is still usually pronounced in the French way, but in Eastern Europe the final consonant is sounded, and this has had some influence in America.

Marguerite   F   French form of >>**Margaret**, also used in the English-speaking world, where its use has been reinforced by the fact that the name was adopted in the 19th century for a garden flower, a large cultivated variety of daisy. *Margaret* was earlier used in English as a dialect word denoting the ox-eye daisy, and the French equivalent was borrowed into English just in time to catch the vogue for deriving girls' names from the names of flowers. See also >>**Daisy**.

Mari   F   Welsh form of >>**Mary**; see also >>**Mair**.

Maria   F   Latin form of >>**Mary**. In the English-speaking world it is a learned revival dating from the 18th century, pronounced both 'ma-**ree**-a' and, more traditionally, 'ma-**rye**-a'. The Latin name *Maria* is actually the feminine of the pre-Christian name >>**Marius**, but it owes its popularity in Christian tradition to being taken as the Latin equivalent of *Mariam*, Aramaic form of the Hebrew name >>**Miriam**.

Mariah   F   Elaborated spelling of >>**Maria**, influenced by female names of Hebrew origin such as >>**Hanna(h)**, ending in -*a* plus an optional final *h*.

Mariamne   F   The form of >>**Miriam** used by the Jewish historian Flavius Josephus, writing in Latin in the 1st century BC, as the name of the wife of King Herod. On the basis of this evidence, it has been thought by some to be closer to the original form of the name actually borne by the Virgin Mary, and has therefore been bestowed in her honour.

Marian   F   Originally a medieval variant spelling of >>**Marion**. However, in the 18th century, when combined names began to come into fashion, it was sometimes understood as a combination of **»Mary** and **»Ann**.

Marianne   F   Extended spelling of **»Marian**, reinforcing the association of the second element with **»Ann(e)**. It also represents a French assimilated form of **»Mariamne**. *Marianne* is the name used for the symbolic figure of the French Republic.

Marie   F   French form of **»Maria**. When first introduced to England in the Middle Ages, it was Anglicized in pronunciation and respelled **»Mary**. This French form was reintroduced into the English-speaking world as a separate name in the 19th century, and is still pronounced more or less in the French manner, although sometimes with the stress on the first syllable.

Mariella   F   Italian pet form of **»Maria**, now sometimes used as an independent given name in the English-speaking world.

Marietta   F   Italian pet form of **»Maria**, now occasionally used as a given name in the English-speaking world. In Gaelic Scotland *Mar(i)etta* is sometimes found as an Anglicized form of **Mairead**, the Gaelic form of **»Margaret**.

Marigold   F   One of the group of names that were adopted from words for flowers in the late 19th and early 20th centuries. The Old English name of the flower was *golde*, presumably from *gold* (the precious metal), in reference to its colour. At some time before the 14th century the flower became associated with the Virgin Mary, and its name was extended to *marigold*.

Marilee   F   Modern coinage, a combination of **»Mary** and **»Lee**.

Marilene   F   Modern coinage, a combination of the name **»Mary** with the productive suffix *-lene*, or else a variant of **»Marilyn**.

Marilyn   F   20th-century elaboration of **»Mary**, with the addition of the productive suffix *-lyn* (see **»Lynn**). Use of the name peaked in the 1940s and 1950s but has since been surprisingly moderate considering the huge popularity of the film star Marilyn Monroe (1926–62). The spellings **Marilynn**, **»Marylyn(n)**, and **»Marilene** are also found.

Marina F From a Late Latin name, a feminine form of the family name *Marīnus*. This was a derivative of *Marius*, a traditional name of uncertain derivation, but even during the early centuries AD it was widely assumed to be identical with Latin *marīnus* 'of the sea'.

Marion F Originally a medieval French pet form of **»Marie**, introduced to Britain in the Middle Ages, and now completely Anglicized in pronunciation.

Marisa F 20th-century elaboration of **»Maria**, with the suffix *-isa* abstracted from such names as *Lisa* and *Louisa*.

Marissa F Variant of **»Marisa**, with the suffix *-issa*, abstracted from names such as *Clarissa*.

Marius M Latin name occasionally used in English and other languages. It is of uncertain origin: it may be connected with *Mars*, the name of the god of war, or perhaps *mas, maris* 'virile'. The Italian, Spanish, and Portuguese equivalent **Mario** is extremely popular, being taken as the masculine form of **»Maria** and therefore associated with the cult of the Virgin Mary.

Marjorie F The usual modern spelling of **»Margery**. It seems to have arisen as the result of folk etymological association of the name with that of the herb *marjoram*. The spelling **Marjory** is also found.

Mark M From the Latin name **»Marcus**, borne by the Evangelist, author of the second gospel in the New Testament, and by several other early and medieval saints. In Arthurian legend, King Mark is the aged ruler of Cornwall to whom Isolde is brought as a bride by Tristan; his name was presumably of Celtic origin,

perhaps derived from the element *march* 'horse', and is
unrelated to the Latin name.

Marlene F Contracted form of Latin *Maria Magdalene*
(see **»Madeleine**). The name is of German origin, but
is now also widely used in the English-speaking world,
normally in a pronunciation with two syllables.
Probably the first bearer of the name was the film star
Marlene Dietrich (1901–92), who was christened Maria
Magdalena Dietrich. The name was further
popularized in the 1940s by the wartime song 'Lili
Marlene'.

Marlon M Name apparently first brought to public
attention by the American actor Marlon Brando (1924–
2004). The name is of uncertain origin, possibly derived
from **»Marc** with the addition of the French diminutive
suffix *-lon*. The actor's family is partly of French
extraction.

Marmaduke M Of uncertain derivation. It is generally
held to be an Anglicized form of the Old Irish name
Mael-Maedóc 'devotee of Maedóc'. The name *Maedóc*
was borne by various early Irish saints, most notably a
6th-century abbot of Clonmore and a 7th-century
bishop of Ferns. Mael-Maedóc Ó Morgair (1095–1148)
was a reformer of the Church in Ireland and a friend of
Bernard of Clairvaux. However, the modern Gaelic
form (from *c.*1200) is *Maol-Maodhóg* (pronounced 'mul-
may-og'), so that the name would have had to have
been borrowed into English before this loss of the *d*.
Marmaduke has never been common except in a small
area of North Yorkshire.

Marna F Swedish vernacular form of **»Marina**, now
occasionally also used in the English-speaking world.
The pet form **Marnie** is well established as an
independent given name.

Marquis M Mainly U.S.: taken from the vocabulary
word denoting the rank of nobility. This derives from

Old French *marchis*, i.e. 'lord of the marches (border districts)'. The spelling was later influenced by the Provençal and Spanish equivalents. Use as a given name may also have been influenced by the Scottish surname *McMarquis*, Gaelic *Mac Marcuis* 'son of »**Marcus**'.

Marsh   M   Transferred use of the surname, in origin a local name for someone who lived on a patch of marshy ground, from Middle English *mersche*. It is also used as an informal short form of »**Marshall**, and possibly on occasion as a masculine equivalent of »**Marsha**, by back-formation.

Marsha   F   Phonetic spelling of »**Marcia**, associated particularly with the American film star Marsha Hunt (b. 1917).

Marshall   M   Transferred use of the surname, derived from a Norman French occupational term, ultimately from Germanic *marah* 'horse' + *scalc* 'servant'. Originally it denoted someone who looked after horses, but by the time of surname formation it had come to mean 'shoeing smith'; later it was used to denote an official whose duties were largely ceremonial. The surname is pronounced the same as the Latin name *Martial* (from Latin *Mars*; cf. »**Martin**). This may have contributed to its use as a given name.

Martha   F   New Testament name, of Aramaic origin, meaning 'lady'. It was borne by the sister of Lazarus and Mary of Bethany (John 11:1). According to Luke 10:38, when Jesus visited the house of Mary and Martha, Mary sat at his feet, listening to him, while Martha 'was cumbered about much serving'. For this reason, the name *Martha* has always been associated with hard domestic work and practical common sense, as opposed to the contemplative life.

Marti   F   Short form of »**Martina** or »**Martine**. Its best-known bearer in Britain is the English comedienne

Marti Caine (1945–96). The spellings **Martie** and
»Marty are also found.

Martin M English form of the Latin name *Martīnus*.
This was probably originally derived from *Mars*
(genitive *Martis*), the name of the Roman god of war
(and earlier of fertility). *Martin* became very popular
in the Middle Ages, especially on the Continent, as a
result of the fame of St Martin of Tours. He was born
the son of a Roman officer in Upper Pannonia, and
although he became a leading figure in the 4th-century
Church, he is chiefly remembered for having divided
his cloak in two and given half to a beggar. The name
was also borne by five popes, including one who
defended Roman Catholic dogma against Eastern
Orthodox theology. He died after suffering
imprisonment and privations in Naxos and public
humiliation in Constantinople, and was promptly
acclaimed a martyr by supporters of the Roman Church.   **m**
Among Protestants, the name is sometimes bestowed
in honour of the German theologian Martin Luther
(1483–1546); *Martin* was used as a symbolic name for
the Protestant Church in satires by both Dryden and
Swift. A further influence may be its use as the given
name of the civil-rights leader Martin Luther King
(1929–68). The spelling **»Martyn** is also found.

Martina F Feminine form of the Latin name *Martīnus*
(see **»Martin**). It was in use from an early period, being
borne by a notorious poisoner mentioned by the
historian Tacitus. The 3rd-century saint of the same
name is of doubtful authenticity. Modern use of the
name in the English-speaking world seems to be the
result of German or Eastern European influence, as in
the case of the tennis player Martina Navratilova (b.
1956 in Czechoslovakia).

Martine F French form of **»Martina**, also used in the
English-speaking world.

Marty M, F Short form of ≫**Martin** or of ≫**Martina** and ≫**Martine**. It has sometimes been used as an independent boy's name in the latter part of the 20th century, being associated particularly with the comedian Marty Feldman (1933–83), the 1960s pop singer Marty Wilde (b. 1938), and the country-and-western singer Marty Robbins (1925–82).

Martyn M Variant spelling of ≫**Martin**.

Marvin M Medieval variant of ≫**Mervyn**. Modern use may represent a transferred use of the surname derived from this in the Middle Ages. It is very popular in the United States, where it is associated in particular with the American singer Marvin Gaye (1939–84).

Mary F Originally a Middle English Anglicized form of French ≫**Marie**, from Latin ≫**Maria**. This is a New Testament form of ≫**Miriam**, which St Jerome associated with a Latin phrase meaning 'drop of the sea' (*stilla maris*, later altered to *stella maris* 'star of the sea'). *Mary* is the most popular and enduring of all female Christian names, being the name of the Virgin Mary, mother of Jesus Christ, who has been the subject of a cult from earliest times. In the New Testament, it is also the name of several other women: Mary Magdalene (see ≫**Madeleine**); Mary the sister of Martha, who sat at Jesus's feet while Martha served (Luke 10:38–42; John 11:1–46; 12:1–9) and who came to be taken in Christian tradition as symbolizing the value of a contemplative life; the mother of St Mark (Colossians 4:10); and a Roman matron mentioned by St Paul (Romans 16:6). The name was extremely common among early Christians, several saints among them, and by the Middle Ages was well established in every country in Europe at every level of society.

Marylyn F Variant spelling of ≫**Marilyn**. The spelling **Marylynn** is also found.

Mason M Transferred use of the surname, which originated in the early Middle Ages as an occupational name for a worker in stone, Old French *maçon* (of Germanic origin).

Mathew M Variant spelling of »**Matthew**.

Mathias M Variant spelling of »**Matthias**.

Matilda F Latinized form of a Germanic personal name derived from *maht, meht* 'might' + *hild* 'battle'. This was the name of an early German queen (895–968), wife of Henry the Fowler, who was noted for her piety and generosity. It was also the name of the wife of William the Conqueror and of the daughter of Henry I of England (see »**Maud**). The name was introduced into England by the Normans, and this Latinized form is the one that normally occurs in medieval records, while the vernacular form *Maud* was the one in everyday use. *Matilda* was revived in England as a learned form in the 18th century. The spelling **Mathilda** is also found.

m

Matthew M English form of the name of the Christian evangelist, author of the first gospel in the New Testament. His name is a form of the Hebrew name *Mattathia,* meaning 'gift of God', which is fairly common in the Old Testament, being rendered in the Authorized Version in a number of different forms: *Mattan(i)ah, Mattatha(h), Mattithiah, Mattathias,* and so on. In the Authorized Version, the evangelist is regularly referred to as *Matthew,* while the apostle chosen to replace Judas Iscariot is distinguished as »**Matthias**. The spelling »**Mathew** is also found.

Matthias M New Testament Greek form of the Hebrew name *Mattathia* (see »**Matthew**), or rather of an Aramaic derivative. The Latin form of the name is *Matthaeus.* In English the form *Matthias* is used in the Authorized Version of the New Testament to distinguish the disciple who was chosen to replace Judas Iscariot (Acts 1:23–26) from the evangelist *Matthew.* However, this distinction is not observed in other languages, where *Matthias* (or a version of it) is often a learned doublet existing alongside a vernacular derivative.

Maud F Medieval vernacular form of **»Matilda**. This form was characteristically Low German (i.e. including medieval Dutch and Flemish). In Flemish and Dutch the letter *-t-* was generally lost when it occurred between vowels, giving forms such as *Ma(h)auld*. The wife of William the Conqueror, who bore this name, was the daughter of Baldwin, Count of Flanders. *Maud* or *Matilda* was also the name of the daughter (1102–67) of Henry I of England; she was married early in life to the Holy Roman Emperor Henry V, and later disputed the throne of England with her cousin Stephen. In 1128 she married Geoffrey, Count of Anjou. A medieval chronicler commented, 'she was a good woman, but she had little bliss with him'. The name *Maud* became quite common in England in the 19th century, when its popularity was influenced in part by Tennyson's poem *Maud*, published in 1855.

Maude F Variant of **»Maud**, the usual spelling of the name in North America.

Maura F Of Celtic origin. St Maura was a 5th-century martyr, of whom very little is known. In Ireland *Maura* is now commonly regarded as a form of **»Mary** (cf. **»Moira** and **»Maureen**).

Maureen F Anglicized form of Irish Gaelic **Máirín**, a pet form of **»Máire**. Among other influences, the name was popularized by the film actress Maureen O'Hara (b. 1920). See also **»Moreen**. The spellings **Maurene** and **Maurine** are also found.

Maurice M From the Late Latin name *Mauricius*, a derivative of *Maurus* (a byname meaning 'Moor', i.e. 'dark', 'swarthy'), borne by, among others, an early Byzantine emperor (c.539–602). It was introduced to Britain by the Normans, and was popular in the Middle

English period, but was not widely adopted by the nobility, and became rare in the 17th century. It is now sometimes believed in Britain and America to be a mainly French name, perhaps because of the enormous popular influence of the French singer and film actor Maurice Chevalier (1888–1972). See also **»Morris**.

Mave F Variant spelling of **»Maeve**, also sometimes used as an informal short form of **»Mavis**.

Mavis F Not found before the last decade of the 19th century. It belongs to the small class of girls' names taken from vocabulary words denoting birds. *Mavis* is another word for the song-thrush, first attested in Chaucer.

Max M Short form of **»Maximilian**, **»Maxwell**, and various other names formed with this first syllable. It is also a popular independent given name.

Maximilian M From the Latin name *Maximiliānus* (a pet form of *Maximus* 'greatest'). This was borne by a 3rd-century saint numbered among the 'Fourteen Holy Helpers'. Although already existing, the name was reanalysed in the 15th century by the Emperor Friedrich III, who bestowed it on his first-born son (1459–1519), as a blend of the names *Maximus* and *Aemiliānus*, intending thereby to pay homage to the two Roman generals Q. Fabius Maximus Cunctator and P. Cornelius Scipio Aemilianus. The name became traditional in the Habsburg family in Austria-Hungary and also in the royal house of Bavaria. It was borne by an ill-fated Austrian archduke (1832–67) who was set up as emperor of Mexico but later overthrown and shot.

m

Maxine F Modern coinage, first recorded around 1930. It is a derivative of **»Max** by addition of the feminine ending *-ine*.

Maxwell M Transferred use of the Scottish surname, in origin a local name from a minor place on the River Tweed, named as 'the stream (Old English *well(a)*) of

Mack'. The latter is a form of **»Magnus**. Maxwell is now also frequently taken as an expansion of **»Max**.

May F Pet form of both **»Margaret** and **»Mary**. The popularity of this name, which was at its height in the early 20th century, has been reinforced by the fact that it fits into the series of month names with **»April** and **»June**, and also belongs to the group of flower names, being another word for the hawthorn, whose white flowers blossom in May.

Maya F Latinate version of **»May** or a respelled form of the name of the Roman goddess *Māia*, influenced by the common English name *May*. The goddess Maia was one of the Pleiades, the daughters of Atlas and Pleione; she was the mother by Jupiter of Mercury. Her name seems to be derived from the root *māi-* 'great', seen also in Latin *māior* 'larger'. In the case of the American writer Maya Angelou (b. 1928), *Maya* is a nickname which she acquired in early childhood as a result of her younger brother's referring to her as 'mya sista'.

Maybelle F Altered form of **»Mabel**, influenced by the independent names **»May** and **»Belle**.

Maynard M Transferred use of the surname, which is derived from a Norman French given name of Germanic origin, from *magin* 'strength' + *hard* 'hardy', 'brave', 'strong'.

Meagan F Recent variant spelling of **»Megan**. The spelling **Meaghan** is also found.

Meave F Variant of **»Maeve**.

Meg F Short form of **»Margaret**, an alteration of the obsolete short form *Mag(g)* (as in **»Maggie**). Until recently *Meg* was a characteristically Scottish form, but it is now used more widely.

Megan F Welsh pet form of **»Meg**, nowadays generally used as an independent first name both within and beyond Wales, but nevertheless retaining a strong Welsh

flavour. The pseudo-Irish spellings **»Meghan** and
Meag(h)an are also found.

Meghan F Recent variant spelling of **»Megan**.

Mehetabel F Biblical name (meaning 'God makes
happy' in Hebrew), borne by a character who is
mentioned in passing in a genealogy (Genesis 36:39).
The name achieved some currency among the Puritans
in the 17th century but had gone out of regular use by
the 19th century. Nowadays, it is chiefly associated
with the poems of the companion (a cat) of Archy, the cockroach in the
poems of Don Marquis (1927). The variant spelling
Mehitabel is also found.

Meical M Welsh form of **»Michael**.

Meilyr M Welsh: traditional name derived from an Old
Celtic name, *Maglorīx*, derived from *maglos* 'chief' +
rīx 'ruler'.

Meinwen F Welsh: modern coinage composed of the
elements *main* 'slender' + *(g)wen*, feminine form of
gwyn 'white', 'fair', 'blessed', 'holy'.

Meirion M Welsh: traditional name, derived from Latin
Mariānus (a derivative of **»Marius**).

Mel M, F Short form of **»Melvin** or **»Melville**, or, in
the case of the girl's name, of **»Melanie** or the several
other girls' names beginning with this syllable. It is also
found independently as an Irish boy's name, having
been borne by a medieval saint who founded the
monastery at Ardagh.

Melanie F From an Old French form of Latin *Melania*,
a derivative of the Greek adjective (feminine form)
melaina 'black', 'dark'. This was the name of two Roman
saints of the 5th century, a grandmother and
granddaughter. St Melania the Younger was a member
of a rich patrician family. She led an austere and devout
Christian life and, on inheriting her father's wealth, she
emancipated her slaves, sold her property, and gave
the proceeds to the poor. She also established several

contemplative houses, including one on the Mount of
Olives, to which she eventually retired. The name
Melanie was introduced to England from France in the
Middle Ages, but died out. It was reintroduced and
became popular in the late 20th century. The spellings
Melany and >>**Melony** are also found.

Melinda F Modern coinage, derived from the first
syllable of names such as >>**Melanie** and >>**Melissa**, with
the addition of the productive suffix *-inda*.

Melissa F From the Greek word *melissa* 'bee'. The
variant **Melitta** is from an ancient Greek dialectal
variant of the same word.

Melody F Modern transferred use of the vocabulary
word (Greek *melōdía* 'singing of songs'), chosen partly
because of its pleasant associations and partly under
the influence of other girls' names with the same first
syllable.

Melony F Variant of >>**Melanie**, perhaps influenced by
>>**Melody**. The spellings **Mellony** and **Mel(l)oney** are
also found.

Melville M Mainly North American: transferred use of
the Scottish surname, which originated as a Norman
baronial name borne by the lords of a place in northern
France called *Malleville* 'bad settlement', i.e. settlement
on infertile land. The name was taken to Scotland as
early as the 12th century and became an important
surname there; use as a given name seems also to have
originated in Scotland.

Melvin M Modern name of uncertain origin, probably
a variant of the less common >>**Melville**. The variant
Melvyn is associated particularly with the film star
Melvyn Douglas (1901–81).

Mercedes F Spanish name associated with the cult of
the Virgin Mary, from the liturgical title *Maria de las
Mercedes* (literally, 'Mary of Mercies'; in English, 'Our
Lady of Ransom'). Latin *mercēdes* (plural) originally

meant 'wages' or 'ransom'. In Christian theology, Christ's sacrifice is regarded as a 'ransom for the sins of mankind', hence an 'act of ransom' was seen as identical with an 'act of mercy'. There are feasts in the Roman Catholic calendar on 10 August and 24 September to commemorate the Virgin under this name. As a given name, this is occasionally used in England, and more commonly in the United States, but normally only by Roman Catholics. It is associated with the American film actress Mercedes McCambridge (b. 1918). A more materialistic association with the high-class brand of German car so named may also be having an influence on the continued use of the name.

Mercia F Latinate elaboration of **»Mercy**, coinciding in form with the name of the Anglo-Saxon kingdom of Mercia, which dominated England during the 8th century under its king, Offa.

Mercy F From the vocabulary word denoting the quality of magnanimity, and in particular God's forgiveness of sinners, a quality much prized in Christian tradition. The word is derived from Latin *mercēs*, which originally meant 'wage' or 'reward' (see **»Mercedes**). The name was much favoured by the Puritans; Mercy is the companion of Christiana in the second part of John Bunyan's *Pilgrim's Progress* (1684). Subsequently, it fell out of use as a given name. In modern use, this is often an Anglicized form of *Mercedes*.

Meredith M, F From the Old Welsh personal name *Maredudd*, later *Meredudd*. This is of uncertain origin; the second element is Welsh *iudd* 'lord'. In recent years the name has sometimes been given to girls, presumably being thought of as the formal form of **»Merry**.

Merfyn M Welsh: traditional name derived from Old Welsh *mer*, probably meaning 'marrow' + *myn* 'eminent'. This name was borne by a shadowy 9th-century Welsh king.

Meriel F Variant of **»Muriel**, a Breton form of the underlying Celtic name.

Merle F, M Probably a contracted form of **»Meriel**, but also associated with the small class of girls' names derived from birds, since it is identical in form with Old French *merle* 'blackbird'. The name came to public notice in the 1930s with the actress Merle Oberon (1911–79). In Britain it is still normally a girl's name; in the United States it is more commonly borne by boys.

Merlin M Usual English form of the Welsh name *Myrddin*. The name is most famous as that of the legendary magician who guides the destiny of King Arthur. It is apparently composed of Old Celtic elements meaning 'sea' and 'hill' or 'fort', but it has been distorted by mediation through Old French sources, which associated the second element with the diminutive suffix *-lin*. The variant **Merlyn** is occasionally given to girls, as if containing the suffix of female names *-lyn*).

Merrill M Transferred use of the surname, which was derived in the Middle Ages from the girl's name **»Meriel** or **»Muriel**.

Merrily F Mainly U.S.: apparently a respelling of **»Marilee**, reshaped to coincide with the adverb derived from the adjective *merry*.

Merry F Apparently an assimilated form of **»Mercy**. In Dickens's novel *Martin Chuzzlewit* (1844), Mr Pecksniff's daughters **»Charity** and *Mercy* are known as *Cherry* and *Merry*. Nowadays the name is usually bestowed because of its association with the adjective denoting a cheerful and jolly temperament. In the accent of Canada and the central and northern United States there is no difference in pronunciation between *Merry* and *Mary*.

Mervyn M Anglicized form of Welsh **»Merfyn**, now also widely used beyond Wales. The spelling **Mervin** is also found.

Meryl F Recent coinage, associated chiefly with the American actress Meryl Streep (b. Mary Louise Streep in 1949). It has also been influenced in part by the ending *-yl* in names such as **»Cheryl**.

Meurig M Welsh form of **»Maurice**, derived from Latin *Mauricius* via Old Welsh *Mouric*.

Mia F Danish and Swedish pet form of **»Maria**. It came to be used in the English-speaking world largely as a result of the fame of the actress Mia Farrow (b. 1945).

Micah M Biblical name (meaning 'who is like Yahweh?' in Hebrew, and thus a doublet of **»Michael**). This was the name of a prophet, author of the book of the Bible that bears his name, and which dates from the late 8th century BC.

Michael M English form of a common biblical name (meaning 'who is like God?') borne by one of the archangels, who is also regarded as a saint of the Catholic Church. In the Middle Ages, Michael was regarded as captain of the heavenly host (see Revelation 12:7–9), symbol of the Church Militant, and patron of soldiers. He was often depicted bearing a flaming sword. The name is also borne by a Persian prince and ally of Belshazzar mentioned in the Book of Daniel. See also **»Michal**.

Michaela F Latinate feminine form of **»Michael**.

Michal F Biblical name (meaning 'brook' in Hebrew) borne by a daughter of Saul who married King David.

Michelle F French feminine form of *Michel*, the French form of **»Michael**. This name is now also used extensively in the English-speaking world (partly influenced by a Beatles song with this name as its title).

Mickenzie F Altered form of **»Mackenzie**, influenced by the name *Mick*, short form of **»Michael**.

Mignonette F Probably a direct use of the French nickname *mignonette* 'little darling', a feminine pet form of *mignon* 'sweet', 'cute', 'dainty'. Alternatively, it may belong to the class of names derived from flower names (the word in English is used for various species of *Reseda*).

Mihangel M Older Welsh form of **»Michael**, representing a contraction of the phrase 'Michael the Archangel'.

Mike M Usual short form of **»Michael**. It is also used as an independent given name, particularly in the United States.

Mikki F Feminine variant of *Micky*, pet form of **»Michael**, or pet form of **»Michaela**, now sometimes used as an independent given name. The spellings **Micki**, **Mickie**, and **Mickey** are also found.

Mildred F 19th-century revival of the Old English female personal name *Mildthrŷth*, derived from *mild* gentle + *thrŷth* 'strength'. This was the name of a 7th-century abbess, who had a less famous but equally saintly elder sister called *Mildburh* and a younger sister called *Mildgŷth*; all were daughters of a certain Queen Ermenburh. Their names illustrate clearly the Old English pattern of combining and recombining the same small group of name elements within a single family.

Miles M Of Norman origin but uncertain derivation. Unlike most Norman names, it appears not to be derived from any known Old French or Germanic name element. It may be a greatly altered pet form of **»Michael**, which came to be associated with the Latin word *miles* 'soldier' because of the military attributes of the archangel Michael. However, the usual Latin form of the name in the Middle Ages was *Milo*. There is a common Slavonic name element *mil* 'grace', 'favour', with which it may possibly have some connection. The name has been modestly popular in England ever since the Norman Conquest. See also **»Milo** and **»Myles**.

Milla F Shortened form of **»Camilla**.

Millicent F From an Old French name, *Melisende*, of Germanic (Frankish) origin, from *amal* 'labour' + *swinth* 'strength'. This was the name of a daughter of Charlemagne. It was adopted by the Normans and introduced by them to Britain.

Milo M Latinized form of **»Miles**, regularly used in documents of the Middle Ages, and revived as a given name in the 19th century.

Milton M Transferred use of the surname, in origin a local name from the numerous places so called. The surname is most famous as that of the poet John Milton (1608–74), and the given name is sometimes bestowed in his honour.

Mimi F Italian pet form of **»Maria**, originally a nursery name. The heroine of Puccini's opera *La Bohème* (1896) announces 'They call me Mimi', and since that time the name has occasionally been used in the English-speaking world.

Mirabelle F French: from Latin *mīrābilis* 'wondrous', 'lovely'; cf. **»Miranda**). *Mirabelle* and the Italian form *Mirabella* were quite common in the later Middle Ages. The form *Mirabel* was found occasionally in France and England as a boy's name. By the 16th century, however, both forms were rare. The Latinate form **Mirabella** also occurs.

Miranda F Invented by Shakespeare for the heroine of *The Tempest* (1611). It represents the feminine form of the Latin gerundive *mīrandus* 'admirable', 'lovely', from *mīrāri* 'to wonder at', 'admire'; cf. **»Amanda**.

Mireille F French name, apparently first used, in the Provençal form **Mireio**, as the title of a verse romance by the poet Frédéric Mistral (1830–1914). The name is probably a derivative of Provençal *mirar* 'to admire' (cf. **»Miranda**). The poet himself declared it to be a form of **»Miriam**, but this was apparently in order to

m

overcome the objections of a priest to baptizing his god-daughter with a non-liturgical name. The name is occasionally also used in the English-speaking world.

Miriam F Biblical name: the Old Testament form of the Hebrew name *Maryam* (see **>>Mary**). Of uncertain ultimate origin, this is first recorded as being borne by the elder sister of Moses (Exodus 15:20). Since the names of both Moses and his brother Aaron are probably of Egyptian origin, it is possible that this is too. It was enthusiastically taken up as a given name by the Israelites, and is still found mainly, but not exclusively, as a Jewish name.

Misty F Modern coinage, apparently from the vocabulary word.

Mitchell M Transferred use of the surname, itself derived from a common medieval form of **>>Michael**, representing an Anglicized pronunciation of the French name *Michel*, introduced to Britain by the Normans.

Moira F Anglicized form of Irish Gaelic *Máire*, a form of **>>Mary**, now used in its own right throughout the English-speaking world. The spelling **>>Moyra** also occurs.

Molly F Pet form of **>>Mary**, an altered version of the earlier pet form *Mally*. It has long been established as an independent given name.

Mona F Anglicized form of the Gaelic name **Muadhnait**, a feminine diminutive of *muadh* 'noble'. It is no longer restricted to people with Irish connections, and has sometimes been taken as connected with the feminine of Greek *monos* 'single', 'only' or chosen with reference to Leonardo da Vinci's painting *Mona Lisa*.

Monica F Of uncertain ultimate origin. This was the name of the mother of St Augustine. She was a citizen of Carthage, so her name may well be of Phoenician origin, but in the early Middle Ages it was taken to be a derivative of Latin *monēre* 'to warn', 'counsel', or 'advise', since it was as a result of her guidance that her son was converted to Christianity.

Monroe M Transferred use of the Scottish surname, usually spelled *Munro*. The ancestors of the Scottish Munros are said to have come from Ireland, apparently from a settlement by the River Roe in County Derry; their name is therefore supposed to be derived from Gaelic *bun Rotha* 'mouth of the Roe'. In the United States the popularity of the given name may have been influenced by the fame of James Monroe (1758–1831), fifth president of the United States. The spellings **Monro** and **≫Munro(e)** are also found.

Montague M Transferred use of the surname, originally a Norman baronial name borne by the lords of Montaigu in La Manche. A certain Drogo of Montaigu is known to have accompanied William the Conqueror in his invasion of England in 1066, and *Montague* thus became established as an aristocratic British family name.

m

Montgomery M Transferred use of the surname, originally a Norman baronial name from various places in Calvados. It has never been common as a given name, although it was given additional currency by the actor Montgomery Clift (1920–66), and during and after the Second World War by the British field marshal, Bernard Montgomery (1887–1976).

Montmorency M Transferred use of the surname, originally a Norman baronial name from a place in Seine-et-Oise. The given name enjoyed a brief vogue in the 19th century.

Monty M Short form of **≫Montgomery** or of the much rarer **≫Montague** and **≫Montmorency**. It is now sometimes found as an independent given name. As a Jewish name, it was originally used as an approximate English equivalent of **≫Moses**.

Mór F Scottish and Irish Gaelic: from the vocabulary word *mór* 'large', 'great'. This was the commonest of all girls' names in late medieval Ireland, and has continued in frequent use in both Scotland and Ireland to the present day.

Morag F Scottish: Anglicized spelling of Gaelic **Mórag**, a pet form of **»Mór**. In the 20th century this name became popular in its own right in Scotland. It is also occasionally used elsewhere in the English-speaking world.

Moray M Scottish: variant of **»Murray**, and the more usual spelling of the placename from which the surname is derived.

Moreen F Irish: Anglicized form of Gaelic *Móirín*, a pet form of **»Mór**. It has now been to a large extent confused with **»Maureen**.

Morgan M, F Welsh: traditional boy's name derived from Old Welsh *Morcant*. The first element is of uncertain derivation, the second represents the Old Celtic element *cant* 'circle', 'completion'. In recent years it has frequently been used outside Wales as a girl's name, perhaps with reference to King Arthur's jealous stepsister Morgan le Fay.

Morley M Transferred use of the surname, in origin a local name from any of the numerous places in England so named.

Morna F Irish and Scottish: variant of **»Myrna**. This is the name borne by Fingal's mother in the Ossianic poems of James Macpherson (cf. **»Malvina**).

Morris M Variant of **»Maurice**. The spelling *Morris* was quite common as a given name in the Middle Ages, but it fell out of use and was readopted in modern times, in part from the surname earlier derived from the given name.

Mortimer M Transferred use of the surname, in origin a Norman baronial name borne by the lords of

Mortemer in Normandy. It was not used as a given name until the 19th century.

Morton M Transferred use of the surname, in origin a local name from any of the numerous places so called. It is also widely used as a Jewish name, having been adopted as an approximate English equivalent of ≫**Moses**.

Morven F This was the name of Fingal's kingdom in the Ossianic poems of James Macpherson. In reality it is a district in north Argyll, on the west coast of Scotland, properly *Morvern*, known in Gaelic as *a' Mhorbhairne* 'the big gap'. *Morven* could alternatively be held to represent Gaelic *mór bheinn* 'big peak'.

Morwenna F Cornish and Welsh: from an Old Celtic personal name derived from an element cognate with Welsh *morwyn* 'maiden'. It was borne by a Cornish saint of the 5th century; churches in her honour have named several places in Cornwall. The name was revived in Wales in the mid 20th century as a result of nationalistic sentiment.

Moses M Biblical name, the English form of the name of the patriarch (**Moshe** in Hebrew) who led the Israelites out of Egypt (Exodus 4). His name is thought to be of Egyptian origin, most probably from the same root as that found in the second element of names such as *Tutmosis* and *Rameses*, where it means 'born of (a certain god)'. Various Hebrew etymologies have been proposed, beginning with the biblical 'saved (from the water)' (Exodus 2:10), but none is convincing. It is now mainly a Jewish name, although until the mid 20th century it also enjoyed considerable popularity among Christians in England, especially among Puritans and Nonconformists.

Moss M Transferred use of the surname derived from the usual medieval vernacular form of ≫**Moses**, or a

m

revival of this form. In Wales it has in recent years also been used as a short form of **»Mostyn**.

Mostyn M Welsh: from the name of a place in Clwyd, on the Dee estuary. The place in fact derives its name from Old English rather than Welsh elements: it appears in Domesday Book as *Mostone*, from Old English *mos* 'moss' + *tūn* 'enclosure', 'settlement'.

Moya F Modern name of uncertain origin; it may be derived from **»Moyra**.

Moyra F Variant spelling of **»Moira**.

Muir M Transferred use of the Scottish surname, in origin a local name representing a Scottish dialect variant of *moor* 'rough grazing'.

Muireall F Scottish Gaelic traditional name, pronounced '**moor**-all', apparently from Old Celtic words meaning 'sea' + 'bright'. The Irish Gaelic form is **Muirgheal**.

Muireann F Traditional Irish Gaelic name, pronounced '**mwir**-an', apparently from *muir* 'sea' + *fionn* 'white', 'fair'. The spelling **Muirinn** is also used, and there has been considerable confusion with **»Maureen** and **»Moreen**.

Muiris M Irish form of **»Maurice**. In part it also represents a contracted form of the Gaelic name *Muirgheas*, which is probably derived from *muir* 'sea' + *gus* 'vigour'.

Muirne F Irish Gaelic traditional name, pronounced '**moor**-nya', originally a byname meaning 'beloved'. The Anglicized forms **»Myrna** and **»Morna** also occur.

Mungo M Scottish: of uncertain derivation. It is recorded as the byname of St Kentigern, the 6th-century apostle of south-west Scotland and north-west England. Having been glossed in Latin by his biographer as *carissimus amicus* 'dearest friend', the name (in its Brythonic form *Munghu*) was taken to represent later

Welsh *fy nghi* 'my dog', i.e. 'my pet'. The Scottish Gaelic form **Munga** is also found.

Munroe M Variant spelling of >>**Monroe**. The spelling **Munro** also occurs.

Murchadh M Traditional Gaelic name, pronounced 'moor-ha', derived from *muir* 'sea' + *cadh* 'battle'. It was borne by many medieval Irish kings and princes. It is Anglicized as >>**Murrough**.

Murdo M Scottish: Anglicized spelling of the traditional Gaelic name *Muireadhach*, meaning 'lord', but said to be a derivative of *muir* 'sea'. The spelling **Murdoch** is now equally if not more common.

Murgatroyd M Transferred use of the Yorkshire surname, in origin a local name from an unidentified place named as 'the clearing (Yorkshire dialect *royd*) belonging to (a certain) Margaret'.

Muriel F Of Celtic origin; see >>**Muireall**. Forms of the name are found in Breton as well as in Scottish and Irish Gaelic, and in the form >>**Meriel** it was in use in the Middle Ages even in the heart of England.

Murray M Transferred use of the Scottish surname, in origin a local name from the region now called *Moray*. The variant >>**Moray** also occurs.

Murrough M Anglicized form of Gaelic >>**Murchadh**.

Myfanwy F Welsh name meaning 'little woman', composed of the Welsh affectionate prefix *my-* + *banwy*, a variant form of *banw*, related to *benyw* or *menyw* 'woman'. Its popularity dates only from relatively recent times, when specifically Welsh names have been sought as tokens of Welsh national identity.

Myles M Variant spelling of >>**Miles**.

Myra F Invented in the 17th century by the poet Fulke Greville (1554–1628).

Myriam F Variant spelling of >>**Miriam**. This is the usual spelling of the name in France.

Myrna F Irish: Anglicized form of Gaelic ≫**Muirne**, now also used elsewhere in the English-speaking world. It is associated with the film star Myrna Loy (1905–93). The spelling ≫**Morna** is also found.

Myron M From a classical Greek name, derived from Greek *myron* 'myrrh'. The name was borne by a famous sculptor of the 5th century BC. It was taken up with particular enthusiasm by the early Christians because they associated it with the gift of myrrh made by the three kings to the infant Christ, and because of the association of myrrh (as an embalming spice) with death and eternal life. The name was borne by various early saints, notably a 3rd-century martyr of Cyzicus and a 4th-century bishop of Crete.

Myrtle F From the vocabulary word denoting the plant (Old French *myrtille*, Late Latin *myrtilla*). This is one of the group of plant names that became popular as girls' names in the late 19th century.

m

N

Nadia F French and English spelling of Russian *Nadya* (a pet form of *Nadezhda* 'hope'). This name enjoyed a considerable vogue in the English-speaking world in the 20th century.

Nadine F French elaboration of **»Nadia**. Many names of Russian origin became established in France and elsewhere in the early 20th century as a result of the popularity of the Ballet Russe, established in Paris by Diaghilev in 1909.

Nahum M Biblical name (meaning 'comforter' in Hebrew), borne by a prophet of the 7th century BC. He was the author of the book of the Bible that bears his name, in which he prophesies the downfall of Nineveh, which fell in 612 BC. This is a well-established Jewish name, which was also popular among 17th-century Puritans in England. It was borne by the minor Restoration dramatist Nahum Tate (1652–1715).

Nan F Originally a pet form of **»Ann** (for the initial *N-*, cf. **»Ned**). It is now generally used as a short form of **»Nancy**.

Nancy F Of uncertain origin. From the 18th century onwards it was used as a pet form of **»Ann** (cf. **»Nan**), but it may originally have been a similar formation deriving from the common medieval given name *Annis*, a vernacular form of **»Agnes**. Nowadays it is an independent name, and was especially popular in America between about 1920 and 1960. The spellings **Nancie** and **Nanci** are also found.

Nanette F Elaboration of **»Nan**, with the addition of the French feminine diminutive suffix -*ette*.

Naoise M Traditional Irish Gaelic name, pronounced 'nee-sha'. This was borne by one of the best-known characters in all Irish legend, the lover of Deirdre, with whom he eloped, even though she was betrothed to Conchobhar, king of Ulster. Conchobhar hounded the lovers throughout Ireland and Scotland, eventually offering Naoise promises of pardon and security. But they were false promises, and Naoise was murdered on his return to Ulster.

Naomh F Irish Gaelic name, pronounced 'neev', meaning 'holy' or 'saint'. This use of the vocabulary word as a given name is a comparatively recent development.

Naomi F Biblical name (meaning 'pleasantness' in Hebrew), borne by the wise mother-in-law of Ruth. The name has long been regarded as typically Jewish, but recently it has begun to come into more general use.

Nat M Short form of **»Nathan** and **»Nathaniel**.

Natalie F French form of **»Natalya**, adopted from Russian in the early 20th century, probably like **»Nadine**, under the influence of Diaghilev's Ballet Russe, which was established in Paris in 1909. The name is now very common in France and in the English-speaking world. It was borne by the actress Natalie Wood (1938–82). She was born Natasha Gurdin, in San Francisco. The spelling **Nathalie** also occurs.

Natalya F Russian: from the Late Latin name *Natālia*, a derivative of Latin *natālis (diēs)* 'birthday', especially Christ's birthday, i.e. Christmas (cf. **»Noël**). St Natalia was a Christian inhabitant of Nicomedia who is said to have given succour to the martyrs, including her husband Adrian, who suffered there in persecutions under Diocletian in 303. She is regarded as a Christian saint, although she was not herself martyred.

Natasha F Russian: pet form of **»Natalya**, now widely adopted as an independent name in the English-speaking world and elsewhere. Like *Noëlle* and **»Noël**, it is sometimes given to girls born at Christmas time.

Nathalie F Variant spelling of **»Natalie**. The *th* is a mere elaboration of the French spelling and has not yet had any effect on the pronunciation.

Nathan M Biblical name, meaning 'he (God) has given' in Hebrew (cf. **»Nathaniel**). This was the name of a prophet who had the courage to reproach King David for arranging the death in battle of Uriah the Hittite in order to get possession of the latter's wife Bathsheba (2 Samuel 12:1–15). It was also the name of one of David's own sons. In modern times this name has often been taken as a short form of **»Nathaniel** or of **»Jonathan**.

Nathaniel M English form of a New Testament name, which is derived from the Greek form of a Hebrew name meaning 'God has given' (cf. **»Nathan**). It was borne by one of the less prominent of Christ's apostles (John 1:45; 21:2), who in fact is probably identical with **»Bartholomew**. The spelling used in the Authorized Version of the New Testament is **Nathanael**, but this is much less common as a given name in the English-speaking world.

Neal M Variant spelling of **»Neil**. The spelling **Neale** also occurs.

Ned M Short form of **»Edward**, originating in the misdivision of phrases such as *mine Ed*. It was common in the Middle Ages and up to the 18th century, but in the 19th was almost entirely superseded in the role of short form by **»Ted**. It has since enjoyed a modest revival.

Neil M Anglicized form of the enduringly popular Gaelic name **»Niall**. Its derivation is disputed: it may mean 'cloud', 'passionate', or perhaps 'champion'. Its most famous bearer in Irish legend was Neil of the Nine

Hostages (died *c*.405 AD), a shadowy king of Ireland, about whom very little is known beyond the fact that he was the founder of the O'Neils. The name was adopted by the Scandinavians in the form *Njal* and soon became very popular among them. From the Middle Ages onwards, this name was found mainly in Ireland, the Highlands of Scotland, and the English-Scottish Border region. In the 20th century it spread to enjoy great popularity in all parts of the English-speaking world. The spellings **»Neal** and **Neale** are also found. See also **»Nigel**.

Nell F Medieval short form of **»Eleanor**, **»Ellen**, and **»Helen**; for the initial *N*-, cf. **»Ned**. It was the name by which Charles II's mistress Eleanor Gwyn (1650–87) was universally known to her contemporaries, and at about that time it also became established as an independent name.

Nelson M Transferred use of the surname, which originated in the Middle Ages as either a patronymic from **»Neil** or a metronymic from **»Nell**. Use as a given name probably began as a tribute to the British admiral Lord Nelson (1758–1805). Nowadays, however, it is universally associated with the South African statesman Nelson Mandela (b. 1918), in whose honour it is often chosen.

Nena F Variant spelling of **»Nina**.

Nerissa F Of Shakespearian origin. It is the name of a minor character in *The Merchant of Venice*, a Latinate elaboration of Greek *nērēis* 'sea sprite'.

Nerys F Welsh: of uncertain derivation, perhaps intended to be from Welsh *nêr* 'lord', with the suffix *-ys* by analogy with other girls' names such as **»Dilys** and **»Gladys**. It was not used as a given name in the Middle Ages, and dates only from the recent Welsh cultural revival; this has been accompanied by a spate of modern coinages of Welsh names, enabling Welsh parents to give their children names reflecting their national identity.

Nessa F Traditional Irish Gaelic name, also found in the form »**Ness**, of unknown origin. It is borne by a character in *Táin Bó Cuailgne* (the Cattle Raid of Cooley), the mother of Conchobhar. This name is also found as a short form of **Agnessa**, a Latinate form of »**Agnes**, and in modern use as a short form of »**Vanessa**.

Nesta F Welsh: Latinized version of **Nest**, a Welsh pet form of »**Agnes**. Nesta was the name of the grandmother of the 12th-century chronicler Giraldus Cambrensis ('Gerald the Welshman').

Netta F Apparently a Latinate variant of **Nettie**, a pet form of »**Annette** or »**Jeanette**. In Gaelic-speaking areas of Scotland it is more probably a feminine form of »**Neil**.

Neville M Transferred use of the surname, in origin a Norman baronial name from any of several places in Normandy called *Néville* or *Neuville* 'new settlement'. First used as a given name in the early 17th century, and with increasing regularity from the second half of the 19th, it is now so firmly established as a given name that it has lost touch with its origin as a surname.

Newton M Mainly U.S.: transferred use of the surname, in origin a local name from any of the very numerous places so called from Old English *nēowe* 'new' + *tūn* 'enclosure', 'settlement'. This is said to be the commonest of all English placenames. The most famous bearer of the surname is probably Sir Isaac Newton (1642–1727), the English scientist.

Ngaio F New Zealand name, pronounced '**nye**-oh': apparently from the Maori word *ngaio* which, among other things, means 'clever'. *Ngai* is also a prefix meaning 'tribe' or 'clan'; the given name may have originated as a tribal name.

Ngaire F New Zealand (Maori) name, pronounced 'nye-ree': of unknown origin. It is usually Anglicized as **»Nyree**.

Nia F Welsh form of **»Niamh**.

Niall M Irish and Scottish Gaelic spelling of **»Neil**. It was strongly revived, even among non-Gaelic speakers, in the 20th century.

Niamh F Irish Gaelic name, pronounced 'nee-uv', from a vocabulary word meaning 'brightness' or 'beauty'. It was borne in Irish mythology by the daughter of the sea god, who fell in love with the youthful Oisín, son of Finn mac Cumhaill (Finn McCool), and carried him off over the sea to the land of perpetual youth, Tír na nÓg. It is now a very popular given name in Ireland.

Nichol M Variant of **»Nicol**.

Nicholas M English form of the post-classical Greek personal name *Nikolaos*, derived from *nikē* 'victory' + *laos* 'people'. The spelling with *-ch-* occurred as early as the 12th century, and became firmly established at the time of the Reformation, although *Nicolas* is still occasionally found. St Nicholas was a 4th-century bishop of Myra in Lycia, about whom virtually nothing factual is known, although a vast body of legend grew up around him. He became the patron saint of Greece and of Russia, as well as of children, sailors, merchants, and pawnbrokers. His feast-day is 6 December, and among the many roles which legend has assigned to him is that of bringer of Christmas presents, in the guise of 'Santa Claus' (an alteration of the Dutch form of his name, *Sinterklaas*). The spellings **Nicolas** and **Nickolas** also occur.

Nicholl M Variant spelling of **»Nicol**.

Nicky M, F Pet form of **»Nicholas** and of **»Nicola**. The girl's name is also spelled **Nickie**, **Nicki**, and **Nikki**.

Nico M, F Modern short form of both **»Nicholas** and **»Nicola**.

Nicol F, M Originally a common medieval vernacular form of **»Nicholas**, current until a relatively late period in Scotland. In modern use it is found more frequently as a girl's name, possibly being taken as a variant of **»Nicole**. The spellings **Nicoll** and **Nichol(l)** are also found.

Nicola F Latinate feminine form of **»Nicholas**.

Nicole F French feminine form of **»Nicholas**, now increasingly common in the English-speaking world.

Nicolette F French pet form of **»Nicole**, also used as an independent given name in the English-speaking world.

Nicoll M Variant spelling of **»Nicol**.

Nigel M Anglicized form of the medieval name *Nigellus*, a Latinized version (ostensibly representing a diminutive of Latin *niger* 'black') of the vernacular *Ni(h)el*, i.e. **»Neil**. Although it is frequently found in medieval records, this form was probably not used in everyday life before its revival by antiquarians such as Sir Walter Scott in the 19th century.

Nigella F Latinate feminine form of **»Nigel**. Adoption as a given name may also have been encouraged by the fact that this is an alternative name (from its black seed) for the flower known as 'love-in-a-mist'.

Nikita F, occasionally M Originally a Russian boy's name, from Greek *Anikētos* 'unconquered, unconquerable'. This was the name of an early pope (*c.*152–160); he was a Syrian by descent and is particularly honoured in the Eastern Church. In recent years, the name has begun to be used in the English-speaking world, mainly as a girl's name, perhaps being taken as an elaboration of **»Nikki** with the feminine diminutive suffix *-ita*.

Nikki F Pet form of **»Nicola**, now sometimes used as an independent given name.

n

Nina F Russian name (originally a short form of names such as *Antonina*), now commonly also used in the English-speaking world.

Ninette F French pet form of **»Nina**. Like **»Nadine**, this was one of the names brought to the English-speaking world from Russian via French in the early 20th century.

Ninian M Scottish and Irish: of uncertain origin. This was the name of a 5th-century British saint who was responsible for evangelizing the northern Britons and the Picts. His name first appears in the Latinized form *Ninianus* in the 8th century; this appears to be identical to the *Nynnyaw* recorded in the *Mabinogi*. The given name was used in his honour until at least the 16th century in Scotland and has recently been revived.

Nita F Short form of various names that end in these syllables, as for example **»Anita** and *Juanita*.

Noah M English form of the name of the biblical character whose family was the only one saved from the great Flood ordained by God to destroy mankind because of its wickedness. The origin of the name is far from certain; in the Bible it is implied that it means 'rest' (Genesis 5:29, 'and he called his name Noah, saying, This same shall comfort us concerning our work and the toil of our hands, because of the ground which the Lord hath cursed'). One tradition indeed explains it as derived from the Hebrew root meaning 'to comfort' (see **»Nahum**) with the final consonant dropped.

Noam M Modern Jewish name, from a Hebrew vocabulary word meaning 'delight', 'joy', 'pleasantness' (cf. **»Naomi**, from the same Hebrew root).

Noble M Mainly U.S.: name derived from the modern English adjective (via Old French from Latin *nobilis*). The idea behind it may have been to hint at high-born origin or to suggest qualities of character. In part there may be some influence from the surname, which arose in the Middle Ages as a descriptive nickname in the first sense.

Noël M, F From Old French *noel*, *nael* 'Christmas', from Latin *natālis diēs (Domini)* 'birthday (of the Lord)'. The meaning is still relatively transparent, partly because the term occurs as a synonym for 'Christmas' in the refrain of well-known carols. The name is often given to children born at Christmas time. The spelling **Noel** is also found, as well as the feminine forms **Noëlle** and **Noelle**.

Nola F Probably a short form of the Gaelic name »**Fionnuala** (cf. »**Nuala**). It may alternatively have been created as a feminine form of »**Nolan**.

Nolan M Transferred use of the Irish surname, Gaelic *Ó Nualláin* 'descendant of Nuallán'. The latter is an ancient Gaelic personal name, originally a byname representing a diminutive of *nuall* 'chariot-fighter', 'champion'.

Nolene F Mainly Australian: name created as a feminine form of »**Nolan**. The spelling **Noleen** is found.

Nona F From the feminine form of the Latin ordinal *nonus* 'ninth', sometimes used as a given name in Victorian times for the ninth-born child in a family if it was a girl, or even for the ninth-born girl. At the present day, when few people have nine children, let alone nine daughters, it has passed into more general, if only occasional, use.

Nonie F Pet form of »**Ione** or of »**Nora**, also used occasionally as an independent given name.

Nora F Short form of names such as »**Leonora** and »**Honora**. *Nora* (Gaelic *Nóra*) was at one time regarded as a peculiarly Irish name; as such, it may be a derivative of »**Fionnuala**, due to confusion of *l* and *r*, although it is more probably a borrowing into Gaelic of Latin *Honora*. The spelling **Norah** is also found.

n

Norbert M From an Old French name of Germanic (Frankish) origin, from *nord* 'north' + *berht* 'bright', 'famous'. The best-known bearer of this name was an 11th-century saint who founded an order of monks. *Norbert* was one of several names of Germanic origin that were revived in Britain in the late 19th century, but it is now more common in North America than in Britain.

Noreen F Anglicized form of the Irish Gaelic name *Nóirín*, a pet form of *Nóra* (see **»Nora**). The spellings **Norene** and **Norine** are also used.

Norma F Apparently invented by Felice Romani in his libretto for Bellini's opera of this name (first performed in 1832). It is identical in form with Latin *norma* 'rule', 'standard', but there is no evidence that this word was the source of the name. In recent times, it has come to be taken in England and the Scottish Highlands as a feminine equivalent of **»Norman**. An influence on the popularity of the compound *Norma-Jean* has been the film star Marilyn Monroe (1926–62), originally named Norma-Jean Baker.

Norman M Of Germanic origin, from *nord* 'north' + *man* 'man', i.e. 'Norseman'. This name was in use in England before the Conquest, and was reinforced by its use among the Norman invaders themselves. The Normans were the inhabitants of Normandy in northern France, whose name is a reference to the Vikings who took control of the region in the 9th century.

Norris M Transferred use of the surname, which is derived from Norman French *norreis* (in which the stem represents the Germanic element *nord* 'north'), originally a local designation for someone who had migrated from the north.

Norton M Transferred use of the surname, in origin a local name from any of the numerous places so called.

Nuala F Irish: short form of the Gaelic name
>>**Fionnuala**. It is now in general use as an independent
given name.

Nye M Pet form of the Welsh name >>**Aneirin**,
representing the middle syllable of that name as
commonly pronounced. The name is particularly
associated with the Welsh Labour statesman Aneurin
Bevan (1897–1960).

Nyree F New Zealand: Anglicized spelling of a Maori
name usually transcribed as >>**Ngaire**. It is relatively
common in New Zealand and has been taken up to
some extent in Britain due to the fame of the New
Zealand-born actress Nyree Dawn Porter (1940–2001).

n

Obadiah M From a biblical name meaning 'servant of God' in Hebrew. This was the name of a prophet who gave his name to one of the shorter books of the Bible, and of two other minor biblical characters: a porter in the temple (Nehemiah 12:25), and the man who introduced King Ahab to the prophet Elijah (1 Kings 18).

Oberon M Variant spelling of ➤➤**Auberon**.

Octavia F Of Latin origin, representing a feminine form of ➤➤**Octavius**.

o **Octavius** M From the Roman family name, derived from Latin *octāvus* 'eighth'. The name was fairly frequently given to the eighth child (or eighth son) in large Victorian families. It is much less common these days, when families rarely extend to eight children, and is more often selected without regard to its original meaning.

Odette F French feminine pet form of the Old French masculine name *Oda*, which is of Germanic origin (derived from a word meaning 'prosperity', 'fortune', or 'riches').

Odile F French: from the medieval Germanic name *Odila* (a derivative of *od* meaning 'prosperity', 'fortune', 'riches'). This was the name of an 8th-century saint who founded a Benedictine convent at what is now Odilienburg in Alsace. She is the patron saint of Alsace.

Ofra F Variant spelling of **»Ophrah**.

Oisín M Gaelic name, from a diminutive of *os* 'stag'. See **»Ossian**.

Olga F Russian name of Scandinavian origin, originally derived from the Old Norse adjective *heilagr* 'prosperous', 'successful'. St Olga of Kiev (d. 969) was a Varangian noblewoman who was baptized at Byzantium in about 957 and set about converting her people. The name was introduced to the English-speaking world in the late 19th century, but retains a distinctively Russian flavour.

Olive F One of the most successful of the names from vocabulary words denoting plants that became fashionable during the 19th century, no doubt partly because an olive branch has been a symbol of peace since biblical times. See also **»Olivia**.

Oliver M From a French name, *Olivier*, recorded as the name of one of Charlemagne's paladins (retainers). In the *Chanson de Roland* Oliver, the close companion in arms of the impetuous Roland, is depicted as a thoughtful and cautious man. Ostensibly his name derives from Late Latin *olivārius* 'olive tree', but Charlemagne's other paladins all bear solidly Germanic names, so it is more probably an altered form of an unidentified Germanic name.

Olivia F Latinate name, first used by Shakespeare for the rich heiress wooed by the duke in *Twelfth Night* (1599). Shakespeare may have taken it as a feminine form of **»Oliver** or he may have derived it from Latin *oliva* 'olive'. In the 1970s it came to be associated with the Australian singer and actress Olivia Newton-John (b. 1948).

Olwen F Welsh: from *ôl* 'footprint', 'track' + *(g)wen* 'white', 'fair', 'blessed', 'holy'. A character of this name in Welsh legend had the magical property of causing flowers to spring up behind her wherever she went.

Omar M Biblical name (apparently meaning 'talkative' in Hebrew) borne by a character mentioned in a genealogy (Genesis 36:11). It has been occasionally used from Puritan times down to the present day in America. More often, however, it is of Arabic origin, as in the case of the film actor Omar Sharif (b. 1932 in Egypt).

Onora F Anglicized form of the Irish Gaelic name *Onóra*, which is from Latin ≫**Honora**. It is the source of the popular shortened form ≫**Nora**.

Oona F Anglicized form of the Irish Gaelic name *Úna* (see ≫**Una**). The spelling **Oonagh** is also found.

Opal F One of the rarer girls' names created in the late 19th century from vocabulary words for gemstones.

Opaline F Comparatively recent coinage: an elaboration of ≫**Opal** with the addition of *-ine*, a productive suffix of girls' names (originally a French diminutive suffix).

Ophelia F The name of a character in Shakespeare's *Hamlet*, the beautiful daughter of Polonius; she loves Hamlet, and eventually goes mad and drowns herself. In spite of the ill omen of this literary association, the name has enjoyed moderate popularity since the 19th century. It was first used by the Italian pastoral poet Jacopo Sannazzaro (1458–1530), who presumably intended it as a feminine form of the Greek name *Ōphelos* 'help'. Shakespeare seems to have borrowed the name, without considering whether it was appropriate for a play set in medieval Denmark.

Ophrah F, M Hebrew name meaning 'fawn'. In the Old Testament it is borne by a man (1 Chronicles 4:14), but it is now more commonly used as a girl's name. The spellings **Ophra**, **Oprah**, and ≫**Ofra** are also used.

Oralie F Of uncertain origin, possibly an altered form of French *Aurélie* (see ≫**Aurelia**). The spelling **Oralee** is also found.

Oran M Irish: Anglicized form of Gaelic *Odhrán*, originally a diminutive of *odhar* 'dun', 'sallow'. The name was borne by St Patrick's charioteer and by various early saints, including a 6th-century abbot of Meath who accompanied Columba to Scotland and is said to have been buried alive by the latter as a foundation sacrifice.

Oren M Biblical name, apparently meaning 'pine tree' in Hebrew, mentioned in a genealogy (1 Chronicles 2:25). This name is in use in the United States in a number of different spellings, including **Orren**, **Orin**, and **Orrin**. In some cases it may be a variant of the Irish name ⟫**Oran**.

Orla F Anglicized form of the Irish Gaelic name **Órlaith**, derived from *or* 'gold' + *laith* 'princess'. This was a popular name in medieval Ireland, now being revived.

Orson M From a Norman French nickname meaning 'bear-cub' (a diminutive of *ors* 'bear'). This was occasionally used as a given name in the Middle Ages, but in modern times it probably represents a transferred use of the surname derived from the medieval nickname. Its most famous bearer of the 20th century was the American actor and director Orson Welles (1915–85).

Orville M Though in appearance a surname of Norman baronial origin, this name was in fact invented (with the intention of evoking such associations) by the novelist Fanny Burney for the hero, Lord Orville, of her novel *Evelina* (1778).

Osbert M From an Old English personal name derived from *ōs* 'god' + *beorht* 'bright', 'famous'. In the earlier 20th century it enjoyed a modest vogue in Britain, being borne for example by the cartoonist Osbert Lancaster and the writer Osbert Sitwell.

Oscar M Old Irish name, apparently from Gaelic *os* 'deer' + *cara* 'friend'. This is borne in the Fenian sagas

o

by a grandson of Finn mac Cumhaill (Finn McCool). It was resuscitated by James Macpherson (1736–96), author of the Ossian poems. It is now also a characteristically Scandinavian name; it was introduced there because Napoleon, an admirer of the works of Macpherson, chose the name for his godson Oscar Bernadotte, who became King Oscar I of Sweden in 1844 (see also **»Malvina**). In more recent times it has been associated with the Irish writer Oscar Wilde (1854–1900), and with the annual awards for achievement in the film industry made by the American Academy of Motion Picture Arts and Sciences.

Ossian M Anglicized form of the Gaelic name **»Oisín**. In Irish mythology this name was borne most famously by the son of the hero Finn mac Cumhaill (Finn McCool), who was carried off by Niamh to Tír nan nÓg, the land of perpetual youth. It was resuscitated in 1760 by James Macpherson (1736–96) as the name of the supposed author of some ancient Gaelic poetry which Macpherson claimed to have translated. In fact he probably made it up.

o

Oswald M From an Old English personal name, derived from ōs 'god' + weald 'rule'. This was the name of two English saints. The first was a 7th-century Christian king of Northumbria, who was killed in battle in 641. Because he was killed by a heathen, his death was counted as a martyrdom by the Christian Church. The second St Oswald was a 10th-century bishop of Worcester and archbishop of York, who effected reforms in the English Church. Except in northern England the name more or less died out after the Middle Ages, but underwent a modest revival in the 19th century as part of the vogue for pre-Conquest English names.

Otis M Transferred use of the surname, in origin a patronymic derived from the genitive case of the medieval given name Ote or Ode (of Norman, and ultimately Germanic, origin; cf. **»Odette**). It came to be used as a given name in America in honour of the Revolutionary hero James Otis (1725–83); in modern times it has been bestowed in honour of the American soul singer Otis Redding (1941–67).

Ottoline F French pet form of *Ottilie*, a variant of **»Odile**. The name acquired some currency in the English-speaking world in the early 20th century, partly due to the influence of the literary hostess Lady Ottoline Morrell (1873–1938).

Owen M Most commonly a Welsh name, derived most probably from the Latin name *Eugenius* (see **»Eugene**) or from an ancient Celtic name meaning 'born of Esos'. *Esos* or *Aesos* was a god with a cult in Gaul. *Owen* is also found as an Anglicization of the Gaelic name **»Eoghan**.

o

P

Pádraig M Irish Gaelic form of >>**Patrick**.

Paige F Evidently a transferred use of the surname *Paige*, a variant of *Page*, originally an occupational name given to someone who served as a page to a great lord. It was taken up as a girl's name in the 20th century in North America, possibly influenced by the popularity of the American film actress Janis Paige (b. 1922). It is now popular throughout the English-speaking world. The spelling **Page** is also found.

Pamela F Invented by the Elizabethan pastoral poet Sir Philip Sidney (1554–86), in whose verse it is stressed on the second syllable. There is no clue to the sources that influenced Sidney in this coinage. It was later taken up by Samuel Richardson for the name of the heroine of his novel *Pamela* (1740). The spelling **Pamella** is a modern variant.

Pandora F Name borne in classical mythology by the first woman on earth, created by the fire god Hephaistos as a scourge for men in general, in revenge for Prometheus' act of stealing fire on behalf of mankind. Pandora was given as a wife to Prometheus' foolish brother Epimetheus, along with a box which she was forbidden to open. She nevertheless did open it, and unleashed every type of hardship and suffering on the world, hope alone being left inside the box. The name itself is ironically derived from the Greek words *pan* 'all', 'every' + *dōron* 'gift'.

Pansy F 19th-century coinage, from the word for the garden flower, which is named from Old French *pensee* 'thought'. This was never particularly popular, and is seldom chosen at all now that the word *pansy* has acquired a derogatory slang sense denoting an effeminate man.

Parker M Mainly U.S.: transferred use of the common surname, in origin an occupational name for a gamekeeper employed in a medieval game park.

Pat M, F Short form of both »**Patrick** and »**Patricia**.

Patience F From the vocabulary word denoting one of the Seven Christian Virtues. The word is derived from Latin *pati* 'to suffer', and was associated by the early Christians with those who endured persecution and misfortune without complaint or loss of faith. This name was a favourite with the Puritans.

Patrice F, M Medieval French form of both the male and female Latin names *Patricius* (see »**Patrick**) and »**Patricia**. In modern French it is used only as a boy's name, but in the English-speaking world it is used mainly as a girl's name.

Patricia F From Latin *Patricia*, feminine form of *Patricius*; see »**Patrick**. There are numerous short forms and pet forms, including »**Pat**, **Tricia**, **Trisha**, **Patty**, **Pattie**, **Patti**.

Patrick M Name of the apostle and patron saint of Ireland (c.389–461), Gaelic *Pádraig*. He was a Christian Briton and a Roman citizen, who as a young man was captured and enslaved by raiders from Ireland. He escaped and went to Gaul before returning to Britain. In about 419 he felt a call to do missionary work in Ireland. He studied for twelve years at Auxerre, and in 432 returned to Ireland. For the rest of his life it is difficult to distiguish fact from fiction. He apparently went to the court of the high king at Tara and made some converts there, then travelled around Ireland making further converts until about 445, when he established his archiepiscopal see at Armagh. By the

P

time of his death almost the whole of Ireland is said to have been converted to Christianity. He is also credited with codifying the laws of Ireland. In his Latin autobiography, his name appears as *Patricius* 'patrician' (i.e. belonging to the Roman senatorial or noble class), but this may represent a Latinized form of some lost Celtic (British) name.

Patsy F, M Pet form of **>>Patricia** or **>>Patrick**. It is generally a girl's name; as a boy's name it is almost completely restricted to Irish communities. Its popularity does not seem to have been seriously affected by its use in derogatory senses in the general vocabulary, in America meaning 'a dupe' and in Australia 'a homosexual'.

Paul M From Latin *Paulus*, a Roman family name, originally a nickname meaning 'small', used in the post-classical period as a given name. Pre-eminently this is the name of the saint who is generally regarded, with St Peter, as co-founder of the Christian Church. Born in Tarsus, and originally named *Saul*, he was both a Roman citizen and a Jew, and at first found employment as a minor official persecuting Christians. He was converted to Christianity by a vision of Christ while on the road to Damascus, and thereafter undertook extensive missionary journeys all over the eastern Mediterranean. His preaching aroused official hostility, and eventually he was beheaded at Rome in about AD 65. He is the author of the fourteen epistles to churches and individuals which form part of the New Testament.

Paula F Latin feminine form of **>>Paul**, borne by various minor early saints and martyrs.

Paulette F French pet feminine form of **>>Paul**. It is also widely used in the English-speaking world.

Pauline F French form of the Latin name *Paulina* (feminine of *Paulīnus*, a derivative of the family name

Paulus 'small') that has long been in use also in the English-speaking world.

Peadar M Irish Gaelic form of »**Peter**.

Pearce M Transferred use of the surname, which is from the given name »**Piers**. It has been a popular name among Irish nationalists since the rising of 1916, led by the writer and educationist Patrick Henry Pearce, who was executed for his part in it. The Irish Gaelic forms are *Perais* and »**Piaras**.

Pearl F One of the group of names coined in the 19th century from words for precious and semi-precious stones. It has a longer history as a Jewish name, representing an Anglicized form of Yiddish *Perle* (see also »**Peninnah**).

Pegeen F Anglicized form of Irish Gaelic *Peigín*, a pet form of *Peig*, the Gaelic form of *Peg*, a pet form of »**Margaret**.

Peggy F Pet form of »**Margaret**.

Pelham M Transferred use of the surname, in origin a local name from a place in Hertfordshire, so called from the Old English personal name *Pēo(t)la* + *hām* 'homestead'. From 1715 a family bearing this surname held the dukedom of Newcastle.

Penelope F Name borne in Greek mythology by the wife of Odysseus who sat patiently awaiting his return for twenty years while, as a supposed widow, fending off a pressing horde of suitors. Her name would seem to derive from Greek *pēnelops* 'duck', and play is made with this word in the *Odyssey*. However, this may obscure a more complex origin, now no longer recoverable.

Peninnah F Jewish traditional name, meaning 'coral' in Hebrew. It was borne in the Bible by the co-wife of Elkanah, the father of Samuel. In modern Hebrew it means 'pearl' and has become a popular name, often being substituted for Yiddish *Perle* and English **≫Pearl**. The spellings **Peninna** and **Penina** also occur.

Penn M Mainly U.S.: transferred use of the surname. The given name is sometimes chosen in honour of the founder of Pennsylvania, the Quaker William Penn (1644–1718).

Penny F Pet form of **≫Penelope**, now sometimes also used as an independent given name.

Perce M Variant of **≫Pierce** or informal short form of **≫Percy**.

Percival M From Old French versions of the Arthurian legend, where the name is spelled *Perceval*. According to Chrétien de Troyes (12th century) and Wolfram von Eschenbach (*c.*1170–1220), Perceval (German *Parzifal*) was the perfectly pure and innocent knight who alone could succeed in the quest for the Holy Grail. Later versions of the Grail legend assign this role to Sir Galahad. The name *Perceval* probably represents a drastic remodelling of the Celtic name *Peredur*, as if from Old French *perce(r)* 'pierce' + *val* 'valley'.

Percy M Originally a transferred use of the surname, but long established as a given name, and now often erroneously taken as a pet form of **≫Percival**. The surname originated as a Norman baronial name, borne by a family who had held a fief in Normandy called *Perci*. As a given name it was taken up in the early 18th century in the Seymour family, which had intermarried with the Percy family. The poet Percy Bysshe Shelley (1792–1822) was distantly connected with this family, and it was partly due to his influence that the given name became more widespread.

Perdita F A Shakespearian coinage, borne by a character in *The Winter's Tale* (1610). The feminine form of Latin *perditus* 'lost', it has a clear reference to the events of the play. The name is now also associated with a (canine) character in Dodie Smith's *One Hundred*

and One Dalmatians (1956), which was made into a
perennially popular film by Walt Disney.

Peregrine M From Latin *Peregrīnus* 'foreigner',
'stranger', a name borne by various early Christian
saints, perhaps referring to the belief that men and
women are merely sojourners upon the earth, their
true home being in heaven. In modern times the name
is rare, borne mostly by Roman Catholics, who choose
it in honour of those saints.

Perry M Pet form of ≫**Peregrine**, or transferred use of
the surname *Perry*, in origin a local name for someone
who lived by a pear tree (Old English *pirige*). In modern
times, it was borne by the American singer Perry Como
(1912–2001).

Perse M Variant of ≫**Pierce**.

Persis F Of New Testament origin, from Greek *Persis*,
originally an ethnic name meaning 'Persian woman'.
This name is borne by a woman mentioned fleetingly
by St Paul: 'the beloved Persis, which laboured much
in the Lord' (Romans 16:12). As a result it was taken
up at the time of the Reformation.

Peta F Modern feminine form of ≫**Peter**, not used
before the 1930s.

Petal F From the vocabulary word for the part of a
flower, also used as a term of endearment.

Peter M English form of the name of the best-known
of all Christ's apostles, traditionally regarded as the
founder of the Christian Church. The name derives, via
Latin, from Greek *petros* 'stone', 'rock'. This is used as
a translation of the Aramaic byname *Cephas*, given
to the apostle Simon son of Jona, to distinguish him
from another of the same name (Simon Zelotes).
'When Jesus beheld him, he said, Thou art Simon the
son of Jona: thou shalt be called Cephas, which is by
interpretation, A stone' (John 1:42). According to
Matthew 16:17–18, Christ says more explicitly, 'Blessed

P

art thou, Simon Bar-jona . . . thou art Peter, and upon this rock I will build my church'.

Petra F Feminine form of **»Peter**, representing a hypothetical Latin name *Petra*; *petra* is in fact the regular Late Latin word for 'stone', of which *petrus* is a byform.

Petronel F From Latin *Petronilla*, originally a feminine diminutive of the Roman family name *Petrōnius* (of uncertain derivation). The name *Petronilla* was borne by a 1st-century martyr, and early in the Christian era came to be connected with **»Peter**, so that in many legends surrounding her she is described as a companion or even the daughter of St Peter.

Petula F Of uncertain origin, not used before the 20th century. It is possibly a Christian coinage intended to mean 'supplicant', 'postulant', from Late Latin *petulāre* 'to ask', or there may be some connection with the flower name *petunia*. Alternatively, it may be an elaboration of the vocabulary word *pet* used as a term of endearment, with the suffix *-ula* abstracted from names such as *Ursula*.

p **Phelim** M See **»Felim**.

Philip M From the Greek name *Philippos*, meaning 'lover of horses'. This was popular in the classical period and since. It was the name of the father of Alexander the Great. It was also the name of one of Christ's apostles, of a deacon ordained by the apostles after the death of Christ, and of several other early saints.

Philippa F Latin feminine form of **»Philip**. In England during the Middle Ages the vernacular name *Philip* was borne by women as well as men, but female bearers were distinguished in Latin records by this form. It was not used as a regular given name until the 19th century.

Phillida F Variant of **»Phyllis**, derived from the genitive case (Greek *Phyllidos*, Latin *Phyllidis*) with the addition of the Latin feminine ending *-a*.

Phillip M Variant spelling of **»Philip**, in part a reflection of the surname, which is usually spelled *Phillips*.

Philomena F From the name of an obscure saint (probably of the 3rd century) with a local cult in Italy. In 1527 the bones of a young woman were discovered under the church altar at San Severino near Ancona, together with a Latin inscription declaring them to be the body of St Filomena. Her name seems to be a feminine form of Latin *Philomenus*, Greek *Philomenēs*, from *philein* 'to love' + *menos* 'strength'. The name became popular in the 19th century, as a result of the supposed discovery in 1802 of the relics of another St Philomena in the catacombs at Rome. All the excitement, however, was a result of misinterpretation of the Latin inscription *Filumena pax tecum* 'peace be with you, beloved' (from Greek *philoumena* 'beloved').

Phineas M Biblical name, borne by two minor characters. One was a grandson of Aaron, who preserved the purity of the race of Israel and deflected God's wrath by killing an Israelite who had taken a Midianite woman to wife (Numbers 25:6–15); the other, a son of the priest Eli, was killed in combat with the Philistines over the Ark of the Covenant (1 Samuel 1:3; 4:6–11). The name is spelled *Phinehas* in the Authorized Version. It has been taken to mean 'serpent's mouth' (i.e. 'oracle') in Hebrew, but it is in fact derived from Egyptian *Panhsj*, originally a byname meaning 'the Nubian' and used as a personal name in Ancient Egypt. *Phineas* was popular among the Puritans in the 17th century, and has been occasionally used since, especially in America.

Phoebe F Latin form of the name of a Greek deity, *Phoibē* (from *phoibos* 'bright'), partly identified with Artemis, goddess of the moon and of hunting, sister of the sun god Apollo, who was also known as *Phoibos* (Latin *Phoebus*).

P

Phyllida F Variant spelling of **»Phillida**.

Phyllis F Name of a minor character in Greek mythology who killed herself for love and was transformed into an almond tree; the Greek word *phyllis* means 'foliage', so clearly her name doomed her from the start.

Piaras M Irish Gaelic name, derived in the Middle Ages from Anglo-Norman **»Piers**. Piaras Feiritéar (1600–53) was a Kerry chieftain and poet. In the 20th century *Piaras* has been used as a Gaelic form of **»Pearce**.

Pierce F English and Irish: variant of **»Piers**, in use in Ireland from the time of the Norman Conquest up to the present day. In many cases it may represent a transferred use of the English surname derived from the given name in the Middle Ages.

Piers M Regular medieval vernacular form of **»Peter**. In the form *Pierce* it survived into the 18th century, although in part this may be a transferred use of the surname derived from the medieval given name. *Piers* was revived in the mid 20th century, perhaps partly under the influence of William Langland's great rambling medieval poem *Piers Plowman* (1367–86), in which the character of Piers symbolizes the virtues of hard work, honesty, and fairness.

Pippa F Contracted pet form of **»Philippa**, now quite commonly used as an independent given name. It was popularized in the 19th century by Browning's narrative poem *Pippa Passes* (1841).

Polly F Variant of **»Molly**, now established as an independent given name.

Poppy F From the word denoting the flower, Old English *popæg*. It has been used as a given name since the latter years of the 19th century, and reached a peak of popularity in the 1920s.

Portia F This is the name of two characters in the works of Shakespeare. The most celebrated of them is an heiress in *The Merchant of Venice* who, disguised as a man, shows herself to be a brilliant advocate. It is also the name of the wife of Brutus in *Julius Caesar*. The historical Brutus's wife was called *Porcia*, feminine form of the Roman family name *Porcius*, which is apparently a derivative of Latin *porcus* 'pig'. The spelling **Porsha** also occurs.

Posy F Pet form (originally a nursery version) of »**Josephine**. It has also been associated with the vocabulary word *posy* 'bunch of flowers' (originally a collection of verses, from *poesy* 'poetry'). It is occasionally used as an independent given name, fitting into the series of names from flowers that arose in the 19th century.

Preston M Transferred use of the surname, in origin a local name from any of the numerous places in England named with Old English *prēost* 'priest' + *tūn* 'enclosure', 'settlement'.

Primrose F One of the several girls' names taken from words for flowers in the late 19th century. The word is from Latin *prima rosa* 'first rose', although it does not in fact have any connection with the rose family.

Prince M Originally a nickname from the royal title, Old French *prince*. This word was introduced to Britain by the Normans. The name is favoured among Blacks in Britain and the United States.

P

Priscilla F Of New Testament origin: from a post-classical Latin personal name, a feminine diminutive of the Roman family name *Priscus* 'ancient'. *Priscilla* was the name of a woman with whom St Paul stayed at Corinth (Acts 18:3), referred to elsewhere as *Prisca*. The name was popular among the Puritans in the 17th century and again enjoyed a vogue in the 19th century.

Proinnsias M Irish Gaelic form of »**Francis**.

Prudence F Originally a medieval form of the Latin name *Prūdentia*, a feminine derivative of *prūdens* 'provident'. The Blessed Prudentia was a 15th-century abbess who founded a new convent at Como in Italy. Later, among the Puritans in 17th-century England, *Prudence* was associated with the vocabulary word for the quality.

Prunella F Latinate name, probably one of the names coined in the 19th century from vocabulary words for plants and flowers, in this case from a diminutive derived from Late Latin *pruna* 'plum'.

Pryderi M Welsh: traditional name, meaning 'caring for' (later 'anxiety'). It is borne in the *Mabinogi* by Pryderi, son of Pwyll, who makes several appearances in the narrative.

P

Q

Queenie F Pet form from the affectionate nickname *Queen*, with the addition of the diminutive suffix *-ie*. In the Victorian era it was sometimes used as an allusive pet form for **»Victoria**.

Quentin M From the Old French form of the Latin name *Quintīnus*, a derivative of the given name **»Quintus**. The name was borne by a 3rd-century saint who worked as a missionary in Gaul.

Quincy M Mainly U.S.: transferred use of the English surname, in origin a Norman baronial name borne by a family that held lands at *Cuinchy* in Pas-de-Calais, Normandy. This was the surname of a prominent New England family in the colonial era. Josiah Quincy (1744–75) was a lawyer and Revolutionary patriot, a close friend of John Adams (1735–1826), second president of the United States (1797–1801). The latter's son, John Quincy Adams (1767–1848), also served as president (1825–9). He may have received his middle name in honour of his father's friend, or it may have been taken from the township of Quincy, Massachusetts, where he was born and where the Adams family had their seat. The spelling **Quincey** is also used.

Quinn M Transferred use of the Irish surname, Gaelic *Ó Cuinn* 'descendant of Conn'. The latter is from a word meaning 'leader' or 'chief'. It may also sometimes be used as a short form of **»Quincy** or **»Quintin**.

Quintin M Variant of **»Quentin**.

Quinton M Variant of **»Quentin**, influenced by the surname so spelled. The surname is a local name from any of several places named with Old English *cwēn* 'queen' + *tūn* 'enclosure', 'settlement'.

Quintus M An old Roman given name meaning 'fifth'. It has been used in the English-speaking world, mainly in the 19th century, for the fifth-born son or fifth-born child in a family.

q

R

Rabbie M Scottish: pet form of **»Robert**, from the short form *Rab, Rob*. It is now often associated with the poet Robert Burns (1759–96).

Rachael F Variant of **»Rachel**, influenced by **»Michael**.

Rachel F Biblical name (meaning 'ewe' in Hebrew), borne by the beloved wife of Jacob and mother of Joseph (Genesis 28–35) and of Benjamin, at whose birth she died. In the Middle Ages and later this was regarded as a characteristically Jewish name, but it is now also widely used among Gentiles.

Rachelle F Elaborated form of **»Rachel**, as if from French, but actually a recent coinage in English.

Rae F Mainly Australian: probably originally a short form of **»Rachel**, but now generally taken as a feminine form of **»Ray** or **»Raymond**, or simply a derivative of *ray* meaning 'sunbeam'. In some cases it may represent a transferred use of the Scottish surname *Rae*.

Raelene F Australian: fanciful coinage of recent origin, from **»Rae** + the productive feminine suffix *-lene*.

Raghnall M Irish Gaelic borrowing of the Old Norse name *Rögnvaldr*, derived from *regin* 'advice', 'decision' + *valdr* 'ruler'. The usual Anglicized form is **»Ranald**.

Rainbow F From the vocabulary word (from Old English *regn* 'rain' + *boga* 'bow', 'arch'). This is one of the names taken from the world of nature in the 1960s under the influence of the 'flower-power' movement.

Raine F Of modern origin and uncertain derivation. It
is possibly a respelling of the French vocabulary word
reine 'queen', or a transferred use of the surname *Raine*
or *Rayne*. The surname is derived from a medieval
given name, a short form of various Germanic
compound names derived from *ra(g)in* 'advice',
'decision'.

Ralph M From a Norman French name, *Raulf*, a
contracted form of the Germanic personal name *Radulf*,
derived from *rād* 'counsel' + *wulf* 'wolf'. The spelling
with -*ph* is due to classical influence in the 18th century.
The spellings **Ralf** and **Rafe** are also found.

Ramsay M Transferred use of the Scottish surname, in
origin a local name from *Ramsey* in the former county
of Huntingdonshire. In the 12th century David, brother
of King Alexander I of Scotland, was brought up at the
English court, and acquired the earldoms of Huntingdon
and Northampton. When he succeeded his brother as
king, he took many of his retainers and associates with
him to Scotland, and some of them took their surnames
with them from places in eastern England. This explains
why some famous Scottish surnames, such as *Ramsay*,
Lindsay, *Graham*, etc., are derived from placenames in
that part of England. Some of these surnames have in
turn gone on to be used as given names. The spelling
Ramsey is also found.

Ranald M Scottish: Anglicized form of the Gaelic name
»**Raghnall**.

Randa F Modern coinage, probably a shortened form
of »**Miranda**. See also »**Randy**.

Randall M Common medieval vernacular form of
»**Randolf**, also used to represent Gaelic »**Raghnall**.
This name fell out of use, but before it did so gave rise
to a surname. Modern use as a given name represents
a transferred use of this surname. The spellings **Randal**,
Randel(l), **Randle** are also found.

Randolf M From a Norman given name, Old Norse *Rannulfr*, derived from *rand* 'rim', 'shield' (or *hrafn* 'raven') + *úlfr* 'wolf'. The spelling **Randolph** also occurs.

Randy M, F Mainly North American and Australian: as a boy's name this originated as a pet form of **»Randall**, **»Randolf**, or **»Andrew**. As a girl's name it may have originated either as a transferred use of the boy's name or else as a pet form of **»Miranda** (cf. **»Randa**). It is now fairly commonly used as an independent name, mainly by men, in spite of the unfortunate connotations of the slang term *randy* 'lustful'. As a girl's name it is also spelled **Randie** and **Randi**.

Ranulf M Scottish: from an Old Norse personal name, *Reginulfr*, derived from *regin* 'advice', 'decision' + *úlfr* 'wolf'. This was introduced into Scotland by Scandinavian settlers in the early Middle Ages.

Raquel F Spanish form of **»Rachel**, brought to public attention by the American film actress Raquel Welch (b. 1940). The spelling **Raquelle** also occurs.

Rastus M Of New Testament origin, where it is a shortened form of the Latin name *Erastus* (Greek *Erastos*, from *erān* 'to love'). This was the name of the treasurer of Corinth converted to Christianity by St Paul (Romans 16:23). In the early 20th century *Rastus* came to be regarded as a typically Black name.

Ray M Short form of **»Raymond**, now also used as an independent given name. In some instances it may represent a transferred use of the surname *Ray*, which for the most part originated as a nickname, from Old French *rei*, *roi* 'king'.

Raymond M From an Old French name, *Raimund*, of Germanic origin, from *ragin* 'advice', 'decision' + *mund* 'protector'. This was adopted by the Normans and introduced by them into England. Subsequently it dropped out of use, but was revived in the middle of the 19th century, together with several other given names of Old English and Norman origin.

Rayner M Transferred use of the surname derived from a Norman personal name. This is of Old French origin (*Rainer*), from a Germanic (Frankish) personal name derived from *ragin* 'advice', 'decision' + *heri, hari* 'army'.

Read M Transferred use of the English surname, which for the most part originated as a nickname for someone with red hair or a ruddy complexion (from Old English *rēad* 'red'; cf. **»Reid**). In other cases, it may have arisen as a local name, from Old English *hrēod* 'reeds' or *rēod* 'cleared land'.

Reanna F Modern coinage, apparently an altered form of the Welsh name **»Rhiannon**. The variant **Reanne** is also found.

Rearden M Variant of **»Riordan**.

Reba F Modern coinage, apparently derived from the first and last syllables of **»Rebecca**.

Rebecca F Biblical, from the Latin form of the Hebrew name *Rebekah*, borne by the wife of Isaac, who was the mother of Esau and Jacob (Genesis 24–27). The origin of the name is uncertain, but as Rebecca was Aramean her name probably has a source in Aramaic. It has always been common as a Jewish name; in England and elsewhere it began to be used also by Christians at the time of the Reformation, when Old Testament names became popular. It was very common among the Puritans in the 17th century, and has enjoyed a tremendous vogue in England in the latter part of the 20th century, among people of many different creeds.

Redmond M Irish: apparently an Anglicized form of the Gaelic name *Réamann*, itself a form of **»Raymond**. An alternative explanation derives it from an Old English personal name derived from *ræd* 'counsel' + *mund* 'protector'.

Reenie F Respelling of **»Renée**, representing an
Anglicized pronunciation of the name. It may also
occasionally be a pet form of various names ending in
the syllable *-reen*, such as **»Doreen** and **»Maureen**.

Rees M Anglicized spelling of the Welsh name **»Rhys**,
in some cases representing a transferred use of the
surname so spelled, which is derived from the Welsh
given name. The spelling **Reece** also occurs.

Regan F Apparently of Shakespearian origin. This is
the name of one of the three daughters in *King Lear*
(1605), a most unattractive character. It is not known
where Shakespeare got the name; he presumably
believed it to be of Celtic origin. It can be identified
with the Irish Gaelic word *ríogan* 'queen' (pronounced
'**ree**-gan'). Modern use has been reinforced by the Irish
surname *Re(a)gan* (Gaelic Ó *Riagáin*).

Regina F From the Latin vocabulary word meaning
'queen'. It was occasionally used as a given name
among the early Christians; a St Regina, probably of
the 3rd century, was venerated as a virgin martyr at
Autun from an early date. In modern use it is normally
borne by Roman Catholics in allusion to the epithet
Regīna Coeli 'Queen of Heaven', a cult title of the Virgin
Mary since the 8th century. It is also found as a Latinization of the traditional Gaelic name **»Rionach**, which
likewise means 'queen'.

r

Reginald M Of Norman origin, derived from
Reginaldus, a Latinized form of **»Reynold** influenced
by Latin *regīna* 'queen'. The full form is now regarded
as very formal, and bearers generally shorten it to **Reg**
in ordinary usage.

Reid M Transferred use of the Scottish and northern
English surname, originally a nickname for someone
with red hair or a ruddy complexion (from Old English
rēad 'red'; cf. **»Read**).

Reine F French vernacular form of Latin *rēgīna* 'queen', probably arising for the most part as an affectionate nickname, but also perhaps with reference to the Virgin Mary, one of whose titles is 'Queen of Heaven'.

Rena F Of recent origin, either an altered form of **»Renée**, or else a variant spelling of **»Rina**.

Renée F French: from the Late Latin female name *Renāta* 'reborn', used by early Christians as a baptismal name celebrating spiritual rebirth in Christ. The name is also used in the English-speaking world, often without the accent and in a highly Anglicized pronunciation (cf. **»Reenie**).

Reuben M Biblical name (said to mean 'behold, a son' in Hebrew), borne by one of the twelve sons of Jacob, and so the name of one of the twelve tribes of Israel. In Genesis 30:14–15, Reuben is depicted as a devoted son to his mother, but he incurred his father's wrath for seducing his concubine Bilhah and on his deathbed Jacob cursed Reuben because of this incident (Genesis 49:4). Despite this, the name has enjoyed steady popularity as a Jewish name. Among Christians (chiefly Nonconformists) it was briefly in vogue after the Reformation and again in the 19th century.

Rex M From the Latin vocabulary word meaning 'king'. This was not used as a personal name in Latin of the classical or Christian periods, and its adoption as a given name seems to have been a 19th-century innovation. Its popularity was increased by the fame of the British actor Rex Harrison (1908–90).

Rexanne F Altered form of **»Roxane** or feminine equivalent of **»Rex**.

Reynard M From an Old French name of Germanic (Frankish) origin, derived from *ragin* 'advice', 'decision' + *hard* 'hardy', 'brave', 'strong'. In French, *renard* has become the generic term for a fox, as a result of the popularity of medieval beast tales featuring *Re(y)nard*

le goupil 'Reynard the Fox'. The name was adopted by
the Normans and introduced by them to Britain.

Reynold   M   From an Old French name, *Reinald*,
Reynaud, of Germanic (Frankish) origin, derived from
ragin 'advice', 'decision' + *wald* 'ruler'. This was adopted
by the Normans and introduced by them into England.
In modern use, the given name sometimes represents a
transferred use of the surname derived from the
Norman personal name. See also **»Ronald**.

Rhea   F   The name borne, according to Roman tradition,
by the mother (Rhea Silvia) of Romulus and Remus,
who grew up to be the founders of the city of Rome. It
was also a title of the goddess Cybele, introduced to
Rome from Phrygia. Its meaning is unknown.

Rheanna   F   Altered form of the Welsh name
»Rhiannon.

Rhett   M   Transferred use of a surname well established
in South Carolina, an Anglicization of the Dutch
surname *de Raedt* (from Middle Dutch *raet* 'advice').
Robert Barnwell Rhett (1800–76) was a South Carolina
congressman and senator, a noted secessionist. The
name was used by Margaret Mitchell in *Gone with the
Wind* (1936) for the character of the black sheep and
charmer Rhett Butler. Like some of the other unusual
names in that novel, it has attained a modest currency.

Rhetta   F   Name coined as a feminine form of **»Rhett**.

Rhiannon   F   Welsh: name borne in Celtic mythology by
a minor deity associated with the moon, and in the
Mabinogi by a daughter of Hyfeidd the Old. It is
probably derived from the Old Celtic title *Rigantona*
'great queen'; it was not used as a given name before
the 20th century.

Rhoda   F   From the post-classical Greek name *Rhoda*,
derived either from *rhodon* 'rose', or as an ethnic name
meaning 'woman from Rhodes' (Greek *Rhodos*). In the
New Testament Rhoda was a servant in the house of

Mary the mother of John, where Peter went after his release from prison by an angel (Acts 12:13). In the Scottish Highlands *Rhoda* is used as a feminine form of **»Roderick**.

Rhodri M Welsh: from an Old Welsh personal name derived from *rhod* 'wheel' + *rhi* 'ruler', borne by a 9th-century Welsh king. The spelling **Rhodrhi** is also used.

Rhona F Of uncertain derivation, apparently originating in Scotland sometime around 1870. The spelling *Rona* is also found, and it is probable that the name was devised as a feminine form of **»Ronald**. It has also been suggested that it may be associated with the Hebridean island name *Rona* (cf. **»Ailsa**, **»Iona**, **»Isla**). In either case the spelling would then have been altered by association with **»Rhoda**.

Rhonda F Modern coinage, a blend of **»Rhoda** and **»Rhona**. It is now often taken to be a Welsh name derived from *rhon* 'pike', 'lance' + *-da* 'good'. The name is associated particularly with the American film actress Rhonda Fleming (b. 1923).

Rhonwen F Welsh: traditional name derived either from *rhon* 'lance' + *(g)wen* 'white', 'fair', 'blessed', 'holy', or from *rhawn* 'hair' + *(g)wen*. It was used by medieval Welsh poets as a form of **»Rowena**, regarded as the progenitrix of the English nation, and is now fairly common in Wales.

Rhydderch M Welsh: traditional name, originally a byname meaning 'reddish-brown'. This was a relatively common name in the Middle Ages and in Tudor times, when it gave rise to the surname *Prothero(e)* (Welsh *ap Rhydderch* 'son of Rhydderch'). It has recently been revived by parents proudly conscious of their Welsh roots and culture. See also **»Roderick**.

Rhys M Welsh: traditional name meaning 'ardour'. The name was borne in the early Middle Ages by various rulers in south-west Wales, such as Rhys ap Tewdur (d.

1093) and Rhys ap Gruffudd (1132–97). See also
»Rees.

Rian M Irish: see **»Ryan**.

Ricarda F Latinate feminine form of **»Richard**.

Rich M Short form of **»Richard**. There was a medieval
given name *Rich(e)*, but it is connected only indirectly
with the modern form. It represents a short form of
several medieval names, including not only *Richard* but
also other names of Old French (Germanic) origin with
the same first element, as, for example, *Rich(i)er* 'power
army' and *Richaud* 'power rule'.

Richard M One of the most enduringly successful of
the Old French personal names introduced into Britain
by the Normans. It is of Germanic (Frankish) origin,
derived from *rīc* 'power' + *hard* 'hardy', 'brave', 'strong'.
It was borne by three kings of England, in particular
Richard I (1157–99). He was king for only ten years
(1189–99), most of which he spent in warfare abroad,
taking part in the Third Crusade and costing the people
of England considerable sums in taxes. Nevertheless,
he achieved the status of a folk hero, and was never in
England long enough to disappoint popular faith in his
goodness and justice. His exploits as a leader of the
Third Crusade earned him the nickname 'Coeur de Lion'
or 'Lionheart' and a permanent place in popular
imagination, in which he was even more firmly
enshrined by Sir Walter Scott's novel *Ivanhoe* (1820).
Among numerous short forms, pet forms, and
derivatives are **Rick**, **Dick**, **»Rich**, **»Ricky**, **Rickie**;
Dicky, **Dickie**; **Richie**.

Richelle F Modern feminine form of **»Richard**, derived
from the first syllable of that name + *-elle*, feminine
diminutive suffix of French origin.

Richie M Pet form of **»Richard**. The suffix *-ie* was
originally characteristic of Scotland and northern
England, but the name is now found elsewhere. In some

r

cases it represents a transferred use of the surname derived from the Scottish pet name. The variant **Ritchie**, probably also a transferred use of the surname spelled thus, is also found.

Ricky M Pet form of **»Richard**, also used as an independent name for boys and (occasionally) girls. As a girl's name various alternative spellings are found, including **Rickie**, **Ricki**, and **»Rikki**.

Ridley M Transferred use of the surname, in origin a local name from any of various places so named. The given name may have been chosen in some cases by ardent Protestants in honour of Bishop Nicholas Ridley (?1500–55), burnt at the stake for his Protestantism under Mary Tudor.

Rikki F Variant spelling of the girl's name **»Ricky**.

Riley M, F In some cases a transferred use of the English surname, a local name from a place so named, for example in Devon and in Lancashire. In other cases it may be a respelling of the Irish surname *Reilly*, which is from an old Irish personal name, *Raghallach*, of unknown origin.

Rina F Short form of **»Katerina** or **»Carina**, or Anglicized form of Gaelic **»Rionach**.

Rionach F Irish: traditional Gaelic name meaning 'royal' or 'queenly', sometimes found in the Latinized form **»Regina**. It is also spelled **Ríoghnach** and sometimes Anglicized as **Rinach** or **»Rina**.

Riordan M Irish: Anglicized form of the Gaelic name **Ríordán**, earlier *Ríoghbhardán*, from *ríogh* 'king' + *bardán*, a diminutive of *bard* 'poet'. Modern use of the given name is influenced by the surname *O'Riordan*, derived from the Gaelic personal name.

Rita F Originally a short form of *Margarita*, the Spanish form of **»Margaret**, but now commonly used as an independent given name. It is associated particularly with the American film star Rita Hayworth (1918–87).

Ritchie M Variant spelling of **»Richie**.

River M From the vocabulary word. This is one of the names taken from the world of nature in the 1960s.

Robert M One of the many French names of Germanic origin that were introduced into Britain by the Normans, derived from the elements *hrod* 'fame' + *berht* 'bright', 'famous'. It had a native Old English predecessor of similar form (*Hreodbeorht*). It was the name of two dukes of Normandy in the 11th century: the father of William the Conqueror (sometimes identified with the legendary Robert the Devil), and his eldest son. It was borne by three kings of Scotland, notably Robert the Bruce (1274–1329), who freed Scotland from English domination. See also **»Rupert**. There are many short forms, pet forms, and derivatives, including **Bob**, **Rob**, **Rab** (Scottish), **»Bobby**, **Robbie**, and **»Rabbie** (Scottish).

Roberta F Latinate feminine form of **»Robert**.

Robin M, F Originally a pet form of **»Robert**, from the short form **Rob** + the diminutive suffix *-in* (of Old French origin), but now nearly always used as an independent name. In recent years it has been increasingly used as a girl's name, partly under the influence of the vocabulary word for the bird. The girl's name is also spelled **Robyn**.

Rochelle F Of uncertain origin, probably a feminine pet form of the French boy's name *Roch* (from Germanic *hrok* 'rest'), borne by a 14th-century saint, patron of the sick. This girl's name is little used in France, though widely used in the English-speaking world. It may in part represent a respelling of **»Rachelle**.

Rocky M Mainly U.S.: of recent origin, originally a nickname for a tough individual. The name came to public notice through the American boxing champion Rocky Marciano (1923–69). He was of Italian extraction, and Anglicized his original name, *Rocco*, into

r

a form that seems particularly appropriate for a fighter. It was later taken up in a series of films as the name of a boxer played by the actor Sylvester Stallone.

Roda F Variant spelling of **»Rhoda**.

Roderick M Of Germanic origin, from *hrōd* 'fame' + *rīc* 'power'. This name was introduced into England, in slightly different forms, first by Scandinavian settlers in the Danelaw and later by the Normans. However, it did not survive beyond the Middle English period. It owes its modern use to a poem by Sir Walter Scott, *The Vision of Don Roderick* (1811), where it is an Anglicized form of the cognate Spanish name *Rodrigo*, borne by the last Visigothic king of Spain, whose vision is the subject of the poem. It is now also very commonly used as an Anglicized form of two unrelated Celtic names: Scottish Gaelic *Ruairidh* (see **»Rory**) and Welsh **»Rhydderch**.

Rodger M Variant spelling of **»Roger**, in part from the surname derived from the given name in the Middle Ages.

Rodney M Originally a transferred use of the surname, but in independent use as a given name since the 18th century, when it was bestowed in honour of Admiral Lord Rodney (1719–92), who defeated the French navy in 1759–60. The surname probably derives ultimately from a placename, but the location and etymology of this are uncertain.

Roger M From an Old French personal name, *Rog(i)er*, of Germanic (Frankish) origin, from *hrōd* 'fame' + *gār*, *gēr* 'spear'. This was adopted by the Normans and introduced by them to Britain, replacing the native Old English form *Hrōthgār*. Roger, Count of Sicily (*c.* 1031–1101), son of Tancred, recovered Sicily from the Arabs. His son, also called Roger, ruled Sicily as king, presiding over a court noted for its splendour and patronage of the arts. The spelling **»Rodger** is also found.

Róisín F Irish Gaelic name, pronounced 'roe-sheen': pet form of *Rós*, the Gaelic form of **»Rose**. The Anglicized spelling **»Rosheen** is also found.

Roland M From an Old French personal name of Germanic (Frankish) origin, from *hrōd* 'fame' + *land* 'land', 'territory'. This was adopted by the Normans and introduced by them to Britain. In Old French literature, it is borne by a legendary Frankish hero, a vassal of Charlemagne, whose exploits are related in the *Chanson de Roland*. The spelling **»Rowland** is also found.

Rolf M Contracted version of an old Germanic personal name derived from *hrōd* 'fame' + *wulf* 'wolf'. As an English given name, it represents in part the survival of a form imported by the Normans, in part a much more recent (19th-century) importation of the modern German name. See also **»Rudolf**.

Rollo M Latinized form of *Roul*, the Old French version of **»Rolf**. This form appears regularly in Latin documents of the Middle Ages, but does not seem to have been used in everyday vernacular contexts. It is the form by which the first Duke of Normandy (*c.*860–932) is generally known. He was a Viking who, with his followers, settled at the mouth of the Seine and raided Paris, Chartres, and elsewhere. By the treaty of St Clair he received the duchy of Normandy from Charles III, on condition that he should receive Christian baptism. Use of this name in English families in modern times seems to be a consciously archaistic revival.

Rona F Variant spelling of **»Rhona**.

Ronald M From the Old Norse personal name *Rögnvaldr* (see **»Ranald**). This name was regularly used in the Middle Ages in northern England and Scotland, where Scandinavian influence was strong. It is now widespread throughout the English-speaking world.

r

Ronan M Irish: Anglicized form of the traditional Gaelic name *Rónán*, a diminutive of *rón* 'seal' (the animal). The name is recorded as being borne by various early Irish saints, but there has been much confusion in the transmission of their names and some of them are also identified as *Ruadhán* (see **»Rowan**). The most famous is a 5th-century Irish saint who was consecrated as a bishop by St Patrick and subsequently worked as a missionary in Cornwall and Brittany.

Rory M Anglicized form of the traditional Gaelic name **Ruaidhrí**, **Ruarí** (Irish) or **Ruairidh**, **Ruaraidh** (Scottish), from *ruaidh* or *rua* 'red-haired', 'fiery' + *rí* 'king'. It is sometimes further Anglicized to **»Roderick**.

Rosa F Latinate form of **»Rose**.

Rosaleen F Variant of **»Rosalyn**, influenced by the suffix *-een* (in origin the Irish Gaelic diminutive *-ín*). 'Dark Rosaleen' was the title of a poem by James Clarence Mangan (1803–49), based on the Gaelic poem *Róisín Dubh*; in it the name is used as a figurative allusion to the Irish nation.

Rosalie F French form of the Latin name *Rosalia* (a derivative of *rosa* 'rose'), introduced to the English-speaking world in the latter part of the 19th century. St Rosalia was a 12th-century Sicilian virgin, and is the patron of Palermo.

Rosalind F From an Old French personal name of Germanic (Frankish) origin, from *hros* 'horse' + *lind* 'weak', 'tender', 'soft'. It was adopted by the Normans and introduced by them to Britain. Its popularity as a given name owes much to its use by Edmund Spenser for the character of a shepherdess in his pastoral poetry, and by Shakespeare as the name of the heroine in *As You Like It* (1599).

Rosaline F Originally a variant of **»Rosalind**. It is the name of a minor character in Shakespeare's *Love's*

Labour's Lost and is used for another, who does not appear but is merely mentioned, in *Romeo and Juliet*.

Rosalyn F Altered form of **≫Rosalind**. *Rosalin* was a common medieval form, since the letters *d* and *t* were often added or dropped capriciously at the end of words after *n*. The name has been further influenced by the productive suffix *-lyn* (see **≫Lynn**). The spellings **Rosalynn** and **Rosalynne** are also found.

Rosamund F From an Old French personal name of Germanic (Frankish) origin, from *hros* 'horse' + *mund* 'protection'. This was adopted by the Normans and introduced by them to Britain. The spelling **Rosamond** has been common since the Middle Ages, when scribes used *o* for *u*, to distinguish it from *n* and *m*, all of which consisted of very similar downstrokes of the pen. 'Fair Rosamond' (Rosamond Clifford) was a legendary beauty who lived at Woodstock in Oxfordshire in the 12th century. She is said to have been the mistress of King Henry II, and to have been murdered by the queen, Eleanor of Aquitaine, in 1176.

Rosanne F Modern coinage, from a combination of the names **≫Rose** and **≫Anne**, probably influenced by the popularity of the given name **≫Roxane**. There are a number of variants, including **Roseanne**, **Rosanna**, and the fanciful respelling **Rosannagh**.

Roscoe M Transferred use of the surname, in origin a local name from a place in northern England named with Old Norse *rá* 'roe deer' + *skógr* 'wood', 'copse'.

Rose F Ostensibly from the vocabulary word denoting the flower (Latin *rosa*). However, the name was in use throughout the Middle Ages, long before any of the other girls' names derived from flowers, which are generally of 19th-century origin. In part it may refer to the flower as a symbol of the Virgin Mary, but it seems more likely that it also has a Germanic origin, probably as a short form of various female names based on *hros*

r

'horse' or *hrōd* 'fame'. The Latinate form *Rohesia* is commonly found in documents of the Middle Ages. As well as being a name in its own right, it is currently used as a short form of **»Rosemary** and, less often (because of their different pronunciation), of other names beginning *Ros-*, such as **»Rosalind** and **»Rosamund**.

Roselle F Modern coinage, a combination of the given name **»Rose** with the productive suffix *-elle* (originally a French feminine diminutive suffix).

Rosemary F 19th-century coinage, from the name of the herb (which is from Latin *ros marīnus* 'sea dew'). It is often also assumed to be a combination of the names **»Rose** and **»Mary**. The spelling **Rosemarie** is also found.

Rosetta F Italian pet form of **»Rosa**, sometimes also used in the English-speaking world.

Rosheen F Irish: Anglicized form of **»Róisín**.

Rosie F Pet form of **»Rose** and **»Rosemary**. It was first used in the 1860s and is now well established as an independent given name.

Ross M Either an adoption of the Gaelic topographic term *ros* 'headland' or a transferred use of the Scottish surname, which is borne by a large and ancient family whose members have played a major role in Scottish history.

Rowan M, F As a boy's name this represents a transferred use of the surname, which is of Irish origin, being an Anglicized form of the Gaelic byname *Ruadhán* 'little red one'. It was borne by a 6th-century saint who founded the monastery of Lothra. As a girl's name it seems to be from the vocabulary word (of Scandinavian origin) denoting the tree.

Rowena F Latinized form of a Saxon name of uncertain form and derivation. It is perhaps from Germanic *hrōd* 'fame' + *wynn* 'joy'. It first occurs in the Latin chronicles

of Geoffrey of Monmouth (12th century) as the name
of a daughter of the Saxon invader Hengist, and was
taken up by Sir Walter Scott as the name of a Saxon
woman, Lady Rowena of Hargottstanstede, who marries
the eponymous hero of his novel *Ivanhoe* (1819).

Rowland M Variant of **»Roland**, or a transferred use
of the surname derived from that given name in the
Middle Ages.

Rowley M Pet form of **»Rowland**, or a transferred use
of the surname, a local name from any of the various
places in England so named.

Roxane F From Latin *Roxana*, Greek *Roxanē*, recorded
as the name of the wife of Alexander the Great. She
was the daughter of Oxyartes the Bactrian, and her
name is presumably of Persian origin; it is said to mean
'dawn'. In English literature it is the name of the heroine
of a novel by Defoe (1724). The variants **Roxanne** and
Roxanna are also found.

Roy M Originally a Scottish name, representing an
Anglicized spelling of the Gaelic nickname *Ruadh* 'red'.
It has since spread to other parts of the English-speaking
world, where it is often reanalysed as Old French *roy*
'king'.

Royle M Transferred use of the surname, in origin a
local name from a place in Lancashire so called. In part
it may have been adopted as a given name because of
association with the vocabulary word *royal*.

Royston M Transferred use of the surname, in origin a
local name from a place in Hertfordshire. Royston is
now widely used as a given name, especially among
West Indians.

Rozanne F Variant of **»Rosanne** or *Roxanne* (see
»Roxane).

r

Ruben M Variant spelling of **»Reuben**.

Ruby F From the vocabulary word for the gemstone (Latin *rubīnus*, from *rubeus* 'red'). The name was popular in the late 19th century and up to the middle of the 20th and is now enjoying a revival.

Rudolf M From a Latinized version, *Rudolphus*, of the Germanic name *Hrōdwulf* (see **»Rolf**). It was introduced to the English-speaking world from Germany in the 19th century. *Rudolf* was a hereditary name among the Habsburgs, the Holy Roman Emperors and rulers of Austria, from the Emperor Rudolf I (1218–91) to the Archduke Rudolf, Crown Prince of Austria–Hungary, who died in mysterious circumstances in 1889. Rudolf Rassendyll was the central character of Anthony Hope's adventure stories *The Prisoner of Zenda* (1894) and *Rupert of Hentzau* (1898). In the early 20th century the popularity of this name was further enhanced by the American silent-film actor Rudolph Valentino (1895–1926). The spelling **Rudolph** also occurs.

Rupert M Low German form of **»Robert**, first brought to England by Prince Rupert of the Rhine (1618–92), a dashing military leader who came to help his uncle, Charles I, in the Civil War.

Russ M Short form of **»Russell**, now also used as an independent given name. In some cases it may represent a transferred use of the surname *Russ*, from Old French *rous* 'red'.

Russell M Transferred use of the common surname, originally from the Old French nickname *Rousel* 'little red one' (a diminutive of *rous* 'red'). Use as a given name may have been inspired by the philosopher Bertrand Russell (1872–1970), who was noted for his liberal agnostic views.

Ruth F Biblical name (of uncertain derivation) of a Moabite woman who left her own people to remain with her mother-in-law Naomi, and afterwards became the wife of Boaz and an ancestress of David. Her story is told in the book of the Bible that bears her name. It was popular among the Puritans, partly because of its association with the English vocabulary word *ruth* meaning 'compassion'. It has always been popular as a Jewish name, but is now also widespread among people of many different cultures.

Ryan M, F Anglicization of the traditional Gaelic name *Ríoghan*, a derivative of *rí* 'king'. The modern given name has been influenced by the surname derived from the ancient Gaelic name, and is associated with the film actor Ryan O'Neal (b. 1941). It is also well established in North America as a girl's name.

r

S

Sabina F From the Latin name *Sabīna* 'Sabine woman'. The Sabines were an ancient Italic race whose territory was taken over by the Romans. According to tradition, the Romans made a raid on the Sabines and carried off a number of their women, but when the Sabines came for revenge the women succeeded in making peace between the two groups. The name *Sabina* was borne by three minor early Christian saints, in particular a Roman maiden martyred in about 127.

Sabrina F From the name of a character in Celtic legend, who supposedly gave her name to the River Severn. In fact this is one of the most ancient of all British river names, and its true origins are obscure. Legend had it that Sabrina was the illegitimate daughter of a Welsh king called Locrine, and was drowned in the river on the orders of the king's wife Gwendolen. Almost certainly it is the name of this legendary figure that is derived from that of the river, rather than vice versa.

Sacheverell M Transferred use of the surname, apparently originally a baronial name of Norman origin (from an unidentified place in Normandy believed to have been called *Saute-Chevreuil*, meaning 'roebuck leap'). It was made familiar as a given name by the writer Sacheverell Sitwell (1897–1985), who was named in honour of his ancestor William Sacheverell (1638–91), a minor Whig statesman.

Sadhbh F Traditional Irish Gaelic name, pronounced 'syve', from an obsolete Irish word meaning 'sweet'. In

Irish legend, Sadhbh, daughter of Conn Cétchathach (Conn of the Hundred Battles), was considered 'the best woman in Ireland who ever lay with a man'. It was a common female name during the Middle Ages and has recently been revived. It is sometimes Anglicized as **»Sally**.

Sadie F Originally a pet form of **»Sarah**, but now generally considered as an independent name. The exact formation is not clear: probably a nursery form.

St John M Name expressing devotion to St John, generally pronounced '**sin**-jen'; it has been in use in the English-speaking world, mainly among Roman Catholics, from the last two decades of the 19th century up to the present day.

Sally F In origin a pet form of **»Sarah**, but in the 20th century normally considered as an independent name. It is frequently used as the first element in combinations such as *Sally-Anne* and *Sally-Jane*. In Ireland it sometimes represents an Anglicization of **»Sadhbh**.

Salome F Greek form of an unrecorded Aramaic name, related to the Hebrew word *shalom* 'peace'. It was common at the time of Christ, and was borne by one of the women who were at his tomb and witnessed the Resurrection (Mark 16:1–8). This would normally have led to its common use as a Christian name, and it is indeed found as such in medieval times. However, according to the Jewish historian Josephus, it was also the name of King Herod's stepdaughter, the daughter of Queen Herodias. In the Bible, a daughter of Herodias, generally identified as this Salome, danced for Herod and so pleased him that he offered to give her anything she wanted. Prompted by her mother, she asked for (and got) the head of John the Baptist, who was in one of Herod's prisons (Mark 6:17–28). This story so gripped medieval imagination that the name Salome became more or less taboo until the end of the 19th century, when Oscar Wilde wrote a play about her

S

and some unconventional souls began to choose the name for their daughters.

Samantha F Of problematic and much debated origin. It arose in the southern states of America in the 18th century, possibly as a combination of *Sam* (from **»Samuel**) + a newly coined feminine suffix -*antha* (perhaps suggested by **»Anthea**).

Samson M Biblical name (Hebrew *Shimshon*, probably derived from *shemesh* 'sun'), borne by a Jewish champion and judge famous for his prodigious strength. He was betrayed by his mistress, Delilah, and enslaved and blinded by the Philistines; nevertheless, he was able to bring the pillars of the temple of the Philistines crashing down in a final suicidal act of strength (Judges 13–16). In the Middle Ages the popularity of the given name was increased in Celtic areas by the fame of a 6th-century Celtic saint who bore it, probably as a classicized form of some ancient Celtic name. The spelling **Sampson**, usually a transferred use of the surname, derived from the given name in the Middle Ages, is also found.

Samuel M Biblical name (Hebrew *Shemuel*), possibly meaning 'He (God) has hearkened' (presumably to the prayers of a mother for a son). It may also be understood as a contracted form of Hebrew *sha'ulme'el* meaning 'asked of God'. Living in the 11th century BC, Samuel, the son of Hannah, was a Hebrew judge and prophet of the greatest historical importance, who established the Hebrew monarchy, anointing as King both Saul and, later, David. In the Authorized Version two books of the Old Testament are named after him, although in Roman Catholic and Orthodox versions of the Bible they are known as the first and second Book of Kings. The story of Samuel being called by God while still a child serving in the house of Eli the priest (1 Samuel 3) is of great vividness and has moved countless generations. In England and America the name was particularly popular among the 17th-century Puritans and among Nonconformists from the 17th to the 19th century.

Sandford M Mainly U.S.: transferred use of the surname (see **»Sanford**).

Sandra F Short form of *Alessandra*, the Italian form of **»Alexandra**. A major influence in establishing this as a common given name in the English-speaking world was George Meredith's novel *Sandra Belloni* (1886), originally published as *Emilia in England* (1864).

Sandy F, M Pet form, originally Scottish, of **»Alexander** and **»Alexandra**, now also used as a girl's independent given name. It is also used as a nickname for someone with a crop of 'sandy' (light reddish-brown) hair. As a girl's name it is also spelled **Sandie**.

Sanford M Mainly U.S.: transferred use of the surname, in origin a local name from any of numerous places in England called *Sandford*. Use as a given name honours Peleg Sanford, an early governor (1680–3) of Rhode Island. The spelling **Sandford** is also found.

Saoirse F Irish Gaelic name, pronounced 'seer-sha': a modern coinage from the vocabulary word meaning 'freedom'.

Sapphire F From the word for the gemstone (via Old French and Latin from Greek *sappheiros*). The Greek term seems to have originally denoted lapis lazuli, but was later transferred to the transparent blue stone.

Sara F Variant of **»Sarah**. This is the form used in the Greek of the New Testament (Hebrews 11:11).

Sarah F Biblical name, borne by the wife of Abraham and mother of Isaac. According to the Book of Genesis, she was originally called *Sarai* (possibly meaning 'contentious' in Hebrew), but had her name changed by God to the more auspicious *Sarah* 'princess' in token of a greater blessing (Genesis 17:15). The variants **»Sara** and **»Zara** are also found.

Sasha F, M English spelling of a Russian pet form of
>>**Alexander** and >>**Alexandra**. It has been used in the
English-speaking world as an independent name,
introduced in the 20th century via France. Use as a
girl's name in the English-speaking world is encouraged
by the characteristic feminine -*a* ending.

Saskia F Dutch name of uncertain derivation, now also
used in the English-speaking world. It has been in use
since the Middle Ages, and may be derived from
Germanic *sachs* 'Saxon'.

Saul M Biblical name (from a Hebrew word meaning
'asked for' or 'prayed for'), borne by one of the first kings
of Israel. It was also the name of St Paul before his
conversion to Christianity (Acts 9:4). It enjoyed some
popularity among the Puritans, but is now once again
mainly a Jewish name.

Saundra F Scottish variant of >>**Sandra**, reflecting the
same development in pronunciation as is shown by
surnames such as *Saunders* and *Saunderson*, originally
from short forms of >>**Alexander**.

Savannah F Mainly U.S.: apparently from the name of
cities in Georgia and South Carolina. Both are on the
Savannah River, ostensibly named with the word for a
treeless plain. However, the river name may be an
adaptation of some other name existing prior to
European settlement. The given name may be taken
directly from the vocabulary word, more under the
influence of its sound than its meaning. The spelling
Savanna is also found.

Sawney M Scottish variant of >>**Sandy**, resulting from
a pronunciation which is also reflected in the surname
Saunders. The name declined in popularity after the
18th century, no doubt adversely affected by the use of
Sawney as a vocabulary word for a simpleton.

Scarlett F Name popularized by the central character
in the novel *Gone With the Wind* (1936) by Margaret

Mitchell, later made into a film. The characters in the novel bear a variety of unusual given names, which had a remarkable influence on naming practices in the English-speaking world in the 20th century. According to the novel, the name of the heroine was Katie Scarlett O'Hara (the middle name representing her grandmother's maiden surname), but she was always known as Scarlett. The surname *Scarlett* is in origin an occupational name for a dyer or for a seller of fabrics, from Old French *escarlate* 'scarlet cloth'. The spelling **Scarlet** is also found.

Scott M Although this was in use as a personal name both before and after the Norman Conquest, modern use in most cases almost certainly represents a transferred use of the surname. This originated as a byname for someone from Scotland or, within Scotland itself, a member of the Gaelic-speaking people who originally came from Ireland. The given name is sometimes chosen by parents conscious of their Scottish ancestry and heritage, but it is now also used much more widely.

Séamas M Modern Irish Gaelic form of »**James**, pronounced 'shay-mus'.

Séamus M Earlier Irish Gaelic form of »**James**; cf. »**Séamas**. This is also used without the accent as a partially Anglicized form of the name.

s

Seán M Irish Gaelic form of »**John**, pronounced 'shawn'. It was derived in the early Middle Ages via Anglo-Norman *Jehan* from Latin *Johannes*. It has always been common in Ireland, but since the 1960s has frequently been chosen (usually without the accent) by parents who have no Irish connections. One influence on its popularity has been the actor Sean Connery (b. 1930), of James Bond fame.

Seanan M Traditional Irish Gaelic name, pronounced 'shan-an', from a diminutive of the vocabulary word *sean* 'old', 'venerable'. It is also spelled **Senan**.

Sebastian M From Latin *Sebastiānus*, meaning 'man from Sebastē' (a town in Asia Minor). It was the name of a 3rd-century saint, a Roman soldier martyred by the arrows of his fellow officers. His sufferings were a favourite subject for medieval artists.

Selena F Variant of ➤➤**Selina**.

Selima F Of uncertain origin. Its first known occurrence is in a poem by Thomas Gray (1716–71), recording the death of Horace Walpole's cat Selima, 'drowned in a tub of gold fishes'.

Selina F Of uncertain origin. It is first found in the 17th century, and it may be an altered form of *Selena* (Greek *Selēnē*), the name of a goddess of the moon, or of *Celina* (Latin *Caelīna*), a derivative of ➤➤**Celia**. The name suddenly became more popular in Britain in the 1980s, partly perhaps due to the television newsreader Selina Scott.

Selma F Of uncertain origin, probably a contracted form of ➤➤**Selima**. It has also been occasionally used in Germany and Scandinavia, probably because it occurs as the name of Ossian's castle in Macpherson's ballads.

Selwyn M Transferred use of the surname, which is of disputed origin. There was a given name *Selewyn* in use in the Middle Ages, which probably represents a survival of an unrecorded Old English name derived from *sēle* 'prosperity' or *sele* 'hall' + *wine* 'friend'. Alternatively, the surname may be Norman, derived from *Seluein*, an Old French form of the Latin name *Silvānus* (from *silva* 'wood'; cf. ➤➤**Silas**). The spelling **Selwin** also occurs.

Senga F Scottish: common in the north-east of Scotland, this name is popularly supposed to represent ➤➤**Agnes** spelled backwards (which it undeniably does).

However, it is more likely to have originated from the Gaelic vocabulary word *seang* 'slender'.

Seònaid F Scottish Gaelic form of **»Janet**, pronounced 'shaw-natch'. The Anglicized form **»Shona** and the semi-Anglicized form **Seona** are also found.

Septimus M From a Late Latin name derived from Latin *septimus* 'seventh'. It was fairly commonly used in large Victorian families for the seventh son or a male seventh child, but is now rare.

Seraphina F Latinate derivative of Hebrew *seraphim* 'burning ones', the name of an order of angels (Isaiah 6:2). It was borne by a rather shadowy saint who was martyred at the beginning of the 5th century in Italy, Spain, or Armenia. The spelling **Serafina** is also found.

Serena F From a Latin name, representing the feminine form of the adjective *serēnus* 'calm', 'serene'. It was borne by an early Christian saint, about whom little is known. In her *Life* she is described as wife of the Emperor Domitian (AD 51–96), but there is no mention of her in any of the historical sources that deal with this period.

Seth M Biblical name (from a Hebrew word meaning 'appointed', 'placed'), borne by the third son of Adam, who was born after the murder of Abel (Genesis 4:25). It was popular among the Puritans (particularly for children born after the death of an elder sibling), and has been occasionally used since. By the 20th century it had become rare. It was used for the darkly passionate rural character Seth Starkadder in Stella Gibbons's comic novel *Cold Comfort Farm* (1932).

Seumas M Scottish Gaelic form of **»James**, pronounced 'shee-mas'; it is also an older Irish Gaelic form (cf. **»Séamas**).

Seumus M Older Irish Gaelic form of **»James** (see **»Séamas**).

Sextus M Traditional Latin given name, meaning 'sixth'. It was taken up in England during the Victorian period, often for a sixth son or a sixth child, but it is now little used.

Seymour M Transferred use of the surname, originally a Norman baronial name from *Saint-Maur* in Normandy.

Shae M, F Modern variant of ➤➤**Shea**.

Shalene F Modern variant of ➤➤**Charlene**.

Shamus M Anglicized spelling of Irish Gaelic ➤➤**Séamus**.

Shane M, F Anglicized form of Irish Gaelic ➤➤**Seán**, representing a Northern Irish pronunciation of the name. In recent years it has also been used as a girl's name.

Shanee F Anglicized form of Welsh *Siani* (see ➤➤**Siân**).

Shanelle F Recent coinage, apparently a respelled elaboration of ➤➤**Chanel**.

Shanna F Recent coinage, apparently an altered, more obviously feminine form of ➤➤**Shannon**.

Shannagh F Variant of ➤➤**Shannah** or a transferred use of the Irish surname *Shannagh*, Gaelic *Ó Seanaigh* 'descendant of Seanach'. The latter is a Gaelic personal name derived from *sean* 'old', 'wise'.

Shannah F Variant of ➤➤**Shanna** or a short form of *Shoshannah*, the Hebrew form of ➤➤**Susanna**.

Shannon F, M From the name of a river in Ireland. As a boy's name, it is at least in part an Anglicization of ➤➤**Seanan** or a transferred use of the Irish surname derived from this, Gaelic *Ó Seanain*'.

Shantelle F Recent coinage, apparently a respelled elaboration of ➤➤**Chantal**.

Shari F Anglicized spelling of *Sári*, the Hungarian form of ➤➤**Sarah**.

Sharlene F Variant spelling of **»Charlene**.

Sharman M, F As a boy's name this represents a transferred use of the surname, a variant of **»Sherman**. As a girl's name it is an altered form of **»Charmaine**.

Sharon F 20th-century coinage, from a biblical placename. The derivation is from the phrase 'I am the rose of Sharon, and the lily of the valleys' (Song of Solomon 2:1). The plant name 'rose of Sharon' is used for a shrub of the genus *Hypericum*, with yellow flowers, and for a species of hibiscus, with purple flowers. The spelling **Sharron** also occurs.

Sharona F Latinate elaborated form of **»Sharon**.

Sharonda F Elaboration of **»Sharon**, with the suffix *-da* abstracted from names such as **»Glenda** and **»Linda**.

Sharron F Variant spelling of **»Sharon**.

Shaughan M Variant spelling of **»Shaun**, probably influenced by **»Vaughan**. The spelling **Shaughn** is also found.

Shaun M, F Anglicized spelling of Irish Gaelic **»Seán**. In Canada it is also found as a girl's name.

Shauna F Name invented as a feminine form of **»Shaun**.

Shaw M Transferred use of the surname, in origin a local name meaning 'wood', 'copse'.

Shawn M, F Anglicized spelling of Irish Gaelic **»Seán**, used mainly in North America. In Canada it is also found as a girl's name.

Shawna F Recently coined feminine form of **»Shawn**.

Shay M, F Variant spelling of **»Shea**. The spelling **Shaye** is also found.

Shayla F Recent coinage, apparently a variant of **»Sheila**.

Shayna F Modern name, either taken from a Yiddish name derived from German *Schön(e)* 'beautiful', or else a variant of >>**Sheena**.

Shea M, F Transferred use of the Irish surname, Gaelic *Ó Séaghdha* 'descendant of Séaghdha'. The latter is a traditional name of uncertain derivation, perhaps meaning 'hawk-like', i.e. 'fine', 'goodly'. The spellings >>**Shay, Shaye**, and >>**Shae** are also found.

Sheela F Variant spelling of >>**Sheila**.

Sheena F Anglicized spelling of *Sine* (Scottish) or *Sine* (Irish), the Gaelic equivalents of >>**Jane**.

Sheila F Anglicized spelling of >>**Síle**, the Irish Gaelic form of >>**Cecilia**. This name has become so common and widespread that its Irish origins are not always recognized. In Australia since the 19th century it has been a slang generic term for a woman. The spellings >>**Sheela, Sheelah**, and **She(e)lagh** are also used.

Shelagh F Variant of >>**Sheila**. The final consonants in the written form seem to have been added to give a Gaelic feel to the name. There is no etymological justification for them.

Shelby F, M Mainly U.S.: transferred use of the surname (now more common in America than Britain). This has the form of a northern English local name, but no place bearing it has been identified. In the U.S. it is associated mainly with Southern families, the chief inspiration for its use as a given name being Isaac Shelby (1750–1826), Revolutionary commander and first governor of Kentucky.

Sheldon M Transferred use of the surname, which originated as a local name from any of the various places so called. Examples occur in Derbyshire, Devon, and the West Midlands.

Shell F Generally, this is a shortened form of >>**Michelle**, respelled by association with the vocabulary word. In some cases it may be a shortened form of >>**Shelley**.

Shelley F, occasionally M Transferred use of the surname, the most famous bearer of which was the English Romantic poet Percy Bysshe Shelley (1792–1822). The surname is in origin a local name from one of the various places (in Essex, Suffolk, and Yorkshire) so named. The name is now almost exclusively female, in part perhaps as a result of association with ≫**Shirley** (the actress Shelley Winters was born in 1922 as Shirley Schrift), and in part due to the characteristically feminine ending -(e)y.

Sheree F Respelled form of ≫**Cherie**.

Sheridan M, F Transferred use of the surname made famous by the Irish playwright Richard Brinsley Sheridan (1751–1816). The surname is from Gaelic Ó Sirideáin 'descendant of Sirideán' (a personal name of uncertain origin, possibly connected with sirim 'to seek'). This is occasionally also used as a girl's name. In the United States the inspiration is probably the Unionist commander General Philip Henry Sheridan (1831–88)

Sherman M Transferred use of the surname, which is derived from an occupational name for someone who trimmed the nap of woollen cloth after it had been woven, from Old English scēara 'shears' + mann 'man'. In the United States it is sometimes bestowed in honour of the Civil War general William Tecumseh Sherman (1820–71).

Sherry F Probably in origin a respelled form of ≫**Cherie**, but now associated with the fortified wine, earlier sherry wine, so named from the port of Jérez in southern Spain. The spellings **Sherrie** and **Sherri** also occur.

Sheryl F Variant of ≫**Cheryl**.

Shevaun F Anglicized form of Irish Gaelic ≫**Siobhán**.

Shilla F Modern coinage, apparently an altered form of ≫**Sheila**.

S

Shireen F Variant of **»Shirin**.

Shirin F Muslim name of Persian or Arabic origin, now beginning to be used quite widely in the English-speaking world. The spellings **Shirrin** and **»Shireen** are also found.

Shirley F, formerly M Transferred use of the surname, in origin a local name from any of the various places (in the West Midlands, Derbyshire, Hampshire, and Surrey) so named. It was given by Charlotte Brontë to the heroine of her novel *Shirley* (1849), whose parents, according to the story, had selected the name in prospect of a male child and used it regardless. *Shirley* had earlier been used as a boy's name, but this literary influence fixed it firmly as a girl's name. It was strongly reinforced during the 1930s and 1940s by the popularity of the child film star Shirley Temple (b. 1928).

Sholto M Scottish: apparently an Anglicized form of a Gaelic name, *Sìoltach*, originally a byname meaning 'sower', i.e. 'fruitful' or 'seed-bearing'.

Shona F Scottish: Anglicized form of Gaelic *Seonag* or *Seònaid*, Gaelic versions of **»Joan** and **»Janet** respectively. In America it is pronounced identically with **»Shauna**, and may be used as a variant spelling of that name. It has also become popular as a Black name, probably in part because it is spelled the same as the name of a central African people.

Shula F As a Jewish name this is a short form of **»Shulamit**. It has been adopted by non-Jews in the English-speaking world as an independent given name.

Shulamit F Hebrew name meaning 'peacefulness', a derivative of *shalom* 'peace'. The name occurs as a personification in the Song of Solomon (6:13): 'Return, return, O Shulamite; return, return, that we may look upon thee'. It is a popular modern Hebrew name. The variants **Shulamith** and **Shulamite** are also found.

Siân F Welsh form of **»Jane**, derived from the Anglo-Norman form *Jeanne*. In the English-speaking world it is sometimes used without the accent.

Sibyl F Variant spelling of **»Sybil**. Even in classical times there was confusion between the two vowels in this word. The variants **Sibyll** (Latinate), **Sibilla**, and **Sibella** (by association with the Italian feminine diminutive suffix -*ella*) are also found.

Sidney M, F Transferred use of the surname, which is usually said to be a Norman baronial name from *Saint-Denis* in France. However, at least in the case of the family of the poet and soldier Sir Philip Sidney (1554–86), it appears to have a more humble origin, being derived from lands in Surrey named as the 'wide meadow'. The popularity of the boy's name increased considerably in the 19th century, probably due to Sidney Carton, hero of Dickens's novel *A Tale of Two Cities* (1859). As a girl's name it is perhaps in part a contracted form of **»Sidony**, and coincidentally represents a metathesized form of **»Sindy**. The spelling **»Sydney** is favoured for girls.

Sidony F From Latin *Sidōnia*, feminine of *Sidōnius*, in origin an ethnic name meaning 'man from Sidon' (the city in Phoenicia). This came to be associated with the Greek word *sindon* 'winding sheet'. Two saints called Sidonius are venerated in the Catholic Church: Sidonius Apollinaris, a 4th-century bishop of Clermont, and a 7th-century Irish monk who was the first abbot of the monastery of Saint-Saëns (which is named with a much altered form of his name). *Sidonius* was not used as a given name in the later Middle Ages, but the feminine form was comparatively popular and has continued in occasional use ever since. The spelling **Sidonie** is also found.

Sierra F Mainly U.S.: apparently from the vocabulary word referring to a mountain range (Spanish, from Latin *serra* 'saw', referring to the toothed appearance). The reasons for its adoption are not clear, but it has enjoyed considerable popularity recently in the United States.

Sigrid F From an Old Norse female personal name derived from *sigr* 'victory' + *fríthr* 'fair', 'beautiful'.

Silas M Of New Testament origin: Greek name, a short form of *Silouanus* (Latin *Silvānus*, a derivative of *silva* 'wood'). This name was borne by a companion of St Paul, who is also mentioned in the Bible in the full form of his name. The Eastern Church recognizes two separate saints, Silas and Silvanus, but honours both on the same day (20 July).

Síle F Irish Gaelic form of ≫**Cecily**, pronounced 'shee-la', derived in the early Middle Ages from the Anglo-Norman form *Cecile*. The Anglicized forms ≫**Sheila**, ≫**Sheela(h)**, ≫**She(e)lagh**, ≫**Shayla**, and ≫**Shilla** are also found.

Silver F, M From the name of the precious metal (Old English *siolfor*). It is sometimes given to babies born with very fair hair. It is also occasionally also used as a pet form of the names ≫**Silvestra** and ≫**Silvester**.

Silvester M From a Latin name, meaning 'of the woods'. It was borne by various early saints, most notably by the first pope to govern a Church free from persecution (314–35). His feast is on 31 December, and in various parts of Europe the New Year is celebrated under his name. The spelling ≫**Sylvester** is also found.

Silvestra F Latin feminine form of ≫**Silvester**.

Silvia F From Roman legend. Rhea *Silvia* was, according to Roman tradition, the mother of the twins Romulus and Remus, who founded Rome. Her name probably represents a reworking, by association with Latin *silva* 'wood', of some pre-Roman form. It was borne by a 6th-century saint, mother of Gregory the Great. Shakespeare used it as a typically Italian name in *Two Gentlemen of Verona*. It is now well established as an independent name in the English-speaking world. The spelling **≫Sylvia** also occurs.

Simeon M Biblical name, from a Hebrew word meaning 'hearkening'. It is borne by several Old and New Testament characters, rendered in the Authorized Version variously as *Shimeon*, *Simeon*, and **≫Simon**. In the New Testament, it is the spelling used for the man who blessed the infant Christ (Luke 2:25).

Simon M Usual English form of **≫Simeon**, borne in the New Testament by various characters: two apostles, a brother of Jesus, a Pharisee, a leper, a tanner, a sorcerer, and the man who carried Jesus's cross to the Crucifixion.

Simone F French feminine form of **≫Simon**, now also quite commonly used in the English-speaking world.

Sinclair M Transferred use of the Scottish surname, in origin a Norman baronial name borne by a family that held a manor in northern France called *Saint-Clair*, probably Saint-Clair-sur-Elle in La Manche. It is an extremely common Scottish surname: the Norman family received the earldoms of Caithness and Orkney. They merged with the Norse- and Gaelic-speaking inhabitants of their domains to form one of the most powerful of the Scottish Highland families. The name of the novelist Sinclair Lewis (1885–1951) may have had some influence on recent use of this as a given name.

Sinda F Variant of **≫Sindy**.

Sindy F Variant spelling of **≫Cindy** that came into use in about 1950 and is most common in America.

Síne F Irish Gaelic form of **≫Jane**, pronounced 'shee-na', derived from Anglo-Norman *Jeanne*. The Scottish spelling is **Sìne**. It is usually Anglicized as **≫Sheena**.

Sinéad F Irish Gaelic form of **≫Janet**, pronounced 'shin-aid', derived from the French form *Jeannette*. In the English-speaking world it is usually written without the accent, as in the case of the actress Sinead Cusack (b. 1948).

Siobhán F Irish Gaelic form of **»Joan**, pronounced 'shiv-awn' or 'shoo-an', derived from the Anglo-Norman form *Jehanne*. It became widely known in the English-speaking world, written without the accent, through the actress Siobhan McKenna (1923–86). The Anglicized forms **»Shevaun** and **»Chevonne** are also found.

Siôn M Welsh form of **»John**, derived from Anglo-Norman *Jean*.

Sioned F Welsh form of **»Janet**.

Sissy F Pet form of **»Cicely** that came into use about 1890 but largely disappeared again after about 1920. In recent years it has undergone something of a revival. The spellings **Sissey** and **Sissie** are also found.

Skipper M Originally a nickname from the vocabulary word *skipper* 'boss' (originally denoting a ship's captain, from Middle Dutch *schipper*), or else representing an agent derivative of *skip* 'to leap or bound'. It is now sometimes used as an independent given name in the United States.

Sky F, occasionally M From the vocabulary word (from Old Norse *ský* 'cloud'). This was one of the names taken from the world of nature during the 1960s under the influence of the hippy and flower-power movements.

Skye F Elaborated spelling of **»Sky**, influenced by the name of the island of *Skye* in the Hebrides, which is of Gaelic origin.

Sofia F Variant spelling of **»Sophia**.

Sofie F Variant spelling of **»Sophie**.

Solomon M Biblical name (Hebrew *Shlomo*, derived from *shalom* 'peace'), borne by one of the great kings of Israel, son of David and Bathsheba, who was legendary for his wisdom (2 Samuel 12–24; 1 Kings

1–11; 2 Chronicles 1–9). The books of Proverbs and Ecclesiastes were ascribed to him, and the Song of Solomon, otherwise known as the Song of Songs, bears his name. It has been sporadically used among Gentiles since the Middle Ages, but is still mainly a Jewish name.

Somerled M Scottish (Highland): from the Old Norse personal name *Sumarlíthr*, probably originally a byname meaning 'summer traveller'. This was the name of the founder of Clan Macdonald, Lords of the Isles from the 12th to the 15th centuries. Variants include **»Summerlad** (by folk etymology); **Somhairle**, the Gaelic form, also used in Ireland; and the Anglicized form **»Sorley**.

Sondra F Of recent origin, apparently an altered form of **»Sandra**.

Sonia F Variant spelling of **»Sonya**.

Sonya F Russian pet form of *Sofya* (see **»Sophia**), popular as a given name in its own right in Britain and elsewhere since the 1920s.

Sophia F From the Greek word meaning 'wisdom'. The Eastern cult of St Sophia arose as a result of misinterpretation of the phrase *Hagia Sophia* 'holy wisdom' as if it meant 'St Sophia'. The name became popular in England in the 17th and 18th centuries. The heroine of Fielding's novel *Tom Jones* (1749) is called Sophia Weston. In the mid 20th century, its popularity was influenced by Italian film actress Sophia Loren (b. 1934). The spelling **»Sofia** is also found in the English-speaking world.

Sophie F French form of **»Sophia**. In the English-speaking world, where it has been popular since the 18th century, it is often taken as a pet form of that name. The spellings **»Sofie** and **Sophy** are also found.

Sorcha F Irish and Scottish Gaelic name, pronounced 'sorr-kha'. It is derived from a Celtic word meaning 'brightness'. In Ireland it has long been considered a

s

Gaelic form of biblical **>>Sarah**, but this is based on no more than the phonetic similarity.

Sorley M Scottish (Highland) and Irish: Anglicized form of the Gaelic name *Somhairle* (pronounced '**sorr**-lee'). See **>>Somerled**.

Sorrel F From the vocabulary word for the plant. The spellings **Sorrell**, **Sorell**, and **Sorel** are also found.

Spencer M Transferred use of the surname, in origin an occupational name for a 'dispenser' of supplies in a manor house. This is the name of a great English noble family, traditionally supposed to be descended from someone who performed this function in the royal household. Its popularity as a given name was influenced in the mid 20th century by the American film actor Spencer Tracy (1900–67).

Stacey F, M Of uncertain derivation, probably a transferred use of the surname, which was derived in the Middle Ages from a pet form of *Stace*, a short form of **>>Eustace**. It is not clear why this name should have become so common in the 1970s and 1980s, mainly as a girl's name, but also used for boys. The spellings **Stacy**, **Stacie**, and **Staci** are also found.

Stafford M Transferred use of the surname, in origin a local name from any of various places so called, most notably the county town of Staffordshire. This was the surname of the family that held the dukedom of Buckingham in the 15th and 16th centuries.

Stanley M Transferred use of the surname, in origin a local name from any of numerous places so called (in Derbys., Durham, Gloucs., Staffs., Wilts., and Yorks.). This is well established as a given name, and has been widely used as such since the 1880s. It had been in occasional use earlier. Its popularity seems to have stemmed at least in part from the fame of the explorer Sir Henry Morton Stanley (1841–1904).

Star F Modern name, a vernacular equivalent of >>**Stella**. The spelling **Starr** is also used.

Steffany F Respelled form of >>**Stephanie**.

Stella F From Latin *stella* 'star'. This was not used as a given name before the 16th century, when Sir Philip Sidney seems to have been the first to use it (as a name deliberately far removed from the prosaic range of everyday names) in the sonnets addressed to Astrophel to his lady, Stella.

Stephan M Variant of >>**Stephen**, preserving the vowels of the Greek name.

Stephanie F From French *Stéphanie*, vernacular form of Latin *Stephania*, a variant of *Stephana*, which was in use among early Christians as a feminine form of *Stephanus* (see >>**Stephen**). The spelling >>**Steffany** also occurs.

Stephen M Usual English spelling of the name of the first Christian martyr (Acts 6–7), whose feast is accordingly celebrated next after Christ's own (26 December). His name is derived from the Greek word *stephanos* 'garland', 'crown'. The spellings >>**Steven** and >>**Stephan** are also found.

Sterling M Transferred use of the surname, a variant of >>**Stirling**. As a given name, however, it is likely to have been chosen because of its association with the vocabulary word occurring in such phrases as 'sterling qualities' and 'sterling worth'. A 20th-century influence on the name has been the American film actor Sterling Hayden (1916–86).

Steven M Variant of >>**Stephen**, reflecting the normal pronunciation of the name in the English-speaking world.

Stevie F, M Pet form of >>**Stephen** and of >>**Stephanie**. A well-known female bearer was the poet Stevie Smith (1902–71), whose baptismal name was Florence Margaret Smith.

S

Stewart M Variant of **»Stuart**.

Stirling M Transferred use of the surname, in origin a local name from the town in Scotland. The placename is of uncertain derivation, perhaps from Old Welsh *ystre Velyn* 'dwelling of *Melyn*'.

Storm F, M Apparently a 20th-century coinage, although it may have been in use slightly earlier. The name is presumably derived from the vocabulary word.

Stuart M From the French version of the surname *Stewart*. This form was introduced to Scotland in the 16th century by Mary Stuart, Queen of Scots, who was brought up in France. The surname originated as an occupational or status name for someone who served as a *steward* in a manor or royal household. The Scottish royal family of this name are traditionally supposed to be descended from a family who were hereditary stewards in Brittany before the Conquest. Use as a given name originated in Scotland, but is now widespread throughout the English-speaking world.

Sukie F Pet form of **»Susan**, very common in the 18th century, but now rare. The spelling **Sukey** is also found.

Summer F From the vocabulary word for the season, used in modern times as a given name because of its pleasant associations.

Summerlad M Scottish: variant spelling of **»Somerled**, being taken by folk etymology as derived from the words *summer* and *lad*.

Susan F English vernacular form of **»Susanna**, always the most common of this group of names. A 20th-century influence has been the American film star Susan Hayward (1918–75). The spelling **Suzan** also occurs.

Susanna F New Testament form (Luke 8:3) of the Hebrew name *Shoshana* (from *shoshan* 'lily', which in modern Hebrew also means 'rose'). The spelling **Susana** is also found.

Susannah F Variant of **»Susanna**. This is the form of
the name used in the Old Testament. The tale of
Susannah, wife of Joachim, and the elders who falsely
accused her of adultery, is to be found in the apocryphal
book that bears her name, and was popular in the
Middle Ages and later. The spelling **Suzanna** is also
found.

Susie F Pet form of **»Susan** and, less commonly, of
»Susanna(h) and **»Suzanne**. The spellings **Suzie** and
Suzy are also used.

Suzanne F French form of **»Susanna**, now also used
in the English-speaking world.

Suzette F French pet form of **»Suzanne**, now also used
in the English-speaking world.

Sybil F From the name (Greek *Sibylla* or *Sibylla*, with
confusion over the vowels from an early period) of a
class of ancient prophetesses inspired by Apollo.
According to medieval theology, they were pagans
denied the knowledge of Christ but blessed by God with
some insight into things to come and accordingly
admitted to heaven. It was thus regarded as a
respectable name to be borne by Christians. The
variants **Sybilla** (Latinate) and **Sybille** (from French)
occur. See also **»Sibyl**.

Sydney F, M Variant spelling of **»Sidney**. It was a
medieval practice to write *y* for *i*, for greater clarity
since *i* was easily confused with other letters.

Sylvester M Variant spelling of **»Silvester**.

Sylvestra F Variant spelling of **»Silvestra**.

Sylvia F Variant spelling of **»Silvia**. It is now rather
more common than the plain form.

Sylvie F French form of **»Silvia**, now also used in the
English-speaking world.

s

T

Tabitha F Aramaic name, meaning 'doe' or 'roe', borne in the New Testament by a woman who was restored to life by St Peter (Acts 9:36–41). It was one of the names much favoured by Puritans and Dissenters from the 17th to the 19th centuries.

Tacey F As a medieval given name this is derived from the Latin imperative *tace* 'be silent', regarded as a suitable admonition to women. As a modern name, it is a pet form of **»Tacita** or perhaps derived from **»Tracy**.

Tacita F From Latin *Tacita*, feminine form of the Roman family name *Tacitus*, originally a byname meaning 'silent'.

Tad M Normally an Anglicized form of Gaelic **»Tadhg**, but sometimes a short form of **»Thaddeus**. It is used as an independent given name, especially in America.

Tadhg M Irish and Scottish Gaelic traditional name, pronounced 'teig': it was originally a byname meaning 'poet' or 'philosopher'. It was widely used in Ireland throughout the Middle Ages. The Anglicized forms **»Tad**, **»Teague**, and **»Teigue** are also found.

Talfryn M Welsh: modern given name, originally a local name, from Welsh *tal* 'high', 'end of' + a mutated form of *bryn* 'hill'.

Talia F Variant spelling of **»Talya** and **»Thalia**.

Taliesin M Welsh: from *tâl* 'brow' + *iesin* 'shining'. This was the name of a legendary 6th-century Welsh poet, and has been revived in recent times.

Talitha F Of New Testament origin: from an Aramaic word meaning 'little girl'. Jesus raised a child from the dead with the words 'Talitha cumi; which is, being interpreted, Damsel, I say unto thee, arise' (Mark 5:41).

Talulla F Irish: Anglicized form of the Gaelic name *Tuilelaith*, pronounced 'til-a-la', derived from words meaning 'abundance' and 'lady' or 'princess'. This name was borne by at least two Irish saints of the 8th and 9th centuries. The spelling **Tallulah** was made famous by the American actress Tallulah Bankhead (1903–68), who inherited the name from her grandmother.

Talya F Shortened form of ≫**Natalya**.

Tam M Scottish short form of ≫**Thomas**.

Tamara F Russian: probably derived from the Hebrew name *Tamar*, from a vocabulary word meaning 'date palm', with the addition of the feminine suffix -*a*. The name Tamar is borne in the Bible by two female characters: the daughter-in-law of Judah, who is involved in a story of sexual intrigue (Genesis 38), and a daughter of King David (2 Samuel 13), the sister of Absalom, who is raped by her half-brother Amnon, for which Absalom kills him. It is rather surprising, therefore, that it should have given rise to such a popular given name. However, Absalom himself later has a daughter named Tamar, who is referred to as 'a woman of a fair countenance' (2 Samuel 14:27), and the name may derive its popularity from this reference. The name is now also used in the English-speaking world.

Tammy F Pet form of ≫**Tamara** and ≫**Tamsin**.

Tamsin F Contracted form of Latinate *Thomasina*, a feminine form of ≫**Thomas**. This was relatively common throughout Britain in the Middle Ages, but confined to Cornwall immediately before its recent revival.

t

Tania F Variant spelling of ≫**Tanya**.

Tanner M Mainly U.S.: transferred use of the common
surname, in origin an occupational name for someone
who treated animal skins to form leather.

Tansy F From the vocabulary word for the flower (Old
French *tanesie*, derived from Greek *athanasia*
'immortal'). It was briefly in vogue as a given name in
the 20th century.

Tanya F Russian pet form of ≫**Tatiana**, now quite
commonly used as an independent given name in the
English-speaking world. The spelling ≫**Tania** is also
found.

Tara F From the name of a place in Meath, seat of the
high kings of Ireland, named with Gaelic *teamhair* 'hill'.
It has been used as a girl's name in America since
around 1940, probably in response to the film *Gone
with the Wind*, in which the estate of this name has
great emotional significance. In Britain it was not much
used before the 1960s.

Tárlach M Irish Gaelic name, pronounced 'tor-lakh': a
modern shortened form of the traditional name
Toirdhealbhach, apparently originally a byname
meaning 'instigator'. It was the name of a high king of
Ireland who died in 1156. The notion that this is a
derivative of *Thor*, the name of the Norse god of
thunder, is probably incorrect. The Anglicized form
≫**Turlough** is also found.

Tarquin M The name borne by two early kings of Rome,
Tarquinius Priscus 'the Old' (616–578 BC) and
Tarquinius Superbus 'the Proud' (534–510 BC). It is of
uncertain, probably Etruscan, origin. The name is now
occasionally used in the English-speaking world.

Tarra F Variant of **»Tara**.

Tasha F Shortened form of **»Natasha**.

Tatiana F Russian: of early Christian origin. This was the name of various early saints honoured particularly in the Eastern Church. In origin it is a feminine form of Latin *Tatiānus*, a derivative of *Tatius*, a Roman family name of obscure origin. The name is now also used in the English-speaking world, though not so commonly as the pet form **»Tanya**.

Tawny F From the vocabulary word denoting a light brown hair colour (Anglo-Norman *tauné*, Old French *tané* 'tanned'). This is probably a modern name created on the lines of examples such as **Ginger** and **»Sandy**. It may also be a transferred use of the surname *Tawney*, which is a Norman baronial name from one of two places in Normandy: *Saint-Aubin-du-Thenney* or *Saint-Jean-du-Thenney*. The spelling **Tawney** is also found.

Taylor M, F Transferred use of the surname, in origin an occupational name for a tailor (Anglo-Norman *taillour*). Use as a given name was influenced by the U.S. president Zachary Taylor (1784–1850), hero of the Mexican War. It is now well established as a girl's name in North America, perhaps partly inspired by the film actress Elizabeth Taylor (b. 1932).

Teague M Irish: Anglicized form of Gaelic **»Tadhg**.

Teal F One of the girls' names taken from birds in the latter part of the 20th century. The teal is a kind of small duck; its name is attested in English since the 14th century. The spelling **Teale** also occurs.

Teàrlach M Scottish Gaelic, pronounced 'tchar-lakh': a modern shortened form of the ancient Gaelic name *Toirdhealbhach*; see **»Tárlach**.

Ted M Short form of **»Edward**.

Teddy M, F Now generally used as a pet form of **»Edward**, although it was originally used of

t

>>Theodore. Teddy bears were so named from the American president Theodore Roosevelt (1858–1919). Occasionally it is also used as a girl's name, in part as a pet form of **>>Edwina**.

Tegwen F Welsh: modern coinage from *teg* 'lovely' + *(g)wen*, feminine form of *gwyn* 'white', 'fair', 'blessed', 'holy'.

Teigue M Irish: Anglicized form of Gaelic **>>Tadhg**.

Teleri F Welsh: extension of the name **>>Eleri**, with the addition of the honorific prefix *ty-* 'your'. Teleri, daughter of Peul, is mentioned in the *Mabinogi*.

Terence M From the Latin name *Terentius*, which is of uncertain origin. It was borne by the Roman playwright Marcus Terentius Afer, and later by various minor early Christian saints. As a modern given name it is a 'learned' back-formation from the supposed pet form **>>Terry**. It has become common in Ireland through being used as an Anglicized form of the Gaelic name *Toirdhealbhach* (see **>>Tárlach**). The spellings **>>Terrance** and **>>Terrence** are also found.

Teresa F Italian and Spanish form of **>>Theresa**. In the English-speaking world the name is often chosen in this spelling by Roman Catholics, with particular reference to the Spanish saint, Teresa of Ávila (Teresa Cepeda de Ahumada, 1515–82).

Terrance M The most common U.S. spelling of **>>Terence**.

Terrell M Transferred use of the surname, a variant of **>>Tyrrell**.

Terrence M Variant spelling of **>>Terence**.

Terri F Mid 20th-century coinage, originating either as a pet form of **>>Theresa** or as a feminine spelling of **>>Terry**. It is now well established as an independent given name, particularly in North America.

Terry M As a medieval given name this is a Norman form of the French name *Thierri*, from Germanic *Theodoric*, from *theud* 'people', 'race' + *rīc* 'power', 'ruler'. This was adopted by the Normans and introduced by them to Britain. In modern English use it seems at first to have been a transferred use of the surname derived from the medieval given name, and later to have been taken as a pet form of ≫**Terence**.

Terryl F Modern coinage, apparently an elaboration of ≫**Terri** with the suffix -*yl* seen in names such as ≫**Cheryl**.

Tess F Short form of ≫**Tessa**.

Tessa F Now generally considered to be a pet form of ≫**Theresa**, although often used independently. However, the formation is not clear, and it may be of distinct origin.

Tex M Mainly U.S.: in origin a nickname for someone from *Texas*. The name of the state derives from an Indian tribal name, meaning 'friends'.

Thaddeus M Latin form of a New Testament name, the byname used to refer to one of Christ's lesser-known apostles, whose given name was *Lebbaeus* (Matthew 10:3). It is of uncertain origin, possibly derived via Aramaic from the Greek name *Theodōros* 'gift of God' or *Theodotos* 'given by God'.

Thalia F Name borne in classical mythology by the Muse of comedy; it is derived from Greek *thallein* 'to flourish'. In recent years has occasionally been used in the English-speaking world.

Thea F Shortened form of ≫**Dorothea**.

Thecla F Contracted form of the Greek name *Theokleia*, derived from *theos* 'God' + *kleia* 'glory'. The name was borne by a 1st-century saint, the first female martyr.

Theda F Latinate short form of the various old Germanic female personal names derived from *theud* 'people', 'race'. It enjoyed a brief popularity in the United States from about 1915 to 1925, due to the popularity of the silent-film actress Theda Bara (1890–1955), the original 'vamp'.

Thelma F First used by the novelist Marie Corelli for the heroine of her novel *Thelma* (1887). She was supposed to be Norwegian, but it is not a traditional Scandinavian name. Greek *thelēma* means 'wish' or '(act of) will', and the name could perhaps be interpreted as a contracted form of this.

Theo M Short form of **»Theodore** and, less commonly, of **»Theobald**.

Theobald M From an Old French name of Germanic (Frankish) origin, derived from *theud* 'people', 'race' + *bald* 'bold', 'brave'. The first element was altered under the influence of Greek *theos* 'god'. This name was adopted by the Normans and introduced by them to Britain.

Theodora F Feminine form of **»Theodore**, borne most notably by a 9th-century empress of Byzantium, the wife of Theophilus the Iconoclast. It means 'gift of God'; the elements are the same as those of **»Dorothea**, but in reverse order.

Theodore M From the French form of the Greek name *Theodōros*, derived from *theos* 'god' + *dōron* 'gift'. The name was popular among early Christians and was borne by several saints.

Theodosia F Greek name derived from *theos* 'god' + *dōsis* 'giving'. It was borne by several saints venerated in the Eastern Church.

Thera F Of uncertain derivation: it could represent a shortened form of **»Theresa**, or be derived from the name of the Greek island of *Thēra*.

Theresa F Of problematic origin. The name seems to have been first used in Spain and Portugal and, according to tradition, was the name of the wife of St

Paulinus of Nola, who spent most of his life in Spain; she was said to have originated (and to have derived her name) from the Greek island of *Thēra*, but the story is neither factually nor etymologically confirmed. The spellings >>**Teresa** and >>**Treeza** are also found.

Thirzah   F   Variant of >>**Tirzah**. The spelling **Thirza** is also found.

Thomas   M   New Testament name, borne by one of Christ's twelve apostles, referred to as 'Thomas, called Didymus' (John 11:16; 20:24). *Didymos* is the Greek word for 'twin', and the name is the Greek form of an Aramaic byname meaning 'twin'. The given name has always been popular throughout Christendom.

Tia   F   Recent coinage, of uncertain derivation. It coincides in form and pronunciation with the Spanish and Portuguese word meaning 'aunt', but this is unlikely to be the source.

Tiana   F   Recent coinage, apparently an elaborated form of >>**Tia** or a shortened form of >>**Christiana**.

Tiara   F   Recent coinage, apparently from the vocabulary word for a woman's jewelled headdress (via Latin, from Greek *tiara(s)*, originally denoting a kind of conical cap worn by the ancient Persians).

Tiernan   M   Transferred use of the Irish surname, Gaelic *Ó Tighearnáin* 'descendant of Tighearnán'. The latter is a diminutive of *tigherna* 'lord'. *Tighearnán* was a popular name in medieval Ireland.

Tierney   F, M   Transferred use of the Irish surname, Gaelic *Ó Tighearnaigh* 'descendant of Tighearnach'. The latter is a derivative of *tigherna* 'lord'. Tighearnach was the name of a 6th-century saint who served as abbot of Clones and later as bishop of Clogher. This is now well established as a girl's name. Its use in North America is due at least in part to the influence of the film actress Gene Tierney (1920–91).

t

Tierra F Recent coinage, of uncertain derivation, ostensibly from Spanish *tierra* 'land', 'earth' (Latin *terra*), but cf. **»Tiara**.

Tiffany F Usual medieval English form of the Greek name *Theophania* 'Epiphany', from *theos* 'god' + *phainein* 'to appear'. This was once a relatively common name, given particularly to girls born on the feast of the Epiphany (6 January), and it gave rise to an English surname. As a given name, it fell into disuse until revived in the 20th century under the influence of the famous New York jewellers, Tiffany's, and the film *Breakfast at Tiffany's* (1961). This has been a popular Black girl's name in America since the 1980s.

Tilda F Shortened form of **»Matilda**.

Tilly F Pet form of **»Matilda**, much used from the Middle Ages to the late 19th century, when it also came to be used as an independent given name.

Tim M Short form of **»Timothy**, also used in Ireland as an Anglicized form of **»Tadhg**.

Timothy M English form of the Greek name *Timotheos*, from *tīmē* 'honour' + *theos* 'god'. This was the name of a companion of St Paul; according to tradition, he was stoned to death for denouncing the worship of Diana. It was not used in England before the Reformation.

Tina F Shortened form of **»Christina** and other girls' names ending in *-tina*; now often used as an independent given name.

Tirion F Welsh: modern given name, from the vocabulary word meaning 'kind', 'gentle'.

Tirzah F Biblical name, meaning 'pleasantness' or 'delight' in Hebrew, borne by a minor character mentioned in a genealogy (Numbers 26:33). It is also a biblical placename. The variants **Tirza**, **»Thirzah**, and **Thirza** are also found.

Tita F Either a short form of names ending in these two syllables, as for example *Martita*, or a feminine form of **»Titus**.

Titus M From an old Roman given name, of unknown origin. It was borne by a companion of St Paul who became the first bishop of Crete, and also by the Roman emperor who destroyed Jerusalem in AD 70.

Tobias M Biblical name: Greek form of Hebrew *Tobiah* 'God is good'. This name is borne by several characters in the Bible (appearing in the Authorized Version also as *Tobijah*). A historical St Tobias was martyred (*c*.315) at Sebaste in Armenia, together with Carterius, Styriacus, Eudoxius, Agapius, and five others.

Toby M English vernacular form of **»Tobias**.

Todd M Transferred use of the surname, which was originally a nickname from an English dialect word meaning 'fox'.

Tom M Short form of **»Thomas**, in use since the Middle Ages, and recorded as an independent name since the 18th century.

Toni F Feminine form of **»Tony**, in part used as a pet form of **»Antonia** but more commonly as an independent given name.

Tonia F Shortened form of **»Antonia**, now also used as an independent given name.

Tony M, occasionally F Shortened form of **»Anthony**, now sometimes used as an independent given name.

Tonya F Variant of **»Tonia**.

Topaz F One of the rarer examples of the class of modern girls' names taken from vocabulary words denoting gemstones. In the Middle Ages this was sometimes used as a boy's name, representing a form of **»Tobias**.

Torquil M Scottish: Anglicized form of the traditional Gaelic name *Torcall*, originally a borrowing of the Old

Norse personal name *Thorketill*, composed of the name of the god *Thor* + *ketill* 'kettle', 'helmet'.

Tracy F, M Transferred use of the surname, in origin a Norman baronial name from places in France called *Tracy*, from the Gallo-Roman personal name *Thracius* + the local suffix *-ācum*. In former times, *Tracy* was occasionally used as a boy's given name. Later, it was also used as a girl's name, generally being taken as a pet form of ≫**Theresa**. It became a very popular girl's name in the 1960s and 1970s. One influence was the character of Tracy Lord, played by Grace Kelly in the film *High Society* (1956); another was Jean Simmons' daughter, named Tracy in honour of Spencer Tracy. The spellings **Tracey** and **Tracie** (female) are also found.

Trahaearn M Welsh: traditional name composed of the intensive prefix *tra-* + *haearn* 'iron'.

Travis M Transferred use of the surname, in origin a Norman French occupational name (from *traverser* 'to cross') for someone who collected a toll from users of a bridge or a stretch of road. It is now regularly used as a given name, especially in America.

Treasa F Traditional Irish Gaelic name, said to be from *tréan* 'strength', 'intensity'. It is now used as the Irish equivalent of ≫**Teresa**.

Treeza F Modern contracted spelling of ≫**Theresa** or Anglicization of Irish ≫**Treasa**.

Trefor M Welsh spelling of ≫**Trevor**.

Tremaine M Transferred use of the Cornish surname, in origin a local name from any of several places named with Cornish *tre* 'homestead', 'settlement' + *men* 'stone'.

Trent M Especially U.S.: from the name of the river that flows through the British Midlands, or a transferred use of the surname derived from it. The given name may in some cases be used as a short form of ≫**Trenton**.

Trenton M Mainly U.S.: from the name of the city in New Jersey, the site of a decisive defeat of the British (1776) by Washington during the American Revolution. The city was founded in the late 17th century by a group of English Quakers under the leadership of a certain William Trent. It was originally *Trent's Town*, reduced within half a century to *Trenton*.

Trevelyan M Transferred use of the Cornish surname, in origin a local name from a place mentioned in Domesday Book as *Trevelien*, i.e. 'homestead or settlement (Cornish *tref*) of Elian'. The latter is an ancient Celtic personal name of obscure origin.

Trevor M Transferred use of the Welsh surname, in origin a local name from any of the very many places in Wales called *Trefor*, from *tref* 'settlement' + *fôr*, mutated form of *mawr* 'large'. Since the mid 20th century it has enjoyed considerable popularity in the English-speaking world among people with no connection with Wales.

Triona F Shortened form of >>**Catriona**.

Trista F Name invented as a feminine form of >>**Tristan**.

Tristan M From Celtic legend, the name borne by a hero of medieval romance. There are many different versions of the popular tragic story of Tristan and Isolde. Generally, they agree that Tristan was an envoy sent by King Mark of Cornwall to bring back his bride, the Irish princess Isolde. Unfortunately, Tristan and Isolde fall in love with each other, having accidentally drunk the love potion intended for King Mark's wedding night. Tristan eventually leaves Cornwall to fight for King Howel of Brittany. Wounded in battle, he sends for Isolde. She arrives too late, and dies of grief beside his bier. The name *Tristan* is of unknown derivation, though it may be connected with Pictish *Drostan*; it has been altered from an irrecoverable original as a result of transmission through Old French sources that associated it with Latin *tristis* 'sad', a reference to the young knight's tragic fate. The spelling **»Trystan** is a mainly Welsh variant.

Tristram M Variant of **»Tristan**. Both forms of the name occur in medieval and later versions of the legend. This is the name of the narrator in Laurence Sterne's comic novel *Tristram Shandy* (1759–67). The variants **Tristam** and **Trystram** are also found.

Troy M, F Probably originally a transferred use of the surname, which is derived from *Troyes* in France. Nowadays, however, the given name is principally associated with the ancient city of Troy in Asia Minor, whose fate has been a central topic in epic poetry from Homer onwards.

Trudy F Pet form of **»Gertrude** or **Ermintrude** (a Germanic name, composed of *irm(e)n* 'entire' + *traut* 'beloved', and introduced into Britain by the Normans), now used mainly as an independent given name. The spellings **Trudie** and **Trudi** are also found.

Truman M Mainly U.S.: transferred use of the surname, in origin a nickname from Old English *trēowe* 'true', 'trusty' + *mann* 'man'. Use as a given name was boosted by the fame of Harry S. Truman (1884–1972), president of the United States (1945–52), although it was in occasional use before he became president. The spelling **Trueman** also occurs.

t   **Trystan** M Variant (mainly Welsh) of **»Tristan**.

Tucker M Transferred use of the surname, in origin an occupational name for a fuller.

Tudur M Welsh: traditional name derived from the Old Celtic form *Teutorix*, composed of elements meaning 'people' or 'tribe' and 'ruler' or 'king'. The earlier spelling **Tudyr** and the Anglicized spelling **Tudor** are also found.

Turlough M Irish: Anglicized form of Gaelic *Toirdhealbhach* (see **»Tárlach**).

Ty M Short form of **»Tyler** and **»Tyrone**.

Tybalt M The usual medieval form of **»Theobald**, rarely used nowadays. It occurs in Shakespeare's *Romeo and Juliet* as the name of a brash young man who is killed in a brawl.

Tyler M, F Transferred use of the surname, in origin an occupational name for a tiler (an agent derivative of Old English *tigele* 'tile'). John Tyler (1790–1862) was the tenth president of the United States.

Tyrone M From the name of a county in Northern Ireland and a town in Pennsylvania. Its use as a given name seems to be due to the influence of the two film actors (father and son) called Tyrone Power, especially the younger one (1913–58).

Tyrell M Mainly U.S.: transferred use of the surname, which is common in Ireland, but of uncertain derivation. It may have originated as a nickname for a stubborn person, from Old French *tirel*, used of an animal which pulls on the reins, a derivative of *tirer* 'to pull'. The spelling **Tyrrell** is also used.

Tyson M Mainly U.S.: transferred use of the surname, which is of dual origin. In part it is a metronymic from the medieval woman's given name *Dye*, pet form of *Dionysia*, and in part it is a nickname for a hot-tempered person, from Old French *tison* 'firebrand'. As a given name it is often taken as an expanded form or patronymic from **»Ty**.

t

U

Uilleam M Scottish Gaelic form of ≫**William**. The Irish form is **Uilliam**, often shortened to ≫**Liam**.

Ùisdean M Scottish Gaelic: traditional name, originally a borrowing of the Old Norse personal name *Eysteinn*, which is from *ei*, *ey* 'always', 'for ever' + *steinn* 'stone'.

Ulick M Irish: Anglicized form of Gaelic *Uilleac* or *Uilleag*. This name probably derives from Old Norse *Hugleikr*, from *hugr* 'heart', 'mind', 'spirit' + *leikr* 'play', 'sport'. Alternatively, it may be a pet form of *Uilliam*, the Gaelic form of ≫**William**.

Ultan M Irish: Anglicized form of the Gaelic name *Ultán*, a pet form of the ethnic name *Ultach* 'Ulsterman'.

Ulysses M Latin form of the Greek name *Odysseus*, borne by the famous wanderer of Homer's *Odyssey*. The name is of uncertain derivation (it was associated by the Greeks themselves with the verb *odyssesthai* 'to hate'). As an English given name it has occasionally been used in the 19th and 20th centuries, especially in America. It was the name of the 18th president of the United States, Ulysses S. Grant (1822–85). It has also been used in Ireland as a classicizing form of ≫**Ulick**.

Una F Anglicized form of Irish Gaelic *Úna*, a traditional name of uncertain derivation. It is identical in form with the vocabulary word *úna* 'hunger', 'famine', but is more likely to be derived from *uan* 'lamb'. In Irish legend Úna is the mother of the hero Conn Cétchathach (Conn of the Hundred Battles). It was also the name of the beloved of the 17th-century poet Tomás Láidir

Costello: banned by her parents from seeing him, Úna
fell into a decline and died, leaving him to mourn her
in his verse. The Anglicized form of the name is
sometimes taken to be from the feminine of Latin *unus*
'one'. It is the name used by Spenser for the lady of the
Red Cross Knight in *The Faerie Queene*: he probably had
Latin rather than Irish in mind, even though he worked
in Ireland for a while. The spellings **»Oona** and **Oonagh**
are also found.

Unity F From the vocabulary word for the quality (Latin
unitās, a derivative of *unus* 'one'). It achieved some
currency among the Puritans, but has been mainly used
in Ireland as a kind of Anglicized extended form of
»Una.

Uriah M Biblical name (from Hebrew, meaning 'God is
light'), borne by a Hittite warrior treacherously
disposed of by King David after he had made Uriah's
wife Bathsheba pregnant (2 Samuel 11). The Greek
form *Urias* occurs in the New Testament (Matthew
1:6). The name was popular in the 19th century, but
possibly through association with the character of the
obsequious Uriah Heep in Dickens's *David Copperfield*
(1850), it has since undergone a sharp decline in
popularity.

Uriel M Biblical name derived from Hebrew *uri* 'light'
+ *el* 'God', and so a doublet of **»Uriah**. It is borne by
two minor characters mentioned in genealogies
(1 Chronicles 6:24; 2 Chronicles 13:2).

Urien M Welsh: name borne by a character in the
Mabinogi, Urien of Rheged. He is probably identical
with the historical figure Urien who fought against the
Northumbrians in the 6th century. The name is of
uncertain origin: it may be derived from the Old Celtic
elements *ōrbo* 'privileged' + *gen* 'birth'.

u

Ursula F From the Latin name *Ursula*, a diminutive of *ursa* '(she-)bear'. This was the name of a 4th-century saint martyred at Cologne. A more recent, secular influence has been the film actress Ursula Andress (b. 1936).

V

Valda F 20th-century coinage, an elaboration of the girl's name *Val* (short form of **»Valerie**) with the suffix *-da*, extracted from names such as **»Glenda** and **»Linda**.

Valene F 20th-century coinage, an elaboration of the girl's name *Val* (short form of **»Valerie**) with the productive feminine suffix *-ene*.

Valentine M, occasionally F English form of the Latin name *Valentīnus*, a derivative of *valens* 'healthy', 'strong'. It was the name of a Roman martyr of the 3rd century, whose feast is celebrated on 14 February. This was the date of a pagan fertility festival marking the first stirrings of spring, which has survived in an attenuated form under the patronage of the saint.

Valerie F From the French form of the Latin name *Valēria*, feminine *Valērius*, an old Roman family name apparently derived from *valēre* 'to be healthy', 'be strong'. The name owes its popularity in France to the cult of a 3rd-century saint said to have been converted by Martial of Limoges.

Valetta F 20th-century coinage, an elaboration of the girl's name *Val* (short form of **»Valerie**) with the ending *-etta*, originally an Italian feminine diminutive suffix. *Valetta* or *Valletta* is (apparently coincidentally) the name of the capital of Malta.

Van M Short form of **»Ivan** or **»Evan**, as in the case of the American film actor Van Heflin (1910–71), born

Emmett Evan Heflin and the Irish folk singer Van Morrison (b. 1945).

Vanessa F Name invented by Jonathan Swift (1667–1745) for his friend Esther Vanhomrigh. It seems to have been derived from the first syllable of her (Dutch) surname, with the addition of the suffix *-essa* (perhaps influenced by the first syllable of her given name). The name became fairly popular in the 20th century, being borne for example by the actress Vanessa Redgrave (b. 1937).

Vaughan M Transferred use of the Welsh surname, in origin a nickname from the mutated form (*fychan* in Welsh orthography) of the Welsh adjective *bychan* 'small'. The spelling **Vaughn** also occurs.

Velma F Of modern origin and uncertain derivation, possibly based on »**Selma** or »**Thelma**.

Venessa F A modern altered form of »**Vanessa**.

Venetia F Of uncertain origin, used occasionally since the late Middle Ages. In form the name coincides with that of the region of northern Italy.

Vera F Russian name, meaning 'faith', introduced to Britain at the beginning of the 20th century. It coincides in form with the feminine form of the Latin adjective *vērus* 'true'.

Vere M Transferred use of the surname, in origin a Norman baronial name, from any of the numerous places in northern France so called from Gaulish *ver(n)* 'alder'.

Verena F Characteristically Swiss name, first borne by a 3rd-century saint who lived as a hermit near Zurich. She is said to have come originally from Thebes in Egypt, and the origin of her name is obscure. This name is now also used in the English-speaking world, where it is taken as an elaboration of »**Vera**.

Vergil M Variant spelling of >>**Virgil**.

Verina F Variant spelling of >>**Verena**.

Verity F From the archaic abstract noun meaning 'truth' (via Old French from Latin *vēritās*). It was a popular Puritan name, and is still used in the English-speaking world.

Verna F Name coined in the latter part of the 19th century, perhaps as a contracted form of >>**Verena** or >>**Verona**, or as a feminine form of >>**Vernon**.

Vernon M Transferred use of the surname, in origin a Norman baronial name from any of various places so called from Gaulish elements meaning 'place of alders'.

Verona F Of uncertain origin. It seems to have come into use towards the end of the 19th century, and may either represent a shortened form of >>**Veronica** or be taken from the name of the Italian city. It became more widely known from Sinclair Lewis's novel *Babbitt* (1923), in which it is borne by the daughter of the eponymous hero.

Veronica F Latin form of >>**Berenice**, influenced from an early date by association with the Church Latin phrase *vera icon* 'true image', of which this form is an anagram. The legend of the saint who wiped Christ's face on the way to Calvary and found an image of his face imprinted on the towel seems to have been invented to account for this derivation.

Vessa F Modern creation, a contracted form of >>**Vanessa** or an assimilated form of >>**Vesta**.

Vesta F From the Latin name of the Roman goddess of the hearth. It is only rarely used as a given name in the English-speaking world, but was borne as a stage name by the Victorian music-hall artiste Vesta Tilley (1864–1952). In some cases it may represent a simplified form of >>**Silvestra**.

v

Victor M From a Late Latin personal name meaning 'conqueror'. This was popular among early Christians as a reference to Christ's victory over death and sin, and was borne by several saints. An influence on the choice of the name in more recent times was the actor Victor Mature (1916–99).

Victoria F Feminine form of the Latin name *Victōrius* (a derivative of **»Victor**), also perhaps a direct use of Latin *victōria* 'victory'. It was little known in England until the accession in 1837 of Queen Victoria (1819–1901), who got it from her German mother, Mary Louise Victoria of Saxe-Coburg. It did not begin to be a popular name among commoners in Britain until the 1940s, reaching a peak in the 1980s.

Vincent M From the Old French form of the Latin name *Vincens* 'conquering' (genitive *Vincentis*). This name was borne by various early saints particularly associated with France, most notably the 5th-century St Vincent of Lérins.

Viola F From Latin *viōla* 'violet'. The name is relatively common in Italy and was used by Shakespeare in *Twelfth Night*, where most of the characters have Italianate names. Its modern use in English has been influenced by the vocabulary word denoting the small pansy-like flower.

Violet F From the name of the flower (Old French *violette*, Late Latin *violetta*, a diminutive of *viōla*). This was one of the earliest flower names to become popular in Britain, being well established before the middle of the 19th century.

Virgil M Mainly U.S.: usual English form of the name of the most celebrated of Roman poets, Publius Vergilius Maro (70–19 BC). The correct Latin spelling is *Vergilius*, but it was early altered to *Virgilius*. Today the name is almost always given with direct reference to the poet, but medieval instances may have been intended to honour instead a 6th-century bishop of Arles or an 8th-century Irish monk who evangelized Carinthia and became archbishop of Salzburg, both of whom also bore the name. In the case of the later saint, it was a classicized form of the Gaelic name *Fearghal* (see **»Fergal**). The spelling **»Vergil** is also found.

Virginia F From the feminine form of Latin *Virginius* (more correctly *Verginius*), a Roman family name. It was borne by a Roman maiden killed, according to legend, by her own father to spare her the attentions of an importunate suitor. It was not used as a given name in the Middle Ages. It was bestowed on the first American child of English parentage, born at Roanoke in August 1587, and has remained in use ever since. Both child and province were named in honour of Elizabeth I, the 'Virgin Queen'. Among modern influences on the choice of the name has been the actress Virginia McKenna (b. 1931).

Vita F 19th-century coinage, either directly from Latin *vita* 'life', or else as a feminine form of the male name *Vitus*. It has been borne most notably by the English writer Vita Sackville-West (1892–1962), in whose case it was a pet form of the given name *Victoria*.

Vivian F, occasionally M Originally a boy's name from an Old French form of the Latin name *Viviānus* (probably a derivative of *vivus* 'alive'), but now more frequent as a girl's name. It was borne by a 5th-century bishop of Saintes in western France, remembered for protecting his people during the invasion of the Visigoths. The spellings **»Vivien**, **»Vyvyan** are also found.

Vivien F, formerly M Earlier generally taken as a variant of the boy's name **»Vivian**. This spelling was quite common in Old French. Its use as a girl's name in the English-speaking world was influenced by Tennyson's *Merlin and Vivien* (1859). This name, from Arthurian legend, may represent an altered form of a Celtic name (perhaps a cognate of the Irish Gaelic name *Béibhinn* 'white lady', pronounced 'bee-**veen**'). The actress Vivien Leigh (1913–67) was christened *Vivian*.

Vivienne F French feminine form of »**Vivien**, used also in the English-speaking world as an unambiguously female form of the name.

Vyvyan M Fanciful respelling of »**Vivian** as a boy's name.

W

Wade M Transferred use of the surname, in origin either a local name from the medieval vocabulary word *wade* 'ford', or else from a medieval given name representing a survival of Old English *Wada*, a derivative of *wadan* 'to go', borne, according to legend, by a great sea-giant.

Waldo M From a Latinate short form of various old Germanic personal names derived from *wald* 'rule'. In America the name is particularly associated with the poet and essayist Ralph Waldo Emerson (1803–82).

Wallace M Transferred use of the surname, in origin an ethnic byname from Old French *waleis* 'foreign', used by the Normans to denote members of various Celtic races in areas where they were in the minority: Welshmen in the Welsh marches, Bretons in East Anglia, and Britons in the Strathclyde region. The given name seems to have been first used in Scotland, being bestowed in honour of the Scottish patriot William Wallace (?1272–1305).

Walter M From an Old French personal name of Germanic (Frankish) origin, derived from *wald* 'rule' + *heri*, *hari* 'army'. This was adopted by the Normans and introduced to England, superseding the native Old English form, *Wealdhere*. It was a very popular name in medieval England, normally pronounced 'Water'.

Wanda F Of uncertain origin. Attempts have been made to derive it from various Germanic and Slavonic roots. It was certainly in use in Poland in the 19th century, and is found in Polish folk tales as the name of a princess. The derivation may well be from the ethnic term *Wend* (see **»Wendell**). The name was introduced to the English-speaking world by Ouida (Marie Louise de la Ramée), who used it for the heroine of her novel *Wanda* (1883).

Ward M Transferred use of the surname, originally an occupational name from Old English *weard* 'guardian', 'watchman'.

Warner M Transferred use of the surname, which is from a medieval given name introduced to Britain by the Normans. It is of Germanic origin, from *war(in)* 'guard' + *heri, hari* 'army'.

Warren M Transferred use of the surname, which is of Norman origin, derived partly from a place in Normandy called *La Varenne* 'the game park' and partly from a Germanic personal name based on the element *war(in)* 'guard'. In America it has sometimes been bestowed in honour of General Joseph Warren, the first hero of the American Revolution, who was killed at Bunker Hill (1775). Among modern influences on the choice of the name has been the film actor Warren Beatty (b. 1937).

Warwick M Transferred use of the surname, in origin a local name from the town in the West Midlands.

Washington M Especially U.S.: transferred use of the surname of the first president of the United States, George Washington (1732–99), whose family came originally from Northamptonshire in England. They had been established in Virginia since 1656. The surname in this case is derived from the village of Washington in Co. Durham (now Tyne and Wear).

Wat M The usual medieval short form of **»Walter**, now occasionally revived.

Watkin M Either a revival of the medieval given name (a pet form of **»Walter** (see **»Wat**), with the diminutive suffix -*kin*), or a transferred use of the surname derived from it.

Wayne M Transferred use of the surname, in origin an occupational name for a carter or cartwright, from Old English *wægen* 'cart', 'waggon'. It was adopted as a given name in the second half of the 20th century, mainly as a result of the popularity of the American film actor John Wayne (1907–82), who was born Marion Michael Morrison; his screen name was chosen in honour of the American Revolutionary general Anthony Wayne (1745–96).

Webster M Transferred use of the surname, in origin an occupational name for a weaver, Old English *webbestre*. Use as a given name in America may owe something to the politician and orator Daniel Webster (1782–1852) and the lexicographer Noah Webster (1758–1843).

Wenda F Recent coinage, an altered form of ≫**Wendy**. There has probably been some influence by ≫**Wanda**. In the early Middle Ages a girl's name of this form was in occasional use on the Continent as a short form of various girls' names containing as their first element the ethnic name of the Wends (cf. ≫**Wendell**).

Wendell M Especially U.S.: from the surname derived in the Middle Ages from the Continental Germanic personal name *Wendel*, in origin an ethnic name for a *Wend*, a member of the Slavonic people living in the area between the Elbe and the Oder. It has been adopted as a given name as a result of the fame of the American writer Oliver Wendell Holmes (1809–94) and his jurist son, also Oliver Wendell Holmes (1841–1935), members of a leading New England family.

Wendy F Already in infrequent use, this name received a huge boost when J. M. Barrie used it for the 'little mother' in his play *Peter Pan* (1904). He took it from the nickname *Fwendy-Wendy* (i.e. 'friend') used for him

w

by a child acquaintance, Margaret Henley. The spelling **Wendi** is also found.

Wesley M From the surname of the founder of the Methodist Church, John Wesley (1703–91), and his brother Charles (1707–88), who was also influential in the movement. Their family must have come originally from one or other of the various places in England called *Westley*, the 'western wood, clearing, or meadow'. The given name was at first confined to members of the Methodist Church, but is now widely used without reference to its religious connotations.

Weston M Transferred use of the surname, in origin a local name from any of the very many places in England named in Old English as 'the western enclosure'.

Whiltierna F Irish: Anglicized form of the Gaelic name *Faoiltierna*, derived from *faol* 'wolf' + *tighearna* 'lord'.

Whitley F Mainly U.S.: transferred use of the surname, a local name from any of various places in England so named. Use as a girl's name may have been influenced by the adoption of »**Whitney** for the same purpose.

Whitney F, M Mainly North American: transferred use of the surname, in origin a local name from any of various places in England so named. In the 1980s its popularity as a girl's name was increased by the fame of the American singer Whitney Houston.

Wilberforce M Transferred use of the surname, in origin a local name from *Wilberfoss* in East Yorkshire. It was taken up as a given name in honour of the anti-slavery campaigner William Wilberforce (1759–1833). It is now sometimes taken as an extended form of *Wilbur*.

Wilbur M Mainly North American: transferred use of a comparatively rare surname, which is probably derived from a medieval female given name composed of Old English *will* 'will', 'desire' + *burh* 'fortress'.

Wilfrid M From an Old English personal name, derived from *wil* 'will', 'desire' + *frith* 'peace'. This was borne by two Anglo-Saxon saints: there is some doubt about the exact form of the name of the more famous, who played a leading role at the Council of Whitby (664); it may have been *Walfrid*, 'stranger peace'. Wilfrid the Younger was an 8th-century bishop of York. The name was not used in the later Middle Ages, but was revived in the 19th century, and enjoyed some popularity then and in the first part of the 20th century. The spelling **Wilfred** is also found.

Wilhelmina F Feminine version of *Wilhelm*, the German form of ≫**William**, formed with the Latinate suffix *-ina*. This name was introduced to the English-speaking world from Germany in the 19th century.

Will M Short form of ≫**William**, in use since the early Middle Ages, when it was occasionally used also for various other given names of Germanic origin containing the first element *wil* 'will', 'desire'.

Willa F Name coined as a feminine form of ≫**William**, by appending the characteristically feminine ending *-a* to the short form ≫**Will**.

Willard M Especially U.S.: transferred use of the surname, which is probably derived from the Old English personal name *Wilheard*, from *wil* 'will', 'desire' + *heard* 'hardy', 'brave', 'strong'.

William M Probably the most successful of all the Old French names of Germanic origin that were introduced to England by the Normans. It is derived from Germanic *wil* 'will', 'desire' + *helm* 'helmet', 'protection'. The fact that it was borne by the Conqueror himself does not seem to have inhibited its favour with the 'conquered' population: in the first century after the Conquest it was the commonest male name of all, and not only among the Normans. In the later Middle Ages it was overtaken by ≫**John**, but continued to run second to

w

that name until the 20th century, when the picture became more fragmented. There are various short forms and pet forms, including **»Will**, **»Bill**; **Willy**, **Willie**, and **»Billy**.

Willoughby M Transferred use of the surname, in origin a local name from any of various places in northern England so called.

Willow F From the name of the tree (Old English *welig*), noted for its grace and the pliancy of its wood.

Wilma F Contracted form of **»Wilhelmina**, which has retained rather more currency (especially in America) than the full form of the name.

Wilmer M From an Old English personal name, derived from *wil* 'will', 'desire' + *mær* 'famous'. This died out in the Middle Ages, but gave rise to a surname before it did so. The modern given name is probably a transferred use of that surname, perhaps adopted in particular as a masculine form of **»Wilma**.

Wilmette F Especially U.S.: a recent coinage, elaborated from **»Wilma** by means of the productive ending *-ette* (originally a French feminine diminutive suffix).

Wilmot M, F Transferred use of the surname, which is derived from a medieval pet form (with the Old French diminutive suffix *-ot*) of **»William**.

Windsor M Transferred use of the surname, which is derived from a place in Berkshire, the site of a castle that is in regular use as a residence of the royal family. Use as a given name dates from the mid 19th century and was reinforced by its adoption in 1917 as the surname of the British royal family.

Winfred M, F Revival of the Old English name *Wynnfrith*, from *wynn* 'joy' + *frith* 'peace', now often confused with **»Winifred**.

Winifred F Anglicized form of the Welsh female personal name *Gwenfrewi*, derived from *gwen* 'white', 'fair', 'blessed', 'holy' + *frewi* 'reconciliation'. This was borne by a 7th-century Welsh saint around whom a large body of legends grew up. The form of the name has been altered by association with ≫**Winfred**.

Winona F Mainly North American: from a Sioux female name, said to be reserved normally for a first-born daughter.

Winston M Although there was an Old English personal name, *Wynnstan*, from *wynn* 'joy' + *stān* 'stone', which would have had this form if it had survived, the modern given name is a transferred use of the surname, a local name from *Winston* in Gloucestershire. Use as a given name originated in the Churchill family: the first Winston Churchill (b. 1620) was baptized with the surname of his mother's family. The name has continued in the family ever since, and has been widely adopted in honour of the statesman Winston Spencer Churchill (1874–1965).

Winthrop M Especially U.S.: from the surname of a leading American pioneering family. John Winthrop (1588–1649) was governor of Massachusetts Bay Colony from 1629, and played a major role in shaping the political institutions of New England. His son (1606–76) and grandson (1638–1707), who bore the same name, were also colonial governors. Their family probably came originally from one of the places in England called *Winthorpe* (named in Old English as the 'village of Wynna').

Winton M Transferred use of the surname, in origin a local name from any of the various places so called.

Woodrow M Transferred use of the surname, in origin a local name for someone who lived in a row of houses by a wood. Use as a given name was inspired by the

w

American president (Thomas) Woodrow Wilson (1856–1924).

Woody M Pet form of **»Woodrow**, now also used as an independent given name. It has been borne by the American folk singer Woody (Woodrow Wilson) Guthrie (1912–67) and the 1940s band leader Woody (Woodrow Charles) Herman (1913–87). The American humorist Woody Allen was born Allen Stewart Konigsberg in 1935.

Wyatt M Transferred use of the surname, derived from a medieval given name representing a Norman French alteration of the Old English personal name *Wīgheard*, from *wīg* 'war' + *heard* 'hardy', 'brave', 'strong'.

Wyn M Welsh: originally a byname from the Welsh vocabulary word *(g)wyn* 'white', 'fair', 'blessed', 'holy'. The name is found in this form from the early Middle Ages.

Wyndham M Transferred use of the surname, which is derived from a contracted form of the name of *Wymondham* in Norfolk, originally named in Old English as the 'homestead of Wigmund'.

Wynne M, F Probably a transferred use of the surname, which is derived from the Old and Middle English personal name *Wine*. The spelling **Wynn** also occurs. See also **»Wyn**.

Wystan M From an Old English personal name derived from *wīg* 'battle' + *stān* 'stone'. St Wistan was a 9th-century prince of Mercia, murdered by his nephew Bertulf. The modern given name is rare, being best known as that of the poet Wystan Hugh Auden (1907–73).

w

Xanthe F From the feminine form of the Greek adjective *xanthos* 'yellow', 'bright'. The name was borne by various minor figures in classical mythology.

Xavier M From the surname of the Spanish soldier–saint Francis Xavier (1506–52), one of the founding members of the Society of Jesus (the Jesuits). He was born on the ancestral estate at Xavier (now Javier) in Navarre. The given name is used almost exclusively by Roman Catholics.

Xaviera F Name created as a feminine form of ➤➤**Xavier**.

Xenia F Comparatively rare given name, coined from the Greek vocabulary word *xenia* 'hospitality'.

Y

Yasmin F Variant of **»Jasmine**, representing a 'learned' re-creation of the Persian form.

Ynyr M Welsh: traditional name of uncertain derivation, probably from the Latin name *Honōrius* (a derivative of *honor* 'renown'). There is a passing reference in the *Mabinogi* to 'the battle between the two Ynyrs'.

Yolande F Of uncertain origin. It is found in Old French in this form, and may be ultimately of Germanic origin, but if so it has been altered beyond recognition. It is sometimes identified with the name of St *Jolenta* (d. 1298), daughter of the king of Hungary. The Latinate form **Yolanda** is also found.

Yorath M Anglicized form of the Welsh personal name **»Iorwerth** or, in some cases, a transferred use of the surname derived from it.

Yorick M The name of the (defunct) court jester in Shakespeare's *Hamlet*. This is a respelling of *Jorck*, a Danish form of **»George**.

York M Transferred use of the surname, which originated as a local name from the city in north-eastern England. The placename was originally *Eburacon*, a derivative of a Welsh word meaning 'yew'. The Anglo-Saxon settlers changed this to Old English *Eofor-wīc* 'boar farm', which in Old Norse became *Iorvík* or *Iork*.

Ysanne F Recent coinage, a blend of the first syllable of **»Yseult** + the given name **»Anne**.

y

Yseult F Medieval French form of **»Isolde**, still
occasionally used as a given name in the English-
speaking world.

Yves M French: from a Germanic personal name
representing a short form of various compound names
containing the element *iv* 'yew'. The final *-s* is the mark
of the Old French nominative case. The name was
introduced to Britain from France at the time of the
Norman Conquest, and again in the 20th century. See
also **»Ivo**.

Yvette F French feminine pet form of **»Yves**, now also
used in the English-speaking world.

Yvonne F French feminine pet form of **»Yves** (or simply
a feminine form based on the Old French oblique case
Yvon; cf. **»Ivon**), now also widely used in the English-
speaking world.

Z

Zachary M English vernacular form of the New Testament Greek name *Zacharias*, a form of Hebrew *Zechariah* 'God has remembered'. This was the name of the father of John the Baptist, who underwent a temporary period of dumbness for his lack of faith (Luke 1), and of a more obscure figure, Zacharias son of Barachias, who was slain 'between the temple and the altar' (Matthew 23:35; Luke 11:51). It was the name of a 19th-century president of the United States, Zachary Taylor.

Zack M Mainly North American: short form of ≫**Zachary**.

Zane M Transferred use of a surname of uncertain origin. It came to prominence as the given name of the American writer Zane Grey (1875–1939), a descendant of the Ebenezer Zane who founded *Zaneville* in Ohio.

Zanna F Modern coinage, apparently a shortened form of *Suzanna*.

Zara F Of uncertain origin. It is sometimes said to be of Arabic origin, from *zahr* 'flower', but is more probably a respelled form of ≫**Sara**. It was given by Princess Anne and Mark Philips to their second child (b. 1981).

Zaylie F Of uncertain origin, perhaps a respelling of the rare French name *Zélie*, an altered form of *Célie*, the French version of ≫**Celia**.

Zeb M Short form of ≫**Zebedee** and ≫**Zebulun**, now occasionally used as an independent given name.

Zebedee M Name borne in the New Testament by the father of the apostles James and John, who was with his sons mending fishing nets when they were called by Christ (Matthew 4:21; Mark 1:20). This is from a Greek form of the Hebrew name that appears in the Old Testament as *Zebadiah* or *Zabdi* 'gift of Jehovah'.

Zebulun M Biblical name, borne by the sixth son of Leah and Jacob. The name may mean 'exaltation', although Leah derives it from another meaning of the Hebrew root *zabal*, namely 'to dwell': 'now will my husband dwell with me, because I have born him six sons' (Genesis 30:20). It appears in the New Testament (Matthew 4:13) in the form *Zabulon*. The spelling **Zebulon** also occurs.

Zed M Especially U.S.: short form of the much rarer full name **Zedekiah**. This name, meaning 'justice of Yahweh' in Hebrew, is borne in the Bible by three separate characters.

Zeke M Especially U.S.: shortened form of ≫**Ezekiel**.

Zelah F Biblical name (meaning 'side' in Hebrew), the name of one of the fourteen cities of the tribe of Benjamin (Joshua 18:28). It is far from clear why it should have come to be used, albeit rarely, as a girl's name in the English-speaking world. It may simply be a variant of ≫**Zillah** under the influence of the placename.

Zelda F Modern name of uncertain origin, possibly a short form of ≫**Griselda**. It came to prominence in the 1920s as the name of the wife of the American writer F. Scott Fitzgerald (1896–1940).

Zelma F Modern coinage, an altered form of ≫**Selma**.

Zena F Of uncertain origin, probably a variant spelling of ≫**Zina**.

Zeph M Especially U.S: short form of the much rarer full name **Zephaniah**. This name, meaning 'hidden by God' in Hebrew, was borne by one of the minor biblical **z**

prophets, author of the book of the Bible that bears his name.

Zephyrine F From French *Zéphyrine*, an elaborated name derived from Latin *Zephyrus*, Greek *Zephyros* 'west wind'. St Zephyrinus was pope 199–217, but there is no equivalent female saint, so it is rather surprising that this name should have survived only in a female form.

Zeta F Of uncertain origin, probably a variant spelling of ≫**Zita**. It also coincides in form with the name of the letter of the Greek alphabet equivalent to English *z* (but not the last letter of the Greek alphabet).

Zillah F Biblical name (from a Hebrew word meaning 'shade'), borne by one of the two wives of Lamech (Genesis 4:19). The name was taken up in the first place by the Puritans, and again by fundamentalist Christian groups in the 19th century.

Zina F Russian short form of **Zinaida** (from Greek *Zēnais*, a derivative of the name of the god *Zeus*), the name of an obscure saint venerated in the Eastern Church. It is also a Russian short form of the rarer given name *Zinovia* (from Greek *Zēnobia*, a compound of *Zeus* + *bios* 'life'). Its adoption as a given name in the English-speaking world probably owes something to its resemblance to ≫**Tina**.

Zipporah F Jewish: common female form of the rare Hebrew male name *Zippor*, from Hebrew *zippor* 'bird'. The girl's name is borne in the Bible by the wife of Moses (Exodus 18:2–4).

Zita F From the name of a 13th-century saint from Lucca in Tuscany, who led an uneventful life as a domestic servant; she was canonized in 1696, and is regarded as the patroness of domestic servants. Her name was probably a nickname from the medieval Tuscan dialect word *zit(t)a* 'girl', although efforts have been made to link it with Greek *zētein* 'to seek'.

Zoë F From a Greek name meaning 'life'. This was already in use in Rome towards the end of the classical period (at first as an affectionate nickname), and was popular with the early Christians, who bestowed it with reference to their hopes of eternal life. It was borne by martyrs of the 2nd and 3rd centuries, but was taken up as an English given name only in the 19th century. The spelling **Zoe** is also found.

Zola F Apparently a late 20th-century creation, formed from the first syllable of **>Zoë** with the ending *-la*, common in girls' names. It coincides in form with the surname of the French novelist Émile Zola (1840–1902), who was of Italian descent, but it is unlikely that he had any influence on the use of the name.

Zula F Modern coinage derived from the tribal name of the Zulus. The Zulu people of Southern Africa formed a powerful warrior nation under their leader Chaka in the 19th century, and controlled an extensive empire. In 1838, under the leadership of their ruler Dingaan, they ambushed and slaughtered a group of some five hundred Boers. This given name is chosen mainly by Black people proud of their African origins.

Appendix

Contents

Unisex Names

Alex	Eden	Kerry	Robin
Alexis	Ellis	Kim	Rowan
Ariel	Evelyn	Kimberley	Ryan
Armani	Finlay	Kit	Sandy
Ashley	Frankie	Laurie	Sasha
Ashton	Gabriel	Lee	Shae
Aubrey	Gene	Leigh	Shannon
Bailey	Georgie	Lesley	Sharman
Beau	Harley	Leslie	Shay
Billie	Hilary	Lindsay	Shea
Billy	Jaime	Logan	Shelby
Blair	Jamie	Loren	Shelley
Bobbie	Jan	Mackenzie	Sheridan
Bobby	Jay	Maddison	Sidney
Brodie	Jean	Madison	Silver
Brogan	Jerry	Mallory	Sky
Brooklyn	Jess	Marty	Stacey
Cameron	Jesse	Mel	Stevie
Casey	Jessie	Meredith	Storm
Cassidy	Jo	Morgan	Sydney
Charlie	Jocelyn	Nicky	Taylor
Chris	Jody	Nico	Teddy
Christian	Jordan	Nikita	Tierney
Christie	Joss	Noel	Tracy
Cody	Jude	Ophrah	Tyler
Courtney	Jules	Pat	Valentine
Dana	Kelly	Patrice	Vivian
Darcy	Kelsey	Patsy	Wilmot
Devon	Kendall	Randy	Winfred
Drew	Kennedy	Riley	Wynne

Religious Names

Biblical Names

Aaron	Enos	Job	Omar
Abel	Ephraim	Joel	Ophrah
Abigail	Esther	Jonah	Oren
Abner	Ethan	Jonathan	Peninnah
Abraham	Eve	Joseph	Phineas
Adah	Ezekiel	Joshua	Rachel
Adam	Ezra	Josiah	Rastus
Adlai	Gabriel	Judah	Rebecca
Amos	Gideon	Judith	Reuben
Ariel	Hannah	Keren	Ruth
Asa	Hephzibah	Keturah	Samson
Benjamin	Hiram	Kezia	Samuel
Beulah	Immanuel	Leah	Sarah
Caleb	Ira	Levi	Saul
Dan	Isaac	Mara	Seth
Daniel	Isaiah	Mehetabel	Simeon
David	Israel	Micah	Solomon
Deborah	Jabez	Michael	Susannah
Delilah	Jacob	Michal	Tirzah
Dinah	Jared	Miriam	Tobias
Edna	Jemima	Moses	Uriah
Eli	Jeremiah	Nahum	Uriel
Elijah	Jeremy	Naomi	Zebulun
Elisabeth	Jesse	Nathan	Zelah
Emmanuel	Jethro	Noah	Zillah
Enoch	Joachim	Obadiah	Zipporah

New Testament Names

Alexander	Jason	Matthew	Simon
Andreas	Joanna	Matthias	Susanna
Andrew	John	Nathaniel	Tabitha
Barnabas	Jonas	Paul	Talitha
Bartholomew	Jude	Persis	Thaddeus
Bethany	Julia	Peter	Thomas
Chloe	Lois	Philip	Timothy
Damaris	Lucas	Priscilla	Zachary
Drusilla	Luke	Rhoda	Zebedee
Elias	Mark	Salome	
Eunice	Martha	Sara	
James	Mary	Silas	

Saints' and Roman Catholic Names

Abraham	Augustine	Bruno	Corin
Adelaide	Aurelia	Candida	Cornelius
Adele	Ava	Carmel	Cosmo
Agatha	Barbara	Cathal	Crispin
Agnes	Barnabas	Cecilia	Cuthbert
Aidan	Bartholomew	Ceinwen	Cyril
Alban	Basil	Chad	Cyrus
Alexander	Beatrix	Christopher	Damhnait
Alexis	Benedict	Ciarán	Damian
Aloysius	Bernadette	Cillian	Daria
Ambrose	Bernard	Clare	Darius
Anastasia	Bethany	Claude	David
Andrew	Blain	Clement	Deiniol
Anthony	Blaise	Colman	Dennis
Apollonia	Boris	Comhghall	Dervila
Ariadne	Brendan	Conan	Dewi
Arnold	Brice	Corbinian	Dolores
Audrey	Bridget	Cordula	Dominic

Donal	Gemma	Laura	Nicholas
Dorothea	Genevieve	Laurence	Ninian
Duncan	George	Leander	Norbert
Dunstan	Georgia	Leary	Odile
Dymphna	Gerard	Leo	Olga
Edan	Germaine	Leonard	Oran
Edgar	Gervaise	Lorcan	Oswald
Edith	Gilbert	Loreto	Patrick
Edmund	Giles	Loretta	Paul
Edward	Gobnat	Lourdes	Paula
Egbert	Godfrey	Lucia	Peregrine
Eithne	Gregory	Lucilla	Peter
Elwyn	Gwen	Ludmilla	Philip
Emyr	Helena	Luke	Philomena
Erasmus	Hilda	Magnus	Quentin
Eugene	Hubert	Malachy	Regina
Eunan	Hyacinth	Malanie	Ronan
Euphemia	Ignatius	Marcella	Rowan
Eustace	Illtud	Marcia	Sabina
Fabian	Isidore	Margaret	St John
Fabiola	James	Mark	Samson
Felicity	Jarlath	Martin	Sebastian
Felim	Jerome	Mary	Seraphina
Felix	Joachim	Matthew	Serena
Ferdinand	John	Maura	Silas
Fergus	Jude	Maximilian	Silvester
Fiachra	Julia	Mel	Silvia
Fillan	Julian	Mercedes	Simon
Finbar	Justin	Michael	Sophia
Finnian	Katherine	Mildred	Stephen
Fintan	Kenelm	Morwenna	Talulla
Flannan	Kevin	Mungo	Tatiana
Flavia	Killian	Myron	Terence
Francis	Lambert	Natalya	Teresa

Thecia	Tobias	Verena	Winifred
Theodore	Ursula	Victor	Xavier
Theodosia	Valentine	Vincent	Zita
Thomas	Valerie	Wilfred	

Regional and Country-Specific Names

Scottish Gaelic Names and other Names associated with Scotland

Aileen	Conall	Evander	Gregor
Ailie	Craig	Ewan	Hamilton
Ailsa	Creighton	Ewart	Hamish
Ainsley	Darragh	Fenella	Iain
Alasdair	Davina	Fergus	Ian
Alec	Diarmaid	Fife	Innes
Alistair	Donald	Fillan	Íomhar
Allaster	Donnchadh	Fingal	Irvine
Angus	Dougal	Finlay	Irving
Annabel	Douglas	Fiona	Isbel
Aodh	Drew	Fionnuala	Isla
Aoife	Duff	Forbes	Jean
Aonghas	Dugald	Fraser	Jessie
Arabella	Duncan	Freya	Jock
Archibald	Edan	Fulton	Keir
Barclay	Eilidh	Gillespie	Keith
Blair	Elsie	Gilroy	Kenneth
Bruce	Elspeth	Gladstone	Kester
Calum	Errol	Glen	Kirstie
Cameron	Erskine	Gordon	Kirstin
Campbell	Euan	Graham	Kyle
Carson	Euna	Grant	Lachlan
Catriona	Eunan	Greer	Lamont

Lennox	Morag	Reid	Somerled
Leslie	Moray	Rhona	Sorcha
Lexine	Morna	Ross	Sorley
Lindsay	Morven	Roy	Stirling
Logan	Muir	Sandy	Stuart
Lyall	Muireall	Saundra	Summerlad
Mackenzie	Mungo	Sawney	Tadhg
Màiri	Murdo	Scott	Tam
Maisie	Murray	Senga	Teàrlach
Maretta	Niall	Seònaid	Torquil
Maxwell	Ninian	Seumas	Uilleam
Meg	Rabbie	Sheena	Ùisdean
Melville	Ramsay	Sholto	Wallace
Monroe	Ranald	Shona	
Mór	Ranulf	Sinclair	

Irish Gaelic Names and other Names associated with Ireland

Aed	Brady	Cathal	Conley
Aengus	Breda	Ceallach	Conn
Aidan	Brendan	Cian	Connor
Aine	Brennan	Ciara	Conovan
Aisling	Brian	Ciarán	Cormac
Alva	Bride	Cillian	Cowal
Aodh	Bridget	Clancy	Daley
Aoibheann	Brigid	Cliona	Damhnait
Aoife	Brónach	Clodagh	Darcy
Art	Cahan	Cody	Darina
Ashling	Caitlín	Colm	Darragh
Barry	Caitrín	Colman	Declan
Béibhinn	Caoimhe	Comhghall	Deirdre
Bláthnat	Cara	Conall	Dervila
Braden	Cassidy	Conan	Desmond

Diarmaid	Fionnuala	Maeve	Orla
Donagh	Flann	Máire	Oscar
Donal	Flannan	Mairéad	Ossian
Dorean	Garret	Mairenn	Pádraig
Duald	Gearóid	Malachy	Patrick
Duane	Gobbán	Malcolm	Peadar
Eamon	Gobnat	Maureen	Pearce
Eavan	Grálnne	Mel	Pegeen
Edan	Grania	Moira	Piaras
Edna	Guaire	Mona	Pierce
Egan	Heber	Mór	Proinnsias
Eileen	Honora	Moreen	Quinn
Eithne	Jarlath	Morna	Raghnall
Elwyn	Kane	Muireann	Redmond
Emer	Kathleen	Muiris	Rian
Eóghan	Kean	Muirne	Rionach
Eoin	Keegan	Murchadh	Riordan
Erin	Keelin	Myrna	Róisín
Ernan	Keenan	Naoise	Ronan
Étaín	Keeva	Naomh	Rory
Ethna	Kelan	Neil	Rosaleen
Eunan	Kelly	Nessa	Rosheen
Evlin	Kennedy	Neve	Rowan
Felim	Kevin	Niall	Sadhbh
Fenella	Kieran	Niamh	Saoirse
Fergal	Killian	Ninian	Séamas
Fergus	Laoise	Nolan	Séamus
Fiachra	Lassarina	Nora	Seán
Fidelma	Lavery	Noreen	Seanan
Finbar	Leary	Nuala	Seumus
Finn	Lennan	Oisín	Shamus
Finnian	Liadan	Onora	Shane
Finola	Liam	Oona	Shannon
Fintan	Lorcan	Oran	Shaun

Shawn	Síne	Tárlach	Ulick
Shea	Sinéad	Teague	Ultan
Sheena	Siobhán	Teigue	Una
Sheila	Sorcha	Tiernan	Whiltierna
Sheridan	Sorley	Tierney	
Shevaun	Tadhg	Treasa	
Síle	Talulla	Turlough	

Welsh Names and other Names associated with Wales

Alun	Deiniol	Gaenor	Heilyn
Aneirin	Delwyn	Gareth	Heledd
Angharad	Delyth	Geraint	Huw
Aranrhod	Dewi	Gladys	Hywel
Arianrhod	Dilwen	Glenda	Idris
Arianwen	Dilys	Glenys	Idwal
Blodwedd	Drystan	Glyn	Ieuan
Blodwen	Dylan	Glyndwr	Ifor
Branwen	Eiddwen	Glynn	Illtud
Bronwen	Eira	Goronwy	Iolo
Bryn	Eirlys	Griffin	Iorwerth
Brynmor	Eirwen	Griffith	Islwyn
Cadell	Elen	Gwen	Lleu
Cadogan	Eleri	Gwenda	Llew
Caradoc	Elin	Gwendolen	Llewelyn
Carys	Eluned	Gwenllian	Lloyd
Catrin	Elwyn	Gwenyth	Madoc
Ceinwen	Emlyn	Gwilym	Mair
Ceri	Emrys	Gwyn	Mared
Ceridwen	Emyr	Gwynedd	Mari
Cledwyn	Esyllt	Gwyneth	Megan
Dafydd	Evan	Gwynfor	Meical
Dai	Floyd	Heddwyn	Meilyr

Meinwen	Myfanwy	Rhonwen	Trahaearn
Meirion	Nerys	Rhydderch	Trefor
Meredith	Nesta	Rhys	Trevor
Merfyn	Nia	Siân	Trystan
Merlin	Nye	Siôn	Tudur
Mervyn	Olwen	Sioned	Urien
Meurig	Owen	Talfryn	Vaughan
Mihangel	Pryderi	Taliesin	Wyn
Morgan	Rhiannon	Tegwen	Ynyr
Morwenna	Rhodri	Teleri	
Mostyn	Rhonda	Tirion	

Names derived from Latin and Greek*

*See also names from mythology and legends

Adrian	Beatrix	Constant	Dorothea
Agatha	Benedict	Constantine	Drusilla
Agnes	Berenice	Cordula	Eustace
Alban	Caesar	Corinna	Fabia
Alexander	Camilla	Cornelia	Fabian
Alexia	Candida	Crispin	Fabiola
Alexis	Cecilia	Cynthia	Felicity
Andreas	Celia	Cyprian	Felix
Andrew	Charis	Cyrus	Flavia
Anthea	Charmian	Damian	Fulvia
Anthony	Chloe	Damon	George
Antonia	Christopher	Daria	Gloria
Apollonia	Clara	Darius	Gregory
Augusta	Classical	Delia	Helena
Augustus	Claude	Dennis	Horace
Aurelia	Claudia	Dion	Horatia
Aurora	Clement	Dominic	Horatio
Barbara	Cleopatra	Dorcas	Horatius
Basil	Constance	Doris	Hortense

Hyacinth	Lyssa	Phoebe	Tacita
Ignatius	Magnus	Priscilla	Tarquin
Isidore	Marcella	Prudence	Titus
Joanna	Marcus	Quintus	Ursula
Julia	Maria	Regina	Valentine
Julian	Marina	Rex	Valerie
Julius	Marisa	Rhea	Vera
Justin	Marius	Rhoda	Vergil
Justina	Martin	Roxane	Verity
Justus	Martina	Sabina	Vesta
Katharine	Myron	Salome	Victor
Katherine	Nicholas	Septimus	Victoria
Laetitia	Nona	Serena	Vincent
Lalage	Octavia	Sextus	Viola
Laurence	Octavius	Sidony	Virgil
Leo	Paul	Silvester	Vita
Livia	Petronel	Sophia	Vivian
Lucia	Philip	Stella	Xenia
Luke	Phillida	Sybil	Zoë
Lydia	Philomena	Tacey	

Names from Overseas now used in the English-speaking World

RUSSIA	Ludmila	Tanya	Gina
Anastasia	Nadia	Tatiana	Lauretta
Anton	Natalya	Vera	Lia
Boris	Natasha	Zina	Mariella
Gala	Nikita		Marietta
Ivan	Nina	ITALY	Mimi
Katerina	Olga		Rosetta
Katya	Sasha	Carlotta	Teresa
Lara	Sonya	Elena	
Larissa	Tamara	Eleonora	
		Francesca	

SPAIN

Anita
Carmen
Dolores
Elvira
Jacinta
Jaime
Lola
Lolita
Mercedes
Raquel
Xavier

FRANCE

Adeline
Adrienne
Aimée
André
Annette
Antoinette
Beatrice
Blaise
Brigitte
Carole
Céleste
Chantal
Christelle
Christine
Claire
Claude
Claudette
Claudine
Colette
Danielle
Delphine
Denise
Desirée
Diane
Dion
Dominique
Elise
Eugénie
Fifi
Francine
Gabrielle
Genevieve
Georgette
Germaine
Gigi
Giselle
Hortense
Isabelle
Iseult
Jacqueline
Jeannette
Jeannine
Joelle
Josephine
Josette
Jules
Julie
Léonie
Lisette
Louis
Louise
Lucille
Madeleine
Marc
Marcel
Margot
Marguerite
Marie
Martine
Michelle
Mignonette
Mirabelle
Mireille
Nadine
Natalie
Nicole
Nicolette
Ninette
Odette
Odile
Ottoline
Paulette
Pauline
Reine
Renée
Rosalie
Simone
Sophie
Suzanne
Suzette
Sylvie
Vivienne
Yseult
Yves
Yvette
Zephyrine

GERMANY, SWITZERLAND, SCANDINAVIA, AND THE NETHERLANDS

Anton
Astrid
Dagmar
Dirk
Heidi
Helga
Inga
Ingrid
Ivo
Karen
Karin
Karl
Katarina
Katrine
Kirsten
Kristen
Kristina
Marna
Mia
Saskia
Verena

Family Names as Given Names

Addison	Burgess	Coll	Errol
Ainsley	Burton	Cornell	Erskine
Alger	Byron	Courtney	Evelyn
Ashley	Cade	Craig	Everett
Ashton	Cadogan	Creighton	Ewart
Aubrey	Cameron	Curtis	Fletcher
Austin	Campbell	Dale	Floyd
Avery	Carlton	Daley	Forbes
Bailey	Carson	Dana	Ford
Baldwin	Carter	Dane	Franklin
Barclay	Cary	Darby	Fraser
Barton	Cecil	Darcy	Fulton
Baxter	Chadwick	Darrell	Garfield
Bennett	Chance	Dean	Garret
Benson	Chandler	Dell	Garrick
Bentley	Chanel	Denton	Garrison
Beverley	Chapman	Denzil	Garth
Blair	Charlton	Desmond	Gary
Blake	Chester	Dexter	Gerrard
Braden	Clancy	Digby	Gilroy
Bradford	Clark	Donovan	Gladstone
Bradley	Clay	Douglas	Gladwin
Brady	Clayton	Dudley	Godwin
Brandon	Clifford	Duff	Goodwin
Brennan	Clifton	Dustin	Gordon
Brent	Clinton	Dwight	Graham
Brett	Clive	Eldon	Grant
Brock	Cody	Elliot	Greer
Brooke	Colbert	Ellis	Greville
Bruce	Colby	Elmer	Hale
Bryce	Cole	Elsdon	Hamilton
Bryson	Coleman	Elton	Hardy

Harlan	Kent	Madison	Pelham
Harley	Kenton	Mallory	Penn
Harper	Kermit	Manley	Percy
Harrison	Kerr	Marsh	Perry
Hartley	Kingsley	Marshall	Preston
Harvey	Kirk	Mason	Quincy
Haydn	Kyle	Maxwell	Quinn
Hayley	Lacey	Maynard	Ramsay
Hedley	Lambert	Melville	Randall
Herbert	Lamont	Merrill	Rayner
Hesketh	Landon	Milton	Read
Hopkin	Lane	Mitchell	Rees
Howard	Lee	Monroe	Reid
Howell	Leighton	Montague	Reynold
Hunter	Leland	Montgomery	Rhett
Innes	Lennox	Montmorency	Richie
Irvine	Leslie	Morley	Ridley
Irving	Lester	Morris	Riley
Irwin	Lewis	Mortimer	Rodney
Jackson	Lincoln	Morton	Roscoe
Jarrett	Lindsay	Moss	Ross
Jarvis	Linford	Muir	Rowan
Jefferson	Linton	Murgatroyd	Rowland
Jenkin	Lloyd	Murray	Rowley
Jocelyn	Logan	Nelson	Royle
Keegan	Lorraine	Neville	Royston
Keenan	Lovell	Newton	Russell
Keir	Lowell	Nolan	Sacheverell
Keith	Lowry	Norris	Sandford
Kelsey	Lucas	Norton	Sanford
Kemp	Lyall	Otis	Scott
Kendall	Lyle	Paige	Selwyn
Kendrick	Lyndon	Parker	Seymour
Kennard	Mackenzie	Pearce	Shannagh

Sharman	Taylor	Vere	Wilbur
Shaw	Terrell	Vernon	Willard
Shea	Tiernan	Wade	Willoughby
Shelby	Tierney	Wallace	Wilmot
Sheldon	Todd	Ward	Windsor
Shelley	Tracy	Warner	Winston
Sheridan	Travis	Warren	Winthrop
Sherman	Tremaine	Warwick	Winton
Shirley	Trent	Washington	Woodrow
Sidney	Trevelyan	Watkin	Wyatt
Sinclair	Trevor	Wayne	Wyndham
Spencer	Troy	Webster	Xavier
Stafford	Truman	Wendell	Yorath
Stanley	Tucker	Wesley	York
Sterling	Tyler	Weston	Zane
Stirling	Tyrrell	Whitley	
Stuart	Tyson	Whitney	
Tanner	Vaughan	Wilberforce	

Names originating from Occupational Surnames

Bailey	Dexter	Mason	Taylor
Baxter	Fletcher	Paige	Travis
Carter	Harper	Parker	Tucker
Chandler	Heilyn	Scarlett	Tyler
Chapman	Hunter	Sherman	Ward
Clark	Kemp	Spencer	Wayne
Bailey	King	Stuart	Webster
Dean	Marshall	Tanner	

Names that denote Royalty, Rank, or Nobility

| Albert | Augustus | Brendan | Cyril |
| Arnold | Basil | Caesar | Cyrus |

Dominic	Eric	Meilyr	Riordan
Dominique	Eugene	Noble	Rory
Donal	Eugenia	Oswald	Roy
Duke	Eugénie	Prince	Royle
Earl	Frederica	Queenie	Ryan
Earla	Frederick	Raghnall	Sarah
Edgar	Gerald	Raine	Skipper
Edith	Griffith	Ray	Tiernan
Edmund	Harold	Regina	Tudur
Edward	Henry	Reine	Waldo
Edwin	King	Rex	Walter
Elmer	Laraine	Reynold	
Elroy	Leroy	Rhodri	
Emyr	Marquis	Rionach	

Names from Mythology and Legends

Greek and Roman

Althea	Evadne	Iris	Penelope
Ariadne	Evander	Jason	Phyllis
Cassandra	Flora	Jocasta	Silvia
Chloris	Gaia	Lavinia	Thalia
Clio	Hebe	Leander	Ulysses
Corin	Hector	Leda	Virginia
Daphne	Helen	Linus	Xanthe
Diana	Hermione	Lucretia	
Doris	Irene	Pandora	

Arthurian and Welsh

Angharad	Blodwedd	Drystan	Enid	Goronwy
Aranrhod	Branwen	Dylan	Gavin	Guinevere
Arthur	Ceridwen	Elaine	Geraint	Heilyn

Iorwerth	Mark	Rhiannon	Tristram
Isolde	Merlin	Sabrina	Urien
Jennifer	Olwen	Taliesin	Vivien
Lancelot	Percival	Teleri	Ynyr
Lleu	Pryderi	Tristan	

Gaelic

Aoife	Dymphna	Finn	Neil
Art	Eóghan	Gobbán	Niamh
Cliona	Fergus	Gráinne	Ossian
Conan	Fiachra	Heber	Sadhbh
Deirdre	Fidelma	Liadan	Una
Diarmaid	Finbar	Naoise	

Names from Literature and Popular Culture

Names associated with Literature

NAME	WRITER/LITERARY INFLUENCE
Aldous	Now known mainly as given name of novelist Aldous Huxley (1894–1963)
Alice	Lewis Carroll: *Alice's Adventures in Wonderland* (1865)
Amber	Kathleen Winsor: *Forever Amber* (1944)
Amelia	Henry Fielding: *Amelia* (1751)
Anthea	First used as modern given name by English poet Robert Herrick (1591–1674)
Audrey	Shakespeare: Touchstone's sweetheart in *As You Like It* (1599)
Beatrice	Dante's beloved

NAME	WRITER/LITERARY INFLUENCE
Beau	P. C. Wren: *Beau Geste* (1924)
Belinda	Sir John Vanbrugh: *The Provok'd Wife* (1697); Alexander Pope: *The Rape of the Lock* (1712)
Beth	Louisa M. Alcott: *Little Women* (1868)
Bianca	Shakespeare: *The Taming of the Shrew* (1593); *Othello* (1603–04)
Byron	First used as a given name in honour of English poet Lord Byron (1788–1824)
Catriona	Robert Louis Stevenson: *Catriona* (1893)
Cedric	Coined by Sir Walter Scott: *Ivanhoe* (1819)
Celia	Introduced to English-speaking world by Shakespeare: *As You Like It* (1599)
Charlotte	Owed much of its 19th-century popularity to Charlotte Brontë (1816–55)
Charmian	Shakespeare: *Antony and Cleopatra* (1606)
Cherry	Charles Dickens: *Martin Chuzzlewit* (1844)
Chloris	Used by the Roman poet Horace as pseudonym of one of his loves and taken up by 17th- and 18th-century Augustan poets
Christabel	Coined by Samuel Taylor Coleridge: *Christabel* (1816)
Clarinda	First appeared in Edmund Spenser: *Faerie Queene* (1596); Robert Burns: four poems *To Clarinda*
Clarissa	Samuel Richardson: *Clarissa* (1748)
Claudine	Heroine of series of novels by French novelist Colette
Colette	Famous as the name of French novelist Sidonie-Gabrielle Colette (1873–1954)
Cora	Coined by James Fenimore Cooper: *The Last of the Mohicans* (1926)
Cordelia	Shakespeare: *King Lear* (1605–06)
Corinna	Used by the Roman poet Ovid in his love poetry

NAME	WRITER/LITERARY INFLUENCE
Cressida	Shakespeare: *Troilus and Cressida* (1602)
Cynthia	Used in the love poetry of the Roman poet Propertius
Darcy	Jane Austen: *Pride and Prejudice* (1813)
Desdemona	Shakespeare: *Othello* (1603–04)
Dorian	Apparently invented by Oscar Wilde: *The Portrait of Dorian Gray* (1891)
Dylan	Associated with Welsh poet Dylan Thomas (1914–53)
Eliza	George Bernard Shaw: *Pygmalion* (1913)
Emily	English novelist Emily Brontë (1818–48)
Esmeralda	Use as a given name dates from Victor Hugo: *Notre Dame de Paris* (1831)
Evangeline	Henry Wadsworth Longfellow: *Evangeline* (1848)
Fingal	James Macpherson: Ossianic poems
Fiona	First used by James Macpherson: Ossianic poems
Fleur	Modern use derives mainly from its use in John Galsworthy: *The Forsyte Saga* (1922)
Gareth	First occurred in Thomas Malory: *Morte D'Arthur* (14th-century)
Geraldine	Invented by English poet Henry Howard (1517–47)
Gloria	First occurred in George Bernard Shaw: *You Never Can Tell* (1898)
Gwendolen	Oscar Wilde: *The Importance of Being Earnest* (1895)
Haidee	Lord Byron: *Don Juan* (1819–24)
Hal	Shakespeare: *King Henry IV* (1596–97)
Harry	Shakespeare: *King Henry V* (1598–99)
Heidi	Johanna Spyri: *Heidi* (1881)

NAME	WRITER/LITERARY INFLUENCE
Hermione	Shakespeare: *A Winter's Tale* (1609)
Imogen	First used in Shakespeare: *Cymbeline* (1610) (owing to misreading of Celtic Innogen)
Irene	John Galsworthy: *The Forsyte Saga* (1922)
Jancis	First used by Mary Webb: *Precious Bane* (1924)
Janice	First used by Paul Leicester Ford: *Janice Meredith* (1899)
Jessica	Apparently originates from Shakespeare: *The Merchant of Venice* (1596–97)
Joan	George Bernard Shaw: *St Joan* (1923)
Jolyon	Modern use derives from John Galsworthy: *The Forsyte Saga* (1922)
Jude	Thomas Hardy: *Jude the Obscure* (1895)
Juliet	Shakespeare: *Romeo and Juliet* (1595)
Justine	Lawrence Durrell: *Justine* (1957)
Kate	Shakespeare: *The Taming of the Shrew* (1593)
Kim	Rudyard Kipling: *Kim* (1901)
Lalage	Horace: *Odes*; John Fowles: *The French Lieutenant's Woman* (1969)
Lara	Boris Pasternak: *Dr Zhivago* (1957)
Laura	Used in love poetry of Italian poet Petrarch
Leila	Lord Byron: *The Giaour* (1813) and *Don Juan* (1819–24); Lord Lytton: *Leila* (1838)
Lesley	First recorded use as a girl's name in a poem by Robert Burns
Lolita	Vladimir Nabokov: *Lolita* (1955)
Lorna	R. D. Blackmore: *Lorna Doone* (1869)
Lucetta	Shakespeare: *Two Gentlemen of Verona* (1590–91)
Lucinda	First found in Cervantes: *Don Quixote* (1605)
Lynette	Alfred Lord Tennyson: *Idylls of the King* (1859–85)

NAME	WRITER/LITERARY INFLUENCE
Malvina	Invented by James Macpherson: Ossianic poems
Manfred	Lord Byron: *Manfred* (1817)
Maud	Alfred Lord Tennyson: *Maud* (1855)
Mercy	John Bunyan: *Pilgrim's Progress* (1684)
Milton	Use of given name influenced by poet John Milton (1608–74)
Miranda	Invented by Shakespeare: *The Tempest* (1611)
Morna	James Macpherson: Ossianic poems
Morven	James Macpherson: Ossianic poems
Myra	Invented by poet Fulke Greville (1554–1628)
Nerissa	First used by Shakespeare: *The Merchant of Venice* (1596–97)
Nicol	Sir Walter Scott: *Rob Roy* (1817)
Olivia	Originates from Shakespeare: *Twelfth Night* (1601)
Ophelia	Shakespeare: *Hamlet* (1600–01)
Orville	Invented by Fanny Burney: *Evelina* (1778)
Oscar	Associated with Irish writer Oscar Wilde (1854–1900)
Pamela	Invented by poet Sir Philip Sidney; taken up by Samuel Richardson: *Pamela* (1740)
Perdita	Coined by Shakespeare: *The Winter's Tale* (1610)
Piers	William Langland: *Piers Plowman* (1367–86)
Pippa	Robert Browning: *Pippa Passes* (1841)
Portia	Shakespeare: *The Merchant of Venice* (1596–97); *Julius Caesar* (1599)
Rabbie	Associated with Scottish poet Robert Burns (1759–96)
Regan	Originates from Shakespeare: *King Lear* (1605)
Roderick	Sir Walter Scott: *The Vision of Don Roderick* (1811)
Rosalind	Poetry of Edmund Spenser; Shakespeare: *As You Like It* (1599)

NAME	WRITER/LITERARY INFLUENCE
Rosaline	Shakespeare: *Love's Labour's Lost* (1594–95)
Rowena	Sir Walter Scott: *Ivanhoe* (1819)
Roxane	Daniel Defoe: *Roxana* (1724)
Rudolf	Anthony Hope: *The Prisoner of Zenda* (1894)
Sacheverell	English writer and art critic Sacheverell Sitwell
Sandra	George Meredith: *Sandra Belloni* (1886)
Selima	First known occurrence in poem by Thomas Gray (1716–71)
Seth	Stella Gibbons: *Cold Comfort Farm* (1932)
Sheridan	Use of given name influenced by Irish dramatist Richard Brinsley Sheridan (1751–1816)
Shirley	Charlotte Brontë: *Shirley* (1849)
Sidney	Charles Dickens: *A Tale of Two Cities* (1859)
Silvia	Shakespeare: *Two Gentlemen of Verona* (1590–91)
Sophia	Henry Fielding: *Tom Jones* (1749
Stella	First used in sonnets of Sir Philip Sidney (1554–86)
Stevie	English poet and novelist Stevie Smith (1902–71)
Thelma	First used by Marie Corelli: *Thelma* (1887)
Tristram	Laurence Sterne: *Tristram Shandy* (1759–67)
Tybalt	Shakespeare: *Romeo and Juliet* (1595)
Uriah	Charles Dickens: *David Copperfield* (1850)
Vanessa	Invented by satirist Jonathan Swift (1667–1745) for his friend Esther Vanhomrigh
Verona	Sinclair Lewis: *Babbitt* (1923)
Vita	English writer Vita Sackville-West (1892–1962)
Vivien	Tennyson: *Merlin and Vivien* (1859)
Wendy	J. M. Barry: *Peter Pan* (1904)
Yorick	Shakespeare: *Hamlet* (1600–01)

Names associated with Film, Television, and Music

NAME	FILM, TV, MUSIC INFLUENCE
Angharad	Welsh actress Angharad Rees (b. 1949)
Anita	Swedish film actress Anita Ekberg (b. 1931)
Arlene	US actress Arlene Dahl (b. 1924)
Art	US singer Art Garfunkel (b. 1941)
Audrey	Belgian actress Audrey Hepburn (1929–93)
Ava	US film actress Ava Gardner (1922–90)
Basil	Character Basil Fawlty in 1970s UK sitcom *Fawlty Towers*
Beau	Character Beau Wilks in Margaret Mitchell's *Gone with the Wind* (1936; filmed, 1939); US actor Beau Bridges (b. 1941)
Bette	US film actress Bette Davis (1908–89)
Bonnie	Infant daughter of Scarlett O'Hara in the film *Gone with the Wind* (1939); character Bonnie Parker in film *Bonnie and Clyde* (1967)
Brigitte	French actress Brigitte Bardot (b. 1934)
Brooke	US actresses Brooke Adams (b. 1949) and Brooke Shields (b. 1965)
Burt	US film actor Burt Lancaster (1913–94)
Cade	Use as a given name originates from Margaret Mitchell's *Gone with the Wind* (1936; filmed, 1939)
Candice	US actress Candice Bergen (b. 1946)
Careen	First appeared in in Margaret Mitchell's *Gone with the Wind* (1936; filmed, 1939)
Carmen	Heroine of Bizet's opera *Carmen* (1875)
Carole	US film actress Carole Lombard (1908–42)
Cary	US film actor Cary Grant (1904–89)
Chandler	Character in US sitcom *Friends*

NAME	FILM, TV, MUSIC INFLUENCE
Charlton	US film actor Charlton Heston (b. 1924)
Christian	US actor Christian Slater (b. 1969)
Clara	Silent film actress Clara Bow (1905–65)
Clark	US film actor Clark Gable (1901–60)
Claudette	French film actress Claudette Colbert (1903–96)
Clementine	Associated with popular song with this title
Cliff	English singer Cliff Richard (b. 1940)
Clint	US film actor Clint Eastwood (b. 1930)
Clyde	Character in film *Bonnie and Clyde* (1967)
Colby	1980s television serial *The Colbys*
Cole	Songwriter Cole Porter (1893–1964)
Courtney	UK jazz saxophonist Courtney Pine (b. 1964); US actress and musician Courtney Love (b. 1965); US actress Courtney Cox (b. 1964)
Dean	US actor and singer Dean Martin (1917–95)
Deanna	Canadian-born US singer and film actress Deanna Durbin (b. 1921)
Delia	English cookery writer and broadcaster Delia Smith (b. 1941)
Demelza	Heroine of Winston Graham's *Poldark* novels, serialized on British television
Demi	US actress Demi Moore (b. 1962)
Dirk	English actor Dirk Bogarde (1921–99)
Dolly	US singer Dolly Parton (b. 1946); song 'Hello, Dolly' (1964)
Dolores	Mexican actress Dolores del Rio (1905–83)
Donovan	Scottish folk-rock singer Donovan (b. 1946)
Doris	US film actress Doris Day (b. 1924)
Dorothy	US film actress Dorothy Lamour (1914–96)
Duane	US guitarist Duane Eddy (b. 1938)
Dustin	US actor Dustin Hoffman (b. 1937)

NAME	FILM, TV, MUSIC INFLUENCE
Dylan	US singer Bob Dylan (b. 1941)
Eamon	Broadcaster Eamon Andrews (1922–87)
Ella	US singer Ella Fitzgerald (1918–96)
Elton	English songwriter and singer Elton John (b. 1947)
Elvira	Heroine of Swedish film *Elvira Madigan* (1967)
Elvis	US rock singer Elvis Presley (1935–77)
Errol	US film actor Errol Flynn (1909–59)
Ewan	Scottish actor Ewan McGregor (b. 1971)
Faye	US film actress Faye Dunaway (b. 1941)
Gary	US film actor Gary Cooper (1901–61)
Gayle	US film actress Gayle Hunnicutt (b. 1942)
Gene	US film actors Gene Hackman (b. 1930), Gene Kelly (1912–96), Gene Wilder (b. 1934)
Gigi	Popularized by the musical *Gigi* (1958)
Gina	Italian actress Gina Lollobrigida (b. 1927)
Giselle	A. Adam's ballet *Giselle* (first performed 1841)
Glenda	English actress and politician Glenda Jackson (b. 1936)
Glenn	US film and stage actress Glenn Close (b. 1947)
Grace	US film actress Grace Kelly (1929–82)
Greer	British actress Greer Garson (1903–96)
Greta	Swedish-born US film actress Greta Garbo (1905–92)
Gwyneth	US film actress Gwyneth Paltrow (b. 1972)
Harrison	US film actor Harrison Ford (b. 1942)
Haydn	Austrian composer Joseph Haydn (1732–1809)
Hayley	English actress Hayley Mills (b. 1946)
Honey	Character in Margaret Mitchell's *Gone with the Wind* (1936; filmed, 1939)
Honor	UK actress Honor Blackman (b. 1926)

NAME	FILM, TV, MUSIC INFLUENCE
Humphrey	US film actor Humphrey Bogart (1899–1957)
India	Character in Margaret Mitchell's *Gone with the Wind* (1936; filmed, 1939)
Ingrid	Swedish film actress Ingrid Bergman (1915–82)
Irving	US composer Irving Berlin (1888–1989)
Isadora	US dancer Isadora Duncan (1878–1927)
Ivor	Welsh actor and songwriter Ivor Novello (1893–1951)
Janis	US rock singer Janis Joplin (1943–70)
Jason	Australian actor Jason Donovan (b. 1968)
Jethro	British rock group Jethro Tull (formed 1968)
Jolene	Song with this title recorded by Dolly Parton in 1979
Jodie	US actress Jodie Foster (b. 1962)
Joni	Canadian folk singer Joni Mitchell (b. 1943)
Jude	Song by John Lennon and Paul McCartney 'Hey Jude' (1968)
Judy	US singer and actress Judy Garland (1922–69)
Keanu	US film actor Keanu Reeves (b. 1965)
Kermit	Frog puppet on the US children's television series *The Muppet Show* and *Sesame Street*
Kim	US film actresses Kim Novak (b. 1933) and Kim Basinger (b. 1953)
Kirk	US film actor Kirk Douglas (b. 1916)
Kylie	Australian actress Kylie Minogue (b. 1968)
Lana	US film actress Lana Turner (1920–95)
Lara	Character in B. Pasternak's *Dr Zhivago* (filmed, 1965)
Lauren	US film actress Lauren Bacall (b. 1924)
Laurence	English actor Laurence Olivier (1907–89)
Leslie	British film actor Leslie Howard (1890–1943)

NAME	FILM, TV, MUSIC INFLUENCE
Liam	Irish actor Liam Neeson (b. 1952)
Lonnie	Scottish pop singer of the 1950s and 60s Lonnie Donegan (1931–2002)
Luana	First used in the film *The Bird of Paradise* (1932)
Lucille	US comedy actress Lucille Ball (1910–89); song 'Lucille', first recorded 1957
Lulu	Scottish pop singer Lulu (b. 1948)
Madonna	US pop singer and actress Madonna Ciccone (b. 1959)
Mae	US film actress Mae West (1892–1980)
Magnus	Icelandic–Scottish journalist and broadcaster Magnus Magnusson (b. 1929)
Marilyn	US film actress Marilyn Monroe (1926–62)
Marlene	US film actress Marlene Dietrich (1901–92); wartime song 'Lili Marlene'
Marlon	US actor Marlon Brando (1924–2004)
Marsha	US film actress Marsha Hunt (b. 1917)
Marvin	US singer Marvin Gaye (1939–84)
Maureen	Irish film actress Maureen O'Hara (b. 1920)
Maurice	French singer and actor Maurice Chevalier (1888–1972)
Meryl	US film actress Meryl Streep (b. 1949)
Mia	US film actress Mia Farrow (b. 1945)
Mimi	Heroine of Puccini's opera *La Bohème* (1896)
Montgomery	US actor Montgomery Clift (1920–66)
Natalie	US film actress Natalie Wood (1932–82)
Nicole	Australian film actress Nicole Kidman (b. 1968)
Norma	Invented by Felice Romani for Bellini's opera of this name (1832); Norman-Jean, the original name of US film star Marilyn Monroe (1926–62)

NAME	FILM, TV, MUSIC INFLUENCE
Nyree	New Zealand-born actress Nyree Dawn Porter (1940–2001)
Olivia	Australian singer and actress Olivia Newton John (b. 1948)
Omar	Egyptian-born actor Omar Sharif (b. 1932)
Oprah	US actress and TV presenter Oprah Winfrey (b. 1954)
Orson	US actor and director Orson Welles (1915–85)
Oscar	Associated with American Academy awards for achievement in the film industry
Otis	American singer Otis Redding (1941–67)
Perdita	Character in *One Hundred and One Dalmations* (Dodie Smith, 1956; filmed by Walt Disney, 1961)
Perry	US singer Perry Como (1912–2001)
Phoebe	Character Phoebe Buffay in US sitcom *Friends*
Prince	US singer Prince (b. 1958)
Prunella	English actress Prunella Scales (b. 1932)
Raquel	US film actress Raquel Welch (b. 1940)
Rex	British actor Rex Harrison (1908–90)
Rhett	Character Rhett Butler in Margaret Mitchell's *Gone with the Wind* (1936; filmed, 1939)
Rita	US film actress Rita Hayworth (1918–87); song 'Lovely Rita' (The Beatles, 1967)
River	US actor River Phoenix (1970–93)
Rocky	Series of films about a boxer starring Sylvester Stalone
Rolf	Australian entertainer Rolf Harris (b. 1930)
Ronan	Irish singer Ronan Keating (b. 1977)
Rowan	English actor, comic, and writer Rowan Atkinson (b. 1955)
Rudolf	US silent-film actor Rudolph Valentino (1895–1926)
Ryan	US film actor Ryan O'Neal (b. 1941)

NAME	FILM, TV, MUSIC INFLUENCE
Scarlett	Character Scarlett O'Hara in Margaret Mitchell's *Gone with the Wind* (1936; filmed, 1939)
Seán	Scottish actor Sean Connery (b. 1930)
Shirley	Child film star Shirley Temple (b. 1928)
Sibyl	Character Sibyl Fawlty in 1970s UK sitcom *Fawlty Towers*
Sinéad	Irish actress Sinead Cusack (b. 1948)
Sophia	Italian film actress Sophia Loren (b. 1934)
Spencer	US film actor Spencer Tracy (1900–67)
Sylvester	US film actor Sylvester Stallone (b. 1946)
Tallulah	US actress Tallulah Bankhead (1903–68)
Tara	Name of the estate in Margaret Mitchell's *Gone with the Wind* (1936, filmed, 1939); UK actress Tara Fitzgerald (b. 1967)
Tiffany	Film *Breakfast at Tiffany's* (1961); character in UK soap *Eastenders*
Tracy	Character Tracy Lord, played by Grace Kelly, in film *High Society* (1956)
Tyrone	US film actor Tyrone Power (1913–58)
Ursula	Swedish born US actress Ursula Andress (b. 1936)
Van	Irish folk singer Van Morrison (b. 1945)
Vanessa	English actress Vanessa Redgrave (b. 1937)
Victor	US actor Victor Mature (1915–99)
Vivien	British actress Vivien Leigh (1913–67)
Warren	US film actor Warren Beatty (b. 1937)
Wayne	US film actor John Wayne (1907–82); English dancer and choreographer Wayne Sleep (b. 1948)
Whitney	US pop singer Whitney Houston (b. 1963)
Woody	US folk singer Woody Guthrie (1912–67); US actor and director Woody Allen (b. 1935)

Themed Names

Names derived from or associated with Flowers, Trees, and other Plants

Anthea	Fern	Laurel	Poppy
Azalea	Fleur	Lavender	Posy
Bláthnat	Flora	Leaf	Primrose
Blodwedd	Hazel	Lilac	Prunella
Blodwen	Heather	Lily	Rose
Blossom	Holly	Linden	Rosemary
Briar	Honesty	Marguerite	Rowan
Bryony	Hyacinth	Marigold	Sharon
Cherry	Iris	May	Sorrel
Clematis	Ivy	Myrtle	Tansy
Dahlia	Jasmine	Nigella	Viola
Daisy	Jonquil	Olive	Violet
Daphne	Juniper	Pansy	Willow
Eirlys	Larch	Petal	

Names derived from Birds' Names

Arlette	Corbin	Linnet	Teal
Arnold	Corbinian	Mavis	Zipporah
Bertram	Kestrel	Merle	
Calum	Lark	Robin	

Names derived from Gemstones, Stones, Metals, and Minerals

Amber	Esmerelda	Margaret	Sapphire
Beryl	Gemma	Opal	Silver
Coral	Jade	Pearl	Topaz
Crystal	Jetta	Petra	
Emerald	Jewel	Ruby	

Names derived from Nature

Aurora	Misty	Sky	Summer
Dawn	Rainbow	Star	
Eira	River	Stella	
Iris	Sierra	Storm	

Names derived from River Names

Alma	Clodagh	Jordan	Shannon
Alun	Clyde	Kelvin	Trent
Cary	Eleri	Sabrina	

Names derived directly from Placenames*

*Most given names that are also placenames derive from family names

Africa	Demelzer	Keighley	Sharon
Ailsa	Devon	Kimberley	Skye
Ariel	Ebenezer	Loreto	Tara
Bethany	Erin	Lorna	Trenton
Brittany	India	Lourdes	Troy
Brynmor	Iona	Morven	Tyrone
Carmel	Isla	Mostyn	Zelah
Chelsea	Israel	Savannah	

Names from Words denoting specific Qualities

Charity	Grace	Hope	Prudence
Chastity	Hardy	Joy	Sterling
Constant	Honesty	Mercy	Unity
Faith	Honor	Noble	Verity
Felicity	Honour	Patience	

Most Popular Names in England and Wales in 2003

(Data from the Office of Statistics)

RANK	BOYS	RANK IN 1998	RANK	GIRLS	RANK IN 1998
1	Jack	1	1	Emily	2
2	Joshua	5	2	Ellie	22
3	Thomas	2	3	Chloe	1
4	James	3	4	Jessica	4
5	Daniel	4	5	Sophie	5
6	Oliver	20	6	Megan	3
7	Benjamin	16	7	Lucy	10
8	Samuel	7	8	Olivia	16
9	William	14	9	Charlotte	6
10	Joseph	9	10	Hannah	7
11	Harry	15	11	Katie	13
12	Matthew	6	12	Ella	38
13	Lewis	18	13	Grace	36
14	Luke	13	14	Mia	77
15	Ethan	47	15=	Amy	11
16	George	17	15=	Holly	27
17=	Adam	21	17	Lauren	8
17=	Alfie	75	18	Emma	15
19	Callum	8	19	Molly	23
20	Alexander	19	20	Abigail	21

Most Popular Names in Scotland in 2004

(Data from the General Register Office for Scotland)

RANK	BOYS	RANK IN 1998	RANK	GIRLS	RANK IN 1998
1	Lewis	4	1	Emma	4
2	Jack	2	2	Sophie	11
3	James	6	3	Ellie	below 50
4	Cameron	5	4	Amy	4
5	Ryan	below 50	5	Chloe	5
6	Liam	15	6	Katie	17
7	Jamie	21	7	Erin	14
8	Ben	39	8	Emily	19
9	Kyle	19	9	Lucy	16
10	Callum	10	10	Hannah	10
11	Matthew	14	11	Rebecca	3
12	Daniel	12	12	Rachel	7
13	Connor	7	13	Abbie	48
14	Adam	26	14	Lauren	8
15	Dylan	22	15	Megan	below 50
16	Andrew	8	16=	Aimee	43
17=	Aidan	41	16=	Olivia	below 50
17=	Ross	3	18	Caitlin	6
19	Scott	9	19	Leah	below 50
20	Nathan	30	20	Niamh	47

Most Popular Names in the Republic of Ireland in 2004

(Data from the Central Statistics Office Ireland)

RANK	BOYS	RANK IN 1998		RANK	GIRLS	RANK IN 1998
1	Sean	2		1	Emma	5
2	Jack	3		2	Sarah	3
3	Adam	5		3	Aoife	4
4	Conor	1		4	Ciara	2
5	James	4		5	Katie	13
6	Daniel	10		6	Sophie	17
7	Michael	9		7	Rachel	7
8	Cian	12		8	Chloe	1
9	David	8		9	Amy	12
10	Dylan	7		10	Leah	27
11	Luke	15		11	Niamh	6
12	Ryan	16		12	Caoimhe	24
13	Aaron	6		13	Hannah	18
14	Thomas	17		14	Ella	94
15=	Darragh	28		15	Lauren	10
15=	Eoin	20		16	Megan	8
17	Joshua	52		17=	Kate	22
18	Ben	48		17=	Rebecca	9
19	Patrick	17		19	Jessica	19
20	Oisin	37		20	Emily	25

Most Popular Names in the United States in 2003

(Data from the Department of Social Security)

RANK	BOYS	RANK	GIRLS
1	Jacob	1	Emily
2	Michael	2	Emma
3	Joshua	3	Madison
4	Matthew	4	Hannah
5	Andrew	5	Olivia
6	Joseph	6	Abigail
7	Ethan	7	Alexis
8	Daniel	8	Ashley
9	Christopher	9	Elizabeth
10	Anthony	10	Samantha
11	William	11	Isabella
12	Ryan	12	Sarah
13	Nicholas	13	Grace
14	David	14	Alyssa
15	Tyler	15	Lauren
16	Alexander	16	Kayla
17	John	17	Brianna
18	James	18	Jessica
19	Dylan	19	Taylor
20	Zachary	20	Sophia

Most Popular Names in Australia (New South Wales) in 2003

(Data from the NSW Registry of Births, Deaths, and Marriages)

RANK	BOYS	RANK	GIRLS
1	Joshua	1	Emily
2	Jack	2	Jessica
3	Lachlan	3	Chloe
4	Thomas	4	Isabella
5	William	5	Sarah
6	Daniel	6	Emma
7	Benjamin	7	Georgia
8	Nicholas	8	Grace
9	Matthew	9	Ella
10	Samuel	10	Charlotte
11	Liam	11	Mia
12	Luke	12	Lily
13	Ryan	13	Zoe
14	Jayden	14	Jasmine
15	Jordan	15	Olivia
16	Alexander	16	Jade
17	Harrison	17	Holly
18	James	18	Caitlin
19	Michael	19	Amy
20	Ethan	20	Ruby

Most Popular Names in New Zealand in 2003

(Data supplied by Statistics New Zealand)

RANK	BOYS	RANK	GIRLS
1	Joshua	1	Emma
2	Jack	2	Sophie
3	Benjamin	3	Ella
4	Samuel	4	Emily
5	Daniel	5	Jessica
6	Jacob	6	Hannah
7	Ethan	7	Olivia
8	James	8	Grace
9	Thomas	9	Charlotte
10	Matthew	10	Georgia
11	Liam	11	Sarah
12	William	12	Paige
13	Caleb	13	Isabella
14=	Luke	14	Caitlin
14=	Oliver	15	Lucy
16	Ryan	16	Holly
17	Jayden	17	Samantha
18	Cameron	18	Brooke
19	Connor	19	Kate
20	Logan	20	Lily

Most Popular Names in England and Wales 1954–2003

(Data from the Office for National Statistics)

Boys

RANK	1954	1964	1974	1984	1994	2003
1	David	David	Paul	Christopher	Thomas	Jack
2	John	Paul	Mark	James	James	Joshua
3	Stephen	Andrew	David	David	Jack	Thomas
4	Michael	Mark	Andrew	Daniel	Daniel	James
5	Peter	John	Richard	Michael	Matthew	Daniel
6	Robert	Michael	Christopher	Matthew	Ryan	Oliver
7	Paul	Stephen	James	Andrew	Joshua	Benjamin
8	Alan	Ian	Simon	Richard	Luke	Samuel
9	Christopher	Robert	Michael	Paul	Samuel	William
10	Richard	Richard	Matthew	Mark	Jordan	Joseph

Girls

RANK	1954	1964	1974	1984	1994	2003
1	Susan	Susan	Sarah	Sarah	Rebecca	Emily
2	Linda	Julie	Claire	Laura	Lauren	Ellie
3	Christine	Karen	Nicola	Gemma	Jessica	Chloe
4	Margaret	Jacqueline	Emma	Emma	Charlotte	Jessica
5	Janet	Deborah	Lisa	Rebecca	Hannah	Sophie
6	Patricia	Tracey	Joanne	Claire	Sophie	Megan
7	Carol	Jane	Michelle	Victoria	Amy	Lucy
8	Elizabeth	Helen	Helen	Samantha	Emily	Olivia
9	Mary	Diane	Samantha	Rachel	Laura	Charlotte
10	Anne	Sharon	Karen	Amy	Emma	Hannah

Most Popular Names in the United States 1954–2003

(Data from the Department of Social Security)

Boys

(Years 1954–1984 are based on 1% samples; 1994 and 2003 on 100% samples)

RANK	1954	1964	1974	1984	1994	2003
1	Robert	Michael	Michael	Michael	Michael	Jacob
2	Michael	John	Jason	Christopher	Christopher	Michael
3	John	David	Christopher	Matthew	Matthew	Joshua
4	James	Robert	David	Joshua	Joshua	Matthew
5	David	James	James	David	Tyler	Andrew
6	William	Mark	John	Daniel	Brandon	Joseph
7	Richard	William	Robert	James	Jacob	Ethan
8	Thomas	Richard	Brian	Robert	Daniel	Daniel
9	Mark	Thomas	William	John	Nicholas	Christopher
10	Gary	Joseph	Daniel	Ryan	Andrew	Anthony

Girls

(Years 1954–1984 are based on 1% samples; 1994 and 2003 on 100% samples)

RANK	1954	1964	1974	1984	1994	2003
1	Mary	Lisa	Jennifer	Jennifer	Jessica	Emily
2	Deborah	Mary	Amy	Jessica	Ashley	Emma
3	Linda	Maria	Michelle	Ashley	Emily	Madison
4	Debra	Susan	Angela	Amanda	Samantha	Hannah
5	Patricia =	Karen	Kimberly	Sarah	Sarah	Olivia
6	Susan =	Patricia	Heather	Stephanie	Taylor	Abigail
7	Barbara	Donna	Lisa	Nicole	Amanda	Alexis
8	Maria	Linda	Melissa	Elizabeth	Brittany	Ashley
9	Karen	Kimberly	Maria	Heather	Elizabeth	Elizabeth
10	Nancy	Elizabeth	Stephanie	Melissa	Megan	Samantha